DISAPPEARING ACTS

Perón was able
to bring labor &
capital together to
avoid social revolution-
balancing act

a dirty war is a
war against its
own - an internal war

DISAPPEARING

 ACTS

Spectacles of Gender and Nationalism in Argentina's "Dirty War"

DIANA TAYLOR

DUKE UNIVERSITY PRESS   Durham and London 1997

© 1997 Duke University Press
All rights reserved
Printed in the United States of America on acid-free paper ∞
Typeset in Minion by Keystone Typesetting, Inc.
Library of Congress Cataloging-in-Publication Data
appear on the last printed page of this book.
Second printing, 2000

Contents

Preface

Public spectacle is a locus and mechanism of communal identity through collective imaginings that constitute "nation" as "an imagined political community." I focus on Argentina's "Dirty War" (1976–83) to explore how public spectacle both builds and dismantles a sense of community and nation-ness, how it both forges and erases images of national and gender identity, how it stirs and manipulates desire, allowing a population insight into events and blinding it to the meaning of its situation, how it presents both an invitation to cross the line between actor and spectator, and a prohibition. But, in a way, this is not so much a study "about" Argentina as about how a small group of power brokers (in this case the military) engenders and controls a viewing public through the performance of national identity, traditions, and goals.

This study began when I inadvertently crossed the actor/spectator line and became suddenly caught up in the Argentine spectacle of gender and nationalism. Like an unsuspecting spectator, I stumbled onto the wrong play. It began on a visit to Buenos Aires and it has led me to various kinds of border cross-ings—geographic, theoretical, political, and disciplinary. While the divides first presented themselves as both politically charged and irreconcilable—U.S./Ar-gentina; "outsider"/"insider"; voyeur/witness; theatre/politics—I've come to view them as conceptual barriers that block political understanding. Good fences don't make good neighbors in my book. Rather than see my work as a back-and-forth motion *across* borders, I've attempted to follow the lead of performance border artists in expanding the in-betweenness, the shared spaces of the border itself.

Disappearing Acts is an interdisciplinary work that draws on performance, feminist, Latin American, and cultural studies to analyze spectacles of gender and nation-ness in the context of the Dirty War. I've included public events from various arenas: military parades and soccer games, the weekly marches by the Mothers of the Plaza de Mayo and the "Open Theatre" festival. Given the atrocity of the political context, characterized by state-organized "disappear-ances," abductions, torture, and murder, the title *Disappearing Acts* may sound oddly flippant. What do cheap theatrics and magic shows have to do with human annihilation? Too much, unfortunately. The title is meant to conjure up not only the military junta's blatant uses of theatricality to terrorize its popula-tion (the "disappearances" being the most devastating and grotesque) but to signal the interconnectedness among the various disappearances taking place simultaneously. Just as human beings disappeared, so did civil society. Discur-sive absences led to empty streets and to missing people, just as missing people and empty streets led to more discursive absences. What has to fall out of the picture, I ask repeatedly, for the militaristic version of a healthy social "body" to make sense? This study explores how systems of terror emanate throughout the public sphere, rippling through newspaper headlines, magazine covers, films, ads, and TV spots. Terror systems transform human bodies into surfaces, avail-able for political inscription.

Public spectacles of terror, of course, are nothing new. From pre-Columbian human sacrifice to the Inquisition, from the witch trials in early modern Eu-rope to the staging of "the terror" in revolutionary France to the Nazi conven-tion in Nuremberg, power relations have been written into and onto the human body. Nor is the ideology I trace here—one that depicts the social body as infirm, feminized, and in need of "cleansing"—specifically Argentine. The idea of disease, degeneration, and deviancy associated with the feminine has long been part of the collective imaginary, and not just in the West, though that is my focus. The "other" is that which is given to be feared: the feminine, the "masses," Jews, homosexuals, and the indigenous populations in Argentina as elsewhere. While different "others" emerge geographically and historically, readers will find the same patterns we've come to associate with the language of conquest, colonialism, fascism, and the new Right.

This work goes against the isolationism of many U.S. studies that automatically situate theories of the body, subjectivity, and positionality within the national discourse as if this were all-inclusive and universally applicable. It expands upon the historical studies of the period that explain state formation while leaving out gender, as if this were incidental, rather than fundamental, to its formulation. It attempts to "look at" history through a performance model that, I hope, will illuminate fractures and tensions that more traditional "readings" will not recognize. It questions the economic versions of the social production of reality that fail to recognize spectacles as the product and producer of group fantasies and desires. It goes against the grain of right-wing nationalists and left-wing "independence" thinkers by challenging the ideology of nation-ness so dear to many Anglo and Latin Americans. For in spite of all the rampant nationalisms of the moment, we live in a global community shaped by international economic policies and plagued by common problems.

In using a performance model to look at political spectacles and spectatorship I engage in a search for better scripts, for better politics. Spectacles cannot be understood as separate entities; they can be understood only as they interface with spectators and with other national and international spectacles. What happened in Argentina during the Dirty War cannot be distanced as another example of atrocity happening in some other country. The crisis resulted from Argentina's entry into the global economic market; thus it is very much a product of a broader agenda, indeed "our" imaginary and "our" global economic system. It is not simply that the neofascist ideology I look at in Argentina pertains to the Western political repertoire. The United States trained Argentine military leaders in the Doctrine of National Security and taught them the methods of repression and torture needed to implement it. The Dirty War, in some concrete ways, played for and to U.S. interests, comprised of the likes of Henry Kissinger, Frank Sinatra, and Ford Motor Company. Nonetheless, the *particular* shape of the crisis—which culminated in the Dirty War with its "disappearances," concentration camps, tortures, and murders—has to do, I propose, with the specific, localized images, myths, and explanatory narratives that populations hold about themselves. Understanding spectacle, then, is dependent on a complex scene of interface: understanding *both* the local cultural specifics of national dramas *and* the way that national and international spectacles interface and produce each other. The performance model also helps spectators define their position vis-à-vis spectacles of violence. Are we complicit? Can we work to end violence, or will we go on "just looking"? My study on spectacle aspires to "academic" activism, a respected ideal in Latin America that, in the United States, has often been deemed a contradiction in terms. My goal is to examine the politics of looking, "just looking," dangerous seeing, and percepticide in order to make active spectators, or witnesses, of us all.

While this project has proved difficult and challenging for me in many respects, the greatest pleasure that I derived from it was feeling that I was working with a community of artists, scholars, friends, and family who made the enterprise possible. I thank Clyde Snow, the forensic anthropologist, for the photograph of Matilde's casket, Howard M. Fraser for lending me valuable material from *Caras y caretas,* and Pablo Rouco de Urquiza, director of the Argentine school of journalism T.E.A. (Taller/Escuela/Agencia), for allowing me to view and copy materials not to be found in Argentina's national archives. I am grateful to those who have helped, challenged, and accompanied me through these crossings. My student Owen Gottlieb taught me more than I taught him about Argentine film. Ken Wissoker, my editor at Duke University Press, has supported me throughout. I am deeply indebted to those who, through their work and in our discussions, guided me through the complexities of lived experience during the Dirty War: Diana Raznovich, Griselda Gambaro, Renee Epelbaum, Alicia Partnoy, Sylvia Molloy, Roberto Gutierrez-Varea, Guillermo Loiácono, Marta Savigliano, Marcelo Súarez-Orozco, Ana María Amar Sánchez, and Tómas Eloy Martínez. (All translations are my own unless otherwise noted.) Others have enriched my perspective through their own work in feminist, performance, and cultural studies: Doris Sommer, Sue-Ellen Case, Richard Schechner, Joseph Roach, Rebecca Schneider, Ross Chambers, Jorge Salessi, Marguerite Feitlowitz, and George Woodyard. And several of the aforementioned did all at once. I owe the deepest gratitude to all those who have been my companions on these crossings. Elizabeth Garrels accompanied me on my initial journey to Buenos Aires and sat with me through the fateful *Paso de dos* and forum that got me involved in this project in the first place. My friends at Dartmouth are a constant source of support, pleasure, and enlightenment. They're always available to read, edit, argue, and discuss the many versions of my work that I've given them. I can't think of anything I've written that isn't also the work of Marianne Hirsch, Susanne Zantop, Laurence Davies, Silvia Spitta, Alexis Jetter, Annelise Orleck, Agnes Lugo-Ortiz, and Diane Miliotis. I hasten to add that the weaknesses and blind spots in the text are entirely my own. The only way I know to thank them is by cooking for them and reading, editing, arguing over, and discussing whatever they put before me. And, as always, Eric, Alexei, and Marina have been with me, cheering me, teasing me, helping me get my bearings when the border crossings became disorienting and I thought I would never find my way home. I thank you all.

1   Caught in the Spectacle

The Scene of the Crime

Utter darkness. Some indiscernible sounds. The sounds grow louder, more distinct. Grunts. Gasps. Rustling in the dark. The lights go up slightly. A mournful, beautiful tango comes out of nowhere. Two figures can be made out, though it's not clear either from their movements or from the noises they make whether they're struggling or having sex. What's happening? Who are they? It's a man and woman. They're in a pit full of mud. It's sex, it seems from the way she sits on his lap, clutching him. He howls, slaps her, pushes her away. He stands up, cinching his pants at the waist. She clings to him. He yells at her. A female voice answers him, but it's not her voice. Where is that coming from? He throws her into the mud, slapping her some more. Kicks her. Pulls all her clothes off her. She tries to get close to him. He grabs her face. Hits her. He screams "Bitch!" He pulls her naked body, exposing her, humiliating her. Though the female voice talks back, it's not hers. She never says a word, just whimpers and crawls back to him. He kills her. The female voice vows revenge. He won't get away with it. He stands defiantly, buttoning up his military jacket as he towers over her prostrate, naked, dead body.

Applause. Weary but seemingly content, Eduardo Pavlovsky, Susana Evans, and Stella Galazzi (the voice offstage) take their bows in the circular tub full of mud.

From the bleachers, I watched in stunned silence. I was disoriented. How to position myself in the face of the spectacle I had just seen? I was trapped—trapped between wanting to see, to make out what was happening in front of me, and not wanting to see once I had made it out. I tried to disbelieve: this couldn't be happening. By moments, the mournful tango and beautiful lighting swept me up to what seemed a lofty plateau of transcendent "meaning" where all this made sense. But her brutalized body brought me back. I wondered what the other members of the audience felt. Were they looking at her destruction, or through it to that lofty beyond? The prolonged applause suggested that this play had resonated with them.

Paso de dos was the hit of the Argentine 1990 season. The show had been sold out for months. What were people expecting to see, I wondered? What was I expecting? I wasn't sure, but having read Pavlovsky's earlier works and the original script for this play (*Voces* or Voices), I anticipated some indictment of the atrocities of the Dirty War. Eduardo Pavlovsky, a psychotherapist/play-wright/actor, had long been a prominent "leftist" and confirmed enemy of the military regime. He had narrowly escaped abduction by the military in 1978 and had gone into exile in Spain until 1980. In the production, Pavlovsky played He, a monomaniacal military man who beat, stripped, raped, and finally killed She, played by Susana Evans, Pavlovsky's wife. What did this graphic representation of sexual violence against the female body say about the Dirty War? What fantasies did it convey about Argentine nation-ness? What function was it performing for the enthralled audience? And what was my role there, anyway?

The play clearly raised questions of national identity and resistance in the context of Argentina's recent tragedy. He, the male protagonist, is a torturer during the Dirty War (or *proceso*) who becomes obsessed with one of his female victims. Even before meeting her, simply hearing about her from his fellow torturers, he confesses later, "I had already created an image of you" (13).[1] "I was obsessed with the thought of possessing you . . . claiming you as a trophy, I was always thinking about your body . . . Overpowering you forcefully . . . suddenly . . . like when an animal catches its prey" (14). He needs her, he says; she is his "NECESSITY. The necessity of our bodies . . . together" (11). His dependency makes him feel vulnerable, violent, and insanely jealous. "Not being with you was like facing the void; the horror was knowing that my intensity could cease at any moment, that it depended entirely on you" (12).

She, the script tells us, becomes caught up in his search for intensity. They engage in a tortuous ceremony during which he inflicts physical pain. She endures the ordeal stoically, but then, the play suggests, he was not torturing her in order to obtain answers. He wanted her to resist, to keep silent, so that the interrogations and sessions might continue and intensify his pleasure. "I wanted to possess your body, your cavities, your smells, each part of your body that I struck; I knew the color of every one of your bruises" (28). He feels compelled to expose and control her interior, innermost parts. Now, after the *proceso* is over, he confesses in a meeting they have arranged, he still needs her— not as a source of intensity but to give him his identity: "I don't understand you. Now you could scream out my name and again you choose to keep quiet, you won't say a word. Confess, you bitch, scream out who I am, who I was . . . Because I existed! Why? Why won't you name me?" (28). Her final choice, at the end of the script, is again to keep silent: she will deny him the hero status enjoyed by the generals who are free to walk down the streets of Buenos Aires. Throughout the play he demands, he interrogates, tortures, and possesses her "entirely" (22), but she "wins." She, not he, the play wants us to believe, holds the ultimate power.

Having read the script, I had been prepared to accept that the play was "about" the torturer's perversity, a term Robert Stoller defines as "the erotic form of hatred" (4). After all, it has been well documented that the Argentine torturers routinely raped their victims. There was even a well-known case in which a victim "fell in love" with her tormentor. There is psychiatric literature that elucidates the phenomenon, known as the Stockholm syndrome.

Or perhaps the text could be seen as critiquing the military's version of masculinity, predicated on the eradication of the "feminine." He, much like Klaus Theweleit's *Freikorps* soldiers, is acutely conscious of being trapped in a highly vulnerable body, a "feminized" body full of holes (*huecos*, 9). He wants a controlled, masculine body, which he tries desperately to discipline: "I want every gesture to make sense. I mean, I want every gesture to have a feeling of spontaneity. I don't want any holes" (9). Pavlovsky the psychoanalyst even has a few lines about castration anxiety to "explain" how the male killer got to be that way: As a child, a bully had beat him up; he complained to his father; his father took him back to the group, promising to hold the other boys back while his son took on the bully one-on-one; the boy, terrified, failed to take on his opponent. His "cowardice" and "weakness" transformed him into a "shit" in his father's eyes. One moment shaped his entire life. Now, shunned permanently by the father, he himself must play out those rituals of intensity one-on-one, on a safe body, the body socially constructed to not fight back, the woman's body. Her body is scripted to allow for his virility; her silence is given to justify his actions; she is passive, he is active, but he depends on her absolutely for his masculinity. Alone, he himself pursues the "fascist aesthetic" (Theweleit 2:197) of turning his body into a well-functioning machine: "I turn my head to the right, now to the left, now to the front again. Pause" (9).

As I watched the play, however, the political critique seemed to recede as the performance replicated and affirmed the fascination with eroticized violence. The female body was sexually exposed and violently obliterated even as the play denounced Argentina's torturers and the imminent *indulto* (the governmental pardon of those leaders of the armed forces found guilty of human rights violations in 1985). While the repetition and displacement of violence against the female body seemed to relate to the historically "real" trauma suffered by the terrorized Argentine social body, the visual frenzy provoked by her abuse seemed closer to pornography.[2] The woman's voice, now separate from the body, reenacted the implicit misogynist violence of the military's discourse which splits the "feminine" into the lofty, disembodied *Patria* (Motherland, literally *belonging to the Father*) and the corporeal, dispensable woman. Intensely beautiful, set to a mournful tango, this production presented the woman as a metaphor for a beleaguered Argentina. Her destruction was somehow coherent, necessary, and, yes, aesthetically pleasurable and morally redemptive. So what was the play about, I asked myself? Was it about sadomasochism? or about torture and the *indulto* (the torturer goes free at the end of the play)?

Not even the commentators could agree about *Paso de dos,* though they, like most of the women and men who watched the play the night I was there, seemed to admire the play enormously. One "reading" of the spectacle that reviewers reiterated was that *Paso de dos* was a *testimonio,* along the lines of Peter Weiss's *The Investigation,* here based on the testimonies of the victims televised during the generals' trials in 1985. As one commentator stated, the play stages Argentina's recent tragedy.[3] Another claimed that it was in the horror of the production that its redemption lay: "*Paso de dos* is horrible. There lies its triumph over a horrible part of our history."[4] Or was this a porn show intended to titillate rather than critique, thus recapitulating paradigms of domination? Her "intimidades" and "intersticios" (22), repeatedly alluded to in the script, were fully exposed female body parts. The poster advertising the production focused specifically on a nude frontal of her in the process of being strangled. Did the sex and violence—indisputably theatre's two major selling points—lure the audience into the tiny cubicle of a theatre? Was the play about quasi-fascist violence, or did it imply that criminal politics were simply a sexual aberration? Pavlovsky, in an interview, called the play a "love story" in which both partners enjoy themselves: "I imagine them enjoying themselves like dogs in this love story."[5] Love or repression? Pornography or docudrama? Was she, like the female captive of the Argentine stag film *El Satario* (ca. 1907–12), just carried away by a horny devil?[6] Was this merely one more macho fantasy of sadomasochism projected yet again onto a social (female) "body," or a politically committed attempt to demythify the violence of Argentina's Dirty War? And how do we decide?

Apparently, the play would have us believe, there are two stories. In the first, the female body is committed to the pursuit of erotic, deathly pleasure, which, the play tries to convince us, is hers, not just his. This, seemingly, is the world of mutual desire and consent. *Paso de dos* seems to be the theatrical equivalent to the narrative of "torture as a love story," best exemplified in Argentina by authors Luisa Valenzuela and Marta Lynch.[7] The woman can't help but give herself up to the powerful, seductive military man. Pavlovsky's "intensity" seems equivalent to Georges Bataille's eroticism, "the assenting to life to the point of death" (11). True, it is the woman who dies, but as Bataille himself insists, that has always been the case: "I must emphasize that the female partner in eroticism" he says, is "seen as the victim, the male as the sacrificer" (18). In Bataille, too, eroticism is tied into male individuation, it "is that within man which calls his being into question" (29). But the annihilation of the female simultaneously serves a collective goal, for when "the victim dies . . . the spectator shares in what [the] death reveals" (22). Again, the split: the dead female body/the redemptive image. She dies so that we (the viewers) might live. Thus, she is positioned as the *other,* the disposable, sacrificial body that marks the viewing audience as implicitly male. Much as in the military discourse that I examine in the following chapter, the *puta* dies, the *Patria* reunites a shattered population. Not only that, she likes it! The conquest is complete and empowers him beyond the actual rape. He has truly penetrated her deepest being: She now has no desire that is not merely the extension of his desire. The play depicts the fatal linkage between male identity, male violence, and male pleasure. The female body (*puta*/women) is simply the inert mass on which that violence and pleasure are acted out. At the end of the production her body is almost indistinguishable from the endlessly malleable mud of the pit. But the play reproduces the violence it sets out to reflect because the spectator's pleasure in *Paso de dos* depends on and develops what Barbara Freedman calls the "coercive identification with a position of male antagonism toward women."[8] As spectators we are required to participate in the misogyny in order to reap the redemptive dividend. Sadism and redemption for the price of one single ticket. The "dead," naked body of Susana Evans lying in the mud fills the house; Galazzi's painful voice offstage allows spectators to share in what the death reveals.

The problematic depiction of female pleasure and desire, as illustrated in the first of the play's two tales, is even more disturbing than the above suggests. It is not only that women are cast as victims to be exterminated for male pleasure, under the misnomer of *female* pleasure. The violence and repression inflicted on women is intrinsic in the very way we are forced to be women. By "Woman" I refer simply to the embodied image of the so-called feminine (as in *Patria*), the cultural construction of gender attributes in patriarchy. By "women," I refer to "real" flesh-and-blood, female-sexed persons—laying aside for the moment the question of whether such a category can even be imagined outside of culture and gender. Feminist scholars have long noted that women are socialized into a sex system that forces them into masochistic submissiveness and obliges them to act out obligatory sexual and gender roles. The play perpetuates the masculinist move of appropriating female desire: her only pleasure comes from participating in his desire, even if it kills her. The depiction of her desire and erotic pleasure as masochistic of course reaffirms the notion that female sexuality develops from the experience of pain, envy, frustration, and humiliation. Thus, as the play suggests, women "like" brutal treatment, enjoy it, need it, respect the hand that beats them. In fact, the acceptance and even pleasure in pain affirm their femininity.[9] This version of feminine surrender confirms the military's political discourse that relocates the masculinist desire for domination onto the feminized population, claiming that "she" desires to be dominated; "she" willingly offers up her subjectivity, even her life, to the superior power.

The disembodied voice in *Paso de dos* seems to tell a different, no less troubled, story. The voice tells us that the play is about national identity, victimization, retribution, and the *indulto*. The military male tries to define himself through violence. Like the junta leaders, He is immune to retribution. Though a couple of junta leaders had been sentenced to jail terms in Argentina's Trial of the Century (1985), She maintains they were proud of what they had done. Her silence, then, had been politically motivated. She wanted to deny him celebrity status. The need to deny torturers a heroic role was a hot political issue in 1990. That year, Emilio Massera, the junta leader most directly linked to the practice of abduction and torture, had been spotted in downtown Buenos Aires, though officially he was in jail. There were rumors (which became reality in December 1990, a few months after I saw the play) that President Menem was about to pardon all the junta leaders, including Videla and Massera, who had been condemned to life imprisonment. Some people even saw the military leaders as national heroes who had come down hard on the enemy. As one commentator stated, "there's talk of monuments to these men, to their heroic war against subversion" (Feitlowitz, 60).[10] "Her" refusal to name him, then, countered the pro-military aggrandizing gesture even as it expressed her unwillingness to be further exposed: "You want me to name you, don't you, to tell everything, all the details. I know that would make you feel better, proud that everyone knows you touched me. You want to be a hero, like the rest, proud once again of what they've done, proud to be walking free, defiant, always on the lookout. Heroes once again" (29). She suspects that her confession of the crimes committed against her would only serve to fuel the public's fascination with sexualized violence and would, ironically, enhance the military's heroic status.

These urgent political issues, however, never really came into focus in the production. Rather, in a cruel irony, the play transformed her pain into public pleasure and titillation. The play performs the "confession" that she attempts to refuse. And while silence, as a strategy of resistance *for women,* needs to be historicized, especially in this scenario of forced "confessions," it has generally been a sign of women's public and political invisibility. This play effectively silenced the woman while ostensibly giving her a voice. There was no desire expressed or envisioned in the performance that was not simply an extension, or an echo, of his desire. He exerted his power to speak, to initiate language; her voice, separated from her body, emanated from the distance of the bleachers. Insofar as the female voice in *Pasos,* like the mythical Echo herself, can't initiate dialogue, her only "power" comes from her refusal to speak, from her silence. But this is hardly *power.* Women have been refused *voz y voto* (voice and vote) throughout much of history. Although the play ostensibly grants her a voice and allows her a quasi-critical response to her predicament, in effect she is cast as an echo. The performance repeated the military's strategy of silencing its public. The population's responses during the *proceso,* scripted into the military performance, only served to give the appearance of open dialogue. As Francine Masiello noted, the military dictatorship attempted "to reduce the interpretative activity of the population to an echo of the official word and abolish the contesting voices of those 'others' opposed to the government" (*Nuevo Texto Crítico* 155). Under the political guise of denouncing victimization and the Dirty War, the play too stages a phony dialogue while it carries out a systematic assault on the "feminine." The female body is destroyed through violence. Her voice vanishes into a metaphor for victimization and is pushed to the outer

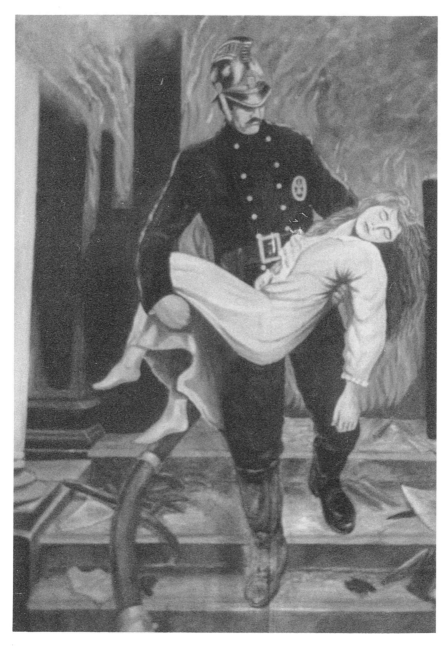

Figure 1. *Police to the Rescue.* (Tucuman Museum of Police, photo by Silvia Spitta)

limits of what, theoretically, was meant to be a collective and "open" exploration into Argentina's authoritarian past.

What struck me most about *Paso de dos,* however, was not the play's misogyny. Rather, it was my realization that this "progressive" play depicts the construction of national identity as predicated on female destruction, just as the military had done. Yet, I kept reminding myself as I sat on the bleachers, this was the *opposition.* But it became painfully evident to me that Pavlovsky's critique of the military was not antithetical to the work's misogyny. The misogyny, rather, was a fundamental bridge or slash connecting the military/antimilitary discourse. In the struggle for national identity, both groups of males were fighting to define and occupy the "masculine" position while emasculating, feminizing, and marginalizing the "other." The painting reproduced in figure 1, which still hangs in the Police Museum in Tucuman, Argentina, graphically illustrates the role of the "feminine" in the conjunction between crisis and male heroism. The house/city/country is going up in uncontrollable flames. An eerie landscape of towering infernos suggests the magnitude of the devastation. While the foregrounded pillars seem to be holding strong, shards of the buildings crash down around the two figures. The littered steps hint at dangers still ahead. The dutiful officer, so straight and surefooted, keeps his eyes on the prize: the unconscious body of a beautiful young white woman with long golden hair. The brushstrokes blend the flames in the background into the waves of her hair. She was almost swallowed up by that furious devastation. She's so white, so inert, so vulnerable one wonders if she's perhaps not dead after all. But his caring eyes, fixed on her in spite of the dangers, suggest not. He can save her. His measured steps, his calm, caring manner, can see them out of the predicament. The three plaques on the wall around the painting explain the true significance of the work—it's not about "her" of course, but about the *Patria.* "Every good citizen has the obligation to sacrifice himself for the liberty of the Patria," says one plaque decorated with crossed rifles. "Whoever serves peace," says one with a trumpet horn, "serves God and the Patria." A third announces that "the promotion and enlightenment of our letters (literatures) are the keys that open the doors of abundance and bring happiness to our people." The crossed swords that decorate this third plaque make one wonder what kinds of "keys" the artist envisioned. This image of the heroic military/police officer rescuing the prostrate young woman is clearly meant to inspire steadfastness and purpose in the viewers—that is, those spared the threat of the flames, or the survivors. She embodies the communal ideals, aspirations, and hopes that "we" cling to and will work to restore. She, too, dies/languishes so that "we" might live. Her suffering evaporates into an image

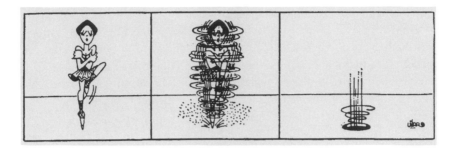

Figure 2. "Disappearing the Feminine," cartoon by Vilar.
(*La Nación*, April 23, 1976, p. A1)

of communal redemption and resolve. Is there something very different in this story of community building than in Pavlovsky's? Even if the play were intended as a critique of the macho military male by a "leftist" male intellectual, it still needed the woman's naked and abused body to express its objections and redeem its audience.

But how to explain the audience's desire to participate in a painful experience by watching this particular play? If the military forbade the public access to all sorts of "sights" and "insights," was the audience now manifesting a need to see, to regain perception, to reclaim insight? Obscenity (etymologically, a term for that which took place offstage, off-scene), after all, is the product of prohibition. Or was the play participating in the blinding of the population that the military promoted—what I will call percepticide[10]—by making what was so obviously visible, the woman's humiliation and destruction, seemingly invisible to the audience and resistant to a critique? Just as the "disappeared" were dragged away in full view of family, neighbors, and other observers, violence against women disappears and reappears as pure metaphor. The brutality and misogyny of the performance made me feel contaminated. Was that, perhaps, the point of this production? In the Dirty War, everyone felt contaminated—those who looked, those who looked away. Maybe this production restaged more than the violence. Maybe it intended to snare spectators (as it had snared me) in the drama of percepticide. Are we at risk if we see, or are we at risk if we don't? What did the enthusiastic applause signify? Did the catastrophe in the play produce an Aristotelian catharsis or release in the spectators? Did *Paso de dos* help us to see *differently*? Or did it recapitulate the very drama of percepticide it purportedly sought to illuminate?

Visibility/Invisibility

The invisible is not what is hidden but what is denied, that which we are
not allowed to see.—Ana María Fernandez, "Violencia y conyugalidad"

Invisibility is one of the most terrifying forms of forgetting and it is against forgetfulness
that our protagonist struggles.—Rodrigo Fresán, *Historia argentina*

Paso de dos tapped into a number of concerns and emotions that ran through
Argentina in 1990, among them the preoccupation with national memory and
forgetting, feelings of complicity and resistance, the desire to see the forbidden
and the need to reimagine community. Seven years had passed since the down
fall of the last military dictatorship and the end of the so-called Dirty War
(1976–83); fourteen years since the first junta of the period started the country
on a *proceso de reorganización nacional* (process of national reorganization,
henceforth referred to as *proceso*), which it claimed would save their *Patria*
from corrosion at the hands of her internal enemies or "subversives"; fourteen
years since the beginning of a period of systematized terror during which thirty
thousand people were abducted, tortured, and permanently "disappeared."

The cultural climate during the Dirty War had been characterized by censorship, blacklisting, and the systematic implementation of terror. Writers, producers, filmmakers, actors, technicians had been threatened and at times killed
by military forces. Interestingly, there had been no obvious break between the
pre-*proceso* and *proceso* cultures: plays were staged, television programs ran
their usual hours, newspapers announced the same number of films, shows,
and concerts, book fairs and other cultural events proceeded, superficially at
least, as before. But the content changed radically as more and more artists were
gagged. The junta declared early on that this war was not only about weapons,
but about "ideological penetration" and about the tensions between "culture
and counterculture, in a moment in which Argentina was experiencing acute
weakness in its social controls."[11] Prohibitions (euphemistically called "guidelines") against unacceptable content came down from above. Cultural content
would harmonize with the *proceso*'s mission—there should be no contradictory
or disturbing images, nothing against church, family, or state.[12] Divorce, abortion, adultery, wife and child and elder abuse all vanished—in representation if
not in life. Images of institutional and generational conflict were to be avoided
at all cost. Stories had to have happy endings.[13] No wonder, then, that artists of
all kinds started censoring and silencing themselves in order to keep their jobs.
The prohibitions were so many, and the language so vague and all-inclusive,
that anything could be construed as subversive. People started burning their

own books. The prohibitions, Argentine playwright Diana Raznovich said, "made fascists of us all, for we were on the lookout for anything that could be construed as 'subversive' in our possessions. I remember going through my books, and burning even my Jewish cookbook, for fear it might be considered subversive."[14] Argentine life became increasingly terrifying even as Argentine culture was reduced to a world of make-believe and happily-ever-afters. The writer/songwriter María Elena Walsh described herself as Alice, struggling through her misadventures in her country/kindergarten. In 1979, in one of the first journal articles published against the *proceso*, she noted the sad state of Argentine writers: "Our pencils are broken, and we all have a huge eraser encrusted in our brains" (*Desventuras*, 18).

Even before the collapse of the junta in 1983, the population had begun its efforts to look at the atrocity of the past decade and leave behind the culture of make-believe. There was a hunger to see, to know. Accounts by people such as Jacobo Timerman, Carlos Gabetta, and Andrew Graham-Yooll had started to surface as early as 1980.[15] When *Nunca Más: Informe de la Comisión Nacional sobre la desaparición de personas* (*Nunca Más: The Report of the Argentine National Commission on the Disappeared*) appeared in 1984, it became an instant best-seller. Copies of *Nunca Más* dotted the beaches as summer vacationers in swimwear read the dreadful testimonies. Thirteen editions of the report were published between November 1984 and May 1986. This period culminated in the very visible trial of the junta leaders in 1985 ("the Trial of the Century"). The nine leaders of the three consecutive juntas that ruled between 1976 and 1983 were tried in a civilian court for crimes against humanity. The five-month trial was televised. The *Diario del juicio*, dedicated exclusively to the trial, came out weekly. *El libro del juicio* (The book of the trial) appeared in 1985. The Asamblea Permanente por los Derechos Humanos (Permanent Assembly on Human Rights), a prominent human rights organization, put out the video *El juicio: Un documento inedito*. The Madres de la Plaza de Mayo continued their marches around the plaza and began publishing their own paper, *Madres de Plaza de Mayo*, complete with its Galería de Represores (a portrait gallery of the military men involved in the repression). During this period, scholars such as Oscar Troncoso compiled and published documents pertaining to the Dirty War. In 1986, Emilio F. Mignone brought national attention to the nefarious role of the Catholic Church in the *proceso*.[16]

During this period, too, plays, films, and songs dealing explicitly or implicitly with the Argentine political situation began to appear. In 1981, a festival of twenty-one one-act plays by major playwrights was staged as Teatro Abierto (Open theatre), in defiance of government censorship. And even after their theatre, the Teatro Picadero, was burnt to the ground, the playwrights and the audience refused to be silenced; the festival moved to another location and the audience, which nightly lined up for blocks to get into the theatre, made a visible show of its support. Films such as Adolfo Aristarain's *Tiempo de revancha* (1981, Time for revenge), Hector Olivera's *No habrá más penas ni olvido* (1983, Funny, dirty little war), Eliseo Subiela's *Hombre mirando al sudeste* (1985, Man facing southeast), and Luis Puenzo's *La historia oficial* (1985, The official story) all contributed to the population's understanding of the historical period it had gone through. Songwriters and singers such as Mercedes Sosa, María Elena Walsh, Susana Rinaldi, Eladia Blazquez, and Teresa Parodi created a sense of communal resistance during and after the dictatorship with songs such as "Porque cantamos," "Como las cigarra," and "Sólo le pido a dios." Mercedes Sosa's rendition of "Sólo le pido a dios" (I only ask God) led a collective cry against the *indulto* (general amnesty) in the massive "No to Impunity" rally in Buenos Aires in 1990: "I only ask God that I never become indifferent" to war, death, or the future. Another line stresses the importance of feeling that one has done everything humanly possible to safeguard against indifference and forgetting.

By 1990, forgetting had become official policy, much against the wishes of certain groups that had vowed never to forget. Two legacies from the Dirty War haunted the new democracy under Alfonsín. The most obvious concerned the antidemocracy pressure of the armed forces and the specter of the disappeared. Alfonsín had initiated the trend toward general amnesty and "reconciliation" in 1986 with his *punto final* policy. He set February 22, 1987, as the date for a "full stop" to new charges of human rights abuses. The Law of Due Obedience followed in June 1987, dismissing charges against all but the commanding officers who ordered the tortures and executions. The other legacy, more difficult for most Argentineans to relate directly to the Dirty War, was the enormous burden of foreign debt, mostly owed to the United States, which the military had accrued to pay for the repression. Alfonsín's government was destabilized both by the two military uprisings threatening to overthrow him and by escalating inflation that rose to an incredible 5000 percent in 1989. The economic situation created a different kind of disappearance: goods vanished from the stores. Instead of discussing Argentina's recent past, people worried about obtaining food and blamed the new democracy for threatening their livelihood. Menem, running for the presidency, accused Alfonsín of unleashing "economic terrorism" on the country.

When Menem became president in 1989, he vowed to bring the economy (and inflation) under control. He succeeded with the help of his minister of

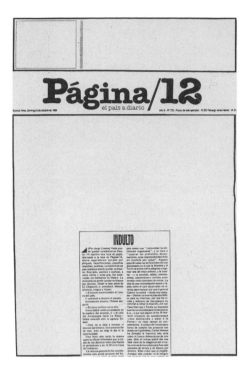

Figure 3. "Indulto." (*Página 12*,
October 8, 1989)

economy, Domingo Cavallo, who imposed strict neoliberal policies and dismantled Argentina's state-run businesses and industries, though the measures
created their own brand of economic misery.[17] But Menem further contributed
to erasing the memory of political terrorism by forgiving even those few who
had been indicted under Alfonsín. Following the third military attempt to overthrow the constitutional government on December 3, 1990, Menem granted a
presidential pardon to six senior officers accused of torturing and murdering
hundreds and thousands of individuals, including Jorge Rafael Videla and
Emilio E. Massera, two of the junta leaders most directly responsible for the
atrocities of the Dirty War. Menem justified his actions by stating that "Argentina lived through a dirty war, but the war is over. The pardons will definitely
close a sad and black stage of Argentine history."[18] *Página 12,* a leftist daily
newspaper, ran a blank front page, with an admonition against the *indulto,*
warning the country about the consequences of not coming to terms with its
past (see figure 3). A special supplement to *Página 12,* dedicated to the recent
past, was titled simply *Memory.* The front page showed nothing but a match
burning in the dark (see figure 4).

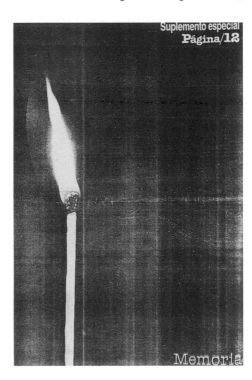

Figure 4. "Memory." (*Página 12,*
Special Supplement. 1994)

On a Thursday afternoon in 1990, as I stood in the Plaza de Mayo witnessing the moving spectacle of the Madres who still continue their weekly demonstrations around the plaza, I wondered: Were these women right? Was closure impossible? Or were the indifferent passersby right—it was over, these women were relics of the past? I asked myself if these public spectacles against forgetting were little more than a public display of the failure of spectacle itself. For in spite of the reports, the films, the songs, the public demonstrations, and the televised trial of the generals, it looked as if the criminals had gotten away with murder. As Menem's term as president proceeded, it became increasingly apparent that Argentina was embarked on a trajectory of what James Petras and Steve Vieux call electoral neoauthoritarianism. The "democracy" functioned within the same authoritarian institutional framework set up by the military and pursued many of the same political policies (5). In 1992, Menem warned students and other protesters that the danger of violent politics was not over and threatened that the "exaggerated use of liberty" could lead to a new wave of "subversion" and "another contingent of the Plaza de Mayo demanding their children."[19] In 1994, Menem was expelled from the Permanent Assembly on

Human Rights when he praised the armed forces' fight against "subversion" during the Dirty War.[20] In 1995, after the first military officer directly associated with the atrocities broke ranks and explained how he and others threw the live but drugged, naked bodies of the "disappeared" into the sea, Menem continued to advocate for silence and forgetting.[21] Let's not "rub salt in old wounds," Menem urged. The new efforts in nation-building under Menem were based not just on commonality and shared experience, but on communal forgetting. As Ernest Renan observed more than a century ago, "the essence of a nation is that all individuals have many things in common, and also that they have forgotten many things."[22]

Crossing the Line

I see only from one point, but in my existence I am looked at from all sides. — Lacan, *Four Fundamental Concepts of Psycho-Analysis*

While *Paso de dos* was a work against forgetting, it was also a play that restaged a scenario that has reappeared throughout Argentine culture since its inception. It depicted the construction of national identity as predicated on female destruction. The struggle for national identity was waged between two kinds of men (conqueror/indígena; liberal/federalists; military/antimilitary), who fought to define and occupy the "masculine" position while emasculating and feminizing the "other." Women have no space in this contest, except perhaps as the contested space itself. The battle in Argentina between the so-called nationalists and progressives during the twentieth century has been staged on and around the female body—be it the metaphorical *Patria*, Evita's wandering corpse, the nude body onstage, or the scantily clad body of the endless number of women who, during the Dirty War, appeared on the covers of national magazines that announced ever escalating acts of horror. Week after week, month after month, and year after year, Argentina's national tragedy was written on the exposed flesh of these feminine bodies. *Paso de dos* did not tell two stories—one about erotic intensity, the other about criminal/national politics— but one tale about a brutal battle for national identity and power between men, which was waged on the body of Woman. Only by controlling She, as Pavlovsky's play makes clear, can He define himself, either as the military man or as the progressive Argentine intellectual. Violence against women, it seems, can miraculously do all at once. It provides pleasure and identity for the male sacrificer-torturer. It thrills the spectator. The image of the bleeding *Patria* once more unites and uplifts the population and, besides, the "bitch" (as the play calls her) is dead. Her life is sacrificed in the interest of communal "meaning." "Cultural norms are reconfirmed or secured," as Elisabeth Bronfen has noted, over Woman/women's dead bodies (181).

During the production of *Paso de dos,* I witnessed how a woman was violently eliminated from the public sphere and transferred to the metaphorical realm of redemptive womanhood. This theatrical "disappearing act" all too clearly illustrated the mechanics of nation-building that I had previously associated with the Dirty War. She was one more in a series of sacrificial women (both "good" and "bad") circling through the Argentine public sphere whose function was to stabilize a patriarchal version of nationhood and manhood, with all its attending values and boundaries.

And I didn't like it. Clearly, I was not the intended spectator nor a welcome critic. My intervention at two subsequent meetings—the first on August 6, 1990, at a public forum on Authority and Authoritarianism in which Griselda Gambaro and Laura Yusem were invited speakers, and a couple of weeks later in a private interview with Pavlovsky—proved explosive. The Authority and Authoritarianism forum was designed to question the authoritarian structures still in place in Argentina and their effect on artists. In her presentation, Yusem, a well-known director who directed Griselda Gambaro's *Antígona furiosa,* among other important plays, was arguing that an artist could be conscious of authoritarian structures and undo them. She, an avowed "leftist" like Pavlovsky, cited *Paso de dos* as an illustration of this dismantling. When I suggested to Yusem that the performance reproduced rather than dismantled the military's authoritarian discourse, she immediately ordered me to be silent. I tried to explain my concern over the eroticized representation of violence by contrasting it to theatrical representations of violence that enable us to recognize brutality as brutality, not as pleasure. I used Griselda Gambaro's work as an example of an Argentinean playwright who very effectively represents a violent situation without eroticizing it. Someone from the audience called me a fascist for trying to restrict or censor what could or could not be shown. Yusem refused to speak to me, except to point out that I wasn't Argentinean, hadn't lived in Argentina during the Dirty War, hadn't experienced torture and therefore knew nothing about it and should keep quiet. Not only that, but the play reflected a true incident. She dismissed me as a "Yanqui feminist."

Standing in the auditorium in front of two hundred people, I suddenly felt trapped in the spectacle of nation-building and dangerous border crossings. I was the observer who had suddenly become the object of scrutiny. I had, unwittingly to be sure, become part of the drama of identity and identification. The fact that my "identity" and alliances as a Canadian/Mexican woman living and working in the United States were not easily reducible to "Yankee" was beside the point. There I was, suddenly "American," from a prestigious academic institution, speaking against authoritarianism but weighing in with a different kind of authority. The positioning itself had a history, re-affirming the old hierarchies and tensions between the "first" and the "third"-worlders, one which I was powerless at that moment to challenge or complicate. As the foreigner, I marked the outside, highlighting the boundary between "them" (Argentineans) and the not-one-of-them (the other *against* whom nationality is always implicitly set up). And though I marked the border, I was by no means out of the picture.

But, I would have said if I'd had the presence of mind, dialogues and alliances are constantly being established between people with significant "differences" to achieve similar ends. Now that we're talking about the Dirty War, we have only to think of the military, economic, and ideological ties between the Argentine junta and the Reagan administration. *And don't forget,* I might have insisted, that national identity is not the only basis for identification and mutual recognition—as the abductions and disappearances of Argentineans by Argentineans made clear. Women, for example, can align across national boundaries to demand that women's rights be treated as internationally recognized human rights. *Furthermore,* the theatre expert in me could have added, isn't there more than a little irony in a director telling an audience member that she can't understand the show because she hadn't lived through the experience? The whole point of theatre is that one doesn't have to go mad to identify with Lear and blind to empathize with Oedipus.

But, as Brecht would have put it, "this is what she was thinking, but could not say" (*Caucasian Chalk Circle* p. 82). In part, it was because (I admit it) I was stunned. But I also vaguely perceived that the explosive confrontation was also about something else. My remarks, which I had intended as *constative,* in J. L. Austin's definition of it as a "statement" conveying my concern regarding the representation of violence, were heard as performative. My words, which did not in themselves qualify as a "speech act," had nonetheless done something— they had provoked, interfered, intervened. That "Yankee" was not so much about my identity as about my audacity in carrying through an imperialist gesture in a specific historical context—the aftermath of the Dirty War—in which many Argentineans were keenly sensitive to the whiffs of international condemnation or disdain.

This day at the forum intensified my interest in the politics of looking. As a theatre and performance studies person, I've always known that my passion for looking is an occupational hazard. But now I wondered if looking always con-

stitutes an intervention. Is an equal, reciprocal exchange possible across borders, between entities that have historically been set up as unequal: "center"/
"periphery," "First" World/"Third" World, "developed"/"developing" countries? And if not, what then? We can't *not* look, because spectacles work internationally. Everything crosses borders, from people to capital, from markets to
armaments to e-mail. Fantasies, too, are exported and imported; staging techniques travel; speech acts echo each other; performances have histories or, as
Joseph Roach would put it, genealogies.[23] The neo-Nazis in the U.S. today who
advocate white supremacy belong to the same world as the neo-Nazis in Argentina with their black shirts and both groups mimic Hitler's performance. The
totalitarian spectacle of the Dirty War arose from our shared cultural repertoire. It was yet another repetition, or iteration, another example of the twice-
behaved behavior that Richard Schechner and Jacques Derrida associate with
the performative.[24] Through what act of negation, of self-blinding, can we
maintain that what happens in another country has nothing to do with us?

Standing there, I felt there was no outside, no unseen see-er who could watch
from a position safely outside the frame. As in the Lacanian field of the "gaze,"
that scopic register that situates us and within whose confines we look at each
other, we were all looking. We were looking, moreover, within a specific specular economy that was historically and culturally determined.[25] Maybe I had just
stepped into that position of the bad woman whose symbolic removal allowed
for the reaffirmation of communal norms and values. Object and observer,
at that moment I certainly felt my seeing to be alienating and oppositional,
though I had aspired for a relationship of reciprocity.

I had to make a decision: keep quiet and forget the incident, or try to
understand the scenario and my role in it. This was shaky ground. I wasn't
standing on some geographic or moral terra firma outside the scenario; I was
right there, playing to and into this web of looks. The seeing both objectified
me and pushed me forward. I, the outsider, had seen, and I had been seen
seeing because I had spoken. So now I was caught *in* the drama where I was cast
as outsider. But *seeing* also goes beyond us/them boundaries; it establishes a
connection, an identification, and at times even a responsibility that one may
not want to assume. When I sat down, Renee Epelbaum, one of the founding
Mothers of the Plaza de Mayo squeezed my hand. After the hubbub wore down
and people had started to leave, Griselda Gambaro tried to reconcile Laura
Yusem and me—"My friends, dear friends, please don't fight," she said, holding
us both. The conciliatory approach did not work. Laura Yusem would not
speak to me again. Her silence was a mechanism to deny my vision.

Pavlovsky, having heard about the exchange, met me at his office with icy

formality and a stack of newspaper reviews of his play in which he had under-
lined references to the woman's victory. She wins! he kept reminding me. She
likes it! Look, the papers themselves say so! He too insisted that the play is
historically "true." It reflected reality. A *montonera* woman had actually fallen in
love with her torturer, they reminded me. What about the 29,999 cases in which
that wasn't true, I asked? Is this a "true" representation of a torturer/victim
relationship? And why, out of 30,000 stories, do you choose to represent that
one? Isn't that already suspect? Moreover, there was a metaphoric transformation going on that allowed the spectators to see She as the embodiment of a
violated Argentina. The fallacy of sexualizing political relations of power is that
the parallel simply doesn't work. The sexualizing of political relations obfus-
cates not only the mechanisms of power, but it obscures too the politicizing of
sexual relations.

Pavlovsky insisted that the play was politically urgent insofar as it addressed
the imminent *indulto*. However, he added, he doesn't write political pamphlets
for the theatre; a work of art has its own laws and logic that don't necessarily
constitute political statements. (There is a difference, he reminded me, between
fiction and reality.) And besides, how could this play be misogynist? After all,
She "wins."

Paso de dos, like the military's representation of its project, wanted everyone
to participate in the fantasy of reciprocal desire. It reproduces and eroticizes the
annihilation of women under the guise of historical veracity, political urgency,
and aesthetic necessity. The problem is that the discourse of nation-building
enacted in *Paso de dos* transcends even extreme political differences. While
Pavlovsky is obviously antimilitary he cannot help but repeat their discourse.
The authoritarian structures activated in his play blurred the distinction between "left" and "right" and went far deeper than any such political pronounce-
ments.[26] The notions of masculinity that he reenacted result in the splitting of
the feminine, a move that historically has proven fatal to women. Women get
killed because of these fantasies in which the male's search for identity, empowerment, and intensity are born out of her splitting and annihilation.

The problem with this play, I realized in talking with Pavlovsky, was not (or
not only) that it was violent, not even necessarily that it represented violence
against women. Given the social environment in which women live it would be
bizarre if theatre did not deal with violence directed at them. But it reaffirmed
the continuity of a misogynist version of Argentine nationhood as well as the
gendered structure of representation itself—onstage and off. This spectacle of
brutalization perpetuated the traditional power relation: the male agent (author or actor) exposes himself to his (male) audience. The woman's body

functions merely as the object of exchange, the common ground that allows the males to position themselves—as agents, author, military in front of their clients, audience, population—all united by the image of the exposed woman. The photograph of *Inga, the Sexy Adolescent,* with her outstretched body and open mouth, is a more graphic example of how representational systems work through (not for) women (see figure 5). "She" is the object "he" looks through. The representation blurs the boundaries between torture and sexual desire. Her limbs "disappear" from view. Her eyes are closed, her mouth open. Her facial expression could connote pleasure, of course, but it could just as easily connote pain. Her body is both naked and inscribed; her only "modesty" lies in the producer's words plastered over sexual organs. Inga's breasts proclaim her a young sex object; her pubis serves as a billboard for showtimes and prices. The male gains insight through her genitals, which, doubling as the ticket window, allow him access. The transaction is a commercial one between producer and viewer—in/sight and access for the price of a ticket. Nor is this transaction an isolated one, either in the photograph or in Pavlovsky's play. The women's bodies on the photographs behind Inga place these examples within a wider representational practice.

As we all know, representations are not innocent, transparent, or true. They do not simply "reflect" reality: they help constitute it. Theatre, as one system of representations, participates in the larger cultural network. Each society is itself a complex system of representations. And each society tells stories about itself— about its origin, challenges, and destiny. The specific nature of the explanatory myths, images, and points of conflict gives each nation its own individual characteristics. The stories resonate with the public because they have been internalized over the years and generations. Yet Pavlovsky's story was very like the military's: the man creates himself through the annihilation of woman; community is solidified through the spectacle of "feminine" sacrifice. Nationhood, for the junta, was built by blows to the female/feminized body, both literally and rhetorically. This Motherland, to paraphrase from Joan Landes's study of the French republic, was "constructed against women, not just without them" (12). So where was this fine line between fiction and reality, between author and authority, that Pavlovsky had insisted on?

This study is my attempt to talk back. I want to advocate for a role that I feel is politically vital in our world of free markets and policed borders today—that of the responsible and educated witness. Rather than act like "good," quiet audience members who willingly suspend their disbelief, I am endorsing the part of the resistant spectator. But I could only dare this undertaking by acknowledging and capitalizing on my own limited perspective, and by using the

Figure 5. *Inga: La sexi adolescente.* (Photo by Eduardo Bottaro)

disciplinary tools that performance, gender, and Latin American studies have put at my disposal. These fields give us the tools to "read" spectacles critically and to extend that analysis to the political field. An analysis of social images (everything from news coverage to posters to the way that "wars" are staged) might reveal trends and tensions that more traditional historical analysis may have trouble recognizing. Performance studies can help us understand how the political dénouement of events are built into the conflictual performance itself. The way a particular event sets up conflict and envisions resolution predetermines the dénouement. No happy endings can possibly be scripted into certain performances of power. Understanding spectacles, with their repeated gestures, might enable us to foresee (and perhaps intervene) in their political dénouement.

Nonetheless, this project has silenced me in various ways. For one thing, I keep reminding myself that I don't belong in Argentina. It's not my problem. I should be turning my fascination with public spectacle on the spectacular rise of the extreme right wing in the United States today. Why not explore how the deep-seated misogyny of U.S. society plays itself out in a wide range of actions— from the escalating attack on welfare mothers to the silencing of powerful professional women such as Anita Hill and Hillary Clinton?[27] Why not look at how U.S. demagogues are currently setting up nation-ness as an oppositional us versus them and, in xenophobic zeal, advocating to turn the population into card-carrying citizens? In the United States, too, we hear the accusations that intellectuals, artists, the media, minorities, feminists, homosexuals, and Jews are part of a conspiracy to erode the social fabric. And even as these groups are blamed for everything from the fall in real wages to the dissolution of "family values," the Right is working overtime to corrode civil liberties. And then there is the virulent antigovernment Right, the "militias" and so-called patriots whose escalating fascistic rhetoric and politics only serve to strengthen the call for more repressive, "antiterrorist" legislation. Here too the "Right" and "Left" have become blurred. But then, of course, people in the United States might tell me that I don't belong here. Maybe I should keep quiet, love it or leave it. I wasn't born in Mexico, so I don't belong there. I've never lived in Canada, so I don't belong there. And, as my research in Argentina has taught me, many people who were not born and raised in a country either feel, or are treated, as if they don't belong there. But I am not willing to contribute to my own silencing. Perhaps a debate on becoming informed and responsible members of a de facto international community that has felt the effects of fascist ideology throughout much of this century would prove more fruitful than the fight to establish who "belongs" and who doesn't.

Other issues have been more difficult to overcome. For one thing, I have felt afraid. I fear for my Argentinean friends who are visible in a society in which their persecutors have not been brought to justice. Do I dare even name them in my study? And I'm afraid for myself, afraid mainly of having my argument misconstrued. I fear that some Argentineans will accuse me of depicting their country as a site of deviance, machismo, and violence—a move that would simultaneously distance Argentina as that undeveloped and dangerous southern other and reaffirm the moral and rational superiority of the developed North. My entire project argues against this. The violence of corporate economic systems that override democratic, humane, and egalitarian values is tied to criminal politics and human misery both in the United States and abroad. The atrocity that occurred in Argentina during the Dirty War was tied into Argentina's entry into the neoliberal world economic "order." As Neil Larsen puts it, "Many, if not most, of the policies of military rule in the Southern Cone can in fact be explained as requirements of the imperialist 'solution' to global capital disequilibrium, whereby the latter's most damaging effects are transferred to the dependent economies of the periphery" ("Sport as Civil Society" 113). Rather than "educate" the Latin Americans about democratic values, I think it's important to recognize that Latin Americans know full well what many citizens of the United States refuse to acknowledge or take to heart: that democracies are shaky institutions indeed. The successful functioning of democratic systems demands more debates, more perspectives, more connections, not fewer. Moreover, global economic systems have no borders, and though we barricade our geographic frontiers and cling to nationalist sentiments, we're all in this together—though the disparity in resources and opportunities reminds us that we're not all in it in the same way. But this acknowledgment, I fear, will bring its own repercussions from those on the Right whose agenda relies on refusing connections between economic injustice and violence.

And even when I deal with these fears, moral and ethical doubts set in. The problems surrounding the representation of violence trap those who would critique it. For one thing, the materials that I've had to study on political violence, abductions, rape, torture, and murder are so profoundly disturbing that I have often felt unable to continue. For another, the horror threatens to destroy the position of the witness—the one that I'm trying to affirm—turning the "looking" instead into that of the voyeur or morbid onlooker. The anxiety of looking and positioning I felt when confronted with *Paso de dos* underlies this entire project. Terror systems collapse positions into sides. Points of conflict become simplified and crystalized. Under siege, spectacles tend to essentialize, visually reaffirming the "given" and seemingly obvious differences within and between the sexes or the races or the classes, even as they "disappear" the traces of the performativity of that construction. The plethora of images, positions, and voices, the multiple points of conflict, and the shifting coalitions that compete for predominance in "normal" times vanish or go underground in a police state. A cartoon by the internationally known Quino shows a public space tightly packed with Big Bad Wolves and Little Red Riding Hoods (see figure 6). We're either the persecutors or the persecuted in this picture. We profit from the violence or we're undone by it. Can we even dream of opening up any other spaces?

Finally, by describing the violence am I not myself open to the very charges I bring against Pavlovsky? Can I help but reproduce the violence by further exposing these materials, the tortures and even performances such as *Paso de dos* and the others I include in this study? Is silence, as *Paso de dos* suggests, the truly heroic response? Again, I feel I have to speak back, even at the risk of falling into the trap. At moments, I admit, I have felt transgressive. I, too, am trafficking in obscenity, though my intention is to make it visible, to drag the ob-scene (or off-stage) *onstage* for critical, Brechtian engagement rather than a blind, celebratory recapitulation across the dead, female body.

Thus, I'm attempting to make space for an involved, informed, caring, yet critical form of spectatorship which, for lack of a better term, I'll call witnessing. The term "witnessing" is highly problematic both in the sense of the Western scientific ideal of the "objective" observer and in the tradition of Greek tragic drama. The first erroneously suggests that the viewer is ideologically and physically positioned outside the frame of the given-to-known/seen. And Greek tragedy, as Augusto Boal reminds us in *Theatre of the Oppressed,* casts viewers as passive onlookers, thus discouraging them/us from active involvement. The role of the Chorus, functioning as official witness, ranges from arrogant blindness (*Antigone*) to ecstatic celebration confined within careful limits (*The Bacchae*). That other famous witness in Greek classic drama, Teiresias, is what we are not—the superhuman seer. Yet, even in this tradition, there are those other witnesses, the shepherd in *Oedipus,* the sentry in *Antigone,* and other mere actors who happen to *see,* who are caught up in the looking and, willingly or unwillingly, assume the duty to pass on the insight. For them, seeing is dangerous; it imposes a "terrific burden" (*Antigone,* l. 288). Though neither the perpetrator nor the victim of events, the witness is a part of the conflict and has a responsibility in reporting and remembering of events. Why, I wonder, do we not have a word that adequately reflects the position of the active, yet all too human, see-er? Why is the witness generally depicted as either passive and disinterested or holy and superhuman? Yet, all (social and human)

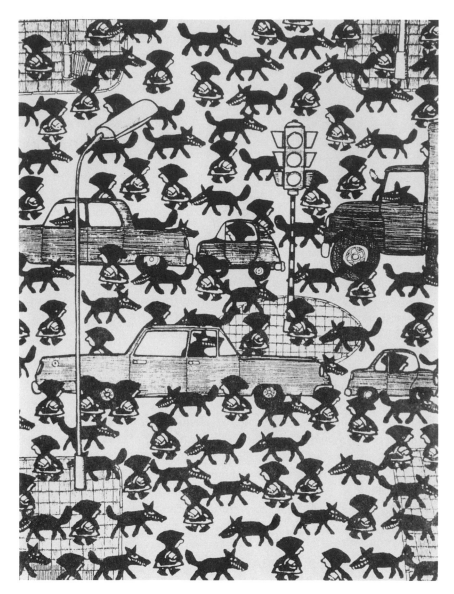

Figure 6. Little red riding hoods and the big bad wolves, cartoon by Quino.
(*Potentes, prepotentes e impotentes,* Buenos Aires: Ediciones de la Flor, 1991)

dramas require spectators/witnesses. We do not all play protagonistic roles in all dramas. Nor are we blind to what goes on around us. Why, then, is the term 'witness' inadequate? Why does Boal conclude that "spectator" too is a "bad word" (154)? Who will fulfill the function demanded of us by Antigone, or the Mothers of the Plaza de Mayo, or others who need us to recognize and do something about injustice or atrocity? My use of the word "witness," however uneasy, is consistent with the one outlined by Shoshana Felman and Dori Laub in *Testimony*. For Laub, the witness is the *listener* rather than the *see-er:* "The emergence of the narrative which is being listened to—and heard—is [. . .] the process and place wherein the cognizance, the 'knowing' of the event is given birth to. The listener, therefore, is a party to the creation of knowledge *de novo* [. . .] the listener to trauma comes to be a participant and a co-owner of the traumatic event: through his [sic] very listening, he comes to partially experience trauma in himself [. . .] The listener, therefore, has to be at the same time a witness to the trauma witness and a witness to himself" (57–58). As active spectator or witness, my goal is to examine the politics of looking, 'just looking,' dangerous seeing, and percepticide. By exploring the erasure of the 'feminine' in community building, my intention is to illuminate that which must be suppressed or repressed for the misogynist version of nation-ness to work—the woman's pain and her extermination. My goal is to make visible again, not the invisible or imagined, but that which is clearly *there* but not allowed to be seen.

2 Gendering the National "Self"

[The] nation by definition situates or "produces" women in permanent instability with respect to the imagined community . . . Women inhabitants of nations were neither imagined as nor invited to imagine themselves as part of the horizontal brotherhood.—Mary Louise Pratt, "Women, Literature and National Brotherhood"

Public spectacles, I have suggested, are the locus for the construction of communal identity. "Communities are to be distinguished," as Benedict Anderson noted, "not by their falsity/genuineness, but by the style in which they are imagined" (15). Public spectacles provide an arena for such imaginings and function as a site for the mutual construction of that which has traditionally been labeled "inner" (from phantoms to fantasy) and that which has usually been thought of as "outer" (political reality, historical facticity). The terms *spectacle, drama, scenario,* and *myth* are not antithetical to historical or material "reality." Rather, they are fundamental to political life, as the political theorist

Antonio Gramsci notes when defining myth as a "concrete phantasy which acts on a dispersed and shattered people to arouse and organize its collective will" (126). Using terms such as *fantasy* and *desire* (and so forth) in the strictly individualistic sense often associated with psychoanalysis hides the contiguousness of the psychosocial. The radical separation of the psychoanalytic from the materiality of the social, I agree with Dominick LaCapra, stems from a misunderstanding of psychoanalysis, which "is misconstrued as a psychology of the individual" when in fact it undercuts the binary between the individual and society (*Representing the Holocaust* 173).

Individual and state formation take place, in part, in the visual sphere through a complicated play of looks: looking, being looked at, identification, recognition, mimicry. This internal network of looks takes place within the overarching structure of the Lacanian gaze, what he calls "the field of the Other" (*Four Fundamental Concepts* 84), in which we are all objects, all part of the spectacle. But that external gaze cannot be understood as an ahistorical, static "given." As Marianne Hirsch puts it, looks are mediated and historicized through what Lacan calls the "image" and the "screen": "The *image* and the *screen* intervene between the subject and the object of the look, structuring the system of representation in which looking takes place . . . the image/screen could thus become the space of ideological opposition and contestation, modulating the effects of the gaze." The external register in which looking occurs undergoes modification because the "screens" (e.g., of race, class, and gender) change. The external image of the desirable, for example, is historicized and localized. Individual and national subjectivity, forged through mutual looking, reaffirm, produce, and reproduce each other in the scopic field.

My emphasis on the visible, however, should not eclipse the power of the invisible, those specters and performative hauntings that help shape what we see. Argentina is a country of ghosts, Tomás Eloy Martínez said when we were talking of the ongoing political presence of absent figures from Facundo to Evita to the "disappeared." To understand Argentina's national "ontology," we have to explore what Derrida calls its "hauntology" (*Specters* 10). But how do we recognize the phantom, this "thing that is not a thing," this thing that, Derrida claims, eludes us as spectators, most of all because we believe that "looking is sufficient" (*Specters* 11)? Perhaps the invisible can be traced through the performative traditions that produce the sense of *nation*. For what is the ghost but the re-appeared, or restored enactment that Schechner defines as performance? Without referring directly to the performative, Derrida nonetheless highlights the reiterative nature of haunting, for phantoms always represent a repetition: "[A] specter is always a *revenant*. One cannot control its comings and goings because it *begins by coming back*" (11, original emphasis).

The contiguousness of the psychosocial is evident in personal, national, and political imaginings. The performative hauntings are historical, as Derrida stresses, but "not dated" (*Specters,* 4). Doris Sommer has examined the ways in which individual sexuality and eroticism have, historically, tied into the erotics of the "state." In her *Foundational Fictions* she asks, "if there were no erotic or sentimental investment in the state, if our identities as modern sexually defined subjects did not take the state to be the primary object and therefore partner on whom our identity depends, what could explain our passion for 'la patria'?" (32). Sommer reads Michel Foucault's study of desire (*The History of Sexuality*) alongside Benedict Anderson's study on nationalism (*Imagined Communities*) to establish the context for "passionate patriotism" (33): "Foucault's hypothesis doesn't really acknowledge a seductive moment in state-celebrated sexuality" (36), while Anderson "doesn't discuss the passions constructed by reading novels, or their ideal gender models that were teaching future republicans to be passionate in a rational and seductively horizontal way" (40). I, like Sommer, am suggesting that "Eros and Polis are the effects of each other's performance" (47). The "passion" for the feminine in Argentina has led simultaneously to the geographic and symbolic expansion of the state, and to the backgrounding or disappearance of women in the name of national order.

While the passion for the feminine may be pivotal in national and nationalist imaginings that are deeply invested in maintaining a strictly fixed ideal of Woman, the terms *woman* and *women* (like *man* and *men*) cannot be considered as either stable or self-explanatory. Though each scenario may be organized around the need to control both historical women and Woman in essentialist and ideal categories, the "screens" change. The various debates themselves concerning gender in Argentina indicate that the categories are socially produced and intensely polemical. There is little "natural" about them. A "real" historical Guarani woman in the sixteenth century would not have thought of herself, or have occupied the same social role, as a Spanish woman of that same century. During the early twentieth century, Argentine physicians claimed that independent women occupied an entirely separate category: the "third" sex. In Argentina today, some Catholic Church officials and other opponents of the women's movement are "declaring war" on everything from the school curriculum to the Beijing conference, accusing feminists of subverting the nuclear family and broadening the gender categories to five: "masculine, feminine, lesbian, homosexual, and transsexual."[1] The debates illustrate the degree to which both the essentialist and constructivist positions are invested in the other, even while we continue to use the terms. As Diana Fuss points out, "While a constructionist might recognize that 'man' and 'woman' are produced across a spectrum of discourses . . . [s]ome minimal point of commonality and continuity necessitates at least the linguistic retention of these particular terms" (4). Similarly, the "state" is neither a given nor natural entity, although the military fetishized it during the Dirty War. The Río de la Plata area of the sixteenth century hardly pertains to the same mental or geographic map as the newly formed Argentine nation of the nineteenth century or the emergent new power of the first half of the twentieth century or the frustrated Argentina of today. Neither gender nor the nation-ness of the "state" are reified categories. Both concepts of gender and state undergo change, reflecting and simultaneously producing each other.

In this chapter, I'll explore the performative traditions, or what Joseph Roach calls "genealogies," that produced the Argentine sense of "nation." Genealogies of performance, according to Roach, transmit social memory through collective participation. These performances take place not only in public events and ceremonies but in written forms as well: "Genealogies of performance," he writes, "approach literature as a repository of the restored behaviors of the past" ("Culture and Performance" in Parker and Sedgwick, 48). Nation-building was predicated on a series of exclusions and violent eradication. Battles for land and national identity have been staged on, over, and through the female body—literally and metaphorically. The performances reiterated the language, methods, and aims of the Conquest: extermination rather than negotiation, all in the name of a higher "good" or order. The conqueror based his sense of supremacy on the subjugation of all others. The conquering male struggled to define himself not only in opposition to other men (the enemy) but also in opposition to the empty, hostile, and feminized environment. "Identity," which folded gender into soon-to-be national identity, was forged through the asymmetrical gesture of exerting power over the feminine.

Since the Spanish conquest in the early sixteenth century, images began to emerge that portrayed the environment as a "disloyal and fearless" *señora* who hates and kills men.[2] In 1540, hungry, exhausted, and disillusioned by the lack of gold or silver, Spanish soldiers concluded that there was nothing for them in the Río de la Plata. Fearing they would abandon their mission, their commander convinced them to go on to Asunción by promising them another natural resource: "mujeres ardientes" or "hot" Guarani women.[3] The political practice of using indigenous women-as-lure, however, was occluded by a new, and soon widespread, version of woman grabbing: the indigenous men were accused of stealing white women, an outrage that then justified the extermination of the indigenous populations.[4] Lucía de Miranda, a *cautiva* (captive) about whom Ruy Díaz de Guzmán writes in *La argentina* (1612), is a loving and loyal wife who is stolen from her husband by the ferocious and treacherous Mangoré and his brother Siripo (the protagonist of the first play by a local author to be staged in Argentina, in 1789). In both cases, the women justified the conqueror's, then colonizer's, expansion into, then possession of, the native lands. The fight to the death against the enemy "other" could be legitimated as a struggle to possess or protect the woman.

Some Argentinean nation-builders blame Argentina's continuing troubles on these performative models of individuation. The *mal,* according to Domingo Sarmiento, writing in the mid-nineteenth century, was that "in Argentine life certain patterns become established—the predominance of brute force, the preponderance of the strongest, authority without limits or responsibilities on those who rule, justice administered without rules or debate" (*Facundo* 14). Ezequiel Martínez Estrada, writing in the 1930s, claimed that "the conquistador had taken possession of all that he surveyed; he was the conquering hero over a vanquished land in which every whim was a command. He had not come to colonize, to remain, or to hope: he came to demand, to despoil, to be obeyed" (8). These thinkers feminized the Latin American continent as a land "with no past" (10). The indigenous populations and their civilizations disappeared, figuratively if not absolutely literally. (The fact that few people realize that there are currently as many indigenous peoples in Argentina as in Brazil illustrates my point: the *invisible* is not just the specter that's there and not there, it's also that which is *there* but not given-to-be-seen.) Indigenous women were cast as the source, though perhaps not the culprits, of racial degradation and ongoing civil strife: "An inconceivable blindness to the future and to his own responsibilities drove the white to beget on Indian women . . . But from that unhappy seeding there sprang forth enemies as did the Spartans from the dragon's teeth" (24–25).

While present scenarios recall a past ur-event and conjure up ghosts, their usefulness lies in transmitting current anxieties, at times appropriating or subverting the role/space of the other, and signaling possible resolution. Whether commentators such as Sarmiento or Martínez Estrada mythify or condemn the violent paradigm, they establish their own claims to "true" masculinity by arguing for or against it. For some, the image of the male who imposes his will by force (*hombría a golpes*) is a desirable one. Women, like the landscape, are obstacles to be tamed, not people with human and civic rights. For those who define themselves as liberal males, in the tradition of Sarmiento, these macho brutes are barbarians, unworthy of being called true men; the "liberal" label is reserved for those who (like themselves) are civilized, those who honor women (in their place). While both models are "patriarchal" insofar as they describe organizational structures in which men dominate women, the "liberal" version is actually more patriarchal in the etymological sense of the word: belonging to the patriarch, the father of the family. For while the Argentine liberals accept and even esteem women in their proper patriarchal position, the "barbarian" or macho model envisions a society basically free of women. The "barbarian" model, like the military model that grows from it, sees male identity (if not biological existence) as produced through a hierarchical, quasi-generational, all-male system. The soldier-male trains and produces other soldiers. This version explicitly distances itself from the family in that it considers the soldier-male (and not the family) the nucleus of the state. Thus male authenticity in both models rests on the careful positioning and control of women—whether under one's boot or under one's wing. As Sarmiento stated, "one can judge the degree of civilization of a nation by the social position of its women" ("De la educación popular" 120).[5] And because both sides compete for national authenticity at the expense of the other, no negotiation or conciliation is possible.

The struggle, as each group aimed to humiliate, humble, and feminize its other, was about gender. It was about claiming the position of power associated with maleness and forcing the other into the "feminine" position of surrender. Gender, then, was not simply the regulatory social system through which each sex assumed and incorporated the attributes assigned to it; it was also performative in that gender roles could be assumed or imposed, either unconsciously and apparently "naturally," or through open or coercive acts of violence. The battle to establish one's own version of masculinity (and, by extension, of femininity) as synonymous with national identity animates struggles in the nineteenth and early twentieth century, as illustrated by the three brief historical antecedents to the Dirty War that I include here. In juxtaposing these antecedents, I do not mean to suggest that there is a direct progression or link between one and the other (Perón was not like Rosas—there is no easy continuity between the two). Rather, I want to illustrate how the thinking about origins, destiny, citizenship, and gender became set in performative traditions deeper than any explicit political position. The traditions reappear, as my earlier reading of *Paso de dos* argued, even in political contexts that were radically opposed. The military and the left-wing armed *montoneros* in the 1970s, one might argue, were appealing to the same myths of heroism and nationhood.

1

As early as the 1830s, the federalist dictator Juan Manuel de Rosas perfected the art of politics as spectacle.[6] His regime (1829–52) set the model for the "macho" nature of authoritarianism that characterizes later manifestations of *nacionalismo,* an ultraconservative, antirevolutionary, Catholic movement that has played a dominant role in the Argentine armed forces throughout much of the twentieth century. Rosas, feared as "the restorer of the laws" and the "Caligula of the River Plate," dictated that men, women, and children had to wear the red band of the Federalists in an outward show of support. The body became inscribed with political meaning, a walking sign, as his critic Domingo Sarmiento put it in *Facundo* (1845), of "the intense love for the person of the Restaurador" (132). Allegiance to Rosas's person and cause was equivalent to national identity. As the Federalist slogan *Mueran los asquerosos salvajes, inmundos Unitarios* (Death to the repulsive Unitarian savages) suggests, political opposition was considered grounds for extermination. "The red band," Sarmiento wrote, "is terror materialized—it accompanies one everywhere, in the streets, in the bosom of the family; one must think of it getting dressed, getting undressed, and ideas are imprinted on us by association" (133). As Rosas came to embody the state, power was materialized and made visible as *fetish*—fetish not so much in the psychoanalytic usage of the term as in the anthropological, as the reification of ideology and power as well as the objectification of desire.[7] As in rituals that endow an icon or mask with all the power and terror of the sacred, the red band was seen as both containing and emanating power. It signaled both belonging and exclusion, rights and prohibition. So, too, Rosas's picture hung everywhere as if it were a sacred icon. Parties and demonstrations of solidarity with the regime were ubiquitous. Faced with the "spectacle of authority," the population was being "taught to obey, to react enthusiastically when it should react enthusiastically, to applaud when it should applaud, to be silent when it should be silent" (Sarmiento 136); in short, to behave like an obedient audience. "Doesn't the population tire of these spectacles?" Sarmiento asked (132).

Rosas's enforced production of national identity involved the double process of elevating women to the symbolic and lofty plane of Woman and simultaneously feminizing and eliminating his enemies. The "good" woman, like his daughter Manuelita, symbolized civility. Other good women, like the *cautivas* (the white women stolen by *indigenas* during their raids on the lands of white ranchers), justified territorial expansion. Abducted from their family and home, they provided an excuse for the continuing campaigns against the *indigenas* in the frontier wars. However, if and when these women were found, their menfolk no longer seemed to want them. As Esteban Echeverría's 1837 *La cautiva* indicates (and as historical records confirm), the women were seen as impure. Echeverría's Brian initially rejects his beloved María on the grounds that her abductors had dishonored her. She has to prove that she killed her captor and defended her own honor before he accepts her. The women's disappearance accelerated the disappearance of the "barbaric savages," but the lack of interest in the women's fate reveals that they themselves were of no great interest.[8] Aside from illustrating these abductions, Echeverría's *La cautiva* also reveals the gender anxiety provoked by Rosas's attack on the masculinity of his enemies. María is the one who plots to get both herself and Brian out of the desert, even though he is so weak she must carry him. She dies only when she learns that her son is dead. Francine Masiello writes: "Echeverría thus posits a curious paradox: in an age when opposition to Rosas can spell only certain defeat for men, women carry the burden of responsibility and survive in masculine pose—but succumb to external threats when they revert to the traditional role of mother" (*Between Civilization and Barbarism* 28). In the disappearance act that accompanies nation-building, women die, even as Woman, transformed into an ideal of stoicism and purity, justifies the attack on the indigenous "interloper."

Appeals for the protection of the ideal Woman, however, served not only to justify geographic expansion. Gender anxiety also underwrote the particular nature of Argentina's political tensions between the *unitarios* and the *federales*. Rosas used violent methods, including torture and assassination, to shape the social body. Commentators such as Sarmiento claimed Rosas modeled himself on the Inquisition to perfect his torments of the flesh.[9] Rosas's *mazorca* (secret police) tortured their enemies by ramming a corncob into their anus and/or castrating them.[10] The attack on sexual identity destabilized traditional concepts of gender in Argentina.[11] Society, historically organized around the recognition of sexual difference, continued to ground divisions along gender lines— but now the line was drawn between the political insiders and their male opponents, who were feminized and marginalized as *others*. As men came to occupy the degraded status of historical women, women were erased as historical subjects. Nonetheless, the idealized realm of the abstract "feminine" (as in Motherland or *Patria*, or Liberty, or Independence) was elevated to the higher plane of male bonding and moral resistance to a brutal dictatorship.

Following the tradition of portraying "true" Argentine identity as a struggle to occupy the male position, oppositional forces used the same strategies to discredit Rosas that he had used against them. Even years after his death, his enemies attributed his popularity to an association with the uncivilized realm of the "feminine," especially the attraction he wielded over "brutish" and "dark" women: "The women of the plebe loved Rosas in an almost animal form . . . More animal in fact because their adhesion and admiration had the same exuberance as the mating urge, and their brief popular encounters, the proportions of copulation . . ."[12] While liberal opponents to Rosas tried to dismiss the macho character of his rule as not-quite-male, both sides tried to negotiate the fine line between power and the feminine. Strong authoritarian leaders are not feminized as long as they control women. Masculinity, in masculinist ideology, is associated with power over, rather than proximity to, the feminine. Clearly, the ability to fix "feminine" difference and distance oneself from it helps explain why powerful leaders are said to fascinate and seduce their subjects: *fascinate*, etymologically, means to cast a spell, to have power over; *seduce* means to lead, or to lead astray. Both terms position the subject as separate from and somehow ahead or above the object. These terms also suggest the sexualized nature of leadership: the power over the susceptible masses, the hocus-pocus dimension of much leadership, then and now, here and there.

Many of the myths and evils we associate with the Dirty War can already be identified in the nineteenth century. Nicolas Shumway in *The Invention of Argentina* points to the most obvious: the appeal to Catholic values exemplified in the Crusades, the Inquisition, and the Counter-Reformation; the radical differentiation between good and evil that allowed for no intermediate or conciliatory ground and that classified as "evil" anything that was not obviously "good"; the deep suspicion of democratic process; the distrust of foreigners; the secret machinations of government; the use of secret police, censorship, and political repression to silence one's opponents; the habit of eliminating (rather than negotiating with) "the enemy"; the tendency to resort to violence to "save" the national "body." Evident too, though Shumway does not mention it, is a profound and abiding misogyny that makes itself felt in the tendency to conflate the "feminine" with all unwanted social groups: indigenous peoples, peoples of African descent, mulattos, foreigners, and barbarians.

2

The second antecedent involves the rise of the Argentine armed forces as a professional body at the beginning of the twentieth century and, specifically, the manner in which it simultaneously posed as the state while feminizing the nonmilitary population. Although this example differs from the first and third in that it lacks a central, organizing figure and is less obviously performative, it was no less instrumental in shaping national subjectivity and institutionalizing the self/other divide—which was once again predicated on gender anxiety and homophobic panic.

The modern, professional, Argentine military was largely formed by German officers, both in Argentina (where they dominated the instruction at the military academies) and in Germany (where promising Argentine military men were sent for training). Many of the military officers were second-generation

Spaniards and Italians who looked back to their countries as models and aspired to emulate their governments. The prevailing ideology in the armed forces was *nacionalismo*. *Nacionalismo* evolved in part from Rosas's federalism, which seems to have endowed it with a "national" quality, though in many respects it resembles fascism and also has its roots in the French Revolution. The *nacionalistas*, like the fascists, belabored grandiose myths of national origin and destiny. Less populist and less future-looking than the fascists, as David Rock notes, the Nationalists were revisionists who "attempted to create blueprints for the future through a mythic reinterpretation of the past . . . The Nationalists encouraged the military to perceive itself as 'the last aristocracy' and the guardian of a 'sacred territory and the Christian way of life,' which answered not to the people or the law but to 'God and history' " (*Authoritarian Argentina* xiv).

From the early twentieth century onward, the military male came to epitomize the Nationalists' aspirations for purity, truth, and grandeur. Nationalist intellectuals and professionals such as the poet Leopoldo Lugones promoted the idea that military men were the "creators of the nation," "defenders of its culture," and "the living symbol of nationality."[13] The civilian Juan R. Beltrán, who taught psychology at the Colegio Militar, wrote of their moral superiority, stating that "within our social milieu, the soldier is the purest, the most uncontaminated element. Because of this significant factor of spiritual purity, of uncontaminated conscience, the soldier is the permanent hope of the country, and the finest present reality of our democracy."[14] The military body was fetishized as the material container of national identity and aspiration. It claimed the position of the male state, guarding over the female *Patria*.

The armed forces created themselves as a homosocial organization that set the standards of behavior and modernity.[15] Homosocial societies are structured around men's relationships to other men, though as Eve Kosofsky Sedgwick notes in *Between Men*, they are "characterized by intense homophobia, fear and hatred of homosexuality" (10). Homophobic anxiety and suspicions ran deep, exacerbated, as Sylvia Molloy has noted, by the trials of high-ranking officers in Germany accused of homosexual behavior.[16] Even the kaiser was said to harbor homosexual sympathies, if not actual tendencies. These incriminations shocked Argentineans, and similar trials were being conducted in Argentina within the year. Then-president Roca tried rigorously to differentiate the military body from the homosexual body through the nature of their performance. He admired "the perfection of the regiments . . . the fifteen thousand corps guards who passed in front of us like automatons."[17] The military soldiers not only enacted their indisputable masculinity, they were also distanced from the homosexual by the mediating figure of the *Patria*. State eroticism made permissible what might otherwise have been seen as male eroticism. The intensely homophobic military defined its version of maleness in opposition to all other versions as non- or dubious maleness, that is, as feminization.

The Nationalists' exaltation of the military male as the "authentic national being" had serious social repercussions for the nonmilitary population of Argentina. The rise to prominence of the armed forces in the early twentieth century coincided with the increased attack on women and nonmilitary men. The huge rise in immigration between the late nineteenth and early twentieth century caused government officials, law enforcement officers, physicians, eugenicists, architects, and other professionals to worry about the increasing number of unattached men and women in Buenos Aires. Donna Guy's *Sex and Danger in Buenos Aires: Prostitution, Family and Nation* studies the anxieties surrounding the large number of single women emigrating to Argentina either as part of the white-slavery business or to escape devastating political or economic situations back home. The existence of these dangerous, disease-spreading others provoked all sorts of social controls and physical/spatial divides. "Good" women were separated from "bad"; the contaminating foreign was cordoned off from the national. Even though prostitution was legal in Argentina, the government's control over the women gave officials a free hand in persecuting other women as well. Businesswomen, waitresses, and factory women all suffered from what Guy calls the "witchhunt" that grew from the search for unregistered prostitutes.

This scenario was complicated by the large number of unattached men in Buenos Aires. Government officials accepted prostitution not only for the pleasure of their own upstanding patriarchs, but also as a preventive measure lest single foreigners resort to even more "unsavory" and anxiety-producing sexual habits. Physicians, psychiatrists, hygienists, and criminologists started taking an avid pseudo-scientific interest in a whole subculture of "feminized" men whom they declared to be a national threat: gay men, hermaphrodites, *simuladores*, and *invertidos*. As Jorge Salessi and Patrick O'Connor note in their essay, "For Carnival, Clinic, and Camera: Argentina's Turn-of-the-Century Drag Culture Performs 'Woman,'" the anxiety over defining and fixing sexual identity was so intense that physicians feared that many hermaphrodites were being falsely labeled. There seemed to be no way of controlling that category; even biology proved an unreliable marker. They feared that men were "passing" as women and "enjoying the sexual advantage of living as and with women."[18] No matter how much patriarchy's defenders might try to fix "woman" as a controllable category, they were threatened by the various ways that women and

Figure 7a. Rosita de la Plata (Teatro San Martin). (Courtesy of Instituto Nacional de Estudios de Teatro, Argentina)   Figure 7b. Rosita de la Plata. (Courtesy of Jorge Salessi)

gay men performed gender in unpredictable ways. Two photographs of "Rosita de la Plata" illustrate the challenges presented to anxious gender watchers. In Figure 7a, Rosita, the famous nineteenth-century actress, looks very mannish indeed dressed up in her equestrian garb and holding her riding crop. In Figure 7b, the second "Rosita" is a gay man dressed as the actress. The caption from the psychiatric journal that ran this study announces that "Rosita" is an "invertido por sugerencia"; that means he let himself be seduced or "suggested" into homosexuality. Where were these poor scientists to draw the gender boundaries when individuals availed themselves of theatrical ambiguity and masqueraded as the other?

Thus uncontrolled women and single (nonmilitary) men were once again grouped together in a feminized zone of deviancy, the "exclusionary zone" of Buenos Aires established in 1908. This zone was both geographic and symbolic, restructuring both city and citizen. Centered in La Boca, a subworld emerged characterized by brothels, pimps, prostitutes, and the tango. Though pushed to the margins, the marginalized tended to imitate and reproduce the norms of the dominant society. Tango, danced first by men, then by men and women, both reenacted and parodied the macho attitude of dominance over the feminized other, male or female. Marta Savigliano, in *Tango and the Political Economy of Passion*, observes that tango, much as the other public spectacles I trace in this study, has also been read as "a struggle for male supremacy waged between men but carried out through women" (58).

The Argentine oligarchy, fearing the large numbers of "dark," dangerous, and economically disenfranchised immigrants, looked to the writings of the European eugenicists for lessons in "improving" the race. In 1904, when the notion of the third sex was introduced, what mattered was keeping women in patriarchy: dependent and subservient to men. Argentine physicians and scientists had kept a close watch for what they considered deviant and degrading elements in the rapidly changing population and singled out the existence of a "third sex . . . made up of women who remain without mates due to emigration to the colonies; or who, due to deviant morals, have renounced or are renouncing marriage."[19] Given the inconclusiveness of biology as a definitive category, "women" were defined by moral values and their adherence to or deviance from cultural norms. This anxiety betrays a recognition of the predominance of "gender" as performative, *doing* one's role in socially regulated ways. As the eugenics movement progressed, however, the concept of "women" (already destabilized) was further atomized. It was not women but *mothers* who mattered, and not the well-being and advancement of individual mothers so much as the control of wombs. As in fascist Europe, nationalist aspirations for purity in Argentina were inseparable from the control of women and their reproductive role. The modern nation needed to modernize notions of female beauty and sexuality. The beautiful woman was increasingly portrayed not only as a product of good breeding, but as herself a good breeder. Kathleen Newman has indicated the rise of a "politicized or civic sexuality" as the new, strong, energetic woman was associated with new, strong, energetic nation-building.[20]

Feminist organizations, grassroots women's movements, and anarchist women resisted what they recognized as the repressive nature of the official policies and, more generally, the patriarchal order. They started newspapers, organized strikes, and advocated for increased civic rights and responsibilities for women. The Centro Feminista Socialista, founded in 1901, began pushing for greater rights and improved living and working conditions. Feminist activists, such as Paulina Luisi writing in 1918, insisted that women "must be freed from the sexual slavery that our society has connected to motherhood."[21]

Magazines such as *Caras y caretas* reflected the social anxiety over signs of

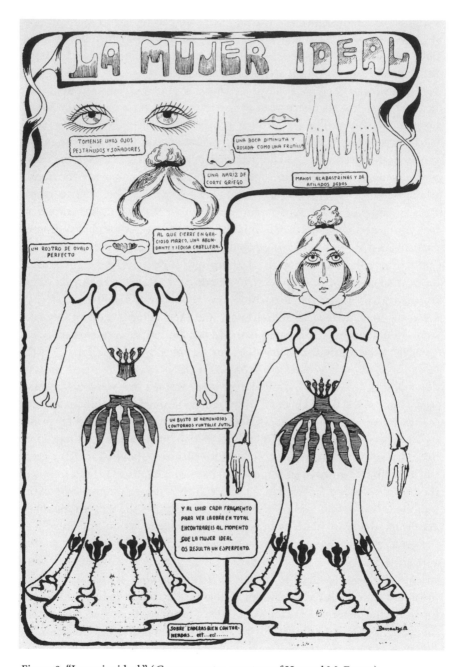

Figure 8. "La mujer ideal." (*Caras y caretas*, courtesy of Howard M. Fraser)

women's growing independence, whether as consumers of the many beauty products advertised in its pages or as "feminists" advocating for social parity, the right to divorce, and political participation (such as the right to vote). Stories published in the magazine by authors Miguel Jaunsarás, Javier de Viana, Evaristo Carriego, Leopoldo Lugones, and many others valorized the long-suffering, dependent, and virtuous woman over the wild, potentially threatening female who seeks her independence—often depicted as synonymous with lascivious pleasure. Cartoons in the same magazine during the first two decades of the twentieth century depicted women as infernal creatures. ("Mother" says the young woman, "I don't want to marry Arthur—he's a skeptic who doesn't believe in hell!" "Marry him, daughter. Between you and me, we'll convince him that hell exists.") Essays taught the public how to "read" women, how to decipher those "looks" (*la mirada femenina*), how to see her soul in her expressions. Women, another article warns, terrify men because they are so expensive. ("Donde se ve que la mujer es más cara que el hombre, y en proporción aterradora para el masculinismo." ["Where one sees that women are more expensive than men to a degree terrifying to masculinism."]) Articles gave advice on how to be a good wife: "The wife's first duty is to love her husband and win his affection"; "No suspicion, no jealousies—those are the vipers of the home"; "Never, under any circumstance, or for any motive, should a wife show that she is unhappy, irritated or angry" (and so on). Figure 8 shows that the "ideal woman" was not considered a human being, but rather, the truncated sum of her parts. She is literally manmade or, rather, un-made—an ironic example of Simone de Beauvoir's position that women are not *born* but *made* through socialization. The man (supposedly) is instructed to take a little of this and a perfect that ("tomense unos ojos") in order to shape the ideal specimen. She must have not only an acceptable shape but, of course, belong to the appropriate race and class. The separate body parts, which theoretically come together to form this woman, "disappear" through metaphoric substitution— her diminutive mouth is a strawberry. The final image and text, moreover, make clear that the whole enterprise is a joke: there is no such thing as a perfect woman. The result, the final caption tells us, is merely an *esperpento,* what Casares's *Diccionario ideológico* defines as "an exaggerated or ridiculous person or thing." Not only is the ideal woman ridiculous, so too is the viewer for even imagining the possibility of such a thing. The violent image of body parts in the cartoon signals the repressive (body-rendering) control exerted by Argentine patriarchy on its women and foreshadows the period of the Dirty War during which women and feminized others were *literally* torn limb from limb.

Though even women of the desired race and class might be viewed suspiciously, Argentine leaders found themselves in the uncomfortable position of needing them anyway. As immigration to Argentina escalated and the native population grew, officials had to come up with a means of controlling not just the population's morals but its racial makeup. Argentine leaders, scientists, and physicians developed a Catholic variation of biological politics to purify their population, instituting programs that controlled marriages, prohibited abortions, and forced pregnant women to register for state monitoring and medical surveillance. The effort at so-called racial hygiene was predicated on the state's ability to reduce women to reproductive agents.[22] The measures were misogynist, based on the assumption that women were unruly elements that needed to be brought into line for national interests. They automatically turned women into antagonists since their individual needs were placed at odds with programmatic demands on their bodies. During these early decades, women became increasingly associated with social deviance. As Francine Masiello notes, dominant discourse perceived "the feminine [as] a threat to the stability of the state; universal suffrage, modernization, and revolutionary ideals form part of a program of subversion."[23] The perception of women as enemies of the state to be dominated in the name of nationhood was one of the cornerstones of the junta's national security doctrine in 1976.[24]

3

The staging and gendering of national subjectivity is perhaps nowhere more evident than during the two terms of Juan Perón's first presidency (1946–55). He and Evita, his second wife, actively promoted his role as the charismatic, populist *Líder* (leader) associated with fascism.[25] Populism, a twentieth-century phenomenon that places "the people at the centre of the nation and State" (Rowe and Schelling 151), conflated love for the person of Perón with love for the state. The image of the *Líder* fused power and sexual prowess. One song, chanted by his followers, alluded to his superhuman sexual potency: "La poronga de Perón/Es más grande que un jamón [Perón's prick is bigger than a ham]."[26] But the "masses," theoretically the privileged party in populism, were the ones feminized and seduced by this staging. "The masses do not think," Perón said, "they feel."[27] The populist rhetoric links Perón's performance with the earlier ones in that it, too, as Doris Sommer notes, celebrates "male activity and female receptiveness as well as a hierarchy of men over women and those dependent beings (i.e., other men) metaphorically understood as women" (*One Master* 7–8).

Perón, cultivating the superhuman image, did everything on a grand scale.

He staged monumental displays of popular support complete with placards of himself and Evita. He forged a sense of national identity, community, and unity through mass mobilization. October 17, 1945, the day he was released from prison,[28] was declared Argentina's most important holiday. As the *Líder*, he used a pseudo-revolutionary language to appeal for the birth of a "new Argentina." Evita, an actress and radio personality, helped shape the image of Perón as a hero in a category with Alexander the Great, Columbus, Napoleon, and José de San Martín and a savior, a new Jesus Christ, while she presented herself as his adoring follower and companion.[29] The two adorned themselves with numerous hyperbolic titles. Perón represented himself as the "Liberator of the Republic." Evita was the "Lady of Hope" and the "Spiritual Leader of the Nation." The "popular," understood as the disempowered groups that adored their leaders, became sucked up into a carefully orchestrated "popularity."[30]

Perón, following a long tradition, specialized in making political allegiance visible. The show of support by his working-class followers, the *descamisados* (the "shirtless" workers), had been instrumental in his rise to power. Workers and peasants would literally strip their shirts off when Perón and Evita paraded before them. Perón and Evita participated actively in the spectacle, seducing and fascinating their audience through a show of sentimentality. Perón delivered his speeches to the *descamisados* in shirtsleeves, unbuttoning the top few buttons. Evita, dressed in her designer clothing, led the flourishing country into the First World of glamorous movie stars and trendsetters. Perón and Evita seduced the population as a Hollywood couple: "Evita y Perón, un solo corazón [Evita and Perón, one heart]." With radio and then television at their disposal, their performance reached ever-wider audiences.

Those who were not won over by love for the *Líder* were controlled in other ways. Perón continued the Nationalist tradition of persecuting his enemies, dismissing university professors, curtailing the press, and purging the Supreme Court. He introduced laws (such as the Ley de Desacato) to criminalize all opposition to authority and to justify police surveillance. He, too, resorted to using secret police to ensure conformity. Instances of police brutality and even torture became routine. Like the military leaders in the 1970s, Perón declared a "state of internal war" in 1951, allowing himself more leeway in attacking his enemies. "Disappearance," torture with the electric cattle prod, and other atrocious specialties of the Dirty War were reportedly practiced by Perón's clandestine forces (Rock, *Authoritarian Argentina* 150). Courses on *peronist* doctrine became mandatory in schools of all kinds, from the military academy to public schools. Evita's ghostwritten autobiography, *La razón de mi vida* (mistranslated as *My Mission in Life* and tampered with by Perón), became required reading.[31] And Perón continued the tradition of appeasing the military with armament acquisitions, special favors, and promotions.

Evita was key to Perón's success for several reasons. First, her flashy good looks enhanced Perón's sexual (though not social) status. (The oligarchy found her, and by extension him, crass and opportunistic. Evita's earlier role as his mistress enhanced Perón's image as a military male rather than as a family man.) Second, she helped orchestrate his position with a theatrical flair—her hair, her figure, her clothes, hats, and jewels, her incendiary speeches, her tireless work for women and the poor attracted national and international attention. More importantly, she was acutely aware of the performative nature of her two roles in Argentine politics, as Eva Perón, wife of the president, and as "Evita," the advocate, almost savior, of the disenfranchised.

> When I chose to be "Evita," I chose the path of my people. Only the people call me "Evita." . . . Men of the government, political leaders, ambassadors, men of business, professional men, intellectuals, etc., who call on me usually address me as "Señora"; and some address me publicly as "Most Excellent Señora" or "Most Worthy Señora," and even, at times, as "Señora Presidenta." They see in me only Eva Perón.
>
> The *descamisados*, on the other hand, know me only as "Evita."
>
> I appeared to them thus the day I went to the humble of my land, telling them that I preferred being "Evita" to being the wife of the President, if that "Evita" could help mitigate some grief, or dry a tear. (*My Mission* 63)

Long before Evita was fetishized in death, she had already made a fetish of herself. As an object of self-representation, Evita far outweighed any "real" subject of representation. While commentators argue vehemently about her "real" motivations and goals, here I'm interested primarily in Evita's self-presentation and the uses made of her image after her death—in representation as opposed to any possible "reality." Evita perfected the performative mode that the nationalist discourse envisioned for Argentine women—her glorious image enlightened the population even as it erased her historical facticity.

Her words, in sharp contrast to her actions, reenacted the "natural" hierarchy of men over women. In words written by others and edited by Perón, Evita compared herself to the *Líder* in images that accentuated the inferior status of women in gendered binaries: "In different ways we had both wanted the same thing: he with intelligence, I with the heart; he, prepared for the fray; I, ready for everything without knowing anything; he cultured and I simple; he great and I small; he master, I pupil. He the figure and I the shadow. He sure of himself, and I sure only of him!" (*My Mission* 43). The link between Perón (as leader of the government) and Evita (as leader of major charity organizations) gendered institutional operations. The relationship allowed Perón to exert power over the masses while he calculated both the desired distance and proximity to the underclass. The general could remain strong, tough, and rational, in charge of important matters such as the economy, the military, and international relations, while Evita picked up, and actually came to embody, *excess*—that which overflowed institutional structures and could not be officially mandated. Her passionate intervention on behalf of the poor, especially women and children, could be construed as "soft," "maternal," a complementary *plus* or add-on to the national well-being.

In practical terms, however, Evita's investment in the poor, particularly in poor women, was fundamental to Perón's political power, for she brought women into the *peronist* movement. Evita was instrumental in getting women the right to vote in national elections, and she organized them into the Peronist Feminine Party. Her success in bringing women into the Argentine political process can still be felt in Menem's current *peronist* government, which recently decreed that one of every three new government posts must go to a woman. Yet, while Evita advocated for women's rights, those rights were framed (by her? by Perón?) strictly within the confines of patriarchy. Women, according to what Evita wrote in her "autobiography," "were born for the home" (*My Mission* 189), but she wanted to ensure that women felt more protected there. She wanted women's work to be respected, and even paid for, arguing that a mother "is the only worker in the world without a salary, or guarantee, or limited working hours, or free Sundays, or holidays, or any rest, or indemnity for dismissal, or strikes of any kind . . . obligations without any rights! Free service in exchange for pain and sacrifice" (190). Yet the answer, according to this blueprint, did not lie in changing or expanding women's roles but in perfecting existing conditions for mothers: "the world really needs more homes every day, and for them more women willing properly to fulfill their destiny and their mission" (190). Thus, Evita distanced herself from feminists, whom the "autobiography" refers to as "ugly" and "old maids" (185), by saying that women who worked in the public realm were "masculinized" and a "strange species of woman . . . which never seemed to me to be entirely womanly" (186). As before, acceptable subjectivity as a woman was constructed against those women who in any way challenged patriarchal values or openly demanded equality. She, a childless public figure who obviously exceeded the stated norms, had to justify her activities by stressing that she was the "mother" of her people. Thus Evita, intentionally or not, continued the notion of a third sex developed by turn-of-the-century physicians and eugenicists to designate women who were not content to accept the domestic role that society forced on them.

The liberation movements Perón and Evita organized for the *descamisados* and for women, respectively, appear ultimately to have been a means of securing their own political position. Perón lost interest in the workers soon after he consolidated power. And, although many Argentines would dispute this, the model that was promoted of Evita, as the embodiment of loyalty and submission to Perón, was not the most promising one for women's equality: "As a woman I belong to him utterly, I am in a manner of speaking his 'slave'; but never have I felt as free as I do now" (*My Mission* 169). Although she was terminally ill with cancer in 1951, when women were first granted the vote in a national election she very publicly cast her vote for Perón from her hospital bed and urged the population to do the same in a radio address. She promised to accompany her *descamisados* "like a shadow, repeating in your ears and consciences Perón's name, until you deposit your vote in the urn as a message of love, faith, and loyalty for the Leader of the people. When each of you deposits the ballot, I want you to think and to know that I will be at your side spiritually to thank you in Perón's name."[32]

Evita's death from cancer at the age of thirty-three in 1952 threw Argentina into a national state of mourning. The working-class sectors of Argentina felt that they had lost the only person who had protected them selflessly. Her body, embalmed in a glass-lidded coffin, was displayed for two weeks. Multitudes crowded the streets to bid farewell. The lines of mourners, according to Marysa Navarro's *Evita*, were thirty blocks long. On July 29, a candlelit procession was organized that culminated in front of an enormous photograph of Evita placed in the Plaza de Mayo. At 8:25, the moment of her death, all the candles were extinguished. The highly orchestrated procession that took Evita's body to lie in state at Congress attracted two million people, and was followed by another candlelit procession that, again, culminated at 8:25. For three years after her death, radio broadcasters would announce the time every day: "It's 8:25 at night, the moment in which Evita passed into immortality." Altars, with huge photographs of Evita, were built to her in public spaces. On August 10, her body was taken to the CGT (the Trade Union Center), where it was to remain until the monument being made to honor her was completed. As the *Nación* announced after her death, Evita had become "an object of exaltation."[33] Perón planned to build an enormous mausoleum for Evita, rivaling Lenin's tomb in size. The statue in her memory was to be larger than the Statue of Liberty.

Both Evita's image and her body became highly charged objects of political tension. She accumulated all the positive and negative power of the fetish, both sacred and repulsive. Her image haunted the country. A thing, an object, a body, she was endowed with superhuman, magical, and even sacred qualities. Not only was her body embalmed, but three wax copies were made of it. For most, she was a saint, the "spiritual leader of the nation," a martyr, a pure, almost virginal figure uncontaminated by base interests. She represented the unending self-sacrifice for her people. For others (mainly the anti-*peronists*, of course), she was a whore, "that woman," "the woman with a whip," a castrating woman who sought to control Perón as well as humiliate and destroy those who saw through her.[34] Both visions were grounded in the anxiety caused by controlled/uncontrollable feminine sexuality. The opposing virgin/whore stereotypes illustrate the manner in which Woman/women generally, and Evita most particularly, can function as the hinge between the "pure" and the "impure," the sacred and the sexual. By possessing Evita's body, fans and foes sought to tap into, or rein in, her extraordinary force. Needless to add, both versions of Evita were profoundly misogynist. In both, she was a dangerous woman, for though she repeatedly stressed women's supporting status in relation to men, her own remarkable power threatened to collapse all gender and even human boundaries. To some, Evita seemed tougher than the toughest man—Perón himself. Her devotees, on the other hand, also dehumanized her by turning her into an object of religious fervor and trying ultimately to sanctify her. Rather than examine the astonishing political career and enduring influence of the illegitimate, working-class, and relatively uneducated Eva Duarte, commentators have tended to use her to uphold or attack either the proscribed role for women in politics or, more commonly, *peronismo* itself. No historical figure that I know of more aptly exemplifies Elisabeth Bronfen's observation that "over her dead body, cultural norms are reconfirmed or secured, whether because the sacrifice of the virtuous, innocent woman serves as a social critique and transformation or because the sacrifice of a dangerous woman reestablishes an order that was momentarily suspended due to her presence" (181). Evita herself, however, understood the power of the fetish in public spectacle and actively participated in her own fetishization.

Evita's body, from the time of her death in 1952 until Perón's return to Argentina in 1973, was the pivotal object in the struggle to control her image and the fetishistic power that continued to emanate from it. Toward the end of 1955, her body was kidnapped from the Trade Union Center. A short story entitled "Esa mujer" (That woman) by the disappeared author Rodolfo Walsh recounts what the kidnapping represented for the men involved. According to Tomás Eloy Martínez's *Santa Evita*, this was not a fictional account. He has the tapes of the interview between Walsh, himself interested in finding Evita's body (though she is never named), and the *coronel* who robbed the body and alone knew of its whereabouts. The *peronists,* a third party in this struggle, frantically look for the body themselves, and make repeated threats on the *coronel's* life and the well-being of his wife and daughter. As they speak, the *coronel* drinks himself into a frenzy in a darkened room, hiding from his enemies:

> "That woman," I hear him [the *coronel*] mumble. "She was naked in the coffin and she looked like a virgin. Her skin had become transparent. You could see the metastases from her cancer, like those little drawings one makes on a foggy glass. . . . There were four or five of us and we didn't dare look at each other . . . When we took her out . . . that repulsive *gallego* . . . jumped on top of her. He was in love with her corpse, he touched her, he stroked her breasts. I punched him on the snout . . ." "But that woman was naked," he says, as if someone were contradicting him, "I had to cover her mount of Venus. I put the shroud on her . . . I told you she was naked, didn't I? A goddess, naked and dead." (*Los oficios terrestres* 13–15)

Although not a *peronist* himself, the *coronel* argues, he did them a favor by protecting their beloved corpse. He relates how they cut off part of her little finger for identification purposes, how they took her out of the building, out of the city, out of the country, and buried her. " 'She is standing!' the Coronel screams. 'I buried her standing, like Facundo, because she was a macho!' " (18). "Where is she, Coronel?" the narrator asks. " 'She's mine,' he said simply. 'That woman is mine' " (19).

In this account of the struggle for the disappeared corpse, Walsh captured the profound though radically contradictory meaning that Evita's body had for Argentines of all political persuasions and the lengths these different men were willing to go to obtain and possess it. Her naked dead body remains at the center of the macho struggle to grab/protect her overwhelming power.

Whatever the specific facts of the saga, Eva's body literally disappeared when *peronismo* became a dirty word in Argentina. It was kidnapped from Argentina, transferred to Italy and later to Spain, only to reappear after Perón's death. When her body arrived once again in Buenos Aires in November 1974, her coffin was accompanied by a wall of armed men (see figure 9). Her body tells a story about the positioning of the feminine on the symbolic level even as it disappears from the literal, material sphere.[35] Her early death cemented the ideal of Evita—self-sacrificing, martyred, and literally disembodied—as the paragon of Argentine womanhood. She, the mother of Argentina, was the image of national unity. Her dead body, though literally reproduced, was nowhere to be found.

Figure 9. "Eva Perón: El día que llegaron sus restos." "Fotos, hechos, testimonios de 1035 dramáticos días: 25 de mayo de 1973–24 de Marzo de 1976" (*Gente*, 1976).

Evita's specter continues to dominate the Argentine imaginary. María Elena Walsh's poem from the early 1980s, "Eva," reenacts Evita's funeral and the "atrocious pilgrimage" of her body. The poem recognizes the deep ambivalence felt toward that figure—the fanaticism it provoked in the underclass, the cynicism in the upper class. "I don't know who you were, but you risked everything." Maybe one day, the poem continues, the image of Evita will bring Argentine women together—those who are against her, those who worship her—not because of what Evita stood for exactly, but because she "had guts." Evita "put women in history," and she stood up to those who opposed her. That courage, if nothing else, can serve as a model for women's empowerment. Gambas al ajillo, a feminist theatre group in Argentina, lugged a coffin (supposedly Evita's) onstage during their 1994 production, *Gambas gauchas* (see figure 10). Everywhere Argentine women go, the Gambas seem to suggest, they have to carry this weight. They have to negotiate with Evita's image because she dominates the social imaginary and occupies one of the few spaces available to women. But it is clear throughout the show that the coffin also has a positive use-value. Irma Roy, a politician who was a radio and TV actress and a candidate to be Menem's vice president in 1994, transformed herself into an Evita look-alike in order to win popular support. She not only lost weight, redid her hair, and took on a 1950s look, but she mimicked Evita's speaking style and even

Figure 10. Evita's coffin. In the play *Gambas gauchas* by Gambas
al ajillo. Buenos Aires, 1994 (Photo by Diana Taylor)

addressed the population as her *descamisados*. Evita is the phantom that dominates the public sphere. Hers is the power of the invisible that shapes visibility itself. She is resuscitated time and again as a sacred relic. The women who perform her speak as ventriloquists—they absent themselves in their bid for public acceptance. They, too, are caught up in the "desiring-machine," both the product and the producers of the same fetishistic spectacle.

Perón was overthrown in 1955 by an extreme right-wing, oligarchic, Catholic, and antipopular coup. Workers were brutally persecuted; *peronismo* became illegal. The noisy clamor, the colors and popular spectacles associated with *peronismo* gave way to a hushed, orderly silence. A decree was issued prohibiting "the images, symbols, signs, expressions, doctrines, articles and artistic works that were or could be taken for the affirmation of peronist ideology."[36] Even so, photographs of Evita did not entirely disappear as she, and *peronismo*, continued to haunt the nation. The political repression of *peronismo* did little to displace the ever more potent shadow of the absent hero and heroine, and provoked new and increasingly more violent forms of resistance and opposition. The anti-*peronists* faced the repercussions of trying to prohibit the use of symbols rather than subverting them to their own ends. They faced the power of the strategically "non-said" over which they had little control.[37] Argentina entered into a period of prolonged civil strife that only began to calm down after the end of the Dirty War.

The decade between the violent coup by General Juan Carlos Onganía in 1966 and the 1976 coup ushering in the Dirty War was particularly turbulent even in the context of a century characterized by coups, uprisings, and repression. The armed struggle between extremist *peronist* and anti-*peronist* forces had made abductions, murders, and other forms of violence all too common since the beginning of the 1970s. The virulent tensions between the factions seemed unresolvable, in part because no clear-cut affinities or agenda united the *peronists*, and no clear-cut ideological differences separated the *peronists* from the anti-*peronists*.[38] There were also extreme left-wing and right-wing factions of *peronismo* with little uniting them except the figure of Perón himself.

When Perón was due to arrive in Buenos Aires after his seventeen-year exile, both the left-wing and right-wing factions of his party turned up at Ezeiza, Buenos Aires's international airport. In what appears to have been an orchestrated ambush approved by Perón, the right wing opened fire on the left. To skirt the massacre, Perón's plane was rerouted to a military base. The Leader was once again safely installed in Buenos Aires and, soon thereafter, in the presidency. He publicly disavowed the *peronist* left wing, primarily made up of the *montoneros*. Surprisingly perhaps, the *montoneros* did not turn on Perón.

They found other ways to explain the treachery, mainly by blaming the evil influence of the "witch" (*brujo*), José López Rega, Perón's right-hand man, and Perón's wife and now vice president of Argentina, María Estela Martínez de Perón (commonly known as "Isabelita").

After Perón's death two years later, the *peronist* and anti-*peronist* groups lost the only remaining symbol of what had united them in the first place. Isabelita, the Argentine cabaret dancer Perón had met in Panama, was now the first female president of Argentina and head of the Argentine armed forces. The anti-*peronist* military actively contributed to the crisis and further destabilized Isabelita's rule. One could argue that the coup actually started in 1974, with Perón's death. If the military leaders—Jorge Rafael Videla, Emilio E. Massera, and Orlando Agosti, who became the junta leaders after the coup—allowed Isabelita to keep power it was for two reasons. Under a constitutional government, the AAA (paramilitary, anticommunist alliance) could undertake the attack on the armed Left. In the two years preceding the 1976 overthrow, the anti-*peronist* Ejército Revolucionario del Pueblo centered in Tucuman, was almost decimated. Moreover, allowing Isabelita ostensibly to retain power set her up to look incompetent. When the time for more repressive measures presented itself, the military leaders could point to her inefficacy to justify their dictatorship. Unlike Evita, Isabelita showed no talent for leadership and was an inept ruler by any standards. Nonetheless, the Argentine political crisis that had been snowballing for decades can hardly be attributed to her lack of experience. In looking at how gender formation converges with state formation, it is significant how she became the lightning rod for hatred from all quarters, even long after she ceased to exert any influence whatsoever on national events.

For months leading up to the coup, the daily papers were filled with photographs and articles highlighting civil disturbances. Paid political advertisements (like those sponsored by the Nationalist organization Liga Pro Comportamiento Humano) called for immediate intervention by the Argentine armed forces. The image of the dangerous, "crazy," "irrational" Left was to a great extent *created* by the various factions on the Right.[39] There were significant numbers of well-meaning, committed students and workers who organized either to protest or resist the increasingly oppressive governmental mandates. They worked in the shanty towns, in community projects, in universities and high schools, and they became involved in all sorts of initiatives to promote social justice and equality that were frowned upon by the junta. But the number of armed antigovernment forces was greatly exaggerated during this period to substantiate the military's assertions that World War III had broken out on Argentine soil. And in the face of this crisis, the government was shown as hysterical and out of control. In its January 22, 1976 issue, the weekly news magazine *Gente* published a two-page photograph of a train explosion with three-quarter-inch headline: "Are We Really Going Crazy?" That same issue ran a feature article on Angola with huge headlines: "You, Argentines, Have the Obligation to Become Informed." The only rational solution, the media suggested, was turning the government over to some good, strong, and rational men.

The military leaders attempted to render *peronismo* ridiculous by mocking Isabelita. Several months before the coup, General Videla had expressed to the "señora presidente . . . that all the errors committed by the government in the period following General Perón's death had, as a common denominator, the presidential figure, that was visibly deteriorated."[40] Isabelita was portrayed not only as an inept president, but as an aggressive and violent woman. The media reminded the population that she had been a cabaret dancer (by implication, little better than a whore). Newspapers quoted her as saying: "I know that some people think that I didn't learn anything. But they're wrong. I didn't spend those twenty years in Europe with the Leader looking at fashion shows." Then, too: "Nobody overturns me . . . Not even Perón." And, "if necessary, I'll have to become a woman with a whip to defend the interests of the *Patria*."[41] Immediately following the coup, Argentine newspapers reported that Isabelita had protested that she couldn't go into exile because she didn't have anything to wear.[42]

The strategy of discrediting Isabelita served a slightly different purpose after she had been ousted. The military advertised her failings publicly to distract from their own criminal machinations. During soccer's World Cup in 1978, one of the most brutal moments of the dictatorship, magazine covers announced to international tourists that Isabelita's misrule was to blame for the Argentine crisis. The magazine *Somos* of May 1978, for example, showed Isabelita looking up as a cherub erased the halo over her head. The headline of the magazine read: "Isabel's Intrigues."

Nor did Isabelita's usefulness as scapegoat end with the military dictatorship. During 1984, her body and reproductive organs were targeted by "progressive" leftist humorists in their weekly magazine, *Hum®* (spelled with the *r* in the *o*, to allude to *humo*, or smoke, hot air), to attack Argentina's new president, Raúl Alfonsín. One cover (see figure 11) has Isabelita up in orbit in a space suit with Alfonsín following her on a rocket/screw, literally screwing her from behind. Another (figure 12) has a grotesque, hugely pregnant Isabelita in hair rollers, rocking as she knits baby clothes; the caption reads "Painless Labor: The Fruits of Reconciliation" (literally "coupling"). A third cover (figure 13) shows a dwarfed Alfonsín, complete with black moustache, suckling at the enormous breast of Isabelita. Another (figure 14) has Isabelita pushing a baby carriage

Figures 11–14. Isabelita, Hum®, #126–129, 1984.

with a baby Alfonsín brandishing a toy sword. The front of the carriage has a sharp pointed face, a caricature of the ex-junta leader Videla, whose prominent nose now resembles a penis with eyes, semi-erect and on the lookout. The grotesque portrayal of Isabelita's pregnant or maternal body embodied the vulgarity and excess that her critics associated with Perón's working-class following. Her hair rollers, her bedroom slippers, her sharp and ugly face all conjure up the social body most intimately associated with Perón. The popular hatred of her emanated and extended—people not only despised her, they could discredit Alfonsín by associating him with her.

As in the case of Evita, a woman once again incarnated everything that the opposition saw as wrong with *peronismo*. But unlike in the case of Evita, no one came to Isabelita's defense. The misogynist images of Isabelita represented an available female body on which the battle for power between men could be played out. The struggles around gender (as "true" male identity and dominance were fought out on female bodies) helped move the focus away from some of Argentina's acute political problems. But they also signaled that women's increased participation in the social arena was perceived as a serious threat to governmental control. By 1978, women enrolled in universities at the same level as men. The irony, of course, was that a university education was seen as a plus for the modern women, enhancing her status as a wife and as a mother. But female university graduates were not encouraged to enter the workforce. They were pressured to put maternal and family "values" over their careers and thus were often limited to part-time employment. And though professional women outnumbered professional men in the workforce more than 2 to 1, they were either relegated to positions of inferior status or paid half a man's salary for comparable work. The normalized sexism hid the fact that almost 1 in 5 Argentine households in the late 1970s was headed by a woman. Moreover, women in low-income jobs were the first to be pushed out of the workforce and back into the home.[43] The number of university women who were unable or unwilling to return to more traditional roles is measured in part by the large number involved in antidictatorship activities. Though most of these were by no means armed opponents, they were viewed as enemies of the state. Working-class women also took on added burdens, such as odd jobs they could do at home as their families became poorer; they organized soup kitchens and other community projects in the *villas miserias,* or shanty towns, that sprang up around the country. The volatile political and economic situation affected the lives of most Argentine women, who had to find some way of coping with the escalating crisis.

Tensions in Argentina were exacerbated by the United States' intervention.

Under Richard Nixon and Gerald Ford, the United States strengthened the armed forces in their war against "subversion"—that is, dissension of all kinds. The military leaders and torturers had been trained in the U.S. School of the Americas, and they continued to receive financial support from the United States for their brutal implementation of the Doctrine of National Security.[44] The U.S. government aligned its national "interests" with the military's. These economic factors, combined with a long tradition of the antiliberal, misogynist ideology known as *nacionalismo,* coalesced to bring about the Dirty War.[45]

3 Military Males, "Bad" Women, and a Dirty, Dirty War

Even the most repressive and the most deadly forms of social
production are produced by desire . . .
—Deleuze and Guattari, *Anti-Oedipus*

The modern state enacts its authority as ghostly, fantasmatic authority. But it would be wrong
to deduce from this . . . that the state is any the less real for that.—Jacqueline Rose, *States of
Fantasy*

"Damnable Iteration": The Military Spectacle

On the day of the last Argentine military coup, or *golpe,* March 24, 1976, the
front page of the daily newspaper, *La razón,* featured an imposing photograph
of a military helicopter abducting the constitutional president, María Estela
Martínez de Perón ("Isabelita"), from the Casa Rosada. Just below the photograph, the headlines for another article boldly announced: "No Public Spectacles." The military leaders had temporarily banned everything public, from
theatre to horse races.[1] They, after all, were the national protagonists, theirs the

mission, theirs the drama. The idea was not merely to seize power—they had done that. Now they wanted to usurp the space formerly associated with civil society. Why was controlling spectacle so vital to their political agenda? Was their "process of national reorganization," as they euphemistically called their war against the civilian population, in itself spectacular? If so, how many spectacles were taking place? Was the coup-as-act part of a larger, consensus-building spectacle unfolding both before and after March 24? Or does its status as singular, direct act put it in a different category altogether?

In "Sport as Civil Society: The Argentinean Junta Plays Championship Soccer," Neil Larsen neatly differentiates between the coup-as-event and the more general consensus-building spectacle that the junta needed to normalize and legitimate its actions. Larsen argues that if "one is able to view the event-form of the 'golpe' as in essence a brief but extremely concentrated civil war ending only in a *military solution*, there then opens up a space for historical interpretation of succeeding events as the struggle to establish a stabilized social *consensus*. It is by means of this consensus that provisional military supremacy (domestic terror) becomes definitive political victory."[2] The coup-as-event, in other words, belongs to a different performative mode than the consensus-producing spectacles needed to make good the coup. The Argentine Dirty War thus seems to present two kinds of events. The first, the coup, posed as a unique event never to be repeated, and the second worked to normalize the situation by extending the temporal and spatial reach of the military men into civil society. This second category would include various forms of public spectacles—the 1978 World Cup analyzed in Larsen's essay as well as other events and images circulating in the public sphere—that the junta used to create a sense of national unity.

I see the spectacles of the Dirty War quite differently. The coup-as-event and the consensus-building project are intricately related. They created not a consensual society but a militarized zone. As the military's display demonstrated, Argentina was at war. The population, confined to spectatorship, was either seduced or coerced into identifying with the military project. Thus, I disagree with Larsen's conclusion that the junta's downfall in 1983 can be attributed to its failure to create a civil society. The junta's disastrous military failure in the Malvinas/Falkland Islands war probably had more to do with its downfall, as did the severe economic crisis that resulted from the huge foreign debt to finance its "war on subversion." Although the various factors clearly contributed to the military's inability to achieve a "definitive political victory," the immediate causes for its dishonor had more to do with failures of war than with failures to lay the basis for peace.[3]

What I will argue here is that the coup-as-event and the consensus-building spectacles converged to feminize the population as it made military violence look necessary, even desirable. Though apparently discrete events, their success and coherence depended on their *iterability*. The "unique" military coup was, after all, only the most recent of six in Argentina alone since 1930. The showing of the instruments, the total occupation of public space, and the mechanical display of rigid, controlled male bodies against which the leader(s) stood tall, illustrate both the mimetic quality of totalitarian performance and the prohibitions built into it: the population was forbidden from mimicking or parodying its gestures. Interestingly, the public exhibition of power was unnecessary from a strictly military perspective, since Isabelita had no one to defend her. The junta leaders were the very men in charge of her armed forces. Rather than whisk her away by helicopter, with a highly visible military backup, they might just as effectively have abducted her by cab. The display of military might was just that: a show, a ritualistic declaration of a "new beginning." The event was not a "brief but extremely concentrated civil war," which, like all wars, presupposes two sides. In 1976 Argentina, unlike the 1973 coup in Chile, for example, no one was fighting back.

The military demonstration of strength was necessary for performative effect. The junta deliberately stressed the ritualistic (and thus quasi-sacred) nature of its endeavor or *proceso*. Like the tripartite ritual pattern identified by anthropologists such as Arnold van Gennep and Victor Turner, the "process" was characterized by a breach (the coup), a moment of crisis or liminality (the Dirty War), and a period of supposed reintegration (*reorganización*).[4] The coup-as-event inaugurated the new beginning, setting the three junta leaders (who had just hours before served under Isabelita) apart from the old order. While claiming to embark on a new beginning, the junta nonetheless promised a return to Argentina's original, albeit long lost, path to glory. The reintegration or restoration of order associated with the ritual process was declared, though never achieved.

This tripartite staging was, by the logic of ritual, citational. It modeled itself on previous coups that were themselves indebted to earlier displays of heroic military prowess. This all too recognizable show signaled invincibility, virility, superior strength. Part of the efficacy of the coup-as-event, then, stemmed from its respect for convention. The public immediately saw it as a *golpe* and reacted appropriately: people vacated the public spaces. The communication was successful though the military show resulted in absenting the addressee (the public). A performance that "disappears" its audience seems to invert the traditional theatrical dependence on presencing. But there is nothing unperformative or antidramatic about a strategy that convinces viewers of the reality and power of that which they are not allowed to see. Pre-Columbian rituals, horror shows, and erotica function on the same principle. The population got the picture and stayed out of the way.

Just as the physical staging of the coup mirrored earlier ones, so did its language. Each coup echoed the terms of previous ones—each promised the end of the old order, the dawning of the new, and progress toward Argentina's glorious future.[5] Though its source of power, the iterability of the performance, needed to be kept hidden. Each junta annulled the past and erased history by mandating a new beginning. Originality, not iterability, was associated with power. The joke of so many "new" beginnings, of course, is that each junta repeated the same slate-cleaning gesture of the one before, monotonously laying claim to originality.

The consensus-producing spectacles entailed different performative strategies, different modes of presencing, and unfolded in a different temporal and spatial framework. As opposed to the coup, which both depended on and disclaimed its iterability, the endless parades, fairs, ceremonies, and events celebrating the military relied openly on repetition. They affirmed the givenness, even naturalness, of the military presence. And unlike the well-produced coup, with its precise orchestration and strict timing, the national crisis seemed to be everywhere, uncontainable, threatening to undermine all structures of social control.

This conflictual scenario legitimated the quest for order even as it gendered the enemy and backgrounded the population. Whether they were regaining control from the hysterical Isabelita or fighting the "subversives" (who were feminized as well), or challenging "La Thatcher," whom they portrayed as delusional for clinging to the Malvinas/Falkland Islands, the junta leaders fetishized male virility into a model of authentic Argentineness.[6] But for all its repetition, the deployment of the scenario was anything but static. The image of the soldier took various guises, depending, among other factors, on the political situation. In the pages that follow I will explore two uses of this image at two moments in the military's quest for national support. The first, presented before the military takeover, is tentative, appealing, almost coy: should we or shouldn't we? The second, occurring after the junta had grabbed political power, was, not surprisingly, bold, declarative, even imperative.

The drawing of a lone soldier circulated in the major centrist newspaper, *La nación*, three days before the coup (see figure 15).[7] It was a pro-military political advertisement featuring a young, innocent-looking soldier preparing for a just, "clean" war. In a style typical of poster art, the soldier sets out into the dark unknown terrain in order to vanquish evil. The medium, a drawing as opposed

Figure 15. The Lone Soldier. (*La Nación*, March 1976.
Paid for by Liga pro-comportamiento humano)

to a photograph, presented warfare as no more than a possibility. The viewer was asked to imagine the good fight, to visualize the good soldier. This was not reality (yet), the drawing implied, but an invitation to consider war. It more than foreshadowed upcoming events; it staged what the armed forces presented as their hesitation, almost reluctance, to take that dramatic, decisive step forward. Where would the action lead? the military seemed to be asking, even as their financial guru, José Martínez de Hoz, was putting the final touches on the undemocratic and backbreaking program the junta would unleash on the workforce a few days later.

The soldier's nervousness emanates from the page. He is truly alone, surrounded by a vast black emptiness. Should he go forward into the dark? Or, his glance over his shoulder suggests, should he watch his back? Where does the enemy lurk—outside in the dark night or within the *pueblo* he hopes will support him? He looks vulnerable, even frightened. He, too, runs the risk of being vanquished and feminized. Which way does heroism lie? Should he fight the good fight? Or should he selfishly, and perhaps with fatal consequences for all, stay out of the fray? The danger of feminization lurks around this figure. The haunted eyes plead for reciprocity and solidarity, pulling the viewer into the frame. The drawing transmits the nervousness of the legitimating project itself. Would the audience respond appropriately to the event?

The emphatic tone and layout of the text counter the soldier's questioning look. "YOU'RE NOT ALONE . . . your nation stands behind you," the caption cries at him. The type attempts to convey the overwhelming, clamoring public support; bold, crowded letters leave no room for contradiction. The speech act aims to create the consensus it desires. The Spanish word *pueblo* collapses both the nation and the "masses" that inhabit it, signaling the military's fantasy of a whole, harmonious country united by war, "his" war. "Yes, your fight isn't easy, but knowing that you've got truth on your side makes it easier. Your war is clean." Days before the coup, the ad elevated Argentina's civil conflict to a "war." But the armed forces' protestations of a "clean" war, maintained in the face of all evidence, finds an ironic and no doubt unintended counterpoint in the drawing's black, murky background. The insistence continues through the short choppy sentences: "Because you didn't betray. Because you didn't vow in vain. Because you didn't sell our your Patria. You didn't think of running away." The negative construction of the appeal, beginning with the opening *no*, sets the soldier ("you") apart from all those implied "thems." Unlike all those enemies and sissies, the soldier had not (and, of course, could not) "run away." Unlike all those international bankers and financiers (usually associated with Jews), the simple soldier had not "sold out" his country. Unlike those treacherous women like Isabelita who had brought it to the verge of chaos, the soldier stood true and firm. The linguistic juxtaposition of the *Sí, no* inadvertently betrays the mixed message, confirmed by the drawing itself. Though the soldier clutches a rifle, the caption assures us he holds nothing but the "truth." "You're not alone," repeated again, urges us to suspend all disbelief. Aloneness becomes transformed into solidarity, a weapon metamorphoses into the objectification of truth. The misrepresentation, more than the darkness, limits our capacity to see clearly, to make out what is really going on in this scenario.

The drawing presents male heroism in opposition to an enemy *other* lurking somewhere in the dark. Danger conflates with femininity, conjured up by all that is dark, threatening, unseen, and inscrutable. This figuration goes beyond the gendered mythic scenario in which the male is the doer and creator of cultural difference.[8] The representation recalls a very specific and violent political practice. Either the soldier will be overcome and subjected to *mazorca*-esque tortures, or he will have to overcome the threatening feminine other.

The image of the lone soldier also gendered the viewer. The eyes of the Argentine population (condemned to passive spectatorship) were fixed on the poster-hero. Viewers were encouraged to identify with him, to see the conflict from his perspective: "You're not alone." Their role was to legitimate, not participate in, the struggle. Cast in a supporting role, spectators were prompted to feel protective, even maternal, toward this innocent young man. But this casting had a double edge: the feminization that allowed for maternal support also posed the potential danger of things feminine. What if the viewers themselves betrayed him? The depiction attempted to control the threat by simply excluding the unreliable public from the frame. No wonder the soldier watched his back. The image brilliantly enacted the control measures exercised by the military; it "disappeared" the viewer. A ventriloquist usurped the population's place, appropriating and silencing the public voice. The dialogue staged here takes place between the young man in the drawing and the reassuring (disembodied) words in boldface type. The strategy presupposed that the spectators would accept those words as their own. The reluctant soldier calls for louder words, ever more emphatic approval. The closing words of the caption echo the opening words—"You're not alone." The circle is closed. What else is there to say? The image of the young warrior male, in a manner typical of fascist iconography, neutralized its violent and sinister message. Who could have imagined by looking at this young soldier that thirty thousand people would be abducted, tortured, and permanently "disappeared" by the military during the next few years?

The junta's self-representation, not surprisingly, underwent radical change

Figure 16. The military junta on parade. (Photo by Guillermo Loiácono)

immediately after it seized power. The decisive step had been taken. The population had not said no to the lone soldier. The photographs included here, taken by photographers who worked for the rigidly censored national and international news service, were reprinted in newspapers throughout the nation to chronicle the "new" climactic moment in the performance.

In its first official pronouncement, transmitted nationally as the helicopter was lifting off, the junta declared itself the "supreme organ of the Nation" ready to "fill the void of power" embodied by "Isabelita."[9] The word *organ* indicates both the fetishistic quality of state power, an abstraction incarnated in the virile personhood of a few select men, and the explicit link between male sexuality and supreme power. The junta consciously represented itself as the model of leadership: male, measured, mature, and responsible, as opposed to Isabelita, who was female, hysterical, unqualified, and out of control. With a show of muscle, the junta undertook its exercise in national-body building, determined to transform the "infirm," inert Argentine masses into an authentic "national being."[10] The imposition of the *proceso* was portrayed as a "coming of age" for the military males, now free from the corrupting feminine presence.[11] In its initial pronouncement the military heralded its ascension to power as the "drawing of a fecund epoch," although the generative process was not, as it recognized, strictly speaking "natural." Isabelita's government was sick, its

Figure 17. All male, Catholic, and strictly hierarchical. (Photo by Eduardo Longoni)

"productive apparatus" exhausted. "Natural" solutions were no longer sufficient to ensure a full "recuperation." As President Videla declared a few months
later, the Mother *Patria* was "bleeding to death. When it most urgently needs
her children, more and more of them are submerged in her blood" (Troncoso,
El proceso 59). In order to save her, the social "body" would be turned inside out
and upside down. The conflict was being fought in the interstices of the *Patria*,
in her bleeding entrails. "Subversion" (i.e., any and all opposition to the armed
forces) was thus transgressive, hidden, dangerous, dirty.

Opposed to the interiority associated with subversion, the military represented itself as all surface: unequivocally masculine, aggressively visible, identifiable by their uniforms, ubiquitous, on parade for all the world to see (see
figure 16). The moving vehicles simultaneously signaled progress and restoration—the junta moved forward to reinstate discipline. Staging order, as in
ritual, would make order happen. The iterability of the performance contributed to the dictatorship's legitimacy. The "restored" nature of the performance
suggested that order itself had been restored. The military display acted, enacted, and reenacted the (new—now more than ever—always) social system: all
male, Catholic, and strictly hierarchical (see figure 17). The display of the
military leaders in church aligned military and sacred power, stabilizing the
former through identification with the latter. The image naturalized the contra-

Figure 18. Unholy trinity. (Photo by Guillermo Loiácono)

diction posed by having armed soldiers positioned around the church. Wasn't the restoration of a universal and static "good" a sacred mission, after all? The unholy trinity (army, navy, and air force) appeared as one entity, set apart as in religious iconography, embodying national aspirations of grandeur. This photograph (figure 18), which zoomed in on the three junta leaders at an air force show, suggested that their attention was transfixed on lofty, transcendent goals. The image distanced them from the surrounding figures: unlike the unruly women immediately behind them, these leaders focused on the matter at hand; unlike the scattered and disorderly men in the background, the junta leaders sat erect. The visual isolation augmented the junta's aura of power by allowing for aggrandizement in terms of scale and by projecting a model of visual domination.

The junta leaders' performed "state" fetishized into a cohesive, visual whole while it feminized the Nation as *Patria*. By embodying the abstract "state," they rendered it visible and identifiable and endowed it with a "sacred and erotic attraction."[12] The erotics of the military's performance, that which made their version of world order *desirable*, stemmed from the exhibitionistic display of potent hard bodies and military hardware (see figure 16). The feminine nation, or *Patria,* mediated the autoeroticism of the military's performance. The armed forces obsessively conjured up the symbolic Woman to keep their homosocial society from becoming a homosexual one. The military men came together in the heterosexual language of "love" of the *Patria*. The caption to figure 19 reads: "The Colonel and the author: two Argentine men identified through their love of the Patria."

The armed forces presented their mission (much as the poster of the lone soldier had) as a shared struggle. They urged the population to participate in mimetic desire by desiring that which they themselves desired: "all the representative sectors of the country should feel clearly identified with the project. In this new stage there is a combat role for each citizen. The task is hard and urgent. It is not without sacrifice, but one takes it on with the absolute conviction that the example will be set from the top" (Troncoso, *El proceso* 108). The junta leaders explicitly set themselves up as models, urging the population to identify with them, to trust in their power to control events and carry the endeavor forward. They spoke as one central, unified subject; their "we" supposedly included everyone.[13] The combat role that the military envisioned for the population (again) was not an active one. Rather, the appropriate attitude was one of blind belief in the scenario, empathy for the struggle and applause for the military effort. In the name of collective well-being (as in classical myths and tragedy) the community was expected to surrender its will to the protagonist. Society as a whole might be in trouble, this paradigm suggested, but as in all tragic drama, only the hero is "born to set it right." This grandiose representation offered a linear progression in which the "climactic moment or goal . . . is an image of perfect immobility" (Bersani and Dutoit 6). The scenario reaffirmed the universality and inevitability of the hegemonic order. Criminal violence claimed the immutability of art.

The junta's self-representation as a model of "authentic" citizenship was both exclusionary and transformative, reenacting an us/them divide. The unitary image left out and denied all other possibilities. But the divide was, on closer examination, more complicated than it appeared. Visually, the spectacle affirmed the centrality and supremacy of the leaders in relation to other military males who were presented as a mass of seemingly identical bodies in military attire (see figure 20). While this junta modeled itself on previous ones, comprised of men in identical uniforms standing just so, it (like the coup-as-act) thrived on the appearance of originality. These leaders were singular; they claimed an authenticity that they denied to their followers. The soldiers crammed into the photograph were destined to imitate. Though expected to emulate their glorious leaders, they themselves were unindividuated, unmarked, compressed (as the photo suggests) into a role that didn't quite fit. Their eyes, directed straight at the camera, are hostile and suspicious. Their somewhat disorderly and de-

Figure 19. "Two Argentine Men Identified through their Love of the Patria/Motherland."
(Raúl Jassen, *Seineldin: El Ejercito Traicionado, La Patria Vencido*)

Figure 20. Military males. (Photo Eduardo Longoni)

fiant body language insinuates a sinister threat: they might be subordinates of the junta, but the photographer better watch his back.

National identity and authenticity, the military staging illustrated, depended on various positions of proximity to the junta leaders themselves. The junta embodied the "national being," the military males imitated them, spectators identified vicariously, and those who were unsympathetic could no longer claim ties to the social body. A complicated play of looks marked lines and degrees of inclusion and exclusion—the junta kept an eye on the military even as the common soldier looked up at it; members of the population might find themselves more comfortable functioning as an undifferentiated audience than being singled out as objects of the military gaze. Exclusion went in tandem with feminization. While the junta embodied masculinity, the masses were feminized. And, as before, gender itself constituted grounds for marginalization: women and nonassimilable men were pushed to the side.

The junta's political power drew from the unequal visual economy it established with the public. The military male might be on display, but he did not return the look. The leaders' disciplined, virile bodies might seduce, but were impervious to seduction. Unlike the lone soldier in the poster, the triumphant soldier denied reciprocity. The military's visual self-referentiality "disappeared" its audience by making it invisible and denying it status as legitimate spectator. The military spectacles extended the percepticide (or blinding) inflicted literally on its blindfolded victims and metaphorically on the population at large. The population was not allowed to acknowledge the violence taking place around it. People had to deny the reality they saw with their own eyes and participate in self-blinding.

The ahistorical scenarios promoted by the junta were useful in obscuring the fact that the economic crisis and political chaos that precipitated the military coup of 1976 were a result, in part, of conflicting economic interests specific to the mid to late twentieth century: international capitalism had the effect of eroding Argentina's social institutions and programs and it clashed with the interests of Argentina's strong labor unions that had gained power during the period of post–World War II prosperity under Perón. It is not coincidental that the junta's dismantling of a constitutional system of collective decision making (such as the dissolution of Parliament and the Supreme Court in the days following the coup) should have been represented in terms of the lone male, situated in a dark vacuum beyond the boundaries of communal life, with only the stars to guide him. Nor should it surprise us that the emphasis on the solitary hero coincided with Argentina's economic drive toward privatization, consumerism, and international capitalism. As the armed forces invaded all public and private spaces, civil society itself "disappeared."

The junta's epic had a beginning and an end; it declared the initiation of a fecund era and tried (ultimately successfully) to legislate a *punto final* (full stop) to accusations of human rights violations. The military's efforts to come to closure by erasing all traces of their criminal actions served as a parody of ritual reintegration. History, as invoked by the junta, was idealized as a founding myth and placed outside, or at the beginning, of what we would traditionally call the historical process. All opposing representations or interpretations of Argentina's national drama were prohibited by the military leaders. Theirs, after all, was the ultimate performance. Declaring an end to conflict and decreeing resolution, they claimed to have put an end to drama. "History," as junta leader Eduardo Massera proclaimed, "belongs to me."[14]

Graciela Scheines, the Argentine author of *Las metáforas del fracaso* (Metaphors of failure), posits that Argentina "is a country that has not yet been founded."[15] She laments what she sees as Argentina's lack of founding myths and acts, arguing that "real foundation is accompanied by epics, heroes, revolutions and heroic gestures." But Argentina, she maintains, is trapped in a circular history, in "cycles of euphorias and frustrations that are typically Argentine. That's what characterizes Argentine failure, everything starts anew and remains frozen in an embryonic state. Nothing comes of it." Here, I have suggested the opposite. The brutal paradigm of national individuation I explore has produced, rather than negated, Argentine history. These heroes and epics dissolved civil society. It's not, as Scheines states, that Argentina "has no history." The problem is that Argentina was founded on myths such as the one staged in the poster of the lone soldier. That image positioned the public and curtailed its ability to respond; it eliminated opposition and vanished not only the feminine but pluralism. But the scenario trapped the military itself. In response to Larsen's argument, I submit that the military, entangled in the scenario of the lone soldier that had helped legitimate it, could not move to another one predicated on more communal and democratic principles that might allow for a civil society. They too were stuck in a scenario that had once served them well. "Damnable iteration," they might have uttered, forever caught in the citational gesture.

Spectacles, I have posited, function as the locus and mechanism of communal identity, the "imaginings" that constitute social systems. They reflect and (re)produce the spatial configurations of the imagined community, establishing both the parameters and organizational structures. By my reading/viewing of the coup-as-event and the consensus-building spectacles of the Dirty War, I am submitting that hermeneutics serves historical analysis. Reading the poster and photographs shows a performative continuity: the junta could not simply switch roles and establish a consensual civil society. The political dénouement of events such as the Dirty War are built into the conflictual performance itself.

What was not visible either in the drawing of the lone soldier or in the military display was the degree of violence that went into the shaping of the military body itself. In their attempts to forge a *ser nacional,* the junta annihilated all traces of the abhorred feminine within themselves and molded their would-be initiates into "holy" killers. "The soldier" as Foucault noted, "has become something that can be made" (135). Rank made "belonging" and hierarchy visible. The soldier's body was codified and denaturalized; body parts took on special meaning. Like the drawing of the "Ideal Woman," the soldier too was a rearrangement of dislocated body parts. Training meant the breakdown of the physical gesture—the hand raised in salute in several separate motions, the specific angle of the hand, the tempo, the bearing of the body, the details of dress. The process of training became an exercise in differentiation. It sorted the men from the nonmen, the boys and "sissies." Drills turned into homoerotic taunting as soldiers were forced to strip naked and were put into small rooms to work out. The intense misogyny and homophobia accompanying the homoerotic nature of the all-male society resulted in a double spectacle: the naked male body of the soldier was exposed for the voyeuristic pleasure of other males even as that exposure was designed to provoke group violence toward the vulnerable male body of the disobedient soldier. The armed forces developed a repertoire of minitortures and rituals of humiliation in order to "harden" its recruits into soldier males. In the *estaqueo* (spikes), a soldier was staked naked to the ground, with arms and legs spread eagle, and left out all night; in the *salto de rana* (frog leap) the soldier was forced to jump up and down; in the *pozo zorro* (foxhole), a soldier was placed and left in a pit in the ground. There were other torments, but one conscript who met with me recounted one session that he remembered particularly vividly. He and fellow soldiers had been ordered to strip naked except for military boots and were then forced to train for hours during a rain storm. When the soldiers broke down and yelled "We're human!" the answer they got was "No, a soldier is not human! A soldier is a survivor." One soldier broke down after days of this brutal treatment and started dancing, naked except for his boots, in front of the others. The conscript recalled the vicarious pleasure in rebellion shared by him and the others who had been forced to submit. The disobedient soldier disappeared. No one ever found out what became of him. "The best of us didn't survive," the soldier summed up. When I asked him to explain who "the best" were, he said, "Those who said 'no.' "

Small wonder, then, that those military males who identified enough with their macho roles to become torturers would boast, "We haven't got mothers or children."[16]

The same epic rendition of "war" circulated also in the public speeches by the junta leaders. Admiral Emilio E. Massera, one of the three members of the first junta and the one most directly associated with the abductions and tortures, described the "war" as ahistorical ("anterior a la política [preceding politics]"), transcendental and "metaphysical" in his collection of speeches, *El camino a la democracia* (17). He maintained that the conflict was "not Argentine but international," but he downplayed the factual economic and ideological tensions leading to it: "it is true, but not the whole truth, that this is a war between dialectical materialism and humanist idealism . . . it is true, but not the whole truth, that this is a war between liberty and tyranny. The truth, the absolute truth, is that here and throughout the world, at this moment, there is a war between those who side with Death and those of us who side with life" (16–17).[17] In one speech, he conjures up the terrifying phantom:

We will not allow Death [feminine, *la Muerte*] to roam freely through Argentina.

Slowly, almost imperceptibly, a horror machine unleashed its iniquity on the unguarded and the innocent, to the incredulity of some, the complicity of others and the stupefaction of many.

A war had begun, a different and oblique war, a war primitive in its techniques but sophisticated in its cruelty, a war we had to get used to little by little, because it was not easy to admit that the entire country was being forced into a monstrous intimacy with blood.

Then the struggle began.

We all suffered losses. Public men and anonymous men, women and children, civilians and military men, those from the Security Forces and the police, all gained a painful notoriety hour after hour on the pages of the newspaper and there was hardly a night in Argentina that did not close with renewed crying.

Surmounting all the obstacles placed before them by self-interested incomprehension, one day, the Armed Forces moved to the offensive. And there, in the Northeast, our valiant comrades from the Army started a patient and risky war. To those men and to all the men from the most diverse units who fought and returned or to those who stayed forever on the battle front, we express our deepest tribute. Then, the Armed Forces initiated the process of reorganization of the Republic . . . (16)

Echoing the beginning of the *Communist Manifesto* (1848), "a spectre is haunting Europe, the spectre of Communism," Massera evokes the terror of femininity. He represents the soldier as innocent, pure of spirit and reluctant to engage in violence but nonetheless bound by honor to take on *la Muerte*, Death the ghostly Woman. Anything was better than the hidden, Oedipal danger of "being forced into a monstrous intimacy with blood." The purity of the soldier male had been threatened; feminine Death was stalking him, waiting to contaminate him or engulf him in blood. The corrupt and insidious feminine body needed to be contained and controlled. She could not be allowed to roam free. The female threat had to be eliminated in order to protect "women and children" and other good citizens who obediently conformed to patriarchal roles. The valiant armed forces presented themselves as safeguarding the world for its distinguished and undistinguished citizens alike. Politicians and other "public men," just like the anonymous population, had to leave the good fight to the soldier males.

The various military spectacles of the Dirty War, I believe, were profoundly interconnected. Through their performance, the armed forces incarnated and made visible an image of eternal, unchangeable social values in the here-and-now of 1976 Argentina. Their show not only miscommunicated a vision of order and hierarchy, but it also obfuscated the fact that the military was waging an attack against its own population. The globalizing focus distracted attention from the bitter struggles among wildly divergent left-wing and right-wing *peronist* forces as well as between *peronists* and the largely anti-*peronist* military. The image of unity promulgated by the junta hid very real personal differences among the three junta leaders and bitter rivalries and tensions among the three branches of the armed forces. The uncontrollable inflation rate, the low production and export rate, and Argentina's uneasy entry into a neoliberal economic system all "disappeared" behind the transcendent, ahistorical view of civil conflict as part of the eternal human condition.

Spectacles, such as the two I have introduced here, are politically powerful in that they encapsulate and transmit the specific plotlines that a population identifies with: dramas of origin, individuation, and destiny, among others. Performative traditions reactivated in moments of civil strife or economic change, seemingly "explain" the current problem and provide models for resolution. Populations may not always be aware of the economic, historical, and/or political tensions that explode in civil conflict, and yet might be seduced into accepting the need to define or defend national identity or authenticity. These public spectacles reflect and (re)produce the spatial configurations of the imagined community, establishing both the parameters and organizational structures (hierarchy/commingling, social actor/spectator, initiates/outsiders) and linking the periphery to the unifying "center." In making communal imaginings visible, spectacles are the glue that holds communities together—glue, because they bond disparate individuals and strangers together in kinship, and glue, too, because they are not "natural" or "authentic" parts of the whole. The metaphor of the glue underlines the nonorganic nature of the scenarios, the "man"-made-ness of the construction. By making obvious that the whole was once otherwise, the constructedness offers the hope that the pieces might one day be imagined otherwise.

Engendering the Enemy: Women in the Military State

Dear Diary: Yesterday was the 24th of March, 1976 and, if we think about it, there are few girls lucky enough to have their history coincide with the history of their country . . . but bang bang bang, Nina got screwed the same day they screwed Isabel Perón.—Rodrigo Fresán, *Historia argentina*

The story of the *proceso,* from the military's point of view, was a story framed by two bad women. It began with the pathetic Isabelita and ended with the castrating Margaret Thatcher, who humiliated the armed forces in the Falkland Islands/Malvinas war. The self-referential and autoerotic nature of the junta's representation and the repression of the feminine in the military discourse should not mislead us to think that women were absent from the scenario. Both the feminine—the *image* of Woman constructed in patriarchy—and women were vital parts of the drama. Women made up one-third of the "disappeared." As university students and community workers, they seemingly posed a threat to the military endeavor. Women also joined armed resistance movements, though they were largely absent from leadership positions. (In fact, women in these movements were usually treated with the same sexist contempt they encountered in other social spheres.)[18] The junta's mythic spectacle simultaneously glorified the feminine—particularly in the image of the *Patria* or Motherland—and targeted active women who resisted or transgressed their assigned role in the social drama.

The good woman, the *Patria,* was the very image of collective harmony. However, the word *Patria,* meaning belonging to or possessed by the Father, already indicates the profound misogyny of the concept. *Patria,* a feminine term for nationhood, is entangled with *patriarchy.*[19] Thus, the word itself alerts us to the slippery positioning of the feminine in this discourse. There is no woman behind the maternal image invoked by the military. The absenting of woman from *Patria* constitutes one of the many disappearing acts of this drama. The maternal is merely the projection of the masculinist version of maternity—patriarchy in drag.

The *Patria,* according to diverse statements by the military leaders, came into being with the armed forces themselves. In *El camino a la democracia,* Massera described the *Patria* born from "man's ingenuity" concomitantly with the birth of the armed forces: "When the uncontainable impulse towards liberty gave birth to the Patria on this soil, with her was born the Army. When the will to being was affirmed in the strategic vision of the liquid realm, the Patria was born in the sea and with her was born the Navy. When man looked at the sky and dominated it through his ingenuity, the Patria was born in the air, and with her was born the Air Force" (58). Massera conceived the *Patria's* boundaries as unlimited, far exceeding the physical markers imposed by cartographers, which he referred to as the "unjust mutilation of geographical limits" (30). Nationhood became as much a physical territory as a longing for heroic transcendence, as much a virginal space to be penetrated by the men of the navy "who fulfill their duty to disembowel its secrets" (32) as an aspiration to male greatness. Throughout *El camino a la democracia*, it becomes clear that Massera's preoccupation with personal authenticity and physical integrity melts into his vision of national boundaries and sovereignty.

According to this discourse (or incest narrative), the military man (who embodies the state) engenders and copulates with the feminine *Patria*, giving birth to civilization. In this scenario the military male embodies masculine subjectivity while the feminine is reduced to the material territory, the body to be penetrated and defended.[20] Insofar as "she" is inanimate, the military male claims sole responsibility for the procreative process: "The West," Massera wrote, "lies deep within us, and we will bring it to the light of day" (50).

During the Dirty War, the good women, in concrete terms, were the ones who supported the military's mission and encouraged it to exercise even more control over the public good. In 1977, the League of Mothers of Families, sounding much like the Christian Right in the United States today, urged their rulers to ensure that "education strengthened traditional and Christian values" and asked that "the media be truly instruments of culture, diffusing good examples and healthy entertainment" (Avellanada 148). In direct retaliation to the use of spectacle by the Madres of the Plaza de Mayo, who pinned photographs of the "disappeared" to their bodies, the military urged and coerced women (many of them government workers) to wear signs punning on *human rights*. These female bodies announced that "Argentines are human and right" (see figure 21).

The politicization of traditionally nonpolitical women was nothing new. The right wing had a long tradition of organizing its women, as Sandra McGee explores in her essay on gender roles in the Liga Patriótica Argentina.[21] Since 1919, Liga women had opposed the forces they claimed corroded the family: women working outside the home, prostitution, moral decay, and feminism. The agenda of the League of Mothers of Families simply followed in that long tradition. Their program, not surprisingly, was reaffirmed by the media that carried interviews and reports on good women, those who were happiest in the home, looking after their children, those whose gravest concern was buying groceries at reasonable prices. In May 1976, the secretary of commerce went on television urging housewives to become vigilant: "why don't you find out what's happening in the family business? What is it doing for the country? The whole country is in this game [literally, match] together . . ." They were warned that their children were in grave danger of being seduced into subversive activity ("Today, education is free, at least classes are. But what happens when he leaves school? What alternatives does a boy have? He hangs around, emigrates, or grabs a machine gun. Is this the country we want for our children?"). This

Figure 21. "Argentines are human and right." (Photo by Guillermo Loiácono)

show, called *Face to Face with Housewives,* was reportedly the program with the highest rating.[22]

The bad woman—as historical subject—on the other hand was conceived as the obstacle to harmony; she (according to the scenario) activated the drama by being uncontrollable, by incarnating the birthplace of evil. Just as the military staged versions of itself on its heroic mission, the opposition was cast or created to fulfill its assigned role. One article, "Las Guerrilleras: La cruenta historia de la mujer en el terrorismo" (Guerrilleras: The bloody story of women in the terrorist movement), states the following:

> Little by little we have got the Argentines to understand that the word "war" reflects a reality. Now we have to get them to understand that war is not peculiar to men. In the *guerrilla,* the woman is *as* or *more* important than the man. She serves as ideologue, she serves as a combatant, she infiltrates all spaces (even the most innocent, the most frivolous, the most banal), she seduces, lies, deforms, gets information, indoctrinates, "keeps a lookout," and she defends herself by attacking the most permeable facets of human sensibility: the respect for pregnancy, maternity and natural feminine fragility. All this makes the war much, much more difficult. Of

course, the problem makes us wonder about its causes. The home, the parents. I would ask every couple with an adolescent daughter: What are you doing so that your daughter doesn't become a *guerrillera?* Unfortunately, next to nothing. They don't control her comings and goings, her friends, the books she reads, the courses she takes. They don't get too alarmed when after dinner she begins her slow and devastating marxist sermon. And what's worse, when they're faced with the evidence that their daughter is part of a guerrilla organization, they become her accomplices—out of love or weakness, which is often the same thing. They only admit their error when it's too late. When they have to enter the morgue to identify her cadáver. (Penguin 17)

Guerrilleras, the article explains, are "unhappy, lonely adolescents" who are initially led astray by a man, but then want to "be" like a man, and finally want to overtake men altogether (13). A *guerrillera* is promiscuous ("mujer de muchos hombres," 14) and will use her sexuality as a weapon of war: "She will try to get pregnant because she knows that she will be handled more gently. She will hold her son in front of her like a shield" (14). She will falsely claim that she has been raped, "creating thus a conflict between her interrogator and his boss" (14). The journalist quotes a high-ranking military official who claims: "As far as I'm concerned, women are worse than men" (15). However, the article goes on to rejoice that once in a while women become pawns in the military's attempt to go after their male partners.

Deviance, associated with femininity, was constructed as "monstrous" and turned into a national spectacle. The armed forces literally exposed the terrorists in their museum of terrorism (called *Museo Histórico Juan Carlos Leonetti*) in Tucuman, displaying life-size mannequins of female terrorists (see figure 22), bloody mattresses, and jars containing preserved body parts of dead terrorists. The newspapers too put the *guerrilleras* on display in reports and interviews that confirmed the armed forces' gendered version of events. In "Declaraciones de una guerrillera detenida" (Declarations by a detained guerrilla), which appeared in *La nación* on March 23, 1976, the day before the coup, the declaration of a young female "subversive" or *guerrillera* (conveniently Jewish) was presented as follows:

Questioned by journalists, the *guerrillera* said she was Miriam Prillertensky, age 20, from Córdoba, married, and a university student. She wore a green uniform with jacket, cap and boots. She seemed tranquil during the press interview and answered all the questions, without exception. She is short, has brown hair and pale skin. During the talk, she took off her cap and then her jacket. At moments in the dialogue, she smiled at the journalists. She made it clear that she was not formulating her declaration to spite her husband who abandoned her when she was wounded in the mountains and who will "certainly try to make a liar out of me saying that I don't belong to the organization and that I was forced to put on this uniform and speak out. All that is untrue: I am doing it all of my own free will." She explained that her *nom de guerre* was "Clarisa" and that she became involved in subversive activities due to her husband, who is on the loose.

The *guerrillera* went on to explain how she had been taught to use firearms and how her organization, the Ejército Revolucionario del Pueblo, was part of an international Marxist movement.

> The objectives of that organization were to take over the government and install a proletarian dictatorship, after which they would eliminate the Armed Forces and private property, expropriate businesses and bring education under state control. They would also do away with the church, with the family as the basis of society, and individuals would be at the beck and call of the State, losing their decision-making capacity. The model states were Cuba and Vietnam. When asked if she believed in democracy, the young extremist answered that "there are many political and economic problems, moreover, I know that this government [Martínez's] is crumbling. To avoid that, the people must be educated to vote for a democratic government. In the last elections [Perón-Perón] the people were not educated to vote as they should have," she said. In closing, she reiterated that she wanted her declaration to warn any young person who wanted to join the ranks of the subversive organizations not to do it, but wanted them to learn from her experiences. (10)

The young *guerrillera* gave voice to the official worldview that internationalist terrorist organizations were going to topple the government and put an end to life as Argentina knew it; that democracy was not necessarily democratic, because people had to be taught how to vote; that the Martínez government was coming down, though, of course, only the military leaders themselves knew how soon. The young *guerrillera*, the black sheep who had strayed from the fold, warned others not to make the mistakes she had. Moreover, she issued her declarations without apparent hesitation, anger, or pressure. Young, smiling, and seemingly honest, she doffed her previous ideology with the same ease with which she took off her *guerrillera*'s cap and jacket.

The young *guerrillera*, though represented as indisputably a public threat,

**ESTO
VIVIO EL
PAIS**

Esta es una mujer ar-
gentina. Pudo haber
elegido el camino de la
paz, del trabajo, del
hogar, de los hijos.
Pudo elegir a favor.
Construir. Pero eligió
el camino de la subver-
sión. Epuñó un arma y
mató. También se hizo
fotografiar en el
monte, armada y ves-
tida con ropa de fajina.
Eligió en contra.

Figure 22. "Exposing Feminine Deviance." Mannequin of a female terrorist on display at the Museo histórico Juan Carlos Leonetti, also known as the "Museum of Terrorism." (Photo by Susan Meiselas, courtesy of Magnum Photos)   Figure 23. "Esto vivió el país" (*Gente*, 1977)

was nonetheless depicted as redeemable on some level. She might still get all the punishment coming to her, but she was not yet a hardened criminal. She was girlish; she had been led astray by a bad man; she smiled charmingly at the journalists; she reaffirmed the military government's fear, methods, and values. Other women, the message was clear, were less redeemable. An article pub-lished in *Gente* carried a photograph of a woman in military attire, standing straight, head back, holding a rifle (see figure 23). The caption reads: "This is an Argentine woman. She could have chosen the path of peace, work, home, children. She could have chosen *for.* To build, be constructive. But she chose the path of subversion. She clutched the rifle and she killed. She even had herself photographed in the mountains, armed and dressed in fatigues. She chose *against.*"[23] Unlike the representation of the heroic soldier male of the poster described earlier, this woman shows no hesitation or reluctance to take up arms. Photographed out in the open, in the wild and dangerous mountains, she has clearly left home and community behind. This was certainly not the woman in patriarchy that the military felt duty-bound to protect. Situated beyond all social structures, she brazenly holds the rifle in front of her. Her stiff and upright body rejects all "feminine" traits. This is the very picture of the third sex, the "masculinized" woman that all the experts had been warning against. Not only that, she "had herself photographed," the ultimate act of defiant self-representation. In all probability, given her stance and attire, the woman photographed as a *guerrillera* belonged to the federal police or some other military-backed organization. The photograph was also conveniently small and blurred.

The danger, of course, was that not all "bad" women looked bad. Several issues of *Gente* in 1976 presented and expanded on the story of Ana María González, a beautiful and innocent young woman whom they claim murdered the chief of police: "This is shocking. Stunning. It makes adjectives impossible," read the opening lines of the article, which goes on to describe the high school student, Ana María González, as a *vedette* (show girl), "wearing a red windbreaker and white stockings, a pistol tucked in her belt" (August 26, 1976, pp. 4–7). The image alerts us to beware of the phallic female. She made friends with a schoolmate, the unsuspecting daughter of the police officer, and insinuated herself into their home. There she planted a bomb under the bed. The article, constructed like a prose poem, rounds off the description by repeating the opening lines: "This is shocking. Stunning. It makes adjectives impossible." It calls on "honest, healthy and conscious Argentines to reflect on the events" (5).

To position resistant women as enemies of the state was simple enough. But what about unarmed women who posed no visible threat to society? The junta also identified the Madres de Plaza de Mayo as terrorists, this time as "emotional terrorists," because the women insisted on obtaining information about their missing children who had been abducted and disappeared by military forces. Here, however, the junta was trapped in a patriarchal discourse that honored motherhood. The junta tried to sidestep the issue by claiming that the women had renounced their right to motherhood by being bad mothers, mothers of subversives. As subversives were considered nonhuman (and were explicitly referred to as such by some, such as Ramón J. Camps), the Madres were thus nonmothers.

The gendering of the enemy on a metaphoric level played itself out on the physical bodies of those detained during the junta's seven years in power. These representations are in no way separable from the experiences of flesh-and-blood people in the lived-in world. In the concentration camp known as Olimpo (Olympus), the distinction between embodied and disembodied "womanhood" (women/Woman) was made brutally evident as military soldiers tortured female prisoners in front of the image of the Virgin Mary.[24] The negative image of the "public" or active woman provoked and enabled the systematic assault on the reproductive organs of all female prisoners held in captivity. Women were annihilated through a metonymic reduction to their sexual "parts": wombs, vaginas, breasts. Abducted women were raped as a matter of course. Testimonies repeatedly allude to guns shot into vaginas and wombs, to breasts being pounded, to buttocks and mouths being ripped open. Women in concentration camps were paraded naked in front of the guards. Women were tortured in front of their husbands as a way of breaking the latter, thus materializing Massera's view that the female body constituted a weak point in the male psyche. Reports that surfaced in Argentina during the recent show-and-tell (the confessions) by members of the armed forces illustrate that women who were going to be "made to fly," that is, who were thrown out of airplanes drugged but alive, had their abdomens slit open so that they would sink into the sea faster.[25] Pregnant women, who made up 3 percent of the disappeared, were often abducted, raped, and tortured simply because they were pregnant.[26] If and when they gave birth they were beaten, humiliated, and usually killed. One woman was thrown out of an airplane alive while she was in her last trimester of pregnancy because "she was ugly, and they were afraid the baby would be ugly, too."[27] One survivor, the physicist Adriana Calvo de Laborde, recounted at the Trial of the Generals that she was seven and a half months pregnant when she was abducted. She was beaten and tortured. When she was due to deliver, she was shoved, blindfolded and handcuffed, into the backseat of a police car. "Lucrecia," one of the very few women known to have tortured during the *proceso,* sat in the back with her. In spite of Calvo de Laborde's screams that her child was being born, the guards did not stop the car, nor did Lucrecia do anything to help her. The baby, a girl, was born and fell onto the floor. Finally Calvo de Laborde was taken to another concentration camp where a physician looked her over while the baby was abandoned on a table and the guards looked on. "With one shove, he took out the placenta and threw it on the floor as he insulted me ... They made me get up, they brought me two buckets of water and made me scrub the floor and wash the stretcher. They made me clean everything. I had to do this in front of the guards, who were all laughing."[28] She was naked—a spectacle for their amusement and deprecation. Finally, the men allowed her to wash her dress and put it on. She was then permitted to pick up and care for her daughter.

Children born in prison were usually given away to military families.[29] The military also tried to destroy mothers in captivity, not only by torturing pregnant women and stealing the children born to mothers who were disappeared, but also by threatening to kill the children of all disappeared women. The assault on political prisoners also was gendered. Women prisoners in jail were allowed no physical contact with their children, a privilege enjoyed by male prisoners. As Alicia Partnoy, one of the few disappeared who "reappeared," states, the military "attacked us as mothers, in our motherhood."[30] Thus the armed forces enshrined the glory of motherhood in the image of the *Patria* even as they targeted women and familial bonds as a way of breaking down the social fabric.

One of the most devastating consequences of a spectacle as pervasive as the military's was that it forced those who resisted it to fight for the same images, icons, and objects of representation. Both the military and its opponents, as I have argued, claimed the right to define the "feminine"—whether women, mothers, or *guerrilleras*. Both sides fought to occupy the moral high ground, which in even the most divergent instances was accompanied by the proximity to the lofty, pure, feminine image. One painful example of this contest is the death of Rodolfo Walsh's daughter, María Victoria, as recounted by Walsh himself in an open letter to friends before he disappeared in 1977.[31] Vicki, as she was known, and four other *montoneros* were ambushed in a house by the armed forces. She and her one-year-old daughter had been sleeping inside the house when the attack started. María Victoria, still in her nightshirt, and a male companion went up to the roof with machine guns. Walsh assumes the role of witness in his recounting: "I have seen the scene with her eyes," he tells us, "the terrace looking over the low houses, the sky at dawn, the siege" (120). He bases his description on a conscript's eyewitness account of the death of his daughter.

> Suddenly, the soldier said, there was a silence. The girl dropped her machine gun, she came up to the edge of the roof and opened her arms. We stopped shooting, though no one had ordered us to, and we could see her clearly. She was a thin little thing, she had short hair, and she was wearing a nightshirt. She started talking to us in a loud but steady voice. I don't remember everything she said. "You don't kill us," the man with her said. "We choose to die." Then they raised their pistols to their temples and killed themselves in front of us. (120)

This account, as painful and moving as it is, seems to me to reproduce the double strategy of simultaneously erasing and elevating the feminine associated with military practice. Even as the military sacrificed "real" historical women, they mythified images of self-sacrificing, pure, and ethereal womanhood. The opposition seemed condemned to replay the same strategies. Even as she faced death, María Victoria had to reenact the image of glorious, self-sacrificing womanhood. No other image could elevate her death to the symbolic level on which the battle of images was being fought. She had to outfetishize the fetish, even as she died. Her self-sacrificing image stuns the soldiers into nonaction. Though she spoke, the informant can't remember what she said. Only her male companion's words make it into the text. But her self-sacrificing image survives and circulates again through her father's text. María Victoria, the young mother, becomes the symbol of a struggle for justice so pure and so lofty that she literally places herself above the contemptible fray. Kathleen Newman, in *La violencia del discurso,* comments on the same passage from Walsh's letter, stating that the "image of the fighting woman, daughter and mother at the same time, standing, with arms raised, dressed in a nightshirt that was too big for her—Walsh writes in the letter that she wore these absurdly large nightshirts—confronting death is, sadly, the counterhegemonic image of Lady Liberty during the years of the dirty war" (26). The counterhegemonic image, as the term itself suggests, is tied to the hegemonic. Even as it tries to break away, it mirrors the hegemonic and its systems of representation that have proved lethal to women. In their struggle to fight back, individual women, too, were forced to erase themselves as material beings as they claimed their existence and validity as icons. Walsh concludes his letter by stating that Vicki could have chosen other paths, but that she chose the "most just, the most generous, the most reasonable. Her lucid death is a synthesis of her short, beautiful life." And though the baby daughter was found sitting on the bed "surrounded by five corpses," Walsh writes that Vicki "didn't live for herself: she lived for others, and there are millions of those others" (120). While her life might have been dedicated to others, "her death," he writes, "was gloriously her own" (120). Well, it was and it wasn't. Even her death tragically repeats the heroic gesture assigned to the feminine. Like the *Patria,* like Pavlovsky's Ella written fifteen years after Vicki's death, "pure" women sacrifice themselves so that they/we might live. Damnable iteration indeed. The glorious image lives on. Communities define and strengthen themselves around these morally uplifting icons. The reality of the baby daughter sitting alone on a bed surrounded by corpses and the body of her dead mother has to fall out of the representation of the "lucid" death to keep it glorious. The female bodies, once again, become excess—they fall out of the picture so that the representation of death and sacrifice will continue its magic of affirming community, whether hegemonic or counterhegemonic.

While women were systematically tracked down as enemies of the state, all enemies were feminized, identified by a whole cluster of stereotypically feminine images: "weak," "lacking in conviction," "complacent" and "guilty" and "guilt-ridden" (Avellaneda 145). Before being killed, men were routinely sodomized—with the *picana eléctrica* or electric cattle prod—as a means of transforming them all into the penetrable, disposable bodies of misogynist fantasies.

Figure 24. Thatcher torched in effigy. (Photo by Guillermo Loiácono)

The entire struggle (repeatedly referred to as a "match" or game), which the junta described in terms of good and evil, was gendered. Human rights organizations were feminized. It was convenient that Isabelita was female so that the junta could associate all governmental ills with her person. And, of course, one of the great ironies of the entire *proceso* was that another woman was seen as putting an end to it. Because the Galtieri junta fell after failing to "recapture" the Malvinas from the British in 1983, Margaret Thatcher was widely represented in Argentina wearing a pirate's patch over her eye—the revenge of the feminine. Galtieri, as well as a great number of Argentine men generally, were heard remarking things like "That woman isn't going to beat us." Articles reported that Thatcher's husband was henpecked—cartoons showed him up to his elbow washing dishes—and their children utter failures. The castrating Thatcher was torched in effigy (see figure 24).

The profound ambivalence underlying the image of the feminine in the military spectacle was (and is) the source of its efficacy and appeal. The mythic version of events offered up by the military made sense, at least to a population shaped by Western tragic thought that has learned to recognize male individuation in terms of female submission and the suppression of the feminine.

The militarist ideology allowed the junta to appropriate once again the interior, familial space closed to it. The junta attempted to align their militaristic *nacionalismo* with Christian family values. Their spectacle was organized somewhat along the lines of *Oedipus Rex*—in dramatic, rather than psychoanalytic, terms. The story sounded familiar, though it responded to the actual crisis. The narrative logic made it compelling. In the new national family, according to the narrative, each member's first obligation was to the father (the junta) and the mother (the *Patria*). Children, potential Oedipuses, became highly suspect. Real women were written out of the narrative. Even traditional roles for women, new Antigones defending the legitimacy of a private space of familial duty, were called into question. Notions of a woman's domestic "sphere," a nonpolitical space, "disappeared" as women were accused of not properly controlling their children. "Señora, ¿sabe Ud. dónde están sus hijos? [Señora, do you know where your children are?]" Like Creon, the junta demanded that women put state interests over familial bonds. The nocturnal raids on homes, the abduction of family members, the practice of raping and torturing loved ones in front of each other revealed the armed forces' uneasiness with the family as a separate space and organizational unit. As the junta had warned, all the interior/private spaces were turned inside out.

The entire spectacle is noteworthy for its enforced absenting of women. Women disappeared into concentration camps and death flights and disappear again behind a language that transforms the feminine into some metaphorical quality or shortcoming that can be applied to members of the population ("feminized masses"), regardless of their sex. How can we think of the material existence of women, especially the disappeared women who left no bodies, in a system that denies them subjectivity? Are they no more than the "enemy" or dangerous *other* in a binary system founded on the sexual divide, part of a male/female *dialectic,* as thinkers such as Simone de Beauvoir suggest? Or are they simply the projection of masculinist fantasies and prohibitions in a closed system whose only referent is male, a *monologic* system or singular phallic order that denies that there even is an *other?* If so, female subjects are forever linguistically absent and unrepresentable. Women who attempt to represent themselves, as Vicki Walsh did, are condemned to reenact the deathly tropes available to them. Does this absence signal the limits of discursive formations themselves and suggest perhaps the possibility of a negotiated existence between discourses, in the margins and fractures? Or does it put in doubt the material existence of real historical beings, situated in discursive formations that erase them? If subjectivity is produced by the entry into culture, as theorists such as de Beauvoir, Foucault, de Lauretis, and Butler have argued, then it is gendered and, more specifically, gendered from the monologic male position in a closed system of self-reference. There are many absences here: the discursive absence of the feminine in a masculinist imaginary; the absence of real, historical women in protagonistic roles in Argentina; the absence of the material bodies of the women who were permanently disappeared from the scenario.

In a discursive system in which women are unrepresentable as subjects, representation seems, by definition, to be male self-representation. The glorious leaders, as objects of the look, inspire both desire and identification. The willing, implicitly feminized spectators give themselves up to the spectacle and allow the heroic male to dream their dreams for them. And what about non-willing spectators? The performance itself excluded them from participation—expelling as non-Argentinian those who refused to suspend their disbelief by identifying with the protagonist: "We cannot and should not recognize as a brother the Marxist, subversive terrorist just because he was born in our Patria. Ideologically he has lost the honor of calling himself Argentine."[32] While Woman in the scenario (as *Patria*) mediates between power brokers, the military male produces meaning and incarnates power. The homosocial bonding taking place in front of the public eye displaces Woman onto a metaphoric level. The military's self-representation and its discourse on the Argentine "authentic being" situates the feminine as the mediating hinge in the triangular formulation of homophobic fear and homosocial desire. While the feminine may be reduced to a site of communication and exchange between men, it is nonetheless indispensable to ward off feelings of homoerotic intimacy.

Recognizing gender performances, then, is central to our understanding of the Dirty War. The misogyny and homophobia of the fantasies were vital to their efficacy. They not only activated the scenario by engendering an obstacle, they also made sense of the urge to overcome the feminine or feminized other. The *Patria*, imagined as a purely symbolic, virginal mother figure, united Argentina's good children who were expected to identify with and model themselves on the national father figures. The "subversives," the incarnation of noncohesion or nonparticipation, were the bad children who threatened to destroy the father and claim the *Patria* for themselves. The flesh-and-blood mothers, as the locus of nonconforming subjectivity, had to be eliminated so that the image of the *Patria* as a unifying maternal body might work. Individual and collective fantasies of control and domination, played out against castrated, feminized, and penetrable bodies (literally and/or metaphorically), meshed into a highly organized system of terror in which hatred of the feminine was not only the consequence but, simultaneously, its very reason for being.

4 The Theatre of Operations: Performing Nation-ness in the Public Sphere

. . . it is how citizens *see* themselves and how they *see* those against whom they define themselves that determines national self-perception . . . the very idea of a nation is itself dependent on this visual realm.—Susan Jeffords, *Hard Bodies*

Performing Nation-ness

"Argentineans," a commentator noted, "were not born Argentineans; their nationality needed to be invented."[1] Rather than posit an essentializing notion of "national character" and attempt to "psychoanalyze" it, I look at how nation-ness is shaped through spectacle, that desiring-machine at work in the "imaginings" that hold a community together. "Nation-ness" captures the *idea* of nation that links disparate phenomenon such as nation, nationalism, and nationality.[2] But it is not just about politics and borders, it's about our way of *imagining* community, of creating and performing civil bonds. While citizens may envision the horizontal, fraternal community described by Benedict Anderson, identification is predicated on the internalization of a rigid hierarchy along the lines of gender, class, and race. Theatrical choreography situates members of the population in relation to each other. The visual arena allows a basis for identification, for in the public sphere "citizens" see themselves as somehow related to other citizens, most of whom (as Anderson notes) they will never meet.

Other scholars have focused on *writing* the nation, examining foundation fictions (as Doris Sommer does) or the literary traditions (as Josefina Ludmer did with the *gauchesca*) or national constitutions, grammar books, and comportment manuals (as the Venezuelan scholar Beatriz González Stephan has done).[3] Although language, literature, and any number of linguistic systems are key in aligning a citizen's sense of identity to a geographic place, becoming a "citizen" is also performative. We might look at theatre (as I do in chapter 8) as one more stage on which nation-ness was played out. Just as gender is a performative act, what Judith Butler describes as an "identity tenuously constituted in time—an identity instituted through a stylized repetition of acts,"[4] nation-ness is also performative. Both gender and nation-ness (which, I will argue, are the product of each other's performance and therefore difficult to imagine separately) are oppositional and exclusionary—just as one is male as opposed to female, one is Argentinean as opposed to something else. Both are inscribed on physical bodies. This does not suggest that either can be "put on" or exchanged at will. But there is a certain range available in enacting them. National/gender characteristics may look "natural," though they become more visibly performative in situations that brutally impose acceptable embodiments of national identity. But even in their everydayness they're performative: discontinuous moments come to appear as constituting a cohesive "reality" that social actors believe in. Doing one's nation-ness/gender "correctly" promises privilege and a sense of belonging, yet involves coercive mechanisms of identification. National/gender identity is not so much a question of being as of doing, of being seen doing, of identifying with the appropriate performative model. This identity is forged in the public sphere—the way we see others and ourselves is key to the process of national recognition and identification. Identification is key to subject formation, though enactments vary from country to country and from period to period.

The performativity of nation-ness involves a double mechanism—on one hand, nation-ness as the sum total of diverse "imaginings" is possible only because very different people imagine they share commonalities and learn to identify as part of a group. On the other, the hegemonic "nation" tends to suppress or appropriate diversity; otherness either disappears or becomes absorbed as sameness. The Dirty War represents an extreme example of the double mechanism of imagining and imposing national/gender identity. The military promoted an image of the "authentic national being" and demanded that the population feel "Argentine" by identifying with their performance of national identity. Everyone had to act and dress a part in the new scenario—from the Mothers of the Plaza de Mayo to students walking to school. The military mandated strict controls on the physical body and on sexuality. Unlike the Brazilian military junta during the same period that encouraged the export of highly eroticized body images to suggest that sexual freedom equaled political freedom, the Argentine military clamped down on the body with a vengeance.[5] Surviving meant "being" Argentinean, or, more specifically, "being seen as" Argentinean in a brutal context that defined patriotism as conformity and nonconformity as subversion.

The performative aspect of the struggle to control Argentinean citizens in no way minimizes those factors that, traditionally, have been thought of as objective or real—that is, the political, economic, historical, social, or ideological tensions that provoked the country's instability and culminated in the Dirty War. On the contrary. I would argue that the way nation-ness has been formulated and enacted in the public arena affects the way politics have been conceptualized, orchestrated, and played out in Argentina throughout its history. Thus, the performative strategies are themselves key factors—ultimately inseparable—from the other, more "objective" events of the Dirty War.

During the Dirty War, the military's spectacle, like Perón's populist spectacles before it, staged national/gender identity in the social arena. The two performances showed two faces of authoritarian power. Both spectacles were undoubtedly displays of masculine domination, yet they looked different and, thus, so did Argentineans. The *peronist* simulacrum of democracy and mutuality seemed antithetical to the brutal dictatorship of the junta. The *peronist* spectacle was organized around the cult of the *Líder*—Perón's and Evita's names were inscribed on streets, buildings, and plazas; public space became associated with their persons. The same gesture, however, absorbed "private" space into the all-encompassing "public": "when one reaches the home of the people one is accompanied by, it is like being in one's own home . . . Speaking the same language, we understand each other easily."[6] Communal cohesion, as in theatre, emanated from *presencing*. Perón and Evita territorialized their followers, and made them at home in what was presented as a shared collective and expansive *peronist* space. Nation-ness became equivalent to *peronismo*—an umbrella that promised to unite even the most disparate members of this imagined community: ("You can't be a good Argentine without being a good *peronist*" was one slogan).[7] Desire for national unity coalesced with desire for the glamorous, powerful, and entwined figures of Perón and Evita. One got read as the other. The visibility of Evita not only intensified popular desire, it made it appear that women too could play a central role in Argentinean nation-ness. Furthermore, Perón specifically encouraged racial and ethnic minorities to join his following. Perón and Evita toasted the poor and the powerless (children, most specifically) as the most deserving of their constituents. As classes, ranks, and races comingled, the rowdy anti-elitist aesthetic signaled a provocation to the established oligarchy. The pseudo-carnivalesque quality of the *peronist* production promised an inversion of the status quo. The taunt went so far that *peronist* supporters vowed to "tocarles el culo a los oligarcas [touch the oligarchy's ass]," thereby defiantly transgressing all the bounds of class and good manners.

The spectacle of the Dirty War, on the other hand, was a theatre of panic, of isolation, silence, and unnaming. The junta's show of male dominance varied from the *peronist* in that it shattered the festivity, the mass demonstrations, the illusion of political participation, the questionable racial and gender inclusivity associated with the *peronist* spectacle. Instead of the physical commingling of bodies, the junta enforced strict separation and control. Public space was reduced and policed.[8] The population was physically compartmentalized and organized in spatial divisions—cells, units, zones. People were not only exposed to surveillance by the armed forces, they internalized the surveillance, monitoring themselves to ensure that they were acting correctly. Instead of an active *Líder* cult, the junta encouraged the population to passively identify with their leaders, who presented themselves as "gentlemen." Argentineans were assigned to spectatorship—watching themselves, looking up to (or out for) the military, scrutinizing others. Instead of encouraging people to demonstrate on the streets and overflow the plazas in shows of political support, the junta emptied the streets and plazas.

The meaning and function of spectacle had changed. The junta entrapped the population through the controls of seeing and being seen. People were pushed back into the supposedly private spaces and, again supposedly, out of politics. Women were confined to more traditional roles. The junta wanted no more Evitas. Racial minorities were disparagingly referred to as *cabecitas negras* (little black heads), revealing a deep racism that to this day continues to marginalize and even disappear indigenous and racially mixed people from the collective imaginary.

Military males alone occupied public space. Silence replaced clamor. Only the military sirens and screams of victims broke the imposed quiet of the Dirty War. All the limits and boundaries enforced on the population emphasized that the military males themselves recognized no boundaries. There was no limit, it seemed, to what they could do and get away with. Transgression became the property of the state. The paramilitary forces in their Ford Falcons would run wild through the streets of Argentina, driving up on curbs and knocking over fruit stands and kiosks, but the general population had to walk the straight and narrow. The *peronist* populist spectacle of national cohesion gave way to atomization. The abductions, disappearances, exile, and inner exile made this, quite literally, a theatre of absenting and deterritorialization. Instead of the pseudocarnivalesque inversion, the junta imposed order, "national reorganization," stasis. The military attempted to stamp out the *peronist* spectacle—they despised and feared it as the spectacle of the unruly, the diverse, the inclusive. During the Dirty War, nation-ness was resemanticized: every gesture was broken down, isolated, scrutinized. The ideal citizens were those who selfconsciously controlled their every act, every word, even as they attempted to create the appearance of a cohesive and natural reality.

The Theatre of Operations

[T]he city is . . . the site of the body's cultural saturation, its take-over and transformation by images, representational systems, the mass media, and the arts—the place where the body is representationally reexplored, transformed, contested, reinscribed. In turn, the body (as cultural product) transforms, reinscribes the urban landscape according to its changing (demographic, economic, and psychological) needs, extending the limits of the city, of the sub-urban, ever towards the countryside which borders it.—Elizabeth Grosz, "Bodies-Cities"

The performativity of nation-ness and gender are coterminous and mutually reenforcing. The sense of geographic expansion that underlines a nation (though is not identical to it) includes both city and rural scapes and has often been expressed in terms of gendered bodies. Sarmiento, for example, described Buenos Aires as a lady reclining comfortably over a vast territory. "She," with her river and her port, is the point of entry that allows the interior provinces contact with the European nations across the sea (12–13). The female body and Buenos Aires, with their respective deltas, conflate into the site of both danger and desire as well as the arena for economic and cultural exchange. The national/state body subsumes both spatial configuration and human embodiment into its larger project. The various discourses that equate human bodies, spatial bodies (such as cities), and state bodies (nations or other imagined communities) indicate the degree to which nation-ness and gender have been naturalized to shape, organize, and valorize space as well as human corporeality: outside versus inside; up versus down; private versus public; functionality (health) versus nonfunctionality (or disease), and so on. Each of the divides is gendered along the lines that assign the outside, up, public, and functioning position to the masculine and the inside, down, private, and nonfunctioning position to the feminine. Thus each "body" is constructed along the various coordinates of space (territory/nation-ness) and gender.

Different societies, in different historical moments, will need different kinds of bodies. Cities and other national spaces contain humans, much as those humans become the containers of social and national images and values. I've come to think of the Dirty War as a theatre of operations, for the expression emphasizes the theatricality, the medicalization, and the violence of the operation exercised simultaneously on social space and human bodies. The theatre of operations served the goals of a new economic age of privatization. The entry into a neoliberal economy required the creation of a social body that would accelerate production yet obediently dissociate itself from the financial fruits of its labor (see figure 25). Breaking bodies literally became a way of breaking unions.[9] Yet the assault was framed in the seemingly incongruous discourses of conquest and Christian "purity." Only by cleansing the social body could Argentina once again achieve glory. The military, the embodiment of the spirit of conquest (with all those historical antecedents) would undertake the heroic struggle.

The armed forces assaulted both civil society and the individual worker/dissident/political opponent at the same time and in the same way. The masculinist discourse on bodies—that feminizes interiority, depth, and malfunctioning/disease, for example—shaped the nature of their attack on both the human body and civil society.

The military unleashed a two-pronged offensive. The first was the "masculine," logical, and seemingly necessary implementation of strategies that were supposedly "up" and aboveboard. The military's control of space and bodies was justified by a rhetoric extolling national health and rational social functioning. The visible was made available to inspection through the official reorganization and redistribution of space into "zones" and the regimentation and surveillance of the human body. As in Bentham's *Panopticon*, power was "visible and unverifiable"[10]—visible because the population could not get away from the military presence, unverifiable because people never knew when they were being watched. Combining militarized and medicalized language, the armed forces exerted authority over the enemy/disease. Medical terminology allowed them to target not only the "disease" but the entire population. Theories of contagion suggest that all people are at risk of catching and spreading the disease; everyone was a candidate for surveillance.

The other prong of the attack was aimed at "feminine" spaces and bodies—those dangerous interiors associated with femininity, occupied by the diseased and deranged subversives who hid underground. The military, while flaunting its visibility, also laid claim to invisibility, appropriating the tactics of the weak, those who, as de Certeau puts it, can never control but only insinuate themselves into, invade, or disrupt the space of the powerful. "The place of a tactic," he writes in *The Practice of Everyday Life*, "belongs to the other" (xix). They could see without being seen. Members of the armed forces wore disguises, carried volumes by Marx or Freud under their arms, and "penetrated" the hidden spaces associated with subversion. Their weapons included torture, bespeaking the sexualized character of the assault. These violations took place in nonvisible places, in the secret detention and concentration camps that the military hid from public view (in the interstices of the *Patria*'s "body," as they put it). There, the military tortured and murdered the disappeared who opposed their Frankensteinian efforts at (national) body building. The feminized underground was imagined as the other, that which was not readily available for scrutiny, the limit, the boundary, the extreme. (This gendering, I believe, partially explains the scopic and discursive insistence on displaying/exposing/violating the female body.) The junta vowed to *operar* and *limpiar* (to operate and clean) the public sphere, exterminating the germs that threatened the well-being of the fragile social organism.[11] The offending body was literally under the knife or *picana eléctrica* (electric cattle prod). Those who were not deemed recoverable died. The well-being of the nation/patient often called for drastic measures.

If spatial configuration participates in nation-ness by locating national identity in a given place, and by shaping and reflecting the way that citizens see themselves and each other, then clearly the sense of a national self undergoes change when space is partitioned and policed. The mechanisms are more visible, because they're extreme, during states of siege. The cities and countryside were divided up into zones that were searched in operatives known as *rastrillos* ("to rake"; see figure 26).[12] Entire neighborhoods were blocked off, one by one, as military forces searched homes asking for identification of all those present and the whereabouts of those absent. These invasive spatial tactics went so far as to reproduce the ghosts, if not the actual bodies, of those whom the military had already disappeared. When those absent from the home were among the disappeared, some Argentines confess to succumbing to the absurdity of making up stories explaining the disappeared person's absence to avoid provoking the irascible and brutal members of the armed forces.[13] Terrified individuals had to stay put; there was no place else to go that would not incriminate friends or family. Buses, cars, and all other forms of transportation were randomly stopped and searched. Messages on the radio and television reminded citizens that it was their patriotic duty to report suspicious-looking individuals. The regimented population, in military fashion, was reviewed, controlled, disciplined, and, at times, punished in full public view. Visibility was key to social control: people had to be available for inspection.

In this theatre of operations, there was a new semiotics of terror. The green light gave the go-ahead for paramilitary and military "task forces" (*grupos de tarea*) to carry out their raids and abductions (see figure 27). These were not, as the term *disappearance* might suggest, invisible affairs. Members of the armed forces in helicopters, military trucks, and jeeps cordoned off the area under siege. The victim was abducted, often yelling and screaming for help, by a group of heavily armed men (see figure 28). The victim would usually be thrown down on the back seat of the waiting car, and the group would drive away, recklessly, flaunting. Yet no one was supposed to "see" or, more specifically, admit to seeing what was going on. (The photograph of the *operativo* was taken from a passing train.)

The term *theatre of operations* connotes not only the performative nature of nation-ness, mediated through the visual sphere, but also the military's flagrant theatricality in destabilizing the population en masse. As if by magic, people disappeared into thin air. Then, just as suddenly, the bodies of disappeared people showed up all over the country—on sidewalks, in trash cans—as messages to the population. In one dramatic display, a group of corpses—all dressed up in suits, with shoes dangling around their necks like neckties—was found tied around the Obelisk, Argentina's national monument of independence, situated at *punto zero,* the dead-center of Buenos Aires. A new sense of communal identity was simultaneously forged and undone around a shared terror. Apprehensive spectatorship united a silent, atomized population. People no longer identified with the space they inhabited. They no longer saw themselves as members of a cohesive community. They felt like strangers in their country, in their city, in their own homes. The scenario became increasingly surreal as the junta disavowed the state terrorism that people saw with their own eyes. News reports failed to mention the escalating number of disappearances that occurred daily throughout the country. The make-believe world traditionally associated with theatre became the official version of reality and was relentlessly transmitted through the media. The military blinded and silenced the population, which had to accept and even participate in the production of fictions.

Each aspect of this theatre of operations—the military, the medical, the theatrical—reflected the same struggle and objectives: men struggled for control and supremacy over the feminized body (Motherland, population, woman). There was a constant crossover from the individual to the social through the attack on the "body." The invisible yet all too obvious practice of torture is just one example of how the three discourses fused into one—the torture was a hidden, hence obscene and fascinating, spectacle that paralyzed both the victim and the population. The performance of torture was medicalized, though of course it was a part of a military operation. Torture annihilated the victim's body and the social "body" simultaneously. One mutilated body, theatrically exposed for the population to see, undid the national sense of self and subverted the judicial, ethical, and social safeguards designed to protect individuals from atrocity. Just as bodies disappeared, so did civil society.

Both the city/country and its inhabitants showed the effects of terror. Parks and streets were empty. The once lively Buenos Aires failed to energize its inhabitants. Curfews were imposed; plazas, bars, and cafés came under surveillance. The "center" of Buenos Aires itself disappeared as movie- and theatregoers, restaurant patrons, and strollers abandoned what had been the city's cultural hub of Corrientes and Lavalle. (Upper-class neighborhoods such as Palermo and Belgrano, considered less resistant to the military project because they benefited economically from its agenda, became the new social centers.) The seemingly "natural" performativity of everyday life transformed into a command performance. The normally stylish and even flamboyant population now wanted to go unnoticed.

The *idea* of an "imagined" community underwent metamorphosis. Argentineans felt as if they were in exile, an internal exile, as the signs, sights, and codes of their familiar environment became progressively stranger and more terrifying. They could no longer read the signs.

The transformation of public space into militarized zone through systems of visual dominance and surveillance affected all social organizations. Military personnel took over positions of power. The universities, the cultural centers, the news services, and government agencies were all run by military men. Argentina's forty-four radio stations and eighteen television stations were state owned and operated. The military's goal was to "purify" the environment by cracking down on ideological contaminants. The vibrant intellectual life was stifled, and those who did not tow the official line were pushed out of universities into the intellectual underground of private tutorials, seminars, and group research projects.[14] With inquisitorial zeal, the junta oversaw book burnings. Theatres were burned; actors, writers, and technicians were threatened and blacklisted.

Figure 25. "Have a coke." (Photo by Jorge Aguirre)   Figure 26. Rastrillo: raking the neighborhood. (Photo by Guillermo Loiácono)   Figure 27. Military operation. (Photo by Guillermo Loiácono)

Figure 28. Victims were abducted in broad daylight. (Photo by Daniel García)

While officials claimed there was no censorship, they imposed "guidelines": "The programs should offer models of Argentineness for each inhabitant of our country . . . exalting the values that conform to the desirable models."[15] The portrayal of conflict on TV was deemed unpatriotic. Even though it is hard to imagine a soap opera without divorce, adultery, abortion, depression, generational problems, economic problems, attempted suicides, and violent offenses, unpleasant realities simply vanished from view. There were no live shows; everything was taped first, then submitted to the censors.[16] The dictatorship's propaganda clearly transmitted its version of the struggle to establish good over evil. The make-believe quality of the programming, presented in the social context of extreme brutality in which ordinary people were dragged screaming off the streets by military forces, endowed the national scenario with a ghostly spectacularity.

Boundaries collapsed between private and public spaces as the entire "private" domain became sucked up into the *proceso* (see figure 29). The junta co-opted the language and space of domesticity. The Motherland was the "house" in which the military had to establish order. One photograph that was widely circulated during the Dirty War showed four male high-school students white-washing the outside of their school. The caption reads: "Let's put the house in order. No, they're not members of any political group and they're not painting

Figure 29. "And they say one can't live in this country!" cartoon by Quino.
(*Potentes, prepotentes e impotentes.* Buenos Aires: Ediciones de la Flor, 1991)

slogans on the wall. They're students from the Otto Krause High School who, of their own accord, decided to whiten the front of the school. There were placards with political slogans on them, dates, calls for meetings and strikes. Now, there is just a neat and white wall. As there should be. As there should have been always. This gesture by young Argentineans is a symptom, a good symptom. Something that makes us think: 'Order begins at home.' "[17]

And in this new militarized "home," families, like armies, were reorganized and hierarchized. There had to be a clear system of command: fathers had to occupy their place of authority; mothers were responsible for household affairs; children had to respect and obey their parents. Parents were designated military proxies and asked to police their children: "Parents are primordial agents in the eradication of this nightmare [leftist ideology]. They must keep watch, participate and report whatever complaint they deem necessary."[18] The military spokespeople and the mass media lauded those who adhered to their roles. The Consejo Publicitario Argentino (Argentine Publicity Commission) put out "Calls for Individual Responsibility," which were ads in papers and magazines directed alternately at women, students, workers, educators, businesspeople, religious leaders, and other sectors of the population: "You who are a woman, you are young, you work, maybe you are overwhelmed by all the risky bifurcations that present themselves on your chosen path. You must avoid those dangers, you must not stray from the main path. One day, when you face your children, you will rejoice that you knew how to do it. This country is what you make of it. Be aware of that responsibility."[19]

The same equation between familial and national duties were relentlessly broadcast throughout the media. Parenting magazines alerted parents to all sorts of "dangers" surrounding their children. Is dancing erotic? How can you tell if your son is effeminate? Two such magazines, *Padres* and *Vivir,* claimed to offer all the "responsible information for parents who want to know everything about their children." Women's magazines (such as *Para ti*) cautioned that words such as *dialogue, bourgeoisie, Latin America, exploitation, structural change,* and *capitalism* should warn parents that their children were being exposed to subversive thinking. Academic subjects such as history, geography, economics, and literature, not to mention prohibited subjects such as psychology, these sources reiterated, were hotbeds of subversive indoctrination. *Gente* and other news magazines also took up the mission of educating parents: "What do you do so that your son won't become a *guerrillero?*"[20]

As society became "reorganized," the physical semiology of the population changed. Adherence to the uniform roles proscribed by the military became synonymous with Argentineness. Political adherence, belonging, "being Argen-

Figure 30. "Like This, NOT Like This." (Illustration in military
flyer circulated through the educational system)

tine" were enacted daily in the public sphere. Being "seen" performing one's
national identity correctly was key to survival. Guidelines dictating appropriate
appearance and behavior for male and female students were issued and enforced throughout the entire educational system (see figure 30):

> Males: short hair, ears visible, no beard, classic trousers, jacket, shirt and
> tie.
> Females: hair pulled back, white apron covering shirt, blouse or sweater,
> shirt buttoned at the neck or white undershirt. If trousers are worn, they
> must be navy blue; no makeup.
> For both sexes: Stand up every time an authority figure enters the
> classroom (professor or older person). Maintain silence in all official cere-
> monies. No smoking. It is prohibited to wear blue jeans or colored cloth-
> ing under aprons. It is prohibited to make a group presentation or a
> collective request. It is prohibited to make any comment that affects the
> principle of authority and hierarchy.[21]

These prohibitions extended to professors and school administrators, who
were made responsible for all infractions and were forced into policing their
students.

The dramas of Argentineness were also enacted throughout the public sphere, particularly by the mass media that extended the military's capacity to invade domestic spaces and redo the body of its citizens:

> between one program and another, there was endless ideological propaganda in which a well-dressed youth with short hair and a tie arrives at the University; another youth, dirty and long-haired, making crazy and frightened gestures, hands him a subversive flyer; a father (the first boy's, of course) finds out about the situation. First, he hesitates, but then he calls the police to inform them of what is happening. A voice (from off) recommends "call the authorities *before* your son becomes involved in some *dangerous business.*" (Adellach, *Argentina* 44)

In this spectacle of control, the "authentic" body (male) of the tidy young man was in sync with military aspirations of order and hierarchy. Conformity had to be visible. The principles of duty, generational trust, and openness were affirmed. Doubt and self-doubt were portrayed as debilitating. The father and son duo (in association with the police) triumphed. They showed the efficacy of the chain of (male) command while the crazy, frightened, structureless, fatherless son tumbled toward doom. The "subversive" boy was associated with femininity—the long hair and the frenzied manner conjured up the enemy as hysterical and effeminate. The image of safety within the system overrode the representation of chaos engulfing those outside it. Along with the idea of order, the ad also insinuated the quasi-fascist opposition of cleanliness and "health" versus dirt, disease, and disorder. The "subversive" boy was both dirty and unhealthy—situated on the brink of mental disintegration. The pamphlets he handled seemed contaminated by their infirm source. Ideas, clearly, were not to be aired and debated; they were categorized as life-threatening and therefore to be shunned unexamined. The population at large was in danger of contagion. The father-son-police alliance kept danger and violence at bay by being obedient citizens (calling the authorities), rather than by assuming protagonistic or active roles in the conflict.

Maintaining visible differences between the sexes, through the use of gender-appropriate uniforms, grooming, and comportment, became paramount. In-between-ness became the zone of deviancy in which homosexuals and independent women "naturally" fell and in which all enemies were cast. However, as in the military ranks, difference *between* males was rigorous and visible as well. Hierarchies such as status, age, and ideological positioning became immediately discernible—worn in one's attitude and attire. Discipline, as Foucault noted, was truly "the art of rank"; it fixed bodies in a militarized system while allowing them to circulate "in a network of relations" (*Discipline and Punish* 146).

Citizens had to make their adherence visible not only by behaving in an orderly, obedient manner but by looking a certain way. If someone "did" their nationality differently it was taken as the sign of an antinationalist or unpatriotic ideology. Individuals policed themselves, internalizing the surveilling eye— Were they doing it right? Was their shirt too flashy, their hair too long? What would their bodies signal to others? The appropriate way to "do" one's nationality was to adhere to strict hierarchies and demarcation lines. Obedient bodies publicly enacted submission.

People not only cultivated the official look, their bodies underwent change. Though they were generally despondent, they became increasingly alert to dangers around them. Their senses and protective instincts became more acute.[22] They learned to "read" others's bodies, a new system of signs and codes, just as they exposed themselves to observation. Was that ordinary-looking man a military infiltrator? What was the meaning of that sound? Was it safe to attend a certain show, read a particular book, or frequent a specific shop? The slightest gesture could attract unwanted attention, as Quino's cartoon makes clear (see figure 31). Interpretation became critical in the most literal sense.

With the general population safely pushed into visible performative categories, the public arena became a theatrical space for the military and their opponents. While the general population dressed up as itself (in its role as obedient citizen), the military and its opponents needed disguises to infiltrate the *other's* space, the space of the "weak." They tried to look like average citizens or students or soccer fans in order to pick up information or identify and track down their opponents.

The opposition, too, often tried to look like "good" Argentineans so that they could successfully enter the spaces otherwise closed to them. However, the media played up the performativity of the enemy while denying that the military used the same tactics. Here too gender played a role, as women opponents were accused of being more deceptive and seductive than their male counterparts. In his article "Las guerrilleras: La cruenta historia de la mujer en el terrorismo" (Guerrilleras: The bloody story of women in terrorism), which appeared in the weekly magazine *Somos*, Carlos Penguin described the *guerrillera* as an accomplished actor, with multiple names and looks: "today she'll wear a blond wig, tomorrow clean cut, the day after tomorrow a red wig. She has an arsenal that includes a variety of items: sunglasses, a freshly washed face, heavy makeup, loose fitting dresses and tight pants. Men have far more limited

Figure 31. "Normality division. Documents, please." cartoon by Quino.
(*Potentes, prepotentes e impotentes* Buenos Aires: Ediciones de la Flor, 1991)

resources" (13). One of the photographs accompanying the article shows two women's wigs hanging next to numerous pistols and assorted ammunition. The innocent-looking Ana María González was presented as a monster by the media not just because she was supposedly responsible for the death of the chief of police, but because she had tricked him: "she was able to introduce herself into the household, her youth was seductive, as was her manner of relating to the family" (17). She had acted as a friend of the officer's daughter; she had deceived him and his family; she had betrayed their trust. That is what makes this story so shocking that *Gente* claims "This [story] is terrifying. Stunning. It makes adjectives impossible."[23]

Everyone was performing. Everyone was trying to look the part that offered them security and relative invisibility (if they wanted to stay out of the fray) or access and information (if they were somehow involved). Even those who did not participate in the political struggle, but who wanted to effect some kind of social change, found that they too had to dress up.[24] Other people, as Griselda Gambaro's play *Decir sí* (*Saying Yes*) suggests, found themselves playing the stooge in a drama that they did not recognize as their own. The rigid state control and the hypertheatricality of the period deterritorialized the population, making people feel like strangers in their own bodies as well as in their own home, city, and country.

Transmitting Terror

To assist in the task of developing a new cultural interpretation, a list of *don'ts* instructed "citizens living in a new age" (see figure 32). The new militarized semiology insinuated itself seamlessly into daily life. This was, as the indications show, a negative space in which *do* disappeared and everything multiplied into an endless series of *don'ts*. This was the world in which anything that wasn't obligatory was prohibited. Road signs, showing a military silhouette bearing arms, warned drivers: "Don't stop or the guard will open fire." Public space itself had been transformed into a no-stop zone.

The visual strategies of dominance used by the junta were simple, repetitive, and banal. The news enacted a public show of death. Daily headlines, trafficking in violence, kept pace with the military's heroic mission: "A Subversive Group Was Annihilated"; "Eleven Extremists Die in 2 Confrontations"; "3 Extremists Die in a Shootout"; "Spectacular Capture on the Corner of Córdoba and Florida"; "Hard Blow to Subversives"; "Extremist Group Kills Policeman"; "Ten Extremists Killed by the Army"; "Three Men Hurt Trying to Detonate a Bomb"; "Seven Men and Six Women Shot to Death"; "Eight Jews Detained"—

Figure 32. "The Dos and Don'ts of a Terror System:
'Everything You Should NOT Do'" (*Gente*, April 1, 1976)

on and on the reports go, sometimes two or three incidents reported on the same page, page after page, day after day. *La nación* even ran a special section for *extremistas*, though, in fact, the newspaper represented the *extremistas* as overflowing all boundaries, much as they reportedly did in "real" life. Reports of bloody confrontations insinuated themselves even into that cloistered section of the paper known as "woman, home, child" (la mujer, el hogar, el niño).

Along with the simplification and repetition of the military's deeds, the media amplified feelings of terror throughout the public sphere—many ads, reports, and news items reiterated the military message. The same battle between men for supremacy was being replayed in social spectacles from ads to soccer games. Those who identified with the military could participate in the conquest. Ford Motor Company, for example, put out a series of ads for Falcon, the car most often used for the military abductions. The ads promoted feelings of male prowess and supremacy by heralding the car and its drivers as "champions." "A history of feats without precedence . . . And you, with your Ford Falcon, will win out on the streets and the highways." The ad traded in death, making the viewer one with the armed, military and paramilitary forces that imposed their dominance on the public roads. The ad created complicity by putting "us" in the driver's seat, identifying "us" with those brave men who controlled the military machine. Ford also celebrated the military's usurpation of power with a full-page ad on January 2, 1977: "1976: Once again, Argentina finds its way; 1977: New Year of faith and hope for all Argentines of good will [Not *all* Argentines, of course, just the "good" ones]. Ford Motor of Argentina and its people commit themselves to the struggle to bring about the great destiny of the Patria."[25]

Chrysler indirectly joined the fray, showing a self-satisfied male consumer who did not enter the fight but who nonetheless profited from it. The large bold caption read: "Efficiency has a price: All the better for You." The ad closed with instructions in another bold line: "Choose, demand, and enjoy: it's your right."[26] Chevrolet circulated images of male prowess and freedom through the picture of a man hang gliding. Peugeot put out an ad showing two boxers in the ring, both looking slightly ashamed. Its ad made explicit the fact that marketing itself was designed around the motif of the struggle between men. The ad read: "An absurd fight [Una pelea absurda]: To us, it seems a strange combat. 'Not elegant' let's say." The ad ends with a bid for understatement: "Peugeot: The brand of the Lion—because it can roar, it whispers . . ."[27] The fight between men was carried out in various international arenas. One government ad extolling the advantages of the same "free" market that was decimating Argentina's national industries depicted global competitors as heavyweight lifters straining for supremacy.[28]

For the segments of the population that could not participate in the conquest, even vicariously by buying a car, the ads offered two other positions. The first placed the viewer in the quest for purity and safety. The defining feature of numerous products was their purity—from canned fruit to sugar. And businesses of all kinds offered up all manner of security measures: Patria locks announced that "security comes first"[29]; Electrocphin, likewise, promised "Total security against aggression."[30] Banks and financial institutions were also dealing in security with ads such as "I sleep very well . . . and you?"[31] Medical and pharmaceutical companies ran anxiety-creating ads such as the one with a large picture of an alarmed baby under the huge caption: "How long will this Argentinean live?" The rest of the caption goes on to assure the reader that improved medical technology had increased the lifespan of the average Argentinean.[32] The other widely publicized option was escape. Travel became "A real necessity. A must," according to Aereolineas Argentinas. But even escape had its sinister overtones, as illustrated in an ad by AereoMéxico: "We're coming to get you today [Hoy venimos a buscarlo]."[33] Through the visual sphere, terror "passed from mouth to mouth across a nation, from page to page, from image to body."[34]

Soccer as a Spectacle of Nation-ness

The battle between males for supremacy against the effeminate other was being staged through various public spectacles, including soccer, Argentina's national sport. On first view, the soccer match seems the antithesis of the military project, with its exuberance, unruliness, and liberating exaltation of nation-ness. And in certain countries, during certain periods, this may well be true. Gilberto Freyre describes Brazilian soccer in 1964 (on the eve of the military takeover) as "Dionysian" due to the racial mix among the players, the improvisation of the techniques, and the "popular" character of its appeal.[35] But soccer in Argentina, especially during the World Cup games held in Buenos Aires in 1978 at the height of the military violence, functioned as the other face of the same masculinist spectacle. Contextualizing the sport is central unless one accepts, as Pierre Bourdieu puts it facetiously, "that there exists a natural need, equally widespread at all times, in all places and in all social milieux, not only for the expenditure of muscular energy, but more precisely, for this or that form of exertion."[36]

Soccer played a vital role in community building in Argentina since it was introduced by the British in the nineteenth century. In part, as Eduardo P. Archetti argues, this is because it is profoundly entangled in imagining community as a "fraternity that is flat and horizontal," in which people are conceived as "fundamentally homogeneous, only superficially divided by status, class, or locality."[37] Historically, he notes, "Argentinean football has constituted a symbolic and practical male arena for national pride and disappointment, happiness and sorrow" (226).

Soccer had a particularly wide appeal during the Dirty War because it bolstered Argentina's floundering sense of community in a period when more and more public spectacles were suspended or policed. It was privileged by the junta, which allowed the soccer match to be played on the day of the military coup, and enjoyed by a population that sought a sense of national identity and continuity in a sport that was perceived as nonpolitical. The World Cup games in 1978 functioned to keep the population's spirits high and its mind on something other than the escalating numbers of disappearances taking place in the country. Newspaper headlines announced that Argentina's woes were due to Isabelita's ineptitude and that the junta was rationally and painstakingly trying to set things right.

This show was more for the benefit of foreign athletes, sports commentators, and tourists than for internal consumption. And though far fewer foreigners arrived than expected due to international awareness of trouble in Argentina,

Figure 33. "The Country that Changed!" President Videla at the 1978 World Cup. (*Somos*, June 30, 1976)

those who did visit the country saw a rather peaceful situation. Though Amnesty International had recommended that foreign visitors keep their eyes open to human rights violations, the presence of Henry Kissinger as the junta's honored guest legitimated the enterprise. After all, the U.S. secretary of state wouldn't socialize with torturers, would he? (Alas, the photos of Kissinger sucking up lobsters with Chile's infamous General Pinochet suggest otherwise.)

While the *montoneros* who remained carried out some offensives, these were limited in scope and not publicized. There were rumors that the *montoneros* intended to blow up the Casa Rosada and that Massera had paid Mario Firmenich, the head of the *montoneros*, $1 million not to disrupt the games. The final match between Argentina and Holland took place under strict security measures, staging a complex net of "looks" as spectators watched and were watched, submitted to visual controls of surveillance. "The biggest team of security men ever assembled in one place in Argentina guarded the stadium, and remote-action cameras watched every section of the crowd."[38] The spectacle destabilized the spectators who became the objects of visual control.

Argentina won. No resistance was possible (see figure 33). Even the opponents were subsumed in the show of national unity. The weekly magazines *Siete días* described the event in terms that literally obliterated the rivals: "No one who had the privilege of being at the River Plate stadium for the final match will be able to erase those hours of Sunday, June 25th: color, fervor, friendship and one single flag."[39] The magazine also pronounced that Argentines were "True Champions" and ran a feature article on the restitution of national honor.[40] One headline read: "Courage, force, potency and total public support"—a winning combination that the junta read as an endorsement of itself. The next page read: "The End of Our Inferiority Complex." The page that followed had a two-page spread of General Videla addressing the jubilant crowd in the Plaza de Mayo from the balcony of the Casa Rosada. The headline ran: "A Vital Triumph for Argentine Unity."

The soccer match not only affirmed the myth of national unity at one of the worst moments in Argentine history, it functioned as a social equivalent to the military spectacle. Soccer reproduced the homosocial, and profoundly homophobic, nature of male bonding in the struggle for dominance over the other, inferior male/team. Soccer too is an all-male spectacle in which trained, professional bodies, in uniforms, exhibit the thrill and identity of team spirit and cooperation. The interaction is intensely physical (hugs, slaps, body contact on field and off), yet the sport is organized against the homosexual urges, fears, and fantasies that attend the homosocial. Here too, conquest is the name of the game. The goal is to affirm the supremacy of the macho self as he triumphs over the "sissy" other. The hero (Maradona, for example) embodies national dreams of grandeur, of asserting oneself and dominating the international stage. The public identifies mimetically with the heroic figure and projects its aggression, as well as its own fears of inadequacy (national inferiority, anxieties relating to masculinity), onto the game and the opponents' fans. Unlike criminal politics, soccer makes explicit that aggression is only a matter of positionality. For the duration of the match, the enemy occupies the other end of the field and it makes no difference who that other might be—though of course for historical and practical reasons some teams are more hated and feared than others. The other is simply the opposition, the rival, the threat to group supremacy. Like the military display, soccer also positions its public. Avid fans (most of them males who had played soccer at some time in their lives) participate from the sidelines. The public, organized by and around the spectacle, becomes a cohesive group—its own "community." And it is overwhelmingly a male community, for only a small percentage of fans are women, on both the local and national levels.[41] As in the political arena, the onlookers or fans *belong*, but they don't *do*. The chosen male hero figure will fight the good fight. Thus the sport is constructive and transformative in the same way that the military spectacle is; it gives the crowd its sense of identity and cohesion through visual identification. The fans, like the population, can recognize each other; their bodies, shirts, and caps announce their allegiance. They are *one* in their chants, under their banners and flags. Yet clearly the dynamic of community building is, like the military endeavor, oppositional: Argentina *against* whomever the opponent might be; us against them.

Key to the success and centrality of the sport in Argentina is that soccer defines not only the group identity of its fans (and in international matches their nationality) but, as Marcelo Suárez-Orozco recognizes, it defines their masculinity. The fans, unlike the population that is gendered feminine by the military spectacle, clearly fights for its masculinity in the soccer stadium. "The fan must define his manliness at the expense of other fans."[42] The aggression that fans demonstrate during games is usually directed toward fans of the opposing team rather than at the players themselves. The chants they sing demonstrate the anxiety that I've described throughout this study, that of differentiating "real" macho (insertive) males from effeminate males, those who are penetrated and humiliated by the macho, that is, rival fans. The fans who sing the chants have "balls," they will "rape" their opposition, they will "fuck" the other team and "break their ass." Their ball will go "through the asshole" of their rivals, who, after all, are "faggots." The "prick" of the owner of their team will penetrate the "ass" of the owner of the rival team. Moreover, one of the songs says, the ultimate victory of the winning side is that they are invulnerable to "touching" or penetration: "La copa, la copa, se mira y no se toca [The cup or trophy can be seen but not touched]." Suárez-Orozco's interpretation of this chant could apply equally well to the sexualized nature of the military spectacle, though he himself does not make the connection between soccer and the military spectacle and ethos: "First and foremost, the cup symbolizes victory and superiority, which in the Argentine cultural context equals power, which equals virility, or masculinity. So the song now reflects through the symbolic equivalences of the cup= victory= macho—an exhibitionist wish to expose one's masculinity which can be 'seen' but 'never touched,' or penetrated in any way" (21). Like the military on parade, this spectacle is about dominance, not reciprocity. The military make themselves available to viewing, but they are invulnerable to the touch. They need not return the look or establish a connection of any kind with their spectators. Power stems from maintaining distance and control. Furthermore, the songs substantiate an observation that I've noted throughout: the macho "insertive" partner does not consider himself homosexual by participating in same-sex intercourse. On the contrary, penetrating the "receptive" partner, whether male or female, simply reaffirms the macho's

Figure 34. "Useful Defeat."
(*Noticias,* July 3, 1994)

virility and superior power. He has overcome, "beaten," and humiliated the "feminized" other. This explains why the macho protects himself violently from any perceived attack to his masculinity—no one will attack him from behind.[43]

Soccer, like several other spectacles of the period, reenacted the drama of male individuation and supremacy. Now, after the end of the Dirty War, it continues to do so. After the national hero, Maradona, was expelled from the 1994 World Cup games, accusations of foreign conspiracy circulated widely in Argentina. As the defeat was internalized, however, the media presented Maradona as embodying the failure of Argentineness itself. The front cover of the weekly magazine *Noticias* (July 3, 1994) ran a picture of Maradona dressed in the national colors under the headline, "Derumbe util [Useful defeat]": "Just as the loss of the Malvinas [Falkland Island] War moved the country away from messianic thinking, Maradona's self-destruction will help educate a transgressive society. The Argentinean proclivity for the quick win, its notion that the ends justify the means, its personality cults that substitute for a viable system, and this puerile impunity have always ended abysmally. The example of Maradona is a great lesson" (see figure 34).

The reporting reproduces the cult of the heroic personality even as it critiques it. It too focuses on the lone hero—the one who has to save the day or lose it. The staging echoes the military self-presentation I discussed in chapter 3. Standing still, his eyes transfixed above head-level, his hand on his heart, the Argentine flag all over him, Maradona embodies national aspirations of grandeur. Responsibility for national "flaws" are individualized and located in the fallen hero. This tragic narrative of failure echoes, and is made equivalent to, the military failure. Being expelled from a *futból* game for "doping" is on a par with the Malvinas, in which almost a thousand untrained young men lost their lives. The "flaws" that bring down Maradona are part of the national "character": hubris, autodestructiveness, transgressiveness. Maradona is a stand-in for a transgressive society—he represents everyone's hopes and dreams; he carries the weight of Argentina's collective sins.

The various dramas, played out simultaneously in the public sphere, seemed trapped in the same gestures, stuck in the same plotline, unraveling toward the same sad, predictable, and seemingly inevitable resolution.

5 Percepticide

Learning to see is training careful blindness.
—Peggy Phelan, *Unmarked*

Being Seen Seeing: Mis/Identifications
in the Scopic Field

The population's reaction to spectacles of power positioned them as much as their physical attire and body language. In order to qualify as "good" Argentineans, people were forced to focus on the given-to-be-seen and ignore the atrocities given-to-be-invisible, taking place around them. Signs indicated what the population was to see and not to see. The society of the spectacle, to borrow Debord's term, ties individuals into an economy of looks and looking. But everyone was also positioned in the larger scopic field of the Lacanian gaze: "In the scopic field, the gaze is outside, I am looked at, that is to say, I am a picture. This is the function that is found at the heart of the institution of the subject in

Figure 35. Girl looking at portrait. (Photo by Jorge Aguirre)

the visible. What determines me, at the most profound level, in the visible, is the gaze that is outside" (*Four Fundamental Concepts* 106). This photograph of a working-poor young girl, looking at a beautiful portrait of a beautiful young woman in the showcase of Buenos Aires's Harrods, illustrates the look/gaze that structures the subject (see figure 35). The beautiful model is the object of the girl's look, but of course she doesn't return the look. The girl, fixed on the photo, sees both what her society equates with ideal womanhood and her distance (measured not only in meters and panes of glass, but in class and race) from the ideal image. As in the "mirror stage," the girl's sense of self comes from a misidentification with the image in front of her. She sees what she has been taught should be a self-reflection, though in fact it is the very picture of what she can never be. Her diminished place in the social hierarchy is visibly reinforced by the steps positioning the portrait above head level. The scruffy jeans, unkempt hair, and bag of oranges slung over the girl's shoulder don't seem to belong to the same universe as the ethereal beauty of the white, madonnaesque model. Both the girl and the young woman, moreover, are actors who function in the public arena of the gaze, susceptible to scrutiny. The photographer, Jorge Aguirre, caught the young girl looking; this photograph captures the complex interchange of looks and the gaze that contribute to the simultaneous formation of the individual and social subject.

What do we learn to focus on? What are we trained to overlook? How do we get the signals?

The two photographs of Argentineans (figures 36 and 37) glued to the events of the Malvinas/Falkland Islands war indicate how communal identity is shaped and how public attention is controlled by the given-to-be-seen. The newspaper kiosks (in these particular examples) served as hubs from which people imbibed their national positionality, the us versus them. There they stand, looking, nervous spectators of a drama taking place all around them. But the staging of the headlines delimits the focus, situating the battlefield (Malvinas) and identifying the enemy (the British). The wall of headlines and posters in figure 36 not only depicts Thatcher as a pirate, but it situates Argentina as the offended party. Spectators are encouraged to enter into the narrative. Individual differences, social inequalities, and criminal politics "disappear" in the staging of a singular "body." The "Now to the Death" poster (at the far left of the kiosk), featuring a Union Jack tattered by bullets, addressed itself to "All Argentines"—to that homogeneous entity it created through the specular act itself. The caption defined Argentines as naturally self-sacrificing and pacifist, yet prepared to fight to the end for "our Malvinas."[1] It alludes to the "many historical antecedents" shaping both the peace-loving disposition of its popula-

Figure 36. Watching the war, 1. (Photo by Guillermo Loiácono)

tion and its spirit of conquest. These two "virtues," so central to the collective imaginary, according to the poster, safely place Argentineans in a long, stable continuum of national pride. Those looking at the headlines were simultaneously isolated in their spectatorship (it is clear they do not know or speak to each other) and united under the banner of "All Argentineans." (The Falkland Islands/Malvinas war offered Thatcher a similar opportunity to reaffirm essential Britishness.)[2]

Seeing not only affirmed feelings of communal struggle and identity, it was also the trap that destroyed communal cohesion. *Dangerous* seeing, seeing that which was not given-to-be-seen, put people at risk in a society that policed the look. The mutuality and reciprocity of the look, which allows people to identify with others, gave way to unauthorized seeing. Functioning within the surveilling gaze, people dared not be caught seeing, be seen pretending not to see. Better cultivate a careful blindness. A network of surreptitious looks positioned and silenced those who did not condone or identify with the military project. These looks shattered community. Instead of kinship, one recognized the "enemy" in the ordinary, the fatal schism between us and, suddenly, *them*.

The triumph of the atrocity was that it forced people to look away—a gesture that undid their sense of personal and communal cohesion even as it seemed to bracket them from their volatile surroundings. Spectacles of violence rendered

Figure 37. Watching the war, 2. (Photo by Guillermo Loiácono)

the population silent, deaf, and blind. Figure 38 shows not only the overt violence to which people were subjected in public avenues during broad daylight, it also shows the self-blinding of the general population—"percepticide." The woman sitting at the table behind the window of the café is hiding her head in her arms. She cannot or will not witness the events taking place in front of her. The military spectacle made people pull back in fear, denial, and tacit complicity from the show of force. Therein lay its power. The military violence could have been relatively invisible, as the term *disappearance* suggests. The fact that it wasn't indicates that the population as a whole was the intended target, positioned by means of the spectacle. People had to deny what they saw and, by turning away, collude with the violence around them. They knew people were "disappearing." Men in military attire, trucks, and helicopters surrounded the area, closed in on the hunted individuals and "sucked" them off the street, out of a movie theatre, from a classroom or workplace. And those in the vicinity were forced to notice, however much they pretended not to. Other spectators who have suffered similar violence—Elie Wiesel watching the Nazis exterminate the man who destroyed one of the chimneys at Auschwitz, Rigoberta Menchú watching her brother being tortured and burned alive—have judged this watching to be the most dehumanizing of acts. To see without being able to do disempowers absolutely. But seeing without the possibility of admitting that

Figure 38. Man being beaten on the street. (Photo by Pablo Lasansky)

one is seeing further turns the violence on oneself. Percepticide blinds, maims, kills through the senses.

What happens to the "witness" in a situation that forces people to participate in the production of denial? The passersby, the neighbors, could not bear witness; they closed the door, shut the curtains, turned off the light. (As the country people who lived near the train tracks leading to Auschwitz told the makers of the film *Shoah*, they saw nothing because they had been told not to look.) Those who saw denied, as if their lives depended on it. For within the economy of the overarching gaze, they too felt vulnerable to detection, abduction, disappearance. The scenario, which reduced most of the population into a credulous, obedient us, blind to the fate of those who were positioned as the hunted, dangerous them, shows how violent situations collapse positions into two sides: for and against; the Big Bad Wolves and Little Red Riding-Hoods. As the military reiterated constantly, the population was either supportive of their mission, or their next target.

Theatre and Terrorism Revisited

Teacher: Nation: prison, bars, Germany, torture.
Voice of the Pupil: Argentina!
Teacher: (beside himself) Germany, idiot!
(He pushes the button. The Pupil howls.)
—Griselda Gambaro, *Information for Foreigners*

Terrorism, with its scenes of torture and abductions, and its enforced misrecognitions or suspensions of disbelief, proved highly theatrical both on a practical and a symbolic level.[3] "Terrorists" (state and antistate forces) dressed their parts and set the drama in motion. The victims, like actors, stood in (albeit unwillingly) for someone or something else. Antagonists appeared on the scene as if by magic; protagonists disappeared into thin air. The revelation of corpses at the appropriate moment was as typical of terrorism as of the Elizabethan stage. Crimes became "unreal," marked only in their theatricality. After all, doesn't theatre allow us to deny what we see with our own eyes? The onlookers, like obedient spectators in a theatre, were encouraged to suspend their disbelief. Terror draws on the theatrical propensity simultaneously to bind the audience and to paralyze it. Theatrical convention allows for splitting of mind from body, enabling the audience to respond either emotionally or intellectually to the action it sees on stage without responding physically. Terrorism in Argentina pushed this convention further, to atomize the victimized population and to preclude the possibility of solidarity and mobilization. No one dared to look to the side for fear that the person standing nearby was a terrorist or military infiltrator. The regimentation of the social and individual body was an example of what Foucault calls "lateral invisibility" (*Discipline and Punish* 200). Everyone was vulnerable; the unexpected attack could come anytime, from anywhere. As the case of Argentina illustrated, acts of terrorism could endow the national frame with a strange spectacularity. An aura of tragedy enveloped the country. The suspense mounted. The crisis seemed fated. The Madres de la Plaza de Mayo, like a Greek chorus, were a physical reminder of the personal and national dramas that violence conspired to erase from history.

The theatricality of the terror and torture in Argentina during the 1970s does not suggest they were either *theatre* or *magic*, but they were designed to look that way.[4] The theatricality of terror challenged playwrights to turn the gaze back onto the blinding apparatus itself. But how to stage "blinding" onstage? Griselda Gambaro, one of Argentina's most prominent playwrights, has spent her professional life making visible the obfuscating theatricality of Argentina's violent politics through theatre since she began writing plays in 1963. Her play,

Information for Foreigners (1973), is one of the most powerful of her thirty plays because she foresaw many of the phenomena related to the transformation of public space, the ghastly creation of a "national being," and the atomization of the population associated with the Dirty War. *Information*, one of her most complex pieces, is a chronicle in twenty scenes set in a house that presents various forms of violence—from theatrical representations of fragments from *Othello* and Lorca's *Blood Wedding* to scientific experiments carried out on human bodies; from scenes of torture and abductions to seemingly "spontaneous" terrorist attacks. The spectators are warned before they enter the house that the show is restricted or, more accurately, prohibited: "No one under eighteen will be admitted. Or under thirty-five or over thirty-six . . . Everyone else can attend with no problem. No obscenity or strong words. The play speaks to our way of life: Argentine, Western, and Christian. We're in 1971. I ask you to stay together and remain silent" (71).[5] The audience is being invited to transgress, to see that which should never be seen. Immediately upon arrival, the audience, like the population, enters a theatre of panic, isolation, silence, and unnaming.

Set explicitly in Argentina in 1971, Gambaro's *Information* not only thematizes but re-creates the climate of terror. The action takes place in a house, a staging that signals the junta's usurpation of domestic spaces associated with feminized interiority and the nation-as-house image so belabored during the dictatorship. The audience, like the Argentine population during the Dirty War, is compartmentalized upon arrival, split up into groups and marked visibly by a color or number, much in the tradition of Rosas's armband. The various groups are led through the house by a Guide, who stumbles into the wrong rooms and unintentionally exposes the audience to cowering, trembling victims of torture and repression. He introduces the different scenes with short excerpts about abductions and murders taken from actual contemporary newspapers, "information" for foreigners. This information is verifiable, accessible both to the audience in the house and to the reading public in and outside Argentina.[6] "Real" politics thus has commingled with the theatrical on all levels. There are two audiences, the groups walking through the house and the reading audience outside Argentina, the "foreigners" of the title; that is, us. The audience follows the Guide down long, dark passageways cluttered with corpses and prisoners, up and down steep, dangerous staircases, in and out of small rooms in which isolated acts of torture or theatrical rehearsals are forever being played out. In one room, actors are rehearsing the final moments of *Othello*. In another, a Mother sings a lullaby from *Blood Wedding* to her child. The highlight of the tour is the visit to the catacombs in the basement, the tombs of martyred Christians. Although a member of the audience (actually an actor) is attacked and abducted by unidentified men, the Guide encourages his group to overlook such violent intrusions. He dispels the incessant, unexpected outbursts of violence as marginal and accidental in relation to the audience's right to entertainment. As screams and shouts echo through the halls, he clamors for amusement and "a little gaiety, dammit!" (115) and grumbles about the bad scripts and the unsavory subject matter. Complaining that "modern theatre is like that! No respect" (107), he nonetheless urges the spectators to enjoy the show. After all, they've paid for it.

The house as theatrical space, like the junta's appropriation of the domestic, subverts the lines of demarcation between public and private. Systems of terror "get us where we live," nullifying the existence of any safe space. The play's use of the house-as-set emphasizes the corrosive and contagious nature of violence that blurs all physical, moral, and judicial frameworks. Scenes of political violence are not limited to prisons and torture chambers but are played out on public streets, in private houses, on human bodies. The takeover of the house, which concurrently signifies the nation, the family home, and the body's protective shell, indicates that the three spaces—social, familial, individual—have collapsed into one. Staging political confrontation on the human body has shattered the limits of personhood, gutted domesticity, transformed society as a whole into a theatre of operations, and given new meaning to the term *environmental* theatre. Like terror that atomizes populations, *Information* deracinates the audience. Gambaro's play as a whole has no plot, no logical "conflict" in dramatic terminology, no climax, no resolution, no characters in any psychological sense—simply fragmented scenes often highlighted for overt theatricality or "over-acting." The work is structured in a play-within-a-play fashion, with various levels of prohibition and transgression. In scene 18, Gambaro introduces a "deformed CHILD-MONSTER, dressed in a floor-length white shirt with lots of lace and frills" (121). There are also numerous other roles, such as Guide, Guard, Tortured Girl, Abducted Man, and, of course, Audience. As in systems of terror, the audience plays a major, and highly disconcerting, role. It makes its way through the dark passages, peering through half-open doors. No one is safe, and the Guide reminds his group to watch their step and their pocketbooks. The house reflects the invasive tactics of terror and torture. Terror deterritorializes; we are all foreigners in this house.

Throughout the tour, Gambaro calls attention to the way that the public's perception is directed and controlled by those in authority. The Guide, for example, physically ushers his group from room to room. He tells them where and when to look, and he censors what the viewers can see: "Excuse me, but the

ladies may not look! (He gestures them away.) Gentlemen, if you like . . ." (89).
Sight is gendered or, perhaps more accurately, visual access is gendered. As in
rituals, only the initiates have the right to see the hidden source of power. And
in the all-male theatre of the Argentine horror show, women are not the see-ers
but the objects to be seen. The source of power in this grim theatre, as in the
military spectacle, is the desiring production that transforms sexualized violence into power. As the Guide thrusts his hand under the tortured woman's
wet dress it becomes clear that power means *power over* the other—either a
woman or a feminized man. It involves transgression, power to exceed accepted
bounds of decency. It involves prohibition, which separates those who are
allowed to see from those who are not. It positions the initiates above the
excluded.

Obedience and respect for the authority of those in power, in this context, is
dangerous indeed. It can lead innocent bystanders to be indirect, and even
direct, participants in torture. At one point the spectators follow the Guide into
another room, where the Milgram experiment is underway. In this scene, Gambaro restages an actual experiment carried out at Yale, Princeton, and Munich
in the 1960s in which pseudo-scientific trappings veil the fact that the experiment is designed to test an individual's capacity for inflicting pain and death
on a stranger on the orders of an "expert." The young man playing "pupil" is
strapped to a chair and given electric shocks by a man playing "teacher." Although the pupil suffers from a bad heart, an "expert" Experimenter urges the
teacher to increase the voltage. While the teacher knows that the shocks could
cause the pupil's death, the Experimenter posits the traditional arguments that
place obedience to authority over personal responsibility: the experiment is
necessary; it is for the greater social good; the man dialing up the lethal voltage
is not responsible for the victim's death. How can people deny a reality that they
know to be true? By listening to an expert telling them that the scene is really
something else, by participating in a drama that inverts roles and changes
names to create the illusion of innocence. The theatricality of the proceedings,
on a practical level, admirably fulfills its real function. It makes people participate in an act they would otherwise find repellent. While most people probably
disagree with the Massuist position that "torture is not merely permissible but
morally mandatory," the Milgram experiment proved that the majority of the
population can potentially be deformed into torturers: 65 percent of the American participants tested inflicted death on the mock pupil; 85 percent of the
German.[7] So torture and torturers are not quite the monstrous other we like to
imagine. And the audience obediently moves from room to room.

The theatricality of torture and terror, moreover, protects the victimizers from the repercussions of their actions by allowing for the split between appearance and reality, the split between action and emotion. A part of the victimizer can carry on the gruesome work, split off to protect the "innocence" and "integrity" of the whole personality. Studies of fascist and Nazi discourse, such as Lifton's *The Nazi Doctors*, Kaplan's *Reproductions of Banality*, and Friedlander's *Reflections on Nazism*, show that the "psychic numbing" and dissociation implicit in splitting also works through the opposite, through doubling.[8] Like the actor, the torturer is simultaneously a monstrous villain and an ordinary citizen, guilty of atrocious acts and guiltless of them. Within this theatrical frame, the room with its props, its scripts for acquiring information, and its professional terminology, the torturers can safely proceed with the annihilation of others. They can maim or kill their victims by convincing themselves that they are doing something else: they are defending themselves and the country from the dangerous enemy or they are carrying out a "necessary" scientific experiment. Even when, or perhaps *especially* when, the tormentors enjoy killing, as in the cases of fascist murderers described in Theweleit's *Male Fantasies*, they must place their actions within a frame that justifies and exonerates them. The theatricality inherent in constructing this "other" reality makes the action "safe" for the torturer.

The theatricality of torture is of central importance in that it circumscribes and positions the audience's role in systems of terror. In *The Body in Pain*, Elaine Scarry proposes that the exercise of violence lends credibility to the tottering regime. She observes that during periods of sociopolitical crisis "the sheer material factualness of the human body will be borrowed to lend that cultural construct the aura of 'realness' and 'certainty'" (14). Torture, that "grotesque piece of compensatory drama" (28), converts the reality of "absolute pain" into the "fiction of absolute power" (27). "Now, at least for the duration of this obscene and pathetic drama, it is not the pain but the regime that is total, not the pain but the regime that is able to eclipse all else, not the pain but the regime that is able to dissolve the world" (56). However, it seems to me that Scarry omits one vital player: the spectator. Torture works on several levels simultaneously. It annihilates the victim. It destroys the victim's family, sometimes into later generations, as when children are forced to watch the brutalization, rape, and murder of their parents ("family torture"). It undermines the immediate community that is involved, and often threatened, but unable to put an end to torture. It affects the larger international community that, even when it does not feel immediately threatened, still feels powerless to put an end to it. The public (national and international) assists in the conversion of pain to power. Terrorism and torture are not designed to prove to the *victims* that the regime has the power to exterminate them—such proof is manifested in the violent act itself. The aim of terrorism and torture is to prove to the population at large that the regime has the power to control it. The public, the one walking through the house and the foreigners reading newspapers, are both in different ways the intended audience of terror's "pathetic drama."

The amplification of torture, through which twenty victims can paralyze an entire community or country, functions by means of its theatricality. Confronted with the reality of torture, our tendency as audience is to identify with the victim. We cannot identify with the torturer without acknowledging the sadistic tendencies that make up part of our (usually) unconscious fantasy world. We feel for the tortured Girl, for the kidnapped Mother. But Gambaro, almost in a Brechtian fashion, does not allow us to identify too closely with them. By over-emphasizing the theatricality of the violence, she makes it apparent that it is intended to trap us. She demonstrates that our identification with the victim is both misleading and disempowering. We are not being victimized; we have a capacity for choice and for action that the victim does not have. Torture and terrorism function most effectively when members of the population feel *as if* they were the victim, *as if* they were next on the list. The arbitrary choice of victims serves to strengthen the identification between public and victim by accentuating the random nature of this atrocity (*It could happen to us*). Studies from the Dirty War indicate that few of the victims were actually militants or had information to give their tormentors.[9] While the aim of torture, according to Edward Peters, is to reduce the victim to "powerlessness" (162, 164), this also holds for the spectator. The systematic implementation of terror, as those who orchestrated Argentina's Dirty War knew, destabilizes the population and therefore makes it easier for the government to maintain power by creating "a climate of fear in which subversion would be impossible" (*Nunca Más* xvii). Scarry mentions that torture collapses the world of the victim (35). But torture also threatens to reduce the world of the public. People do not like to talk or think about *real* (unaestheticized, uneroticized) violence. Hence, there is less and less people can think about, watch, read, and say. The equation established by Scarry, that "the prisoner's steadily shrinking ground ... wins for the torturer his swelling sense of territory" (36), also holds true for the innocent bystanders. They, too, make it possible for torture to continue by giving up ground, by not daring to venture forth into that realm of knowledge. While we, the audience sitting in distant lands, may not fear the violent intrusion of victimizers into our homes, we fear giving up our peace of mind. If we understood that the practice of torture is tied to financial interest, that torturers are not monsters but people who are trained to do what they do, and that lack of public interest makes atrocious politics possible, we might have to do something about it or else consider ourselves complicitous.[10] The very existence of torture is threatening, but in fundamentally different ways. It threatens the lives of the victims; it paralyzes the immediate population; it undermines the distant spectators' sense of well-being, our easy assumptions about human nature and the civilization we live in.

Terror deconstructs reality, inverts it, transforms it into a grotesque fiction. Accounts from the Dirty War show that the victimized population wrote its own dramas; these people must have moved, they must be some place, any place except in that no-place in which they are being brutalized and assassinated. Terror creates its own looking-glass world, concrete even if it does not appear on city maps. Old maps no longer correspond to or guide us through this world. The theatricality of torture and terrorism tempts us to rethink our world, to somehow accept or make room for these performative acts within our canon of the admissible, thus producing normative changes. The flagrant theatricality of Gambaro's scenes, however, warns us against accepting the theatrical or magical solutions to political conflict and cautions us against thinking of the nonvisible spaces as nonspaces. What happens to the characters who go offstage? What do magicians do with all those bunnies? Actors go backstage to their dressing rooms; bunnies go back to their cages; abduction victims end up in torture chambers and unmarked graves.

The theatricality of terror exceeds the mechanics of staging atrocious acts. Terror, the tour through this haunted house shows, functions like a social transformer. As the audience walks down the dark corridors, it becomes clear how terrorism manipulates social fears and inverts cultural symbols. The audience's reaction, as it stumbles in the dark, up and down stairs, signals that terror plays with potent images of the unknown, the pit, darkness. It capitalizes on infantile fantasies; the torturers exploit fears of destruction, dismemberment, and suffocation. The screams resounding through the loudspeakers emphasize that this kind of destabilizing violence works through amplification; twenty victims can hold an entire society hostage. Phantoms loom over a cowering population. The hideous intrusion of children's songs and games into the play illustrates how terror pushes the population to regress to those early areas of experience that prove the most overwhelming and the hardest to decode. The spectators simply do not understand what is happening. One approaches as an adult and turns away as a frightened child incapable of action. Cultural norms enter and come out skewed. The innocent are called enemies. People disappear. Mothers are raped. And the transformation is real, not illusory. It actually changes society. In this nation-house, new creatures are being brought into existence—not only the child-monster, that "authentic national being," but a new, silent population. The general public does in fact become complicitous and guilty by participating in the transformation. The victims are found guilty; the torturers are acquitted.[11] Torture turns bodies inside out by violence, but it also turns our moral and judicial systems upside down. This, Gambaro's house shows, is an unnatural universe; the lights go on and off throughout the play. Light becomes dark, the visible becomes invisible.

Dealing in invisibility does not, as Anthony Kubiak suggests, make the military's terror untheatrical: "State terrorism (by far the more virulent of the two forms of terrorism) typically relies on the non-theatrical in-visible techniques of torture, clandestine operations, disappearances, and night-time bombing runs."[12] Aside from pointing out that "night-time bombings" are highly visible, it is important to realize that dealing in disappearance and making the visible invisible are also profoundly theatrical. Only in the theatre can the audience believe that those who walk offstage have vanished into limbo. So the theatricality of torture and terror, capable of inverting and fictionalizing the world, does not necessarily lie in its visibility, but rather in its potential to transform, to recreate, to make the visible invisible, the real unreal. Perhaps the fact that we know what is going on and yet cannot see it makes the entire process more frightening, riveting, and resistant to eradication.[13]

Given that the theatre's art of controlling the visible has been used to incapacitate the population and preclude its constructive participation, how could Gambaro hope to communicate the atrocious reality of terrorism and torture *through* theatre? One might ask if Gambaro's play is not itself a variation of a form of torture called "showing the instruments." Does Gambaro want to further terrorize an already terrorized audience? Does she want to inflict violence on her actors? Or are we, the audience, the victims that have stumbled into the wrong play? Is she accusing us of being complicitous in the atrocity? By stripping the spectators of their conventional invisibility and placing them in the (Lacanian) lethal field of other, or as (Sartrian) objects of another's gaze in a situation where danger and death are everywhere, is she not victimizing them?[14] And, by representing the violence through the theatre, which is always involved on some level with the buying and selling of pleasure, is she not, inevitably, falling into the trap of rendering violence pleasurable? The theatrical act by definition skews the process of victimization: the actress playing the Tortured Girl in Gambaro's play is there of her free will; real torture victims are not. Doesn't the theatrical event, then, necessarily add the element of *consent*, which differentiates theatrical violence, or even sexual sadomasochistic violence, from torture?

The dangers of representing violence are manifold, as I've noted throughout this study. But Gambaro, unlike some of her contemporaries, is well aware of them. Clearly, she never inflicts actual pain on the actors or spectators; the actors do not have their heads literally submerged in water; the Tortured Girl sits soaking wet near the tub—the idea is that she has just emerged from the *submarine*. Other actors disappear offstage rather than to their deaths. The audience members, she specifies in the stage directions, are never involved in the action against their will. This is theatre, not torture. Simply reproducing violence would not help elucidate the mechanism of social manipulation that Gambaro illuminates through this most manipulative work. The other questions are more difficult to answer. Gambaro's ethical concern with the representation of violence differs, to a degree, from that voiced by Adorno, or by playwrights depicting the horrors of the Holocaust who try to preserve the unaestheticized memory of an event in the past. The Gambaro of *Information* was living in a society that was becoming increasingly terrifying. The only way to survive in a criminalized society, she felt, was to challenge it, to challenge its myths, its distortions, its monsters. Faced with a life-threatening situation, Gambaro simply felt she had no choice but to respond to it. Now, several years after I began thinking about the reproduction of violence in this play, I would admit that her depictions of atrocity are violent—too violent to stage the play as it was written. Gambaro herself resists the idea of producing the play, realizing perhaps that the violence of the period provoked her to respond with violence. But why? Why is this play, that shows no actual acts of violence, so threatening? Because we can't distance ourselves from the violence. Because it doesn't happen to the "othered" body onstage, whose violated or mutilated corpse serves as a stand-in that deflects violence from us. Because the victim looks back at us, returns and challenges our gaze—just as the victims who were abducted, yelling and screaming, during the Dirty War. What are we going to do about it? In Gambaro's play, we the spectators are both the victims and the accomplices. This is our drama, our violence, our dilemma. National and international spectators are confronted with the brutality of political violence that we can't aestheticize, find beautiful or morally uplifting. The play shatters our sense of community, rather than allow for community building *over her dead body,* as Pavlovsky's *Paso de dos* does, for example. This play is painful, too painful to stage, because we're part of it. Though Gambaro demystifies the violence, it still hurts us. Or maybe it hurts *because* she demystifies violence and our role in it. The subject matter is unpleasant, and we, like the Guide, can complain about the unsavory scripts. Gambaro's intrusions into traditional realms of pleasure are as unwelcome as the mandatory review of emergency procedures on our pleasure cruise, as the Guide jokes: "Come in," he says to the group, "watch your step. All that's missing is a 'fasten your seatbelts and refrain from smoking.'" However, with the waves of indiscriminate violence washing over Argentina, as well as other parts of the world, Gambaro warns that we must learn to see violence in its many guises, we must recognize our role and the role of people "just like us" in maintaining it. She is not demanding "information" from us but offering it: "information for foreigners." As R. I. Moore points out in his preface to Edward Peters's *Torture*, "ignorance has many forms, and all of them are dangerous" (vii). This "information" empowers the audience, local and foreign alike.

The emphasis in *Information*, then, is not on the violent acts themselves, but on the audience's role as spectators watching the violence, on the act of watching itself. There are many ways of watching, some empowering, some disempowering, some associated with wisdom (clairvoyance), some with perversity and criminality (voyeurism). Watching is a powerful tool of the totalitarian states: Big Brother is watching. Like the panopticon, surveillance functions "ceaselessly" and "the gaze is alert everywhere."[15] Gambaro, however, challenges the dangerous fiction that watching in itself can somehow empower the spectator or control violence. Although the Guard reassures the Tortured Girl that she is safe because people are watching, the audience will see the Girl's corpse turn up before the end of the play. The myth runs deep that the public, local as well as international, can miraculously avert violence by watching it. The word *watch* in groups dedicated to ending political and racial violence, like *Americas Watch* and *Klanwatch,* indicates the quasi-magical power we attribute to watching. The play shows, however, that watching, in and of itself, never saved anyone. *Americas Watch, Klanwatch, Amnesty International,* and similar organizations do not simply watch. Another young Girl in a different scene is singing sweetly when a man (supposedly an audience member) walks up to her and suffocates her in front of the whole group. Four hospital attendants are called to the scene: they zip the Girl's body into a plastic shroud and away they go. Did the audience save her? Watching, potentially empowering when it forms part of a broader network, can be extremely disempowering when reduced to the spectator's passive "just watching."

Is watching itself a form of violence? Is it a form of torture (known in Argentina as "family torture") in which we must look on as someone we love is humiliated or destroyed before our eyes? Or is watching the unauthorized or even criminal scopophilia of voyeurism?[16] The beam of the Guide's flashlight accidentally falls on a prisoner, cowering in a corner: "he raises his head, surprised and frightened. He covers his sex with his hands" (71). The spectators, paying customers, are suddenly cast in the role of Peeping Toms. Worse still, having paid for tickets to a restricted play we might have anticipated the nudity and violence, indisputably the two major selling points of commercial theatre. Violence is tied into sexual desire, all right, but here it is our desire—our desire to "*see* the other naked."[17] Here, however, we catch a glimpse of things we do not want to see: a body under a tarp, a naked man gagged and stuffed in a cage, a murder. Faced with this twisted version of what we were paying for, we are shocked into considering, perhaps for the first time, what our expectations were and what we thought we were buying. What are we doing in this theatre? After paying for our tickets, do we merely feel an obligation to get our money's worth? Are we perverted? We are on dangerous ground.

The desire to *see* is nowhere so prominent as it is in the theatre or cinema. We go to the theatre to see, to hear. Christian Metz, in *The Imaginary Signifier*, writes that cinema "is only possible through the perceptual passions." Seeing and hearing are sexual drives, powerful but subliminal, different from other sexual drives in that they function through distance and absence. Metz notes the importance of *lack* or *absence* in fueling this erotic desire: perceptual drives "always remain more or less unsatisfied . . . the lack is what it wishes to fill, and at the same time what it is always careful to leave gaping, in order to survive as desire" (58–59). Barthes also links desire to absence and distance when describing an erotic photograph: "The erotic photograph [unlike the pornographic] does not make the sexual organs into a central object; it may very well not show them at all; it takes the spectator outside the frame, and it is there that I animate this picture and that it animates me—as if the image launched desire beyond what it permits us to see" (*Camera Lucida* 59). Lack, absence, distance, beyond . . .

Gambaro does not allow for the distancing of scopic pleasure, nor for the more vital distancing of voyeuristic pleasure. If, as Metz (following Freud) argues, "voyeurism, like sadism in this respect, always keeps apart the *object* (here the object looked at) from the *source* of the drive (the eye)" (59), Gambaro on the contrary abolishes that distance by having us stumble on what we do not want to see. We are in the same room. This naked body does not, as in cinema, exist in the realm of the imaginary, pure celluloid; it is materially present. The victim returns our look. And unlike traditional theatre that still maintains distance even as the actors and audience coexist within the same four walls, here the member of the audience actually knocks into, or stumbles against, a naked body. Unlike theatre that eroticizes or aestheticizes nudity and violence by covering as much as it reveals, Gambaro's theatre simultaneously exposes violence and draws us into it. The audience sees the utterly raw nakedness of another human being without the erotic distance, the accompanying sympathy, love, or desire that renders the sight tolerable or titillating. Gambaro, moreover, calls attention to the fact that those perceptual desires or "passions" have already been socialized and politicized in ways we do not realize. Theories linking desire to a visual lack fail to account for what we feel standing in front of the half-open doors leading to torture chambers. Is the "beyond" here a visual lure? Is our reluctance to look a reluctance to satisfy our desire, a reluctance to see lest we satiate (terminate) desire itself? Is it not, rather, the horror of witnessing real absence, a case of political absenting, that is, disappearance? If we actually saw it, we might have to do something about it. The lack, then, is of a fundamentally different nature when we move to the physical and political arena of abductions and atrocity. There is nothing safe, erotic, innocent, or gratifying about this vision that inverts traditional theatrical perception, producing pain, perhaps even shame, but precluding pleasure. Intolerable sight, sight that traps both seen and seer, captures both the revolting sight and the viewer's revulsion, all in the same frame.

The same point also holds for the audience's feelings of transgression. Creeping through the halls, peeping into dark rooms, the spectators act like intrusive children, stumbling on the primal scene. Originally, however, the prohibition against transgression, much in the manner of taboos, was conceived by populations to consolidate power in the name of protecting humanity. Theatrical representations and rituals originally mediated between the human and the divine, supposedly shielding humans from the awful (in the sense of holy). Examples as culturally diverse as Euripides' *The Bacchae* and pre-Columbian ritual stress the danger of transgression, of *seeing* that which exceeds human comprehension. The power of the superhuman, like Zeus in all his splendor, threatens to blind and destroy the human.

Gambaro, however, demystifies the notion of transgression and challenges its politics: What is behind those doors and why do we not have legitimate access to it? Fears of transgression obfuscate the mechanics of power rather than protect the sensibilities of humanity. Whether the sanctum sanctorum is the pre-Hispanic *cue,* the parental bedroom, the masking societies of West Africa, the Pentagon, or Oz, the public is excluded from the production and reproduction of power: hence the masks, the hideous sculptures, the admonitions. The politics of the awesome have given way to the politics of the awful: political secrecy replaces taboo; the off-scene has become the obscene; terrorism, like ancient gargoyles, compels us and repels us with its horror. The "hidden" nature of torture, abductions, and other scenes of atrocity frighten us away from seeing and recognizing them by appealing to ways of seeing we consciously or unconsciously associate with *bad* seeing, perversion, voyeurism, and transgression. We are socialized to avert our eyes from sexually charged sights. Binding the sexually charged image with annihilating violence tempts us to look away. We do not want to feel like peeping children at keyholes, like voyeurs, like perverts. We do not want to feel complicitous. Yet the identification with peeping children and perverts is a misleading one; although spectators may have no place in the bedroom, the same does not hold for the political arena. There, the public gives up its place and its right to participation at its peril: torturers can get away with murder.

In order to be empowered by seeing, to be able to look back at the monstrous gargoyles without turning into lifeless stones, we must see beyond the theatrical frame and decode the fictions about violence, about torturers, about ourselves as audience, about the role of theatre in this "pathetic drama." Gambaro develops a dangerous theatre, one that provokes audiences to resent and reject theatrical manipulation, one that shocks and disrupts, that breaks the frames of theatrical tradition in order to make the invisible visible once again. Gambaro challenges spectators, both national and international, to give up the comfort of deniability.

Information for Foreigners exposes the theatricality of terror, the way it shapes our perception and paralyzes us as bystanders. Gambaro draws attention to how theatre's illusionist qualities can be manipulated to control not only *what* people see and *how* they see it, but how they can deny the reality of what they see and know to be true, for example the practice of torture and criminal politics. The population in and outside Argentina knew what was going on during the 1970s. Did anyone really not know that the Argentine military government systematically terrorized its people between 1976 and 1982? Did anyone really not know that the U.S. government supported the military with economic aid and training?[18] The question is, how can the public's attention be diverted so that it can dismiss that knowledge and claim innocence? Robert Skloot's introduction to his anthology *The Theatre of the Holocaust* focuses on some of the issues I have raised here. He asks: "How could these horrifying events occur in one of the most civilized and advanced nations of the world? Why did most of the free world remain aloof to the plight of the Jews and other persecuted minorities . . . Had we been involved in the events of this time, how would we have behaved?" (10). The point, *Information* makes clear, is that these questions are not hypothetical. This in no way suggests that the terrorism holding Latin America hostage compares with or is "like" the Holocaust, although some scholars maintain that "what happened in Argentina in the years that followed 1976 was probably closer to what happened in Germany after 1933 than anything else in the Western world during the past four decades."[19] The Holocaust was a unique historical event. It ended, but atrocity and fascism live on; the tactics of terror, the bureaucratic and systematic extermination of countless victims continues in camps and torture chambers. By juxtaposing the catacombs with traditionally theatrical scenes, with torture, with terrorist attacks, Gambaro forces us to relinquish our comforting assumptions about violence, our claims to deniability, innocence, and quietism, and instead urges us to understand what prompts it and how we participate, either as voyeurs, investors, bystanders, or victims. In a way, *Information* submits the audience to its own Milgram experiment: Will its members continue to follow the Guide and passively participate in the situation? Will we ask for our money back or walk out of the show? As the spectators move from room to room or turn the pages of the newspaper for "information," the question is being answered. The response is not hypothetical; the play will not allow us to split off. We are involved, we are the spectators. Whether we peep through those half-closed doors or glean our information from the newspapers, this is our show. Can we stop just watching and end it? If not, as the Guide says, we might as well enjoy it: we're paying for it. As the Guard complains, "We're the ones who bear the brunt of this show" (124).

6 Disappearing Bodies: Writing Torture and Torture as Writing

Much like the corpse, empty of its soul, representations of death refer to an absence of full meaning by signalling the presence of meaning elsewhere . . . both conceal and reveal at the same time; both are doubled in that they point to what is absent and to their own act of representing.—Elisabeth Bronfen, *Over Her Dead Body*

Initial Problems of Representing Disappearance and Torture

Writing about the disappeared and torture, as well as writing *on the writing* about them, is as difficult as it is urgent. The difficulty lies not only in navigating the troubled waters between those who, in the tradition of Adorno, insist that the atrocities committed defy language and representation and those who insist that only through denunciation, which necessarily involves representation, can crimes be brought to light and similar ones be avoided in the future.

There is another problem that I feel needs to be examined before the first issue can even be addressed: the *desaparecidos* (the disappeared) are, by definition, always already the object of representation. The flesh-and-blood victims, forcefully absented from the sociopolitical crisis that created them, left no bodies. Those disappeared. The victims reemerged as icons, either as "subversives" (for the military government) or as the "disappeared" (for the Madres and other human rights activists)—powerful, conflicting images that reintroduced the missing into the public sphere as pure representation. Somewhere behind those images, and simultaneously occluded and illuminated by them, one imagines the "real" bodies: male bodies, female bodies, some pregnant, almost all young bodies. Thousands and thousands of tortured and mutilated bodies, dead bodies, bodies dumped into mass graves marked "NN" (*Non Nombre,* or no name), or cut into pieces and burned in ovens, or thrown into the ocean from military planes. The reality of their ordeal becomes unreal to us through the very process of trying to illuminate it. How to think about these bodies that we know exist(ed) but that have vanished into thin air? And how to think about those vanishings?

The struggle to represent the absent bodies became central to the battle of images between the military and the Madres during the Dirty War. "Subversive" or "disappeared"? The attempts to identify and label the absent bodies were also key in settling the historical record during the redemocratization process that included the public trial of the military leaders. How many people actually disappeared? What happened to them? Who was responsible? Even after many Argentines began to "forget" about the disappeared, efforts to understand what happened during the Dirty War continue to be of paramount importance to those involved both in national and worldwide human rights organizations as well as to all the international lawyers, forensic specialists, physicians, scholars, and advocates who investigate and provide the evidence of atrocities, past and present. Moreover, a large number of the Madres of the Plaza de Mayo continue the practice of keeping the disappeared "alive," refusing to participate in the exhumation and identification of their children's corpses, in an effort to bring the perpetrators to justice. Thinking about the disappeared, then, involves several different issues: the "real" existence of the men and women and children who disappeared; disappearance as a strategy of terror; and disappearance as a disavowal of death, a resistance strategy that has kept various issues and figures "alive" in Argentina, from the seemingly immortal Evita to the victims of the Dirty War.

The necessity of writing and documenting, that is, of *representing* the "real" existence of the missing bodies does not make the task any easier nor the position of the reader/witness any less complicated. Those who compiled the information in *Nunca Más: The Report of the Argentine National Commission on the Disappeared,* created by then President Raúl Alfonsín, state: "In drawing up this report, we wondered about the best way to deal with the theme so that this chapter did not turn into merely an encyclopedia of horror. We could find no way to avoid this. After all, what else were these tortures but an immense display of the most degrading and indescribable acts of degradation, which the military governments, lacking all legitimacy in power, used to secure power over a whole nation?" (20). For the sake of clarity, I will divide the various kinds of writings/representations about the disappeared into five subgroups.

In the first group, I place the evidence given by the disappeared who survived their ordeal (the so-called reappeared) and who testified before groups such as the Argentine National Commission on the Disappeared, human rights organizations, and the 1985 Juicio (or Trial of the Generals). These oral testimonies were delivered in public settings and written for the record. The experience of testifying potentially empowers the survivors, the assumption behind the graphic descriptions being that the accurate accounts of torture and political violence will help restore justice and bring political change. But for those of us reading these reports who are not in a position to effect direct change or ensure justice, the detailed accounts of victimized bodies in their painful materiality threaten to place us in the position of "just watching"—a position often associated with voyeurism and morbidness, even disempowerment. What are we doing reading these accounts? How should we interpret the fact that *Nunca Más* became a best seller, a ubiquitous presence on the beaches where Argentines vacationed during the summer it was released? Even the title sounds like a bad joke, as the escalating number of atrocities since 1976—from Guatemala to Rwanda to Bosnia—scream for ever more never-mores. What to make of the fact that the cover of *El libro del juicio* announces its sadistic contents with the same exuberance associated with works of pornography? Understanding that even the best intentioned and politically necessary reports on torture can be both perversely titillating and disempowering, groups such as Amnesty International attempt to empower the broader population. They too do so through "literature," which often chronicles first-person oral accounts by survivors to persuade us that our support can indeed change the way human beings are treated the world over.

In the second group, I place the testimonial writings by "reappeared" victims, such as Alicia Partnoy's *The Little School: Tales of Disappearance and Survival in Argentina* and Jacobo Timerman's *Prisoner Without a Name, Cell Without a Number.* These accounts, unlike the evidence given by these same people before human rights commissions, are "literary" representations, necessarily removed from the events that took place in the past. Although these writings, like the *testimonios* of Rigoberta Menchú, Domitila Barrios, and others, want to communicate collective suffering and incite the reader to activism, the way they are constructed places them closer to literary autobiographies than to *testimonios.* As Alicia Partnoy herself makes clear, the literature written by those who survived disappearance serves a different function and addresses a different audience than the accusations and descriptions that those same writers brought forth in front of human rights groups.

In the third group, we have the representation of these bodies by others. The photos paraded by the Madres, for example, are powerful evocations of their loved ones that, arguably, inadvertently hide the very violence they aim to reveal. The smiling, forever youthful faces communicate an image of personal wholeness and integrity that elides the decomposed "real" bodies (see figure 39). The photos, like magic fetishes, keep the dead and brutalized bodies forever "alive." They tempt us to see them as "natural" and transparent manifestations of the "real." Thus it seems treasonous to resist that view by insisting on the iconic quality of these photographs. It is as if the recognition that the photo works as a powerful icon in the battle to establish meaning and set the record were somehow incompatible with the victims' humanness, undermining thus the very authenticity that supports the political struggle. The political exigencies seem to beg for the uncritical acceptance of the object as the thing itself. On the other hand, the skulls and bones of the disappeared, brought forth as evidence of government criminality by the forensic specialists investigating the atrocities, give the opposite picture—irrefutable reality devoid of humanity, merely the remains of an unimaginable individual who is forever absent (see figure 40). These bones, the real remains of the real people, fail to say anything about the *desaparecidos,* the ghosts of the forever missing that haunt the Argentine political scene. In various ways, and for different purposes, these photos, reports, pictures, X rays, and note cards have been put forth as material equivalents for the missing victims of repression. The strategy of objectifying the "missing" was used by both the military and its opponents. The military went so far as to literally substitute representation for the "real" person, as in the case of baby Matilde, who was stolen by the members of the armed forces after they had killed her parents and two young siblings in what they claimed was a confrontation with five armed extremists. The perpetrators buried her socks and pacifier in a fifth empty coffin with her name on it (see figure 41). As in fetish worship, the essence of the represented is magically condensed in the object. The signifier, as Taussig noted, erases the signified.

Figure 39. "Madres de Plaza de Mayo." (Photo by Cristina Fraire)

Figure 40. "Anatomy of Terrorism: Trial of the Generals, 1985." (Photo by Daniel Muzio)

Moving to the fourth, less "real" level of representation involves examining the fictionalized and aestheticized renditions of these bodies in the novels, plays, and films that abound on the subject. As the intended goals of such descriptions are more ambiguous than in the previous groups, it can seem scandalous and at times even cruel of the artists to undertake such a project in the first place. What's to be gained, one might ask, by making a film as painful as *La noche de los lápices* (The night of the pencils), which depicts the abduction, torture, and murder of the group of adolescents who protested the increase in bus fare? or the scene from *Funny Dirty Little War* in which a good and innocent man is being tortured in a children's classroom (another "little school") under the disapproving gaze of the portraits of the illustrious Argentine founding fathers that grace the walls? How can novelists such as Luisa Valenzuela and Marta Lynch (to name just two) and dramatists such as Eduardo Pavlovsky, Roma Mahieu, Griselda Gambaro, Diana Raznovich, and Ricardo Monti (among others) produce a body of work about the violence inflicted on these victims without reproducing and capitalizing on that violence? And even when the aims are laudable, how can one represent the disappeared, by definition unrepresentable? During one of our interviews, I asked Diana Raznovich (also a noted cartoonist) to take ten minutes to sketch me her image(s) of the disappeared. The four sketches (figures 42) she produced illustrate how artists (and scholars) are left literally holding the bag of their signifiers. The signified, banished to some offstage or off-scene, lies beyond the realm of visibility. We have no access to the signified, who will forever prove inaccessible to representation.

In the fifth group I place myself, and scholars like me, who examine this "body" of material. How can we do so without further "exposing it" and fueling the public fascination with violence? What are our aims? Are we capitalizing on the suffering endured by others—for reasons that might include the need to establish a sense of cultural superiority over that violent "other" or for professional advancement? Even if our intent is to participate in ending brutality, how can we talk terror, as Taussig asks in *The Nervous System*, without being undone by it? or, perhaps as real an issue, without being self-indulgent and narcissistic? It is "a matter of finding the right distance, holding it at arm's length so it doesn't turn on you (after all it's just a matter of words), and yet not putting it so far away in a clinical reality that we end up having substituted one form of terror for another. But having said this I can see myself already lost, lost out to terror" (11). Is talking terror always talking about me?

Notwithstanding the traps and complexities of representing political vio-

Figure 41. Matilde. (Photo by Clyde Snow)

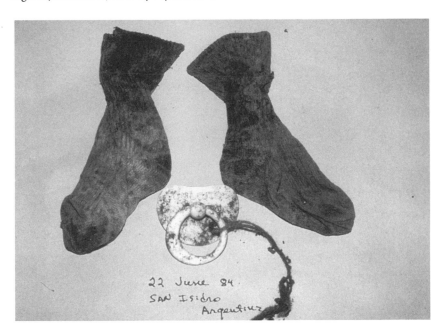

22 June 84.
San Isidro
Argentina

Figure 42. Representing disappearance, four sketches by Diana Raznovich.

lence, all these venues seem absolutely necessary to me. As I see it, we have no choice. *Not* representing real political violence and atrocity only contributes to its legitimization and perpetuation. Rather than *whether* we should attempt such an undertaking, the question is *how* to represent this violence, how to think and write about these bodies? What do these invisible bodies *mean?* Who determines that meaning? How are we being asked to respond to these representations that make conflicting tugs on us as witnesses, spectators, artists, activists, and scholars? How do we hold onto the significance of the "real" body even as it slips into the symbolic realm through representational practices?

These disappeared bodies are the linchpin in different, often ideologically opposed narratives that tie into, or run into, the national fantasy founded on radical differentiation—between good and evil and between national (Argentinean/non-Argentinean) and gender (male/female) identity. Similar fantasies underlie other terror systems. There is such a déjà vu quality to the scenario that one wonders how anyone can think of them as Argentine. They are only Argentinean insofar as they have been rewritten into myths of national being. These bodies are the linchpin in this narrative, in part because they have no clear meaning beyond their individual, biological facticity: their meaning is a product of their entrance into culture through social construction, gendering, positioning, representation. It's hard to even imagine a body prior to the social construction that produces subjectivity. Assuming there is a "real" body *before* or somehow distinguishable from the cultural construction of it, how can we begin to think of it?

Scholars such as Michel Foucault, Teresa de Lauretis, Judith Butler, and Homi Bhabha stress that "subjects" are the product of judiciary and cultural systems; hence, there can be no *before.* In defining *women,* Teresa de Lauretis refers to "the real historical beings who cannot as yet be defined outside of those discursive formations, but whose material existence is nonetheless certain" (*Alice Doesn't* 5). Judith Butler goes further to suggest "there may not be a subject who stands 'before' the law, awaiting representation in or by the law. Perhaps the subject, as well as the invocation of the temporal 'before,' is constituted by the law as the fictive foundation of its own claim to legitimacy" (*Gender Trouble* 2–3). The implications of this possibility are far-reaching. For feminist studies, it questions if the group we call women can even be said to exist before or outside the patriarchal definitions of them. What factors provide the basis for thinking of these bodies before their entry into culture as gendered beings—their organic sex? their hormones? their chromosomes? Can these still be regarded as stable sex markers in this technological age of sex-change operations and hormonal treatments?

The issue gets even more complicated when raised in relation to the atrocities of the Dirty War. Along with the sex/gender conundrum, similar questions arise around the notion of national identity. Entry into or expulsion from the judiciary and cultural system came to depend on the performance of nationness. If there is no subject *before* the law, if subjects are produced by the very systems that claim human subjectivity as their basis (law, culture), then the disappeared, as the military leaders said all along, do not exist. The military rhetoric, with its myths of origin, identity, and destiny, repeatedly stress that they—the male protagonists of Argentine history—came into being, and were coterminous, with the *Patria*. Their entry into culture (they insisted) marked the origin of culture (*Patria*). They both claimed subjectivity and extended it to those who identified with their mission. Everything before the appearance of the soldier male was inert, untamed matter—a nebulous, unfathomable, feminine, prehistoric *before*. If the juridical and cultural systems that simultaneously sustained and were sustained by this discourse produced subjectivity (as in the military's aim to create an "authentic national being"), then what happens to those who fall outside the system? All those they considered subjects, "authentic" Argentineans (as opposed to the other Argentineans), were subjects before the law, that is, had legal rights. The others, the so-called subversives, lacked humanity and subjectivity according to the military government and thus had no legal status or rights. They fell outside or beyond the law—and consequently, as the Argentine official confessed in 1995, they literally fell (that is, were *pushed* by military men) out of airplanes while they were still alive.[1] As General Ramón Camps said, "It wasn't people that disappeared, but subversives."[2] The military discourse produced the subjects, or nonsubjects, over which it presided. Nonhuman nonsubjects do not exist in juridical systems.

If we cannot appeal to the biological facticity of these missing bodies outside or *before* the law, what can we hold onto? Without respect for the inviolability of the body's boundaries—its rights and autonomy prior to any law or culture— the individual would become nothing *but* representation in a system divided into the self-defined/dominant group and its disposable, interchangeable others. Yet even this basic concept of materiality is tied into cultural and juridical debates. What can we agree on as basic rights for all human beings? Death penalty advocates would not maintain that all people have a right to life. And societies cannot agree when rights come into play (birth? conception?). Anyone who has listened to "pro-lifers" justifying the killing of doctors who perform abortions—as well as the secretaries, escorts, family members, or other people remotely involved in the process—understands that the "right to life" is highly ideological. The debates signal the points of conflict within our culture and cannot be said to exist outside or prior to that culture. Thus, any attempt to think about the material facticity of the body poses problems. Nonetheless, I feel the urgency of holding onto the material body even if that body's existence and meaning cannot at the present be fully theorized. In dealing with the Dirty War, and other situations in which collective fantasies and phobias are embodied and fought out on human bodies, it seems to me imperative to guard against seeing the *othered* body as *only* the container of social anxieties, *only* the negative marker of social difference and stratification, *only* the embodiment of other people's fears and passions to be annihilated or absorbed at will. It seems yet another cruel act of disappearance and erasure to accept, as Edmundo Desnoes does in "The Death System" (on Susan Meiselas's moving photographs of criminal politics in El Salvador), that "bodies are obstinate signs" positioned on either side of a violent history: "There are two kinds of bodies . . . the bodies that are against history and the bodies that are on the side of history."[3] Are bodies no more than signs? Are the only two positions—once again—*for* and *against*? But how to hold onto the materiality of the individual body even as we accept the social production of subjectivity?

Only by disentangling the gendered tropes constructed in terms of individual, social, and political *bodies* from the master narrative on the "authentic national being" can we begin to examine the significance of the "real" biological and historical materiality of the victimized women, men, and children. I am proposing the inverse route, with the same final aim as the one mapped out by Barbara Ehrenreich in her foreword to volume 1 of Klaus Theweleit's *Male Fantasies*. Ehrenreich warns that in confronting fascist violence, "the reader's impulse is to engage in a kind of mental flight—that is, to 'read' the murders as a story about something else, for example sex . . . or the Oedipal triangle . . . or anything to help the mind drift off. But Theweleit insists that we see and not 'read' the violence" (xi; ellipses in original). My theory is that violence of the kinds described by Theweleit, and that I describe here, is carried out according to a script with a thread of narrative logic. The reader does not make this story up, neither does the spectator, nor—most importantly—does the victim. But those who control and protagonize the narrative, that is, those who are directly or indirectly responsible for the violence, encourage us spectators/readers to buy into the story, to identify with the protagonists, to empathize with their mission and to otherwise participate in making sense of it all. I thus agree with Laura Mulvey when she writes that "sadism demands a story, depends on making something happen, forcing a change in another person, a battle of will and strength, victory/defeat, all occurring in a linear time with a beginning and an end" (14). However, this "story" generally represents the perspective of the sadists and not that of the victims. Playwrights, as noted earlier, risk coercing the audience into participating in the violent acts and fantasies if, like the military, they encourage their public to accept the tormentors' point of view. But not buying into the story does not mean that there isn't one, or that it doesn't shape the way in which events unravel. So while dealing with the story is complicated, I feel, unlike Ehrenreich, that we must first "read" and dismantle the narrative before we can understand the nature of this violence. It seems to me urgent to consider the acts of torture and disappearance as acts of sociopolitical de-composition and re-composition governed by collective fantasies prioritizing certain kinds of bodies congruent with the nation's self-image.

Labeling "Subversion"

During the Dirty War, the term *subversive* denoted radical undifferentiation; anything or anyone who opposed the government in any way could be considered subversive. Subversives, the military stressed, were not only those who bore arms against the government—any and all "ideological" opposition constituted a crime. In a cruel inversion of the tree of life, the Air Force Academy in Buenos Aires drew up a Tree of Subversion with forty-seven branches representing various crimes. The crimes ranged from progressive Catholicism to Protestantism to Judaism, from alcoholism and prostitution to divorce and homosexuality, from human rights to women's rights and pacifism. Any not covered by a specific branch fell into branch 16: *others*.[4] Furthermore, anyone associated with or sympathetic to this expanding and amorphous group of subversives might well become the next victim.

The radical undifferentiation at work linguistically in labeling subversives led to undifferentiation in terms of "real" material bodies. The military's habit of throwing the corpses into the ocean or into unmarked graves signaled the ultimate obliteration of individuality and differentiation. As bones mingled indiscriminately in common pits or on the ocean floor, the military reduced all difference to sameness; it undermined bodily boundaries and covered up distinctions of gender, class, ethnic origin, religion, and age. These absented bodies, *theoretically*, no longer existed, told no story. Or sometimes complicitous medical examiners and coroners made the bodies tell the wrong story, stories of armed confrontations that never took place, stories of dead babies who actually were adopted by military families.

In these pages, then, I will examine both the unmaking and remaking of the human body in relation to the master narrative. The unmaking (to use Elaine Scarry's term) or *decomposition* involves the disappearance, torture, and murder of the victims; the remaking or *recomposition* involves attempts made by oppositional forces (from human rights advocates to the Madres to artists to scholars) to make these disappeared bodies visible again to the national and international community. According to the junta leaders accused of human rights violations in the widely publicized trials of 1985, these atrocities never happened. When the reports could be proved, the leaders shrugged them off as "excesses" committed by overzealous underlings. But even in the face of these denials, the thousands of bodies—with evidence of fractures, burns, punctures, and bullet holes—continued to tell their stories.

Torture as Writing: Decomposition

... when there is within a society a crisis of belief—that is, when some central idea or ideology or cultural construct has ceased to elicit a population's belief either because it is manifestly fictitious or because it has for some reason been divested of ordinary forms of substantiation—the sheer material factualness of the human body will be borrowed to lend that cultural construct the aura of "realness" and "certainty."—Elaine Scarry, *The Body in Pain*

Devised, in theory, to wring information from threatening enemies of state, the system of disappearance, torture, and murder of military opponents during the Dirty War served fundamentally to reconstitute the Argentine population and turn it into a docile, controllable, feminine "social" body.[5] By means of abduction, social actors vanished from the public arena; by means of torture, they reentered culture, but it was now a culture of terror. Torture was the military's preferred instrument for the re-creation of the individual and political body. Through torture, national and gender markers were inscribed onto the victims' flesh. Inscription, as Joseph Roach notes, produces "bodily images and behaviors," and these bodies were indeed ideologically produced in record time (158). The process was tied directly into the discourse on the *Patria* and the military's explicit aspiration of creating a new "authentic national body." What I am proposing, then, is that the gendered violence taking place in the discourse of the symbolic *Patria* was being played out on the "real" bodies of the victims in order to shape a new symbolic entity: the national being. The "real" bodies were used as the battleground, the geographic terrain, on which were fought the military's fantasies of Argentina's identity and destiny.

The assault on spaces previously deemed private or safe (such as homes) coincided with the appearance of 342 concentration camps, in which a new subjectivity would be hammered out. The body strapped on the metal frame before the torturer was considered the sign of excess, that which could not be contained by the normative, exclusionary image of the "authentic national being." And it was read very much as an "obstinate sign" in the process of creating this new culture. One of the camps most notorious for this violent transformation of the body politic into the desired image (or, if that failed, its elimination) was Olimpo, named after the Greek home of the gods. The name emphasized the same racist proclivities that the eugenicists had displayed in the early twentieth century. Here in Olympus techniques for racial and cultural improvement would attempt to turn Argentina's mixed population into a Hellenic, godlike one. The unredeemables were disposed of. Jewish prisoners were brutalized by guards dressed in Nazi SS uniforms shouting anti-Semitic insults. Also in Olimpo, women were beaten and tortured in front of the statue of the Virgin Mary to signal just how far they had deviated from the acceptable norm. The backdrop for the torture scenario, then, bespoke the cultural values and hierarchies evident in the Junta's rhetoric on national authenticity.

In the torture scenario, the torturer (like the military leaders) claimed total control of the social "body." Torture functioned as a double act of inscription: first, in the sense of *writing the body* into the nationalist narrative and, second, in the sense of *writing on the body*, taking a living body and turning it into text—a cautionary "message" for those on the outside.

Writing the body set up a triangular formulation: it established author-ity (of the military leaders who manipulated the discourse), it cast the torturers as the pen or instrument of inscription (as the midwives in the creation of the new national being), and it turned the victim into the producible/expendable body-text. The process required a story, a sadistic plotline in which the good guys overpower the bad. Male- and female-sexed bodies were turned into the penetrable, "feminine" ones that coincided with the military's ideal of a docile social and political body. Torture rehearsed on the individual body the violent engendering and gendering of the entire social body. Both bodies were *de-* and *re*constructed simultaneously.

The "story" behind the torture, often developed by the torturers, was organized as a sexual encounter, usually entailing motifs associated with foreplay, coupling, and penetration. From hundreds of testimonies by men and women describing acts of fondling, rape, sexual battering, and humiliations as well as death blows and shots aimed at the reproductive organs, I have chosen one, related by Antonio Horacio Miño Retamozo, that accentuates the narrative logic behind the various acts. However, what happened to him was in no way exceptional. In *Nunca Más,* his testimony is prefaced by the statement: "it was the usual sequence of events" (29). Antonio Horacio Miño Retamozo told the Argentine National Commission on the Disappeared: "At night the 'female voice' would arrive, a well-known officer of the *Gendarmería* who spoke in falsetto. The first thing he would do was to stroke one's testicles in anticipation of the pleasure of his task" (*Nunca Más* 31). Then, in a perverse parody of the sexual act, the guards coupled him with another prisoner: "They put me on the bed on top of him and when they applied the electric prod to me, he would jump too" (31). The guards literally staged their assault against Miño Retamozo as a homosexual act, thus "feminizing" the enemy in the cultural understanding of the feminine as the penetrable. Notwithstanding excursions into "deviant" sexual behavior, the military men's own participation in the scenario remained "heterosexual" in the particular understanding of that term that has developed historically in Argentina. Thus the sexual process involving the victim was carried to its "natural" conclusion: a new person was to be born from the reproductive act. Miño Retamozo was taken into the torture chamber, a room full of instruments with a metal table with straps, called the *parilla* or grill. The table resembled the birthing table in an operating room. From it, the new being would materialize. He remembered being tortured by the *picana* or electric cattle prod, which the "specialist" (torturer) "handled like a scalpel . . . guided by a doctor who would tell him if I could take any more" (30):

> The interrogations later became shorter, but the electric prod was more intense, savagely seeking out the sphincters. The worst was having the electrodes on the teeth—it felt as if a thunderbolt was blowing your head to pieces—and a narrow string of beads, which they put in my mouth and which were very difficult to swallow because they induced retching and vomiting, thus intensifying the ordeal, until finally they forced me to swallow them. Each bead was an electrode and when they worked it seemed like a thousand crystals were shattering, splintering inside one and moving through the body, cutting everywhere. They were so excruciating that one couldn't even scream or groan or move. They produced convulsions which, if one hadn't been tied down, would have forced one into the foetal position. This left one shaking for several hours with all one's insides one huge wound . . . (30)

The sequence of events mimicked the sexual process—from the arousal, to the electrifying commingling of bodies, to the probing at the sphincters, the forceful entry of little explosive beads into the man's body, the convulsions, retching, and groans that the beads induced, followed by the materialization of the powerless, trembling body of "one" who longs to assume the foetal position. He is both the vulnerable motherless child and the aching childless mother—the empty body, convulsed with pain, whose "insides" are nothing more than "one huge wound."

What was the point of this ordeal, according to the narrative? To create a new, national being. Was the wretched victim expected to rise again, a changed individual? Clearly the torturers, like the military spokesmen, were trying hard to mold a new breed. As the perfectible human being was perceived as the military male, the sole protagonist in this Argentine epic, "he" clearly needed training. Miño Retamozo recounts an act of collective punishment that passed as "training": "A person calling himself 'Lieutenant' came and said that he was giving us military training . . . They took us to what I imagine was a large room; they surrounded us and began to hit us all over, but especially on the elbows and knees; we would crash into each other, blows were coming at us from all sides, we would trip and fall. Then, when we were completely prostrate on the floor, they started throwing ice-cold water on us and with electric prods they would force us to our feet and take us back to the place we had come from" (30). Alas, the test proved, these pathetic beings lacked the courage and discipline necessary for the new national being. If the "subversives" were in fact unrecoverable, as this collective exercise in military discipline and self-control seemed designed to confirm, it was not for lack of trying to make men of them.

In writing about torture, it seems fundamental to differentiate between the torturer's story and perspective and that of the victim. The "training" Miño Retamozo endured meant one thing to his tormentors and something completely different to him. In this testimony, the survivor/narrator attempts to pull back from his body during this recalled experience of torment. He tries to displace the violence onto some other linguistic body ("one" and "your"). Yet he never disengages his view from his own lived experience; we are never invited (as opposed to much fictional representation) to join the guards in looking voyeuristically at the body from a position of safety somewhere *above* the victim. While he experiences the metonymic reduction of his personhood to a feminine "wound," he never (unlike the torturers) interprets that as feminization. And while his body is being reconstituted as homosexual and later female by his tormentors, his lived experience of his body has little to do with this narrative construction. Moreover, while the ordeal was set up as a sexual encounter by the torturers, Miño Retamozo never acknowledges it as such and never speaks of being sexually aroused. The sexualization of the ordeal is the torturer's doing, not the victim's. Representing the ordeal of torture as in any way sexually gratifying is the trap that writers fall into when depicting it. Writers such as Eduardo Pavlovsky, as we saw, buy into the torturers' version of events and extend that version onto the victims as well. It's from the perspective of the torturers—positioned outside and above the prostrate body of the victim—that many fictional portrayals represent the act of torture.

By rewriting the victim's body as feminine, torture brings together a whole constellation of gendered images that appear in the military's rhetoric—death, pain, violence, though clearly inflicted by the military males, were all "feminine." One form of torture that Jacobo Timerman describes involved "a session with the 'machine,' . . . what the guards called 'a chat with Susan' " (6–7). The torturer "advised me to spill everything, told me that he'd had plenty of experience and that a person my age winds up dying in Susan's arms because his heart can't withstand the electric shocks for long" (7). The violence was symbolically committed by women; dying equaled copulation with feminine death. Torture functioned as both transition and transformation, an uninterrupted passage from the feminine world of birthing into the feminine realm of pain and death. As such, "dying in Susan's arms" collapsed the images of the mother and the lover; traditionally comforting images of fusion with the feminine in fact signaled destruction. In the act of torture, the torturer placed the victim's pain into a narrative—the victim yearned for wholeness and unity with the feminine (Susan), but Susan turned out to be the site of death and decomposition.

The sexual motif in the torture narrative raises important questions about gender, sexual orientation, and the military males as well. What does it suggest about the male torturers who received sexual gratification from probing male and female bodies? Would they perceive this as *homosexual* desire? And who was the new being born of this torture-as-birthing process?

Argentine torturers, it goes without saying, did not consider themselves homosexual for raping their male victims. However, as I've suggested, the gender divide in Argentina has historically been less a matter of male/female sexual organs than of insertive/receptive sexual positions. Jorge Salessi, using turn-of-the-century works by José Ingenieros (Pathology of sexual functions, 1910) and José María Ramos Mejía (The Argentine multitudes, 1899), traces sexual differentiation back to the differentiation between the active or "insertive" position (encoded masculine) and the passive or "receptive" position (encoded feminine). The active or insertive "partner" (whether male or female) takes the male position while the passive or receptive "partner" was positioned female. Same-sexed intercourse was not considered homosexual; that term (or the Spanish term *invertido*) was reserved for the individual who did not accept the appropriate (passive/active) position assigned to her or him, respectively. Only passive males or active females were considered *invertidos*. Continuing in this tradition, torturers could actively inflict sexual torture on male and female victims without calling their own sexual desires into question. On the contrary. Asserting one's active, insertive role served to underline the "macho" character of the torturer and the "effeminate" character of the victims regardless of their sex. As one of the torturers explained: "Some soldiers did have a problem with learning to torture. But the conditioning was that if you don't torture, you're weak."[6] The act of penetration in torture, then, reenacted the moment of radical differentiation between male and female and between males themselves. Thus, it was not simply a differentiation grounded on the biological facticity of sexual organs but, rather, a reorganization of the social and political "body" into active (male) and passive (feminine/effeminate) positions that had more to do with the us/them divide than with biological sex differences. This recasting dramatically expanded the numbers of people who now fell into the feminine category: female-sexed members of the population, regardless of their active or passive roles, were biologically female; male-sexed individuals who had been rendered passive either directly by torture or indirectly by the culture of fear were also now part of this effeminate mass. Most of the population fell into this socially designated "inferior" status through the direct and indirect repercussions of torture.

The self-referentiality of the monologic gender system in which the defining subject is male and the "female" is merely the projection of the male fear or desire is carried even further here. The erasure of female subjectivity is absolute—"she" disappears into an indiscriminate group of noninsertive others. Females, Jews, "inverts," and all others occupy the same symbolic space as outsiders ready to subvert the system.[7] But the system itself is clearly all-male: all-insertive, active, and aggressive, the new protagonist with the "spirit of conquest, aggressive and vital" that Massera envisioned (*El camino* 51). Male identity, as imagined in this masculinist structure, no longer needs the female other, except perhaps for the symbolic *Patria*. He re-creates himself. Again, this thinking had already been prefigured in the turn-of-the-century pseudo-scientific material that Salessi analyzes. Maleness is *biologically* equated with greatness and leadership. Ramos Mejía describes male leaders as physically exuding a seductive fluid that "in fortunate men flows from their eyes, their mouths, their hands, and from what other parts of their bodies I do not know. They have a peculiar aura full of carnal exhalations that irresistibly seduce the imagination and the always agitated sense of women . . . The same thing happens with the masses, who have more or less the same deficiencies as women" (26). When this view of the military male as exuding bodily fluids and self-creating becomes incorporated into the Dirty War mythology, the act of torture becomes the birthing process for the new national being. Thus, gender anxiety, in combination with a self-referential, all-male gender system, has everything to do with torture and the atrocities of the Dirty War. The gender hierarchy is reproduced in torture, which, like the insertive male sex it is modeled on, "define[s] itself around an asymmetrical gesture, that of the penetration of the body of one person by the body—and specifically by the phallus—of another."[8] Torture, in this context, accomplished three ends at once. It wrote the "subversives" out of the national epic, all in the name of creating an "authentic national being." It reaffirmed a masculinist signifying economy in which the military male produced and reproduced himself as sole protagonist in the drama of national reorganization. And it laid the basis for a self-regenerating military state, one which, as Salessi concludes, "harness[ed] homosexual desire and transform[ed] it into a homosocial nationalist military discipline" (75).

So multiple beings were created through torture. Torture was an exercise in national body building, both in terms of the nation and in terms of the military men themselves. It was considered a privilege to belong to that select group of men who practiced torture. Thus the torturer was differentiated from the lowly, though often no less brutal, guard. The military men, actors in the drama of national reorganization, raised themselves over the infirm, bloody *Patria* they aimed to protect and from the unrecoverable microbes (disguised as fellow Argentines) who threatened to destroy Western Civilization. The new, authentic body was the military male himself. He was the one who did not bleed or cry, who did not crash into others during "exercises," who did not lie prostrate waiting to be violated or pushed around. The tortured bodies of the victims were necessary. They *made a difference* in that they made "difference" visible, to paraphrase Ross Chambers's insight that, "in a world of social discourse, all differences are ideologically produced, but some are produced as 'differences that make a difference,' and others as 'just differences.'"[9]

The bodies were not only written into the narrative, the narrative was branded and marked on the body of the victim. The practice of torture marks the convergence of writing (in the traditional sense) and writing on the body. The metaphors—the individual body, the social body, the body politic—literally coalesce in torture. All receive the impact of the instrument of inscription; all take on a new shape following the ordeal.

Writing Torture: Alicia Partnoy Talks/Writes Back

My revenge is to survive to tell this story.—Alicia Partnoy, introduction,
Revenge of the Apple/Venganza de la manzana

While torture is accompanied by writing—writing the victim into the nationalist narrative by literally writing on the victim—writing also provides the victims of torture and atrocity a way back from atomization and disconnection. In her collection of short stories, *The Little School: Tales of Disappearance and Survival in Argentina* (1986), in her bilingual book of poetry, *Revenge of the Apple/ Venganza de la manzana* (1992), and in her play *Casa de papel* (Paper house, unpublished), Alicia Partnoy not only denounces the violence inflicted on her and a whole generation of Argentine young people (her "revenge"), but she also works toward personal recomposition. As the title of her story collection suggests, she writes about two processes simultaneously: disappearance and survival.

Alicia Partnoy began writing about the experiences that she and her fellow prisoners went through as *desaparecidos* in the concentration camp known as the Escuelita (Little School) because she felt she had to. As one of the approximately 1,500 of the 30,000 disappeared to "reappear," she felt compelled to speak for herself and for those who had not been so lucky. "If the intent of the represser is to silence, then speaking out is a defiance, a small victory."[10] But writing about atrocity is never easy, as Partnoy constantly reminds us, and she was gradually able to do so only because she had first spent several years *talking* about what happened: "I came to the U.S. in December 1979, under the Carter Administration, as a refugee. My English was not very good, but I wanted to tell my story to everyone, the bus driver, the person at the cash register of the supermarket, everyone. I wanted them to know that my friends had not been released. Then I started talking to people in the human rights movement. It helped me feel less powerless. After a while I started writing short stories."[11] Thus, like Rigoberta Menchú's and Domitila Barrios's *testimonios,* Partnoy's narrative has a basis in orality and reveals a commitment to denounce ongoing atrocity. Partnoy, too, wants to make witnesses of her interlocutors. Her retelling became even more frustrating and exhausting after the military men involved in the atrocities were granted amnesty in 1986.[12] Her writing about the time she spent in the concentration camp and in a women's jail in Buenos Aires as a political prisoner is accompanied by her writing about her writing, about the process that she feels saved her humanity and integrity.

For Partnoy, each of the two processes—decomposition and recomposition— requires a different register. The facts of Partnoy's case (her political activism as a university student, her membership in a *peronist* organization) are contained in her statements to human rights groups, in her introductions to both of her published books, and in the appendices to *The Little School,* that is, in her nonliterary material. Her short stories, poems, and play work around the violence and reenact a survival strategy that she learned in the concentration camp: to distance herself from the biological facticity of the torture and death taking place around her and to cling to an overriding need for human connectedness and wholeness. A necessary step in her survival, her writings of both types seem to suggest, was to learn which writing could do which. She describes first thinking about these issues in prison (where she was given a pencil and notebook) in her introduction to *Revenge of the Apple/ Venganza de la manzana*:

> Our prisoner doesn't write new poems. It would hurt her immensely to search for words to describe the past three and a half months of her life in a concentration camp where torture, executions, sexual harassment, hunger, and the certainty of imminent death haunt the victims. How could she bear, in the solitude of this cell, to write about the loss of her closest friends, killed by the military after months of torment in that secret detention place? Where could she find the spiritual strength to write about her eighteen-month-old daughter, left behind, and whom the torturers insisted they were going to kill? What words could express the horror of knowing that a baby born in that place, cynically called the Little School, was "adopted" by one of his mother's torturers? (11)

Rather than focus on the atrocity that she had lived through—the decomposition—Partnoy tells how "she," the writer/victim in this representation, began the process of recovery by connecting to her past by writing down the titles of all the poems she had written in her life. Then she performed the poems for her fellow prisoners ("a truly captive audience") in the showers, where they also staged plays. The shower was "a large area whose location at the end of a long corridor gives artists and audience the necessary time to flee or jump under the water when the guards approach" (13). These performances created community even under the most atomizing social conditions. "Many years later," Partnoy continues in the introduction, "the woman will come to the realization that the recovery of her old poems in that notebook amounted to the recovery of her soul, her history" (12). Only toward the end of her introduction does Partnoy finally reconcile the existence of "the woman" who is written and the woman who is writing, admitting, "Yes, I am the woman of this story" (16).

Alicia Partnoy's story is typical of thousands of disappeared people, and her writings stress the ordinary, rather than extraordinary, nature of it. She insists she has luck, not ingenuity, to thank for her survival.[13] And what kept her going was not personal heroism, she insists, but a sense of connectedness and solidarity. Along with her contemporaries, students like herself between the ages of eighteen and twenty-five, Partnoy realized that she could be abducted at any moment. She decided to stop breast-feeding her baby "not because it was time but because I was afraid that I would be disappeared or arrested. I didn't want them to take me away without having gone through this process with her."[14]

When her mother asked how she could put herself at risk having such a young child, Partnoy answered: "It's because of my child that I am doing this. My daughter gave me strength. I was willing to risk everything for her. But that was because I wasn't alone. There was a whole movement."

The vision of a better world, Partnoy claims, put her in the Escuelita, then in a woman's prison, and, finally, into exile. Here I will examine the two voices that Alicia Partnoy developed to write about decomposition and recomposition—about disappearance and torture on the one hand and the human struggle to survive and overcome on the other.

> They cut off my voice
> so I grew two voices
> into different tongues
> my songs I pour . . .

These two voices do not reflect the plural subjectivity associated with *testimonios*. Rather, on the most superficial level, the two voices indicate the two kinds of writing undertaken by Partnoy, the testimonial reports/documents and her literary autobiographical stories, poems, and play. The nonliterary voice documents injustice, names names, identifies places. It speaks directly to political action: "I leave the writing about torture for my work with Amnesty International. I write about what happened and the people who read it go out and do something about it" (interview). In her literary writing, Partnoy encapsulates and backgrounds the violence. Recomposing the disappeared, rather than documenting their destruction, is what matters. And desperate to keep her audience, Partnoy "talk[s] about things that people can relate to. I talk about my nose, feet, slippers, things that are in the normal world. I did not dare to go into the world of things that I saw, like torture. I don't know how to write about torture, not yet" (interview). In her poem "Testimony" she counters those who accuse her of omission. The tone of her reply in the poem suggests that she feels that descriptions of torture would be out of place, perhaps even perverse, in stories about the disappeared. Thus it is perhaps not a question of ability ("I don't know how to write about torture") but a decision to keep the two voices separate—to speak, as she says, through a different ink:

> They say
> I have not managed
> to forcefully convey the pitiless rage
> of the cattle prod.
> They say that in matters such as this

nothing must be left
open
to the imagination or to doubt.
I take out
the Amnesty report
and begin speaking through that ink.
I urge: "Read." (*Revenge* 97)

Testifying before organizations dedicated to ending human rights violations requires assuming a certain positionality and voice. If the military wrote the bodies into the narrative through torture and murder, the survivor offers up the body for a different reading. Physicians interpret the evidence of the marks and injuries. The body becomes the exhibit, the material facticity equated with proof. The victim "describes in detail almost unbearable to read the system of licensed sadism the military rulers created in their country" (*Nunca Más*, introduction, xi). The descriptions of torture cling tenaciously to the body—the wounds, blows, and shocks administered to the flesh, as in the case of Miño Retamozo. The persons describing the violence seem trapped in the body/mind split provoked by their torment in their efforts to keep their personhood out of the picture. It is as if the survivors, separating themselves from the violence inflicted on them in and through the body, negated the totalizing and engulfing nature of pain by isolating it onto the body. Here, too, we have omissions; these acts of description, like the act of torture, disconnect the victims from all the thoughts, feelings, and personal ties that make life meaningful. If, in torture, the tormentor looks beyond the excruciating pain of the victim's body and sees "national security," in these reports the reader looks beyond the victim's pain and sees the monstrosity of which some people are capable. As the introduction to *Nunca Más* announces, "Its story has two themes: ultimate brutality and absolute caprice" (xvi). In both accounts, the victim's pain is effaced in the name of some larger issue. The depersonalized nature of these accounts, of course, reflects the dehumanizing nature of torture: "the presence of pain is the absence of the world," as Scarry notes (37). The depersonalization is accentuated by its mediated quality—members of human rights panels listened to and wrote up the descriptions. Thus, these reports have a bureaucratic air to them. *Nunca Más* lists Partnoy's disappearance simply thus: "On 12 January 1977 Alicia Partnoy was kidnapped in Bahía Blanca and taken by Army lorry to the 5th Corps headquarters, where she was blindfolded and hooded shortly after giving a statement. She was taken in a vehicle to a house where, throughout the first night, she heard her husband screaming as he was tortured (file No. 2266)"

(207). This section of *Nunca Más* highlights only Partnoy's abduction and her husband's torture. The report later notes the fate of the people who died in the Escuelita, the people who, in *The Little School,* we come to see as individuals. Benja, María Elena, and Zulma, known by her nickname Vasca, were killed in a staged confrontation with the military. The *desaparecidos* were injected with anesthetic and shot at close range. Their bodies were placed in a deserted building and newspaper reporters were called in to cover the so-called armed confrontation.[15] These bodies were literally written into the script promulgated by the military and substantiated by the press. Their corpses provided the material evidence (albeit fraudulent) of armed opposition. When the bodies were exhumed, the cadavers told a different story. In a different section of *Nunca Más* Partnoy is again mentioned, this time testifying to the torture and brutality suffered by "a dozen seventeen year olds, all of them pupils of the State Technical School No. 1" (319).

The omissions in *Nunca Más* concerning Partnoy's own suffering are introduced in a personal statement by Partnoy before a medical committee interested in the short- and long-term psychological effects of torture and abuse on victims. In *The Breaking of Bodies and Minds: Torture, Psychiatric Abuse, and the Health Professions,* edited by Eric Stover and Elena O. Nightingale, Partnoy describes the concentration camp at length, outlines the daily routine, identifies the guards, specifies the inhuman methods of torture and abuse inflicted on the disappeared, and tells a little about her friends who died there. She describes her abduction in the following manner:

> On 12 January 1977 I was home alone with my daughter, Ruth, when I heard the doorbell ring incessantly. It was noon. I walked down the hallway which separates the apartment from the main door. When I arrived, someone was kicking the door. I asked, "Who is it?" and they answered, "The army." At that instant, I recalled all the stories I had heard over the past year of people being tortured and disappearing after their abduction by the army. Out of fear, I ran through the hallway and climbed over the back wall. They began firing at me from one of the neighboring roofs. My daughter, who had followed me through the passageway to the door, burst into tears. (45–46)

The first-person account, the physical situatedness of the narrator, the inclusion of feelings such as fear and helplessness, the impact of the display of violence on other family members (Partnoy's daughter), all give the reader a sense that people's worlds (not reducible to physical bodies) were being threatened and destroyed. Violence attacks interconnected bodies and bonds—the individual, the family, the social—threatening to undo them simultaneously. And it is precisely those human connections, as Partnoy's testimony reveals, that are targeted. Partnoy relates being forcefully removed from one world and brutally resocialized into another, populated by her ghostly fellow prisoners in the Escuelita: blindfolded, "I was then taken to a room and forced to lie down on a mattress. There, with hands tied behind my back, I listened all night long to the voices of men and women: 'Sir, water,' 'Sir, I want to go to the bathroom,' 'Sir, bread.' But no one responded. On several occasions, a guard would enter and hit someone or shout insults" (46). Partnoy also remembers hearing her husband being tortured through the night, though she had convinced herself it was not he, but an animal, who was being subjected to such excruciating pain. The next day, she says:

> I was taken to the kitchen to be interrogated by five or six men. At one point, one of the men put an electric prod against my head and shouted "Machine," which is what they call the electric shock torture. They also placed a gun barrel on my temple and pressed the trigger. Later they brought in my husband and told him to tell me of his torture. He could barely speak because his mouth was sore and his tongue hurt from biting it so often during the electric shocks. After beating me and threatening to make me into soap for being Jewish, I was taken back to the room where I had stayed the night before. (46–47)

This evidence expands our understanding of torture; it was not just others who were tortured, as the *Nunca Más* account implies (the husband and the seventeen-year-olds). The mock execution, the showing of the instruments, watching a family member being destroyed, the ethnically motivated insults, and prolonged existence in a life-threatening situation also constitute torture. This account suggests, too, that Partnoy was deprived of agency—"they" did everything: interrogate her, threaten her, bring the husband in, and take her back to the cell. Torture denies the victim a voice: "he could barely speak," remembers Partnoy of her husband, and the terror of it all cuts off her voice as well.[16] Insofar as torture works through amplification, the systematic nature of the assaults also affected the voice of large sectors of the Argentine population who opted not to speak out against the atrocity.

After documenting ten pages of evidence by Partnoy and her ex-husband, the researchers studying torture point to the long-term effects that persist long after the injury itself is over: "People who have been tortured must learn to come to terms with the experience, and they face problems of reintegration with their families and society. In cases of exile, refugees must also learn to adapt to a new culture" (55). The problems they outline clearly plagued Alicia Partnoy and her family. Torture not only undoes the body, but all the personal ties that make up family and community. Instead of trust, individuals, families, and the society as a whole are plagued by suspicions of betrayal; instead of togetherness, people are isolated; instead of communication, there is generalized silence and misinformation; instead of people comforting each other, every act becomes one of self-preservation and hostility.

Torture destroys both horizontally, across these interconnected bodies, and vertically, through the generations. Partnoy observes that it attacks three generations simultaneously: the target generation; their parents, who wonder if they are further endangering their children's lives by doing too much or too little to bring about their release; and their children, most of whom would never see their parents again and who would be taught that, in any case, their parents had been "subversives," undeserving of life. The vertical direction of torture is particularly evident in the military's treatment of women. As Carmen González notes, the military sought not only to eliminate them without a trace, but it wanted to erase all traces of their progeny.[17] The military targeted women both as the enemy (for being active and independent) and as links to the enemy (the enemy males to whom they were married or attached). Moreover, certain kinds of torture were especially designed for women. Sexual torture aimed at violating the female body is one example. But the tormentors also directed their attacks at women as mothers by threatening to kill their children (a form of assault not directed at fathers).[18] Thus, torture shattered communal and generational bonds. Alicia Partnoy and her ex-husband both survived, though their marriage did not. For their daughter, the short- and long-term effects of her parents' disappearance were devastating in that she never again felt she had a home or belonged to a family. Alicia Partnoy's brother, whose life became "absurd," committed suicide. As one survivor put it: "If when I was set free someone had asked me: did they torture you a lot? I would have replied: Yes, for the whole of the three months . . . If I were asked that same question today, I would say that I've now lived through seven years of torture" (*Nunca Más* 20).

The other voice, the one that we hear in the short stories, poems, and play, has a different reason for making itself heard. In part, this voice continues and expands the work of the other, denunciatory one. This writing is testimonial (specifically the Latin American genre *testimonio*) in intent though not in structure. Testimonial writing is a continuation of the struggle by other means, as René Jara suggests in his introduction to a collection of essays, *Testimonio y literatura* (1). As Doris Sommer notes, *testimonios* "are not written for individual growth nor for glory . . . [but are] part of a general strategy to win political ground."[19] But Partnoy's stories differ from *testimonios* in that, though they struggle *against* those who directed or participated in the atrocity, they are also a *struggle to* deal with the long-lasting effects of violence. Thus perhaps they have more in common with the testimonies given by Holocaust victims. As Dori Laub points out in *Testimony,* the "survivors did not only need to survive so that they could tell their story; they also needed to tell their story in order to survive" (78). Thus there is a personal urgency and immediacy to the retelling that differs from the impersonal tone that characterizes both the oral accounts and the *testimonio.* Although *testimonios* such as Rigoberta Menchú's and that of Domitila Barrios de Chungara and oral testimony such as that offered by survivors of the Dirty War were recorded in the midst of (or soon after) ongoing atrocity, there is a striking *not-about-me* quality to their presentation.

These "tales of disappearance and survival" are an odd generic mix of autobiographical and testimonial literature. Like *testimonios,* Partnoy's accounts began as oral presentations to the listener, or series of listeners, whom she hoped would help end the atrocity in Argentina. She insists that the story she has to tell is not about her, her struggle, or her heroism, but about the struggle and fate of a whole generation. Thus Partnoy's intention, like Menchú's and Barrios's is to represent herself as the spokesperson for the collective subject involved in a political struggle. Readers in *testimonios* are asked not to identify but to act as witness to the events.

Throughout the "tales," there is a tension between the testimonial intent to record the disappearance and death of a group of individuals and the literary effort to make those individuals come alive once again—this time for the reader. There are, I believe, two main reasons for this tension. For one, the requirements imposed by the publishers of *The Little School* steered the stories from the testimonial toward the autobiographical. Second, Partnoy's own struggle to heal herself and bring the disappeared back to life pertains more to the literary realm than to the testimonial. Autobiography and *testimonio,* Sommer notes, pertain to two different modes of conceiving subjectivity, political agency, and historical process. Autobiography is a Western construct that conflates "human culture and history with the lives of extraordinary individuals" (" 'Not Just a Personal Story': Women's Testimonios and the Plural Self" in Schenk and Brodski, 110). *Testimonio,* on the other hand, reflects an antihegemonic and minority practice committed to representing "the people as agents of their own history" (115). Partnoy's intention was that *The Little School,* originally made up of thirteen stories, would be a *testimonio.* Unlike Menchü, however, she had no mediator, no one to chronicle her tales and make them available to a reading public. Though the stories were written in Spanish, Cleis Press gave Partnoy a contract for her book, asking that the volume be translated into English and that more stories be added.

> They wanted me to talk more about myself in the book. Most of the stories were about my friends who never reappeared. But the editor told me that the reading public would want to see me in the stories. I didn't want the book to be about me; I wanted a collective voice; I wanted it to be about a whole generation. But I was desperate to get the book published. So I started to write the new stories about me—"My Names," "My Nose," "Birthday." By writing more about me I became the main character in the book. It was a dangerous situation because I did not want to give the impression that I was a special person, that I could go through torture and not show any signs of damage. We were all together in this movement for social change. I kept telling reporters, "I am not a special person, I am an ordinary person like everybody else." But I feel that the book conveys a different message. (interview)

Though Partnoy advocates for the plural subjectivity of the "we" associated with the *testimonio*, she fears that the autobiographical sections risk transforming the collective into the heroic status accorded the singular "I" of autobiography. Thus the publishing process in itself provoked a split between the individual (Partnoy) and group that the military itself was not able to effect.

By writing literary works accessible to a general public, Partnoy hoped that the tales of disappearance and survival would reach a wider audience that could witness and condemn the atrocity. Her purpose was to go beyond the factual limits of human rights reports in order to describe the experience of disappearance, the fears of succumbing to inhumane treatment by losing one's humanity, the tiny moments of personal triumph in a system designed to destroy personhood. Yet, unlike Menchú's *testimonio,* which has caused considerable anger among the ruling elite in her home country, Guatemala, Partnoy's stories have never been published in Spanish and are hardly known in Argentina. Argentines who did not belong to the human rights community, she surmises, were not interested in what she had to say.

Unlike the evidence given by survivors to human rights organizations, these stories do not detail the torture or suffering endured by the victims, though the sounds of blows and screaming are always in the background. In fact, on first view, the stories seem strangely removed from the atrocities that they nonetheless elucidate. The titles themselves seem mundane: "Birthday," "A Puzzle," "Toothbrush," "Bread," "My Nose," "My Names." The stories feature different characters, all of them based on fellow *desaparecidos:* Graciela, who is nine months pregnant, Vasca, María Elena, Benja, and Alicia Partnoy herself and her husband, referred to only as "Ruth's Father." The world in which the prisoners exist, bound, blindfolded, half-starved, abused, sexually harassed or violated, and in constant fear of death, is the same chaotic, nightmarish world of *Nunca Más* and other writings.

The opening story of the volume, "The One-Flower Slippers," offers a good indication of Partnoy's literary strategy throughout. She writes around the violence, as if writing could somehow isolate, circumvent, and neutralize atrocity. The violence inflicted on Partnoy, first in her abduction and then in her incarceration in the Escuelita, is doubly displaced, first onto "she," the protagonist of the story, and then onto a pair of slippers. It seems as if the fate of the nameless protagonist, though clearly Partnoy herself, could only be understood through the fate of the slippers. Here is her "literary" version of her abduction, the opening section of *The Little School:*

> That day, at noon, she was wearing her husband's slippers . . . She had always waited for them to come at night. It felt nice to be wearing a loose house dress and his slippers after having slept so many nights with her shoes on, waiting for them. She realized who was at the door and ran towards the backyard. She lost the first slipper in the corridor, before reaching the place where Ruth, her little girl, was standing. She lost the second slipper while leaping over the brick wall. By then the shouts and kicks at the door were brutal. Ruth burst into tears in the doorway. (25–26)

In the Escuelita, they gave her new slippers, one of which was adorned by an incongruous plastic flower. She and her friend Vasca, who was never to reappear, broke the rules by peering down at it through their blindfolds and laughing quietly: "The flower, a huge plastic daisy, looked up at them from the floor . . . that one-flowered slipper amid the dirt and the fear, the screams and the torture, that flower so plastic, so unbelievable, so ridiculous, was like a stage prop, almost obscene, absurd, a joke" (28). And while the slippers become part of her daily routine at the Escuelita, ultimately it signifies the fate of most of Partnoy's fellow *desaparecidos* whom she would never see again: "The day she was transferred to prison, someone realized that she should be wearing 'more decent' shoes. They found her a pair of tennis shoes three sizes too big. The one-flowered slippers remained at the Little School, disappeared" (28).

Backgrounded in this same story, confined to one paragraph, Partnoy discovers that her husband lies wounded in the concentration camp, describes how the guards threaten to torture her with electricity, and finds herself losing her humanity: "Her heart shrank a little more until it was hard as a stone. 'We must be tough,' she thought, 'otherwise they will rip us to shreds.' Fear carved an enormous hole in her stomach when she stepped down onto the cement floor of the 'machine' room and saw the side of the metal framed bed like those used for torture" (27). Nothing more—no clarification, no elaboration. "Was she tortured?" the reader asks. The narrative progression sets up demands that Partnoy refuses to satisfy. Rather, the paragraph break brings readers up short and challenges us to ask What do we mean by torture? The next paragraph begins: "She does not remember exactly the day it all happened" (27).

Partnoy's distancing herself from the violence she underwent simultaneously typifies and tries to overcome her experience as victim. Like Miño Retamozo's account of his torture in *Nunca Más,* she too displaces the violence linguistically by shifting from the first-person to the third-person. It is as if the "I" telling the story could no longer, or could no longer *bear to,* connect with the "I" who lived it. That distancing, part of a survival strategy, protects against direct access to the past, which becomes recoverable in and through representation. Partnoy says that she wrote the opening segment in the third-person because "the moment of detention goes through my mind like a movie," an analogy that conveys both the repetitive, intrusive recollection of past trauma that haunts victims of torture and the distancing and displacement through representation that allows some of them to cope with, and somehow delimit, the memories.[20]

Partnoy's literary account of her experience differs profoundly from her testimony before the Argentine Commission on the Disappeared and her account featured in *The Breaking of Bodies and Minds* not in terms of content—they are all factual—but in tone and intent. *The Little School* tries to humanize the disappeared, who, again, disappear behind the numbers. In "The One-Flower Slipper," Vasca is alive; she laughs. Partnoy focuses less on the atrocity than on the absurdity of their shared situation and their tactics for coping with it. She focuses on the mundane, on the details (the plastic flower) that the ordinary reader can visualize. The slipper has all the power of what Roland Barthes, in writing about photography, would call the "punctum" or the "partial object" (*Camera Lucida* 43). The punctum, writes Barthes, has "a power of expansion" (45). The absurd flower opens up a world of unthinkable inhumanity in a manner more immediate, perhaps more meaningful, than any bureaucratic report can do. Unlike the *testimonio* that always keeps us out and denies us entry or identification on some level, Partnoy's narrative begs us to follow her footsteps. By anchoring the readers to the slipper, Partnoy takes us into a world that many of us would like to believe is utterly foreign and inaccessible. The slipper, with that garish flower that we can all conjure up before our eyes, helps us overcome our resistance to the dirt, blood, screams, and torture that we might not be able to face on our own. It also helps Partnoy retrace her steps to that terrifying moment of captivity and disappearance; it walks her past the pain of her baby standing helplessly and terrified in a doorway; it moves her to recall her husband's pain; it becomes the shared object of the truncated gaze that unites her with her dead friend.

Beginning with the opening story, Partnoy indicates that the dangers facing the disappeared were not only the brutality of the assaults they experienced or the near certainty of their death—as if these were not enough. Bound and hooded, they are threatened not only by literal percepticide that threatened the general population on a less concrete but perhaps no less "real" level. Partnoy's tales of disappearance call attention to her struggle to resist her own dehumanization. In an effort to survive, the prisoners found themselves in danger of becoming like their torturers, distancing themselves from the pain of their fellow victims and turning them into "animals." Within the world of *The Little School,* Partnoy does not represent herself as connecting to her husband's pain. In the story, "Ruth's Father," she depicts him babbling endlessly, undone by torture but trying to hold onto the memory of an integrated self: "I'm not an animal . . . Don't make me believe I'm an animal. But that's not my scream; that's an animal's scream. Leave my body in peace . . ." (94). Little by little, the memory of all loving relationships receded, and Partnoy could no longer remember her child's face. "If only I had her picture. But again, maybe it's better this way. If I could look at a picture of her face, I would surely cry . . . and if I cry, I crumble" (79).

The victims' bodies, bound and assaulted, are turned into the source of confusion and pain for the victims themselves. The torturers and guards treat the victims as worthless objects who, they sincerely believed, did not deserve life. But in these stories Partnoy pays little attention to the tormentors, as if she took their brutality for granted. She is not interested in simply documenting their abuses or analyzing their psychological motivations or perverse desires. In the spirit of Rigoberta Menchú's oral testimony, edited by Elisabeth Burgos-Debray in *I . . . Rigoberta Menchú,* and Lilian Celiberti's *Mi habitación, mi celda* (My room, my cell) written in collaboration with Lucy Garrido, Partnoy's intent is to tell a collective tale, a story about the suffering and courage of a persecuted generation and people. Nonetheless, in a more overtly literary mode, she takes liberties with the "I" that authenticates *testimonios* to make the victims come alive for the reader. Sometimes Partnoy uses the third-person to describe what is clearly her own experience, yet she sometimes uses "I" to identify with people like Graciela ("They knew I was pregnant. It hadn't occurred to me that they could torture me while we were traveling" [53]). At other moments, the "I" is again Alicia Partnoy ("every day, when I wake up, I say to myself that I, Alicia Partnoy, am still alive" [43]). Her stories are a literary disavowal of death, another bid for "Aparición con vida." Thus, the decomposition, outlined for human rights reports, gives way to recomposition—the recuperation of a lost community, the reaffirmation of a besieged self, and the recovery of the disappeared, reappeared once again through the process of writing.

But writing stories, albeit literary in nature and testimonial in intent, poses its own risks for the survivor/witness/author. As an author of these autobiographical stories about a terrifying past, Partnoy experiences the conflicting pulls and obligations between the writer (who has obligations to a reading public) and the written (Partnoy as a character/witness whose obligations lie with her own lived experience and that of the missing). While all autobiographical writers feel these pulls, the particularly horrifying nature of Partnoy's past further complicates the act of representation. The doubling of the voices—the writer/written split shared by all writers of autobiography—is directly linked to Partnoy's experience of dissociation as a victim of atrocity. It represents an effort to compartmentalize and somehow contain violence. In and of itself, the doubling is a response to brutality that, paradoxically, undermines psychic wholeness in an attempt to protect it. For doubling is not only a representational phenomenon but also a survival strategy, what Robert Jay Lifton defines in *The Nazi Doctors* as "an active psychological process, a means of *adaptation to extremity*" (422; original emphasis). Lifton explores how doubling enabled tormentors to function in a culture of systematized murder, to see themselves as humane and reasonable human beings, to reconcile themselves to their environment and avoid guilt (418–29). Doubling necessarily involves splitting ("They cut off my voice/so I grew two voices") but differs from it in degree. Doubling is a mechanism that strives to keep the personality together rather than allow the radical split or schizophrenic break that completely dissociates one part of the personality from the other or from its environment at large. What Partnoy's writing illustrates, however, is that victims also experience doubling as a protective strategy that works to maintain their sense of psychic integrity, albeit at a cost. Thus writing as a reenactment of the doubling/splitting phenomenon into a writer/written relationship is as much a continuation of the effects of victimization as its representation.

Writing also provides a therapeutic way of dealing with the long-term effects of the torture, of exerting control over a series of events in which one had no control. If distancing and partial dissociation are features of doubling that remain with the victim long after the traumatic incident is over, then literary writing affords the survivor an acceptable alienation technique to write around violence and toward recomposition. The aesthetic framing of events allows for the separateness between author and character that makes representation possible.

Nonetheless, the aesthetic distancing in itself poses risks, this time for the reader as well as for the author. Representing disappearance and atrocity, even if the writer was once a disappeared person herself, runs into the same problems that Elisabeth Bronfen identifies with representations of death in general. Representations of death (and disappearance) "both conceal and reveal at the same time; both are doubled in that they point to what is absent and to their own act of representing" (85). The act of representation calls attention to the unbridgeable gap between Alicia Partnoy the reappeared writer and Alicia Partnoy the *desaparecida* and her friends in the Escuelita. This distance is accentuated by Partnoy's alternating use of "I" and "she" in referring to herself and others. Though Partnoy's intention in referring to herself as "she" or "the woman" in her writing is to put her character on the same level as the other disappeared, the distancing also accentuates that the Alicia Partnoy who lived through the atrocity is no longer the Alicia Partnoy who survived to tell the story. The representational process itself bespeaks the necessary distancing of terror onto the *not-me*. Terror directed at *me* is, as all accounts of torture attest, unspeakable. One of the results of the changing narrative perspective, then, is that it makes all the people equal as characters in a series of stories, all equidistant from Partnoy the author. Thus there can be no unmediated connection between Partnoy the survivor and Partnoy the *desaparecida*. The mediating factors include the representational process itself and the ongoing effects of atrocity on Partnoy the survivor.[21]

But reading mediated forms of testimonial writing does not prepare critics for the particular hybrid literary/testimonial nature of Partnoy's stories, which produce conflicting pulls on the author/survivor, character/survivor, and the reader. These stories destabilize the reader much as the "I"/"she" destabilizes the author/survivor/literary subject. As testimony, their direct link to the "real," to the world of unspeakable inhumanity, supersedes literary criticism. How could we conceivably quibble over their literary value? Wouldn't the work's aesthetic achievement in and of itself neutralize its "real" efficacy, as if there were such a thing as the "beautiful" representation of atrocity that did not disengage itself (i.e., transcend) the real? As stories, however, both the author and the reader must evaluate the effectiveness of the representation of the terrible "real." Do they illuminate or obscure the very real pain inflicted on the *desaparecidos*? Partnoy's stories are, after all, finished products. Or are they?

This kind of representation reflects the continuing effects of victimization. It enables Partnoy to deal with the past and present effects of her ordeal and is, thus, inextricable from her status as survivor. She is a reappeared person, a category that has the same continuous temporal quality to it that the term *disappeared* gives to the dead and that links her to them. She, though alive, will never be "over" the ordeal—there is no "over."

Staging Torture

With an audience, torture becomes an art, the torturer an author, the onlookers an audience of connoisseurs.—Susanne Kappeler, *The Pornography of Representation*

Reports on torture differ in goals and methodology from "aesthetic" writings on torture by artists who wish to allow the general audience some entry into its prevalence and social implications. Unlike the writing of survivors such as Alicia Partnoy, who writes both to denounce criminal politics and to heal or recompose herself, artistic representations of atrocity have been accused, by thinkers such as Adorno, of subjecting the victims of violence to even more pain and degradation. I have argued that the problems regarding the representation of violence are too complex to condemn all efforts outright. Nonetheless, the dangers of reproducing the conceptual frameworks and blind spots under attack haunt me. And no Argentine playwright of the period I am focusing on so visibly attacks and re-creates the problems of violence as Eduardo Pavlovsky.

The degree to which Eduardo Pavlovsky's *El Señor Galíndez*, written and staged in 1973, reproduces and replicates the masculinist discourse that I have described in relation to the Dirty War is uncanny. Even before the concentration camps for political dissenters proliferated throughout Argentina following the military coup of 1976, Pavlovsky depicts the creation of a homosocial society constructed by means of the violence (including torture) inflicted on the feminized social "body." This, in itself, is not surprising. The masculinist discourse has deep roots in Argentine history. Political unrest throughout the century had precipitated military reprisals, and torture in Argentina has unfortunately long been a method of social control.[22] During the turbulent period of the early 1970s, playwrights such as Pavlovsky and Griselda Gambaro had already foreseen the direction Argentina's future would take under military rule. Plays such as Gambaro's *The Camp*, written and staged a full ten years before the 1976 coup, depicted the concentration camps run by fascist guards. Thus the fact that playwrights such as Pavlovsky wrote plays about torture a few years before the 1976 coup was symptomatic of the times.

What I find interesting about *El Señor Galíndez* is that the play situates the violence against the feminine body squarely within the context of nation-building. The play illustrates the connection between political violence and the creation of the "our national being" (*Galíndez* 51). However, it does so in the same way that the military discourse does—by covering up the violence against women and pretending that misogyny is incidental, rather than fundamental, to the national project of re-creating a national being. *El Señor Galíndez,* while written as a denunciation of torture, unwittingly eroticizes the practice of torture and exploits women, all the while suggesting that violence against women does not pertain to the realm of the political. Pavlovsky would no doubt deny that his work fuels, rather than demystifies, the erotic dimension of torture. But that is what makes torture so difficult to write about, what makes it so tempting to accept the torturer's version of events and constitute the act as a sexual encounter. The question is how to write about this narrative of male individuation predicated on the erasure of the "feminine" without falling into it.

The plot of *El Señor Galíndez* can be summarized as follows. Eduardo, a pleasant-looking young man, waits impatiently in a room that the spectator (the playwright specifies) should find rather "strange" and "secret" (9). The audience's vision is carefully controlled by the lighting, which "delimits the acting space. Beyond this limit—nothing, darkness, black" (9). The only opening to this room is a hole in the floor through which the protagonists appear. The room is equipped with metal furniture: a couple of chairs, a table, a metal bed, a cabinet. Pictures and clippings of actresses, models in bathing suits, and soccer players are pasted up here and there. He waits, he reads comic books, he makes small talk with Doña Sara, the unpleasant sixty-five-year-old housekeeper. When Beto and Pepe finally enter, they insult the young man, who explains apologetically that he has been sent to train with them. He passed a "test" indicating he was suited for this kind of "job"; he has read books by Galíndez, their mastermind, on the nature of the profession, and now he is being sent by Galíndez for some practical experience. The kind of work these men dedicate themselves to does not become clear until later in the play and, as Jacqueline Bixler notes, the word *torture* is not used once in the play ("Toward a Reconciliation"). Beto and Pepe are a team; they "work" and often spend hours, even days, in this tiny room waiting for orders from Galíndez. Much as in *Waiting for Godot,* a play that influenced Pavlovsky profoundly, Galíndez never appears onstage. He conveys his orders by phone. Galíndez instructs them to take care of Eduardo and to await further orders. Beto, excited after speaking with Galíndez, confesses: "I swear, every time I talk to him I feel this urge to work" (30). Fifteen hours go by—the tension increases. Beto and Pepe take a violent dislike to the young man and on occasion beat and insult him. Pepe does his exercises and Beto passes the time reading a text and studying for an accounting course he is taking. Pepe gets more and more agitated. He asks Beto if he beats his wife. Beto says no, "it's not right to hit a woman" (34). Pepe beats his "chick," he confesses, but she likes it. It stimulates their sex life and helps her reach orgasm.

Beto, seemingly the more "civilized" and studious of the two, reveals a more brutal side when he calls his wife and daughter on the phone. While he dotes on his little girl, his hostility toward his wife is palpable. After he tells her to "go fuck herself," he hangs up (36). The hours go by. The men's anxiety reaches such a pitch that they suspect Galíndez of being two people, not one. They fear that he will give them contradictory orders to force them to fail. They speak of el Flaco (skinny), a fellow torturer who received contradictory orders and finally killed himself after being reprimanded and accused of not following orders.

Finally, Galíndez calls again to tell the men that he is sending them a "surprise" (37). Eduardo is sent out to retrieve the two packages and comes back with two blindfolded women, Coca and La Negra (Blackie). Pepe exclaims: "It's brilliant, Beto! The two packages are two whores! He outdid himself!" Beto reads the note accompanying the packages: "Courtesy of the house. Signed, Galíndez" (39). The men eye the two blindfolded women: "(Beto takes off his belt and whips the table with it. The girls jump, afraid. Pepe grabs one of them from behind. Beto stands in front of the other.)"

> Beto: Take your blindfold off! Go for it! Take it off! (Each time she tries to take it off he hits her hand. Pepe signals to Eduardo to join in. The three thoroughly enjoy the scene. The girls try to dodge the blows and slaps . . . Eduardo kicks one on her backside . . . He sticks his hand up La Negra's sweater.) (40)

When the men finally allow the women to remove their blindfolds, the women start to laugh; they (like Pepe's woman) apparently like the abuse and think it normal. "(La Negra looks at the three men and starts to roar with laughter.) Look Coca! Look where they've sent us! I thought these were great dudes! But look at them, they look like prisoners!" (40). The women both find Eduardo attractive and start flirting with him. A party begins in which the three men take turns fondling the two women. Eduardo undresses Coca from behind as Beto kisses and caresses her in front and Pepe, drinking from a whiskey bottle, toasts "the great Argentine people" (42) as Coca's body becomes exposed. As the men finish disrobing both of them, they discover that the women have tattoos: La Negra has San Martín de Tours, patron saint of Buenos Aires, and Coca has Perón wearing a presidential band imprinted on her body. After threatening to kill her for being a *peronist*, Pepe finally calms down and invites the "beautiful peronista" to "start a long trip with me. We're going to fly to the clouds. Do you want to fly with me?" (44). Coca consents and he lays her on the bed. He rapidly switches the bed into an upright position and asks Eduardo to tie her hands and feet. Coca, "completely naked" as the stage directions indicate, faces the audience. "Pretty little body, you have" (44), Pepe says, as he goes to the cabinet for his instruments. "Do you know the neurological points?" (44), Pepe asks Eduardo. The lesson has begun. "It's good to start out with a whore," Pepe states, passing on the old wisdom that many a father has given his son. Eduardo is suddenly deaf to Coca's entreaties and when both torturers ask him where he wants to start he answers "the breasts" (44). "OK, the breasts, but no talking! In this business we don't talk. We let others do the talking here" (44). Beto holds the screaming Negra down as Pepe and Eduardo map out Coca's body into "neurological zones" (45). Pepe wets Coca's body with a siphon and plugs in the electric *picana* or cattle prod. He encourages Eduardo to start the operation, which clearly Eduardo is about to do.

Then the phone rings. Galíndez tells them to get rid of the girls because prisoners are being delivered to them in ten minutes. The men pressure the women to dress; they threaten to kill them if they squeal, and they blindfold them. Eduardo takes them back out to the street, insulting them as they go. The lights dim, the room undergoes a subtle transformation by means of lighting and becomes transformed, unambiguously, into a torture chamber. The men take out their instruments, check them, and get them ready. Beto "only leaves out a very large, phallic-looking metal instrument" (46). They put on their cloaks and rubber gloves. While they wait, they start preparing Eduardo.

> Pepe: You should see the faces they make on this stretcher. You'll never forget it.
> Beto: Out there they act like machos, you know? They plant bombs. Kill our innocent companions. But when we put them here on this stretcher and we touch them with these instruments (pause), they shit on themselves! They pee on themselves! They ask for their mothers!
> Beto [*sic*]: You've got to remember that for each job well done here, there are thousands of people out there paralyzed by fear. We act through irradiation. That's the great beauty of this technique. (47)

Just then, the phone rings again. Beto answers. Galíndez informs them that the operation is postponed. He orders them to leave things as they are, go home, and take a break. Pepe becomes hysterical, telling Beto that the voice on the other end was not Galíndez, that they're being set up. Beto maintains his composure throughout the brief conversation. When he hangs up, Pepe becomes even more upset and threatens to find out who this Galíndez character really is. Beto tries to calm him down; he reminds Pepe that he killed a student last time they "worked" due to his overzealousness. A rest will do him good. Besides, "who cares who Galíndez is?" . . . "I think all of us . . . all of us work for Galíndez" (50). Beto and Pepe change their clothes and prepare to leave. Eduardo takes up the metal *picana,* "caresses it" (50), and begins to read from Galíndez's book:

> EDUARDO: We cannot overemphasize the enormous effort that our vocation implies. Only with this faith and with this will can we achieve the degree of mental preparation that we need to succeed at our task. Faith and technique are, then, key in this group of privileged men . . . with an exceptional mission. (50; ellipsis in original)

As Eduardo mimics the preparation for torture he learned from Beto and Pepe, he continues:

> The entire nation now knows about our profession. Our enemies know about it too. They know that our creative and scientific work is our trench. And each and everyone of us has to fight in this definitive war against those who intend, by means of exotic ideology, to destroy our way of life, our national being. (51)

As the lights go down, the telephone rings and Eduardo picks up the mouthpiece "with a martial gesture": "Yes, Señor Galíndez!" (51).

This play, then, links violence to the military rhetoric depicting the military males as self-sacrificing "exceptional beings" embarked on a heroic "exceptional mission" to defend Argentine values and create a new "national being." Galíndez's "text" sounds like vintage Massera: "Every morning the Patria waits for us to reaffirm our total submission to her, that anonymous and discrete submission that can only come of a pure heart" (*El pais* 90); or President Videla's first proclamation after the coup: "in this war without trenches against delinquent subversion . . . there is a battle position for every citizen. The task is arduous and urgent. It is not without sacrifices, but one will undertake it with the absolute conviction that the example will be predicated from the top down" (qtd. in Troncoso, *Proceso,* 108). Pavlovsky captured the lofty-sounding, self-righteous tone that characterizes much of this language. He has illuminated the dirty underside of what the generals tried to pass off as a clean war. He understands how the words themselves have been emptied and co-opted in order to make the military narrative sound plausible: they refer to defending nation-hood rather than to civil bloodshed; they explain the military's actions in terms of the self-sacrifice of altruistic "pure hearts" rather than as self-interest in maintaining political power; they invoke words such as *faith, purity,* and *vocation* to cover up the systematic practice of abduction, torture, and death that awaited all those perceived as dissenting from this all-encompassing project of national reorganization.

Pavlovsky also captures the relationship between the "text" (or nationalist narrative) and its executioner (if a morbid pun is permissible when writing about this grim subject). The image of Eduardo holding the *picana,* the penlike instrument that rewrites the human body, and reading the Galíndez text while he stands in front of the stretcher that will hold the next victim, concretely exemplifies the triangular formulation between author (narrative/author-ity), instrument (torture/*picana*/pen), and the body-as-text that I proposed earlier.

But while the victim's body is literally *written on,* both the victim's body and the torturer are *written into* the masculinist discourse, albeit in different ways. As Eduardo's reading makes clear, the torturer identifies himself as the heroic subject à la lone soldier who sets off into the unknown to fight the good fight. He assumes his scripted role, overcomes obstacles, passes the "tests" and becomes a Man or hero. Though separated from his community, the story goes, his heroism helps him found a new community based on nobler values. Eduardo enters an alien and hostile situation where he is at first shunned and humiliated; he perseveres and passes the torture test to become one of those few exceptional men who will create the new national being. The new being born of the violent ordeal is the torturer himself. Eduardo, at the end of the play, now belongs to that larger "body" of men in contact with and represented by Galíndez.

So far, so good. Pavlovsky's intention was clearly to call attention to the ubiquity of the practice of torture in Argentina. But, he admits, the spectators know this already: "Our aesthetic problem was to resolve on stage (scenically) what everyone (even the spectators) knew: in our country torture is practiced in many 'places'" (introduction 11). He depicts the generalized character of military power that the torturers, and most of the Argentine public, tend to concentrate in one individual. For clearly it is not one individual's drive for power, not one man's desire or personal fantasies that mobilize a political rhetoric and practice that has continued in one form or another for an entire century. Who is Galíndez? Does it matter? Isn't Galíndez—like Videla, Massera, Agosti, Viola, Galtieri, and the rest of the generals associated with this period—only a name one associates with a much wider phenomenon? Is he one person or two? or twenty? It is misleading, as Beto understands, to think of authoritarian regimes in terms of individual leaders. Pavlovsky notes too that while power may be diffuse, its diffuseness when perceived as such provokes an identity crisis in political subjects. Part of the anxiety underlying authoritarianism is exactly this longing for clear definition and precise, differentiating boundaries. Beto and Pepe constantly wonder about Galíndez, who he is, if he is to be trusted. Does his voice sound the same today as it did yesterday? Is that the same voice Beto overheard virtually condemning his buddy, el Flaco, to death? The representation of these torturers underlines the dependency of their sense of self on identifiable figures of power.

However, while illuminating one side of torture, by making it visible onstage and by placing it within an authoritarian epic scenario, Pavlovsky simultaneously eclipses another side of that process—the fact that the epic drama of male individuation, and the violence stemming from it, is predicated on the erasure of women. This occurs, I believe, because Pavlovsky feels his true challenge is an aesthetic one, to resolve aesthetic and political needs in the representation of torture in theatre. And, I must assume, he resolved this need for aesthetic pleasure by exposing the naked body of a young woman. Woman/women function as the space on which the brutal practice of torture plays out. Her body, moreover, captivates the spectator. Like it or not, we, as onlookers, are coerced by the spectacle into the position of Kappeler's "connoisseurs."

Let's look at Pavlovsky's plot again. The scenic space occupied by the men suggests the "feminine" space of mythic narrative. It is small and totally self-enclosed; access to it is through a small hole. As described by Lotman, "The elementary sequence of events in myth can be reduced to a chain: entry into closed space—emergence from it . . . In as much as closed space can be interpreted as 'a cave,' 'the grave,' 'a house,' 'woman' (and correspondingly, be allotted the features of darkness, warmth, dampness), entry into it is interpreted on various levels as 'death,' 'conception,' 'return home' and so on; moreover all these acts are thought of as mutually identical."[23] Why should this space be feminized, when most people would agree that torture is almost invariably a male practice? Why not associate torture with a "male" space—an office, for example, as Griselda Gambaro does in *The Camp* or as Peter Barnes, the British playwright, does in representing the institutionalization of atrocity in *Auschwitz?* But from the first moment of Pavlovsky's play, the "feminine" is collapsed into a generalized threat, a secret and strange place that is the site of death, sexuality, and conception. The new man (Eduardo) will be born here. By passing his rite of initiation on a whore's body he will become one of the boys. "She" (Coca as the embodiment of the feminine) is the obstacle he must overcome. She has "enemy" written all over her, the *peronist* emblem literally inscribed on her skin. As a "whore," she is already guilty, a participant, somehow "asking for it," according to societal norms. Thus, Pavlovsky makes the viewing of her humiliation acceptable. The battle against the feminized masses that throughout the century have been alluded to as agitated and deficient (in Ramos Mejías's words) is staged by Pavlovsky on her body. Strapping her to the table, Beto marks her body into "zones," analogous to the combat "zones" the military refer to. Eduardo hesitates as he approaches Coca's naked body with the *picana* in his hand. Her body has come to stand for the "Argentine people" that Pepe toasts as his companions strip her. Will he prove up to the task? Of course. He refuses to hear her pleas. He triumphs over her and over anything that was "soft" and humane within himself. His rebirth as a new man is predicated on the erasure of the feminine body.

The problem, as I see it, is not that Pavlovsky represents the misogyny that underlines the military discourse on nationhood. That is what I myself am trying to do. What is troubling is that Pavlovsky reproduces and aestheticizes the violence against women without challenging or even addressing the phenomenon. It's as if he does not see it as *violence.* He presents the brutality as sex, kinky sex perhaps, but not violence. As such, it seemingly belongs to the realm of the "normal" rather than the world of aberrant political behavior he has chosen to focus on. The way the play is set up, with the torture sessions promised and postponed by Galíndez, it seems as if the violence or the torture has not happened yet. The violence, supposedly, has been deferred. The fact that women are forced to endure the immediate threat of torture (Coca) and to watch the torture of someone else (La Negra) is overlooked. However, both these ordeals are recognized by Amnesty International and other human rights organizations as true forms of torture. David William Foster, in "Ambigüedad verbal y dramática en *El Señor Galíndez* de Eduardo Pavlovsky," does call the violence against the women "torture." However, he notes quite rightly that the scene functions to show up the men, not to illuminate the phenomenon of social and political violence against women: "soon, the spectator (and the prostitutes) will become aware of the horrible fact that the men's amusement consists in torturing them. This fact leads to the crucial recognition scene of the play in which we understand, along with the women, that for Pepe, Beto, and Eduardo, torture constitutes not only a profession but a means of erotic gratification" (105; my translation). Thus the issues the play poses concern male desire, male destiny. Why did they become like this? Why do they do what they do? What will become of them? The woman's body provides the transparent screen on which the "real" (male) motives will be revealed. We, as audience, tend to look straight at her but, simultaneously, straight through her to see and "read" the all-male narrative that is written and rewritten on her. She functions as pure surface. Again the woman's body is the occupied, blank territory that men will inscribe, fight over, and ultimately dominate in order to become "real" men. The focus of the play is so narrow, sharp, and compelling that other Latin American theatre commentators, including two of the most prominent— Jacqueline Bixler and Frank Dauster—fail to note the violence that befalls these women, who, in their respective commentaries, remain unnamed.[24] How does this blind spot get created? And what does it do to our understanding of the practice of torture, which, theoretically, the play sets out to illuminate?

Pavlovsky's *Galíndez* reproduces—and fails to challenge—a misogynist discourse predicated on the objectification and erasure of women. From the first moment, when the spectators see the pictures of the actresses and the models in bathing suits, it becomes clear that we have entered a masculinist signifying economy in which women are merely commodities of exchange. The same holds true when the two women enter the room; they are presented as sexual objects that money can buy, gifts to be exchanged among men. The desire that produces these sexual objects as a venue of interchange and communication is clearly all male. Male bonds—not male-female ones—are at stake in this transfer. Women serve only as mediators (literally gifts) in the process of male bonding, in the construction of a homosocial political system sustained through the regulation of male desire.

Desire, however, is socially constructed and mediated. In *Galíndez,* desire functions as an instrument of social control. Galíndez sends the men a gift that strengthens their longing—not for the women, but for direct contact with him, their leader. They want nothing more than to meet him, be flattered and accepted by him. Pepe reassures himself: "Galíndez loves us. Doesn't he compliment us on our work all the time?" (27). Here we see a modernized, technologically transmitted version of the dictator/leader as hero that Ramos Mejias describes as physically exuding a seductive fluid. Galíndez is the desired figure, the one the men long to meet, please, and emulate. Desire keeps the men functioning in their claustrophobic room. Desire makes them dependent on the unseen, adulated figure of Galíndez. Their desire is his power. Desire for Galíndez is, ironically, a desire for the invisible, the *power* of the invisible—even as it is the "disappeared" who are tortured. The figure of the woman, in this triangular formulation, functions mainly to keep the desire from becoming blatantly homosexual. Thus it seems to me fruitless to address issues of power and political structures without addressing the desire and gender that enables power to produce and reproduce itself. Bonding is channeled through the

female body. Eduardo comes of age by means of Coca. A tightly knit, homosocial community is founded on this regulation of desire, the passing around of
women.

The female, of course, is denied subjectivity, volition, and individuality—it is
not her desire that motives the exchange. These women are throwaways, the
men get rid of them as soon as they stop using and abusing them. In terms of
the representation, they are functionally dead when the men dispatch them.
There is no conceivable role they could occupy except that of victim—with the
possible exception of bitch/hag who basically stands outside the process of
producing and reproducing power. In *Galíndez*, however, that role is already
taken by the ugly, nasty old woman, Doña Sara. The mother role, given to Beto's
wife, functions according to the Latin American tradition that confines it to the
nonvisible space offstage. And even she, the mother, Beto indicates, is not all
she should be.

Pavlovsky, however, does not simply indicate that these are the roles allotted
women in an all-male system such as the Argentine military. While neither
uplifting nor oppositional, that position would have been understandable.
However, the play suggests that the situation afforded women and the "feminine" is somehow normal and that the violence that befalls them is really
nothing out of the ordinary. Pavlovsky presents domestic violence, violence
against women, and political violence in the same play as if they were somehow
discrete occurrences, thus failing to make any connections between them. How
is the *hombría a golpes* (manhood by blows) associated with wife beating related
to the *golpe de estado* (the blow to a state, or coup), prefigured as feminine? The
violence is inherent in the masculinist discourse, permeating both the political
and social arenas, that socializes men to define themselves in terms of power
and domination. Wherever that discourse prevails, women will be erased physically or metaphorically.

The play focuses events so that political torture (which is not depicted onstage) is considered real and important, while the torture of naked women
(which is depicted onstage) is not the "real" thing and is hardly worth noting.[25]
How can these blind spots blur our "reading"? How does the kind of distortion
manifested in this play get set up? "Through what act of negation and disavowal," to echo de Beauvoir's question, "does the masculine pose as disembodied universality and the feminine get constructed as disavowed corporeality?" The female body, the play suggests, is nothing but the battleground
("disavowed corporeality") on which these military men fight out their aspirations to male individuation and epic grandeur ("disembodied universality").

Unlike the testimonies given by actual victims of torture, *Galíndez* situates the spectators/readers on the side of the torturer. Like the torturers themselves, we look at the naked female body strapped to the table and fail to grant her individuality, to understand her pain, to remember her name. As in actual acts of torture itself, we are placed in the torturer's position of standing outside the pain and looking voyeuristically at the naked body. Rather than demystify a set of relations that enables torture to occur, Pavlovsky further exploits the female body by putting it on display to titillate an implicitly male audience. He, like Galíndez, uses the female body as an object of exchange, a gift for the audience. The naked female body continues to mediate between Galíndez and his men, between Pavlovsky and his implicitly male audience.

Torture plays, unfortunately, now make up an entire subgenre in Latin American and U.S. Latino theatre. They vary in quality, length, and intent—from Enrique Buenaventura's three-page *La tortura* to Ariel Dorfman's international "hit" *Death and the Maiden* to María Irene Fornes's *The Conduct of Life* (to name a few). The popularity of the subgenre makes it even more urgent to examine the representational traps facing playwrights. While similar issues challenge other authors, playwrights face one specific quandary illuminated by Brecht when he said that theatre's business is to entertain people; its only passport is fun. Theatre's need to please the audience (on some level) traps playwrights into trying to represent violence aesthetically. This was Pavlovsky's challenge, as stated in his introduction: "Our aesthetic problem was to resolve on stage (scenically) what everyone (even the spectators) knew: in our country torture is practiced in many 'places' " (11). Is it possible or desirable to speak of a beautiful and pleasurable depiction of torture? If not, where will the pleasure come from? Rather than produce the pleasure by reproducing the old epic narrative of male individuation that has received rave reviews for the past twenty-five hundred years, it may be time to explore other possibilities. How to resist that scenario? and if one does, where does the pleasure come from? One possibility, the one opted for by Griselda Gambaro in *Information for Foreigners,* is the pleasure of resistance that stems from nonidentification. Another possibility is to follow Laura Mulvey's lead: "It is said that analyzing pleasure, or beauty, destroys it. That is the intention . . ." ("Visual Pleasure and Narrative Cinema"). Maybe after my analysis, Pavlovsky's play will seem a little less desirable. There is a kind of aesthetic pleasure in Buenaventura's minimalist script that illuminates but never "shows." Or, as in Diana Raznovich's *Desconcierto,* the audience might be asked to witness what happens to women in nation-building. In order to change the conceptual paradigms that have proven so dangerous we, too, can find pleasure in destroying the old desires, in making them undesirable, and thus moving toward changing desire itself.

7 Trapped in Bad Scripts: The Mothers
of the Plaza de Mayo

Liberty is the proud mother of the Republic and its children; to
lose her, in any way, would be to lose that which we love most.
Let's protect her and conserve her.—Jorge Rafael Videla, "Recuerda el país su gesta patria," *La nación,* May 25, 1976.

The Mothers of the Plaza de Mayo

Arm in arm, wearing their white head scarves, the Mothers of the Plaza de Mayo slowly walk around Argentina's central square. Some carry huge placards with the smiling faces of their missing children. Others hang small photographs around their necks. Turning their bodies into walking billboards, they carry banners demanding "Aparición con vida," that their children be brought back alive. On any given Thursday afternoon at 3:30, hundreds of women meet in the square to demand justice for the human rights violations committed by the brutal military dictatorship that abducted, tortured, and permanently "disappeared" thirty thousand of their children. The plaza, facing the presidential palace, lies in the heart of Buenos Aires's political and economic center. Businessmen and politicians hurry to and fro, sometimes crossing the street to distance themselves from the Mothers. The women continue to talk and comfort each other as they walk, stopping every so often to gather around the microphone and loudspeakers from which they and their leader, Hebe de Bonafini, broadcast their accusations to the country's president. *Where are our children? We want them back alive! Why did their torturers and murderers get away with murder? When will justice be done?* Until these issues are resolved, the women claim, the Dirty War will not be over. Nor will their demonstrations.

The staging of the Madres' tragedy is instructive not only to human rights activists but also to those who study the performance of politics in public spaces and to those concerned with the role of gender in civil conflict. For one thing, the entire scenario of "national reorganization" set in motion by the military was highly theatrical. By this, I am referring not only to the obvious spectacularity of the confrontations, the public marches, the ritualistic orchestration of events, the struggle to control public space and attention, the display of instruments, images, and icons. I am also referring to the script or master narrative used by the military, which "explained" and energized the public battle of images and worked to transform the "infirm" social "body" into a passive (i.e., "feminine") one. The Argentine scenario, then, like all scenarios, invoked a script, complete with plotline and roles. For another thing, the Madres, a group of nonpolitical women, organized one of the most visible and original resistance movements to a brutal dictatorship in the twentieth century. Theirs was very much a performance, designed to focus national and international attention on the junta's violation of human rights. The terrifying scenario in which the Madres felt compelled to insert themselves was organized and maintained around a highly coercive definition of the feminine and motherhood which the women simultaneously exploited and attempted to subvert. The spectacular nature of their movement, which cast the "Mother" in a central role, inspired and influenced numerous other political women's groups throughout Latin America, the United States, the Middle East, and Eastern Europe.[1]

I recognize that using the term *performance* to describe the Madres' activism might appear flippant—What could be more *natural,* one might object, than women looking for their missing children? How could that be considered *performance?* Does the term trivialize the very real nature of their pain? Performance, as I mentioned earlier, is usually perceived as the antithesis of the "real," as if it provokes no concrete repercussions. Anyone familiar with the Madres' movement knows full well how real and courageous it is and would never minimize the violent repercussions—from harassment to abduction to murder—that followed their demonstrations. But *performance*, as I use the term throughout this study, does not suggest artificiality; it is not "put on" or antithetical to "reality." Rather, throughout this study I have followed Richard Schechner's concept of performance as "restored" or "twice-behaved behavior." I will argue that the "restored" nature of the Madres' display served several purposes simultaneously and offered the women a way of coping with their grief and channeling it to life-affirming action. It also brought motherhood out of the domestic closet as the Madres demonstrated the predicament facing women in Argentina and the world over. Traditionally, mothers have been idealized as existing somehow beyond or above the political arena. Confined to the home, they have been made responsible for their children. But what happens to the mothers who, by virtue of that same responsibility to their children, must go looking for them outside the home and confront the powers that be? Do they cease to be mothers? Or must onlookers renounce notions of mothers as apolitical? By socializing and politicizing motherhood, as the Madres did, they were only reacting to the history of socialization of mothers as nonpolitical, tangential figures in patriarchy. Their transgression of traditional roles made evident how restrictive and oppressive those roles had been. Thus their performance of mothers as activists challenged traditional maternal roles and called attention to the fact that motherhood was a social, not just biological, construct.

Thus the concept of performance allows a discussion of the Madres' movement from its most practical level involving the weekly marches in the Plaza de Mayo to its most theoretical—Are *mothers* or *women* groups that need political representation? Or are they already the product of such representation?[2] The individual women who came to be known as the Madres performed traditional, domestic duties for most of their lives. They were dedicated to their homes and families. Few had a degree in higher education or had ever worked outside the home. They were very much the kind of women that Evita had appealed to in her speeches addressed to those who were "born for the home," those who accepted their "profession as women" (*My Mission* 189–90). Hebe de Bonafini recognized this, stating that the figure of Evita continues to represent, "in spite of all its contradictions, an emblematic image of liberty" (qtd. in Diago 216).

The seemingly contradictory character of motherhood that is at once essentialist ("born for") and acquired/performed ("profession") is at the basis of Evita's philosophy, the Madres' demonstration, and contemporary feminist thinking about what (if anything) constitutes *women* as a discrete social or political category. Nowhere is this theory clearer than in the political constitution of the category "women" that Evita brought into public focus. For Evita, "women" were those who accepted their domestic roles. Those who did not— regardless of their biological sex—were accused of "want[ing] to stop being women" (*My Mission* 185) and dismissed as "a strange breed of woman . . . which never seemed to me to be entirely womanly!" (186). Evita sought to extend political visibility and representation to women as she defined and constituted them. Thus, as Butler notes, women are not simply a preexisting category of political subjects in need of representation: women are the *product* of political representation. Only one kind of woman, the one who accepts her domestic "destiny" and "mission" (190), is a *real* woman according to Evita. Thus only one kind of women's movement was possible. The other, the one led by "feminists," said Evita, "seemed to me ridiculous. For, not led by women but by those who aspired to be men, it ceased to be womanly and was nothing!" (186).

In speaking of the Madres' movement in terms of performance, then, I wish to make the connection between the public and ritualistic display of mourning and protest orchestrated by the Madres, and the notion of motherhood and womanhood as a product of a coercive system of representation that promoted certain roles as acceptable for females and eclipsed (and at times literally "disappeared") other ways of being.

The Madres' Movement: An Overview

The Madres' strategy, like the military junta's, was performative and communicative. Their aim was to insert themselves into the public sphere and make visible another version of events. For those unfamiliar with the Madres, I include a brief overview of their movement. At 11 A.M. on Saturday, April 30, 1977, fourteen Madres first took to the plaza to collectively demand information concerning the whereabouts of their loved ones. The women had met in government offices, prisons, and courts looking for their missing children. As soon as they got to the square, the women knew they had miscalculated; while the Plaza de Mayo is the political, financial, and symbolic center of Buenos Aires, it was empty on Saturday mornings. They realized immediately that they had to make a spectacle. Only by being visible could they be politically effective. Only by being visible could they stay alive. Visibility was both a refuge and a trap—a trap because the military knew who their opponents were but a refuge insofar as the women were only safe when they were demonstrating. Attacks on them usually took place as they were going home from the plaza.

So the Madres started meeting on Thursday afternoons at 3:30. They walked counterclockwise around the obelisk in the plaza right in front of the Casa Rosada. They started wearing white kerchiefs to identify themselves publicly as a group. They turned their bodies into walking billboards, carrying banners, placards, and photographs of their children. Gradually, the number of women grew. They belonged to different social classes (54 percent working class) and religious groups and came from different parts of Argentina. Most of the disappeared were in their early twenties, 30 percent were working class, 21 percent were students, a third of the victims were women. In July there were 150 Madres. Public response to their activities was mixed. Though Amnesty International had sent a mission to Argentina in 1976 and reported on the disappeared, neither the government nor the general public paid much attention. Most Argentines tried to ignore the Madres who tried to make the "disappearances" visible. Some Argentines crossed the street to distance themselves as much as possible from the women. Some passersby insulted them; others whispered support and solidarity. On October 5, 1977, they placed an ad in *La prensa* demanding the "truth" about 237 disappeared persons, accompanied by pictures of the victims and the signatures and identity card numbers of the Madres. They got no reply. Ten days later, hundreds of women delivered a petition with twenty-four thousand signatures demanding an investigation into the disappearances. The police tried to disperse them, spraying tear gas at the women, shooting bullets into the air and detaining over three hundred of them for questioning. Foreign correspondents, the only ones to cover the event, were also arrested. News of the Madres and their anti-junta activities soon spread internationally. The battle for visibility commanded more and more attention. Largely due to the public recognition and financial support from human rights groups from the Netherlands, Sweden, France, and Italy, the Madres were able to survive politically and financially. In 1977, President Carter sent Patricia Derian, U.S. assistant secretary of state, to investigate the accusations of human rights abuses; she estimated that three thousand people had been executed and five thousand disappeared (Simpson and Bennett 279). The United States cut military aid to Argentina and canceled $270 million in loans. Although the junta tried to dismiss the Madres as *locas* (madwomen), they realized they had to get rid of them. So in December of that year, they infiltrated the Madres' organization and kidnapped and disappeared twelve women, including the leader of the Madres, Azucena de Vicenti, and two French nuns. But the Madres continued to return to the plaza. During 1978, the military intensified its harassment and detentions of the Madres. In 1979, it became impossible for them to enter the plaza, which was cordoned off by heavily armed police. The women

Figure 43. Las Madres raiding the Plaza de Mayo. (Photo by Daniel García)

would stand around the plaza and raid it—dashing across the square before the police could stop them, in order to remind the world and themselves that this was still their space (see figure 43).

In 1979, the Organization of American States (OAS) sent the Inter-American Human Rights Commission to Argentina. The Madres organized to bring mothers from all over the country to testify before the commission in Buenos Aires. As many as three thousand people lined up at a time to testify before the commission (Navarro "Personal," 253). The junta, unable to block the investigation, launched its own counterattack of inscribing slogans on people, mimicking the visual strategies the Madres used. They made up posters and used bodies as walking billboards marked with a pun on human rights: "Somos derechos y humanos [We are right and human]." In that year, practically banished from the plaza, the Madres formed the Association of the Madres de Plaza de Mayo. In January 1980, the Madres returned to the plaza, ready to face death before relinquishing it again.

Over the years, the Madres' notion of motherhood gradually became political rather than biological. Each came to consider herself the mother of all the disappeared, not just her own offspring. Their spectacles became larger and increasingly dramatic. They organized massive manifestations and marches, some of them involving up to two hundred thousand people: the March of Resistance in 1981, and again the following year; in 1982 the March for Life and the March for Democracy; in 1983, at the end of the last military junta, they plastered Buenos Aires with the names and silhouettes of the disappeared (see figure 44). In 1986, when it became clear that Alfonsín's government would do nothing meaningful to punish those responsible for the atrocities, they staged the March for Human Rights as a procession of masks (see figure 45).

However, redefining motherhood has also been problematic for the Madres. Individually, many Madres admitted that they had lost hope of finding their children alive: "We know we're not going to find our children by going to the square, but it's an obligation we have to all the *desaparecidos*" (qtd. in Fisher 153). The tension between the biological death of their children and the living political issue of disappearance and criminal politics placed them in a conflicted situation. Were they now simply the mothers of dead children? If so, should they claim the dead bodies offered up by forensic specialists, accept compensation, and get on with their lives? Did they need to hold onto the missing bodies in order to bring the military to justice and continue their political movement? Could the Madres, now a political organization, survive the death of their children? By 1986, the dilemma had split the group in two.[3] The group that now calls itself the Madres de la Plaza de Mayo, headed by Hebe de Bonafini (as opposed to the Línea Fundadora (Founding Group) headed by Renée Epelbaum) felt committed to keeping the *desaparecidos* alive. They demanded "Aparición con vida [Back alive]" for all the disappeared (see figure 46). However, their list of the disappeared no longer includes the children of the Línea Fundadora. The Línea Fundadora, on the other hand, continues to work to bring the perpetrators to justice. They too travel, lecture abroad, and document their history with the names of both the victims and victimizers left off other lists or written out of other histories. Both groups, made up mainly of women in their sixties and seventies, continue to march around the Plaza de Mayo.

Some Problems with the "Mother" Problem

The Madres' movement, most scholars would agree, is full of contradictions. Their conscious political aim was to incriminate the Argentine junta and bring their children's torturers and murderers to trial. They succeeded in seriously damaging the junta's legitimacy and credibility—aided by Argentina's failing economy and the military's own gross errors in judgment, particularly in the Falklands/Malvinas war. They also saw nine leaders from the three successive

Figure 44. Silhouettes of the disappeared. (Photo by Cristina Fraire)

Figure 45. "March for Human Rights." (Photo by Raphael Wollmann)

juntas face the most publicized trial in the country's history.[4] The Madres staged one of the most powerful, courageous and influential resistance movements of our times. In Suárez-Orozco's words, they "turned an interrupted mourning process (no bodies, hope, uncertainty) around and articulated out of their maternal pain and rage (their words) and survivor's guilt one of the most visible political discourses of resistance to terror in recent Latin American history. The mothers, by coming together to find out what was done to their children, subverted the silence and the centrifugal isolationism imposed during the years of terror by forcing public debate over the years of terror" ("The Heritage of Enduring a 'Dirty War' " 491).

Without diminishing the importance of what scholars such as Sara Ruddick have called the Madres' "politics of resistance" (227), commentators interested in the Madres and other women's political groups in and outside Latin America have pointed out the many contradictions posed by their movement—a movement that destabilized the military but left a restrictive patriarchal system basically unchallenged. The Madres won significant political power, but they claim not to want that power for themselves but only for their children. The women's shared struggle for missing children bridged class and religious barriers in Argentina, but the Madres have not politicized those issues. They

Figure 46. Hebe de Bonafini and the Madres demanding
"back alive!" (Photo by Guillermo Loiácono)

recognize that "women are doubly oppressed, especially in Catholic-Hispanic countries" (Fisher 155), and they have formed alliances with women's coalitions in Nicaragua, El Salvador, Uruguay, Colombia, Chile, and other Latin American countries. But they are not feminists, if by feminism one refers to the politicization of the female's subordinate status.[5] The Madres left the confines of their homes, physically and politically, but they have not altered the politics of the home, for example, the gendered division of labor; after coming home from their demonstrations most of them still cooked and did housework for their remaining family, even in those cases in which the husbands were at home full time. The Madres took to the streets in order to protect their children and families; nonetheless, their political activity estranged many of them from the surviving family members who were not prepared to accept the women's new roles: "They say if you stop going to the square, you're one of us again. My family now are the Mothers of the Plaza de Mayo," says one Madre (qtd. in Fisher 156). Having left home, they have established a new *casa* (home) for their new family. There, they continue their unpaid labor, their political activity. There, too, they nurture the young people who come to talk to them: "We cook for them, we worry about their problems, we look out for them much as we did for our children" (qtd. in Diago 187).

How to explain these contradictions? Some commentators, such as Beatriz Schmukler and Laura Rossi, both from Argentina, gloss over the contradictions; they "are not interested" in examining them (Rossi 146). Rather, they focus on the positive aspects of the movement and dismiss its limitations. Other commentators stress the importance of gender in regard to the women's political activism. "The Madres are notable in that they are strictly a woman's movement," writes the Argentine sociologist María del Carmen Feijoó.[6] Elsewhere, she and Mónica Gogna stress that it was the women's idea to go to the square and that their men had little faith in the strategy.[7] Suárez-Orozco notes "the very important gender bifurcation" evident in the fact that the Madres "turned private pain, rage and terror into a *collective* project of resistance, while fathers of the disappeared turned inward, often isolating themselves from any collective projects, often going into major narcissistic depressive states and developing high morbidity and death rates" ("The Heritage of Enduring a 'Dirty War' " 497). The question, for some Argentine commentators, was merely *which* gender identity the Madres were performing. One Argentine journalist put it simply: the Madres were the only ones who had balls. Hebe de Bonafini herself refers to having balls, suggesting perhaps that by rejecting their legitimate roles as domestic mothers, the Madres had crossed the gender line (Diago 82). Laura Rossi disagrees. It's not that the Madres had "balls." "Rather it is precisely this lack that constitutes the Madres of the Plaza de Mayo. Their access to politics is a product of this lack. Absence of the son . . . The Madres perform [literally *make*] politics starting from the empty void simultaneously covered over and revealed by the nostalgic and grotesque metaphor—having balls. Their power lies in not having them but, rather, in their lack. Theirs is not the power of force but the power of weakness—the strength," and here Rossi quotes an unidentified Spanish feminist, "that generates from that hole within . . . the power of the cunt" (152). Rossi concludes her study on the Madres noting that with "the power of the cunt the Madres ignited the wick of powerlessness. Through powerlessness, they changed reality in a way that power itself was not able to achieve" (153). Others scoffed at the Madres' "weakness" as a "female luxury."[8]

Performing Motherhood

Some of the contradictions can be understood, I believe, by distinguishing between the Madres' performance of motherhood and the essentialist notions of motherhood sometimes attributed to them and which, in all fairness, the Madres themselves often accentuate. Although much has been written about the Madres' strategy of politicizing motherhood, little has been said about the fact that motherhood—as a role—had already been socialized and politicized through patriarchy. Thus it is always already performative. What we see, then, are conflicting performances of motherhood, one supporting the military's narrative, one defying it.[9] Once they decided to march, the Madres' self-representation was as theatrical as the military's. The Madres' movement did not begin when the individual mothers became acquainted in their search for their children; it originated when the women consciously decided to protest and agitate *as* mothers. That *as* marks the conceptual distance between the essentialist notion of motherhood attributed to the Madres and the self-conscious manipulation of the maternal role—understood as performative— that makes the movement the powerful and intensely dramatic spectacle that it has been. María del Rosario, a Madre, wrote a poem in August 1977 that conveys the women's consciousness of their participation as *role* in the Argentine tragedy:

> With our wounds exposed to the sun, Plaza de Mayo,
> We show you these Argentine mothers . . .
> historical witnesses to the nation,
> in silence, like beaten dogs,
> we walk across your paving stones.
> (Qtd. in Fisher 89)

The women, most of whom had no political background or experience, realized that they were a part of a national spectacle and decided to actively play the roles that had traditionally been assigned to them: the beaten dogs watching in silence, the underdogs, the powerless who cannot speak yet nonetheless witness and testify to the crimes. Yet they shifted the site of their enactment from the private sphere, where it could be construed as essentialist, to the public, where it became a bid for political recognition by means of what U.S. scholars would call "identity politics." The Madres' decision to make their presence visible in the plaza, stage center so to speak, was a brilliant and courageous move. While the plaza had been the locus of Argentina's community building, no one had used it as the Madres did, much less during a state of siege in which public space was heavily policed. They perceived and literally acted out the difference between motherhood as an individual identity (which for many of them it was) and motherhood as a collective, political performance that would allow women to protest in the face of a criminal dictatorship. "We show you these Argentine Mothers," writes María del Rosario in a self-conscious expression of mother-hood somewhat different from the "we" who performs it because it is mediated through the public space of the "you" (the plaza) that transforms their identity from an individual to a political one. María del Rosario speaks, but the Madres are silent. The role of mother was attractive, not because of its "natural" or essentialist qualities, but because it was viable and practical. It offered the women a certain legitimacy and authority in a society that values mothers almost to the exclusion of all other women. It offered them, they believed, a certain protection against retribution—for a military that sustained itself on Christian and family values could hardly attack a group of defenseless mothers inquiring after their missing children. It offered them visibility in a representational system that rendered most women invisible, for, among the few roles open to Argentine women, the suffering mother is the most popular and certainly the most socially rewarding. As the dramatist Diana Raznovich observes in *Casa Matriz,* her play about a "substitute" mother rented from an agency which specializes in fulfilling its client's fantasies, "You can't ask for a more tragic effect . . . I am the suffering mother *par excellence.* Dressed in black, scrubbing, weeping . . . I am the Great Suffering Mother, the Mother immortalized by the tango. Literature is full of me. I'm the biblical mother, 'in sorrow thou shalt bring forth children.' I'm the holy Mother. Just look at these big fat tears!"[10] As the Madres recount how they dressed down as dowdy old women and became quick-change artists—some of them slipping on less traditionally motherly attire to escape arrest—playing the role of mother was also fun and empowering. For once, they manipulated the images that previously had controlled them.

Unfortunately for women generally, and Latin American women particularly, there are few good roles.[11] The Madres attempted the seemingly impossible—a public demonstration of maternal protest, in itself a contradiction in terms. From a representational point of view, the image nullified itself even as it came into being. "Public" women in Latin America, as Jean Franco notes, are considered prostitutes or madwomen—that is, nonmothers, even antimothers.[12] Evita was very aware that to augment her political efficacy she had to downplay her visibility. Perón was "the figure," she said, and "I the shadow" (qtd. in Fisher 9). *Good* mothers are invisible. They do not gather in groups; they stay home with their children. And as the childless Evita once had said, "the home is the sanctuary of motherhood and the pivot of society. It is the appropriate sphere in which women, for the good of their country and for their own children, fulfill their patriotic duty daily" (qtd. in Fisher 9). She resolved the contradiction by declaring herself "the mother of my people," working in the "great home of the Motherland."[13]

The Madres tried to overcome the limitations intrinsic to the role of motherhood by modeling themselves on the Virgin Mary, the ultimate mother who transcends the public-private bind by carrying her privacy with her even in public. Thus, Christian and Jewish women alike initially played the Mater Dolorosa and exploited a system of representations and stereotypes that had so effectively limited most forms of visibility and expression: "At first they marched as if in ritual procession: faces serious, eyes turned upward in supplication, heads covered . . . peaceful, rapt, pleading" (Diago 29). For the Madres, the boundaries of domesticity were also inside and outside. Hebe de Bonafini, for example, has been known to demonstrate in her bedroom slippers to underline the hominess, and thus nonthreatening aspect, of their movement. The women may have stepped outside the home momentarily, the slippers suggest, but they take their home with them wherever they go. The virginal role allowed the women to perform traditionally acceptable "feminine" qualities: self-sacrifice, suffering, irrationality.

Again, the statements from various mothers indicate that the choice of the qualities was based more on accessibility and viability than on their political or ideological commitment to traditional values.[14] Even as they took one of the most daring steps imaginable in their particular political arena, they affirmed their passivity and powerlessness. They, as the poem makes clear, exposed their wounds. They were both Christ and Mary, victim and witness. As Feijoó notes, they incorporated a "feminine logic based on respect for the traditional role of women, who are thought to be altruistic and vicarious. This made it possible for women to reject a conventional political model of participation based on the 'rational calculation of costs and benefits' and to substitute another one based on 'sacrifice.' Despite its sex role conventionality, traditionalism became a daring gesture, an indictment of its original meaning of passivity and submission."[15]

Yet even that virginal role—sanctified by Argentine society though it was—did not protect the women for long. The women's public exposure resulted in their being ostracized from the church. They had gone beyond the representational constraints of the role: pain was permissible, perhaps, but not anger. Silence, maybe, but not protest. As Monsignor Quarracino commented: "I can't imagine the Virgin Mary yelling, protesting and planting the seeds of hate when her son, our Lord, was torn from her hands."[16] But the hypocrisy of the church was made painfully visible in the campaign, organized by the Madres, of "reappearing" the missing through silhouettes. The silhouette in figure 47 of the disappeared pregnant woman and her husband, riddled with bullet holes, is positioned next to the icon of the Virgin Mary. It reminds viewers that for the church, only some women are special, only certain maternal bonds are valued. The others "disappear."

The Madres attempted to manipulate the maternal image that was already

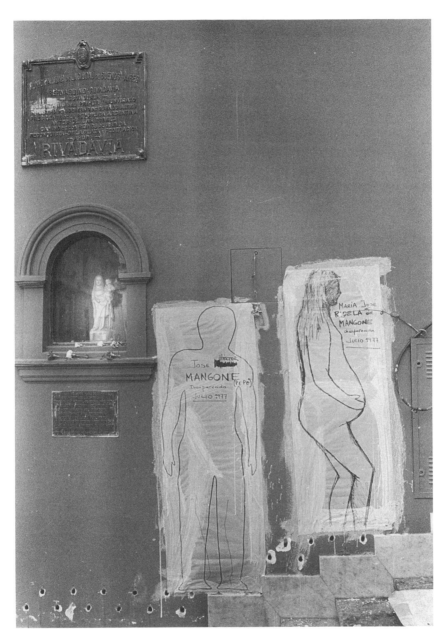

Figure 47. Inscribing the walls of the Metropolitan Cathedral.
(Photo by Guillermo Loiácono)

overdetermined by the state. The "motherhood" performed by the Madres was, after all, designed by the patriarchal system they lived in. The military attempted to capitalize on women's traditional duties and exploit them further by pressuring mothers to police their children. Through the media, they reminded the women repeatedly that it was their patriotic responsibility to know where their children were, who they kept company with, and what they were doing: Do you know where your child is? How did you bring up your child? The Madres turned that reasoning around, claiming that it was precisely their maternal responsibilities that took them to the plaza in search of their children. This was, the Madres made believe, a *private* matter, a *family* matter. If the personal had become political, and the Madres had to take to the streets, it was not because they were feminists but because the military had blurred private-public distinctions by raiding homes and snatching children in the dead of night. One of the most interesting political conflicts of the period, then, was the struggle to define and control "motherhood." In opposition to the church and the state that attempted to lock women in passive, domestic roles, Hebe de Bonafini came to identify the Madres as those who had left their patriarchal home behind and "who have broken with many of the aspects of this system we live in" (qtd. in Fisher 157).

The Madres threatened the military's all-male parade in part because they refused to comply with the military's version of events and forget about their children, in part because they embodied the birthing capabilities that the junta had claimed for itself. Moreover, they destabilized the visible field and resemanticized the terms of the struggle. They responded to the military spectacle with a spectacle that inverted the focus. What had been invisible before—domestic women as well as "subversives"—was now visible for the world to see. Ironically, the women made invisible by patriarchy and disappeared into the home became the spokespeople for the disappeared. By "outing" the disappearance of their children they came out as disappeared themselves. They appeared as the disappeared. The women, by exposing the missing, also exposed themselves. And unlike the military, they showed their wounds rather than their instruments. Or, rather, the Madres' wounds were their instruments. By exposing themselves, sacrificing themselves, they sought to expose the violent politics the military tried to cover up. Through their bodies, they wanted to show the absence/presence of all those who had disappeared without a trace, without leaving a body. Clearly, the confrontation between the Madres and the military centered on the physical and semantic location of the missing body—the object of exchange in this battle of images. While the military attempted to make their victims invisible and anonymous by burying them in unmarked graves, dumping their bodies into the sea, or cutting them up and burning them in ovens, the Madres insisted that the disappeared had names and faces. They were people; people did not simply disappear; their bodies, dead or alive, were somewhere; someone had done something to them. Instead of the military's ahistorical forgetting, the Madres inscribed the times and dates of the disappearances. Instead of dismembering, remembering. The Madres challenged the generals' claim to history by writing themselves and the disappeared into the narrative, literally as well as figuratively. Their bodies, inscribed with names, dates, and faces, were "written into the message," to borrow a phrase from Ross Chambers.[17] Opposed to the image projected by the junta of a lone, heroic male leaving family and community behind, the Madres emphasized community and family ties. Instead of the military's performance of hierarchy, represented by means of rigid, straight rows, the Madres' circular movements around the plaza, characterized by their informal talk and pace, bespoke values based on egalitarianism and communication. While the soldiers' uniforms, paraphernalia, and body language emphasized the performative aspects of gender, the Madres too were highly conscious of the importance of their gender role, specifically their maternal role, and played it accordingly. The Madres also had their "uniforms," though these may not have been immediately identifiable as such. They presented themselves as elderly, physically weak, and sexually nonactive women. Yet they resisted even the most brutal treatment. When the military tried to force the women from the plaza, they marked their presence indelibly by painting white kerchiefs around the circle where they usually walked. Instead of the empty streets and public spaces mandated by the military curfew, the Madres orchestrated the return of the repressed. Buenos Aires was once again filled with people; spectacular bodies, ghostly, looming figures who refused to stay invisible. The armed forces were, once again, in the ludicrous position of having to police ghosts (see figure 48). The public spaces overflowed with demonstrators as the terrorized population gradually followed the Madres' example and took to the streets (see figure 49).

The Madres' spectacle and script relied as much on myth making as the military's did. They too had to justify their actions by appealing to "nature." Hebe de Bonafini expresses the Madres' belief that "our movement stems from our identity as mothers. Mothers are the ones that breast-feed, raise and look after their children. This is historically true. If the child [son] is in trouble, it is the mother that comes to his help. If he's taken prisoner, it is she who defends him and visits him in jail. The mother-lion is a very central figure" (qtd. in Diago 121). This rhetoric, which sounds as suspect as the military discourse, is not, I would claim, an expression of the Madres' belief in woman's place in the

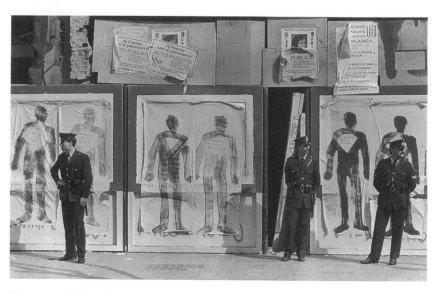

Figure 48. Policing ghosts. (Photo by Guillermo Loiácono)

"natural" order but, rather, an attempt to ground their identity politics and legitimate their struggle. So too their use of spectacle looked "natural" and simple. They, like the military, also stressed universal, immutable, and eternal values. They represented motherhood as something forever fixed. They seemingly adhered to the tradition of women's lamentations that dates back more than twenty-five hundred years to Greek drama, in which women express protest through public demonstrations of pain and sorrow. In Argentina's tragic scenario, the Madres embodied "pity" while the military males staged "terror." But pity and terror are inextricably linked. As the Greek theatre scholar Gilbert Murray notes in his foreword to *The Trojan Women*, "pity is a rebel passion. Its hand is against the strong, against the organised force of society, against conventional sanctions and accepted Gods . . . it is apt to have those qualities of unreason, of contempt for the counting of costs and the balancing of sacrifices, of recklessness, and even, in the last resort, of ruthlessness . . . It brings not peace, but a sword" (7). The military, quick to pick up the threatening quality of the Madres' pitiful display of their wounds-as-weapons, branded the rebellious women *emotional terrorists*.

Commentators find it hard to agree on the short- and long-term effects of the Madres' activism. During the Dirty War, the Madres provided the families of the disappeared a model of resistance to atrocity as well as a network of

Figure 49. Taking to the streets. (Photo by Guillermo Loiácono)

communication and support. The Madres would find out information about a detained or disappeared person and transmit it nationally. The women raised money to allow families around the country to travel to ask about their missing children or to visit a political prisoner. The Madres' organization contributed money to raise the children of the disappeared who had been left behind with relatives or friends. Long term, however, some commentators stress that the Madres changed little in Argentina. Some say that the Madres' grassroots movement lacked any lasting organizational structure. Clearly, the women called international attention to civil rights violations taking place in Argentina. But though the Madres' spectacle was a powerful manifestation of personal courage and moral resistance to oppression, it did little to stop international aid to the armed forces. Carter took the atrocity seriously and cut aid to Argentina, but the United States under Reagan increased its support of the armed forces and their "war" on subversion. The downfall of the military and the "end" of the Dirty War came with the Argentine invasion of the Islas Malvinas, the British-owned Falkland Islands, that lie off its coast. Plagued by a crashing economy and an increasingly irate population, the military decided to bolster its popularity by taking the islands. But the armed forces miscalculated Britain's resolve to keep the islands, for one thing, the islands have substantial oil deposits, for another, Margaret Thatcher herself needed a boost in popular opinion. The humiliating defeat of the Argentine military, which was also held responsible for the deaths of almost a thousand very young and untrained conscripts, brought down the last of the three juntas.

However, there is perhaps a different way of looking at the long-term changes that, indirectly perhaps, stemmed from the Madres' movement. Although the Madres did not politicize the situation of women in Argentina, social conditions improved for women after the end of the Dirty War. Jane Jaquette sees a connection between human rights advocates and feminists growing as a response to violence against women. The fact that women could talk about rape and violence against women as a political crime and human rights issue empowered feminists to decry those crimes in the domestic arena, in which 95 percent of the victims are women.[18] But this indirect connection may hold for other areas as well. The danger that accompanied the junta's display of male virility and impunity led to a more general realization of the dangers attending the socialization of macho masculinity and *hombría a golpes* (maleness by blows). The fact that the Madres had been so visibly active in the search for their missing children might have influenced the creation of Law 23.264, passed in 1985, that finally gave mothers equal rights with fathers in the care and custody of their children (*patria potestad*). With the return to democracy, several women's rights that had been suspended under the military were reinstated. Family planning, prohibited during the dictatorship, became legal again in December 1986 (Decree 2274); divorce was reinstated in 1987 (Decree 23.515). Laws were passed defending women in the workplace; equal pay for equal work and equal opportunity programs were initiated to protect women from discrimination in the labor force. Laws protecting women from sexual harassment were passed in November 1993 (Decree 2385). In order to increase women's role in the political process, a law passed in 1991 (Ley del 30%) mandated that at least 30 percent of the candidate pool for every elected office be made up of women. As a result, in 1993 women held 13.6 percent of the seats in the Senate. While none of these gains can be related to the Madres' movement in any clear-cut way, the Madres' subordinate status was also written into their message on human rights and was politicized by groups other than their own—specifically, feminist groups.

Questions as to the efficacy of the Madres' movement in the political realm are locked into two interconnected issues: their use of identity politics and their use of performance. How can identity politics effectively liberate political actors from stereotypes and systems of representation that have previously precluded political activism? Ross Chambers posits a double hypothesis pertaining to identity politics: "(1) to have a cultural identity (in the sense of an individual's being subsumed into a categorized group on the assumption of self-sameness) is tantamount to being appropriated into the position of cultural mediator or mediating other, with respect to a community of differentiating communicating subjects—a community whose own cultural status is 'forgotten' by its members while it is in fact constituted by the construction of the cultural other that mediates it—then (2) that other who is inscribed, however faceless and namelessly, in the community's messages as the object of an appropriating gesture is also, inevitably, included in that community's affairs, and forms part of its culture, by virtue of the very gesture that seeks to distance it" ("No Montagues" 9–10). In my reading, the Madres' use of identity politics, following Chambers's model, and their move for political visibility are, on one hand, self-defeating because they are drawn into (appropriated by) the discourse and logic from which they are trying to differentiate. They are sucked into a battle of images that is played through them, and around them, which allows for the communication of individuated subjects (politicians) while they themselves remain faceless and nameless (the Madres). The women's attempt to identify politically as mothers, following Chambers's thinking, amounts to falling into the negative "feminine" stereotype that they need to avoid in order to be politically effective.

This same problem plagues their performance. The Madres played into a national fantasy predicated on sexual difference that explains male potency and dominance and the female's lack thereof. Much as the military's performance was a display of virility, the Madres' spectacle was a public display of *lack*. They made it evident that they had no previous political identity or background, no expertise—they were just housewives; they had no power, no weapons, just absence, missing children (whom they repeatedly refer to as *sons*, thereby eliding the daughters once again), who were no longer there. Locked in a quasi-Oedipal *script* (as opposed to *complex*) that has problematized generational and family boundaries for thousands of years, the Madres mediated between warring fathers and sons. While consciously performing motherhood, the Madres were trapped in a bad script. They even perpetuated the Oedipal framing of events by repeatedly asserting that they had been made pregnant by their children (Diago 79). The potential for equality and power, the women claimed, could only be regained by means of the restitution of the missing member, the lost phallus. They represented themselves as nothing but the empty conduits through which the phallus (penis) passed to produce the new Man: "the day will come when one of our sons, whoever he might be, will cross the Plaza de Mayo and enter the Government Building; and that young man, that man will be our son" (Diago 169). The women speak of themselves as the furrow in which the seed of the future was planted (Diago 169). "Today," Marguerite

Bouvard writes, "the Mothers continue to speak of giving multiple births, of creating offspring who will continue the revolution they have initiated, which is at once political, social and humanitarian. An editorial in their newspaper proclaimed, in May, 1990, 'Last Thursday the Mothers in the Plaza felt as if they were giving birth again because of all the Latin American children who were present meeting with Argentine youth.' "[19]

The political dénouement of this national fantasy was predictable, built into the fantasy itself. The "son," according to the scenario, cannot afford to ally himself with the weak mother. He must identify with the father and bypass her to join the ranks of power. Like the lone soldier male, he may cast one nostalgic look behind. National reconciliation leaves women on the sidelines, somehow marginal to the happy ending. As one Madre describes: "We helped the political parties . . . thanks to us marching at the front, they were able to open a way to elections. If not, they wouldn't be where they are today, in Congress" (qtd. in Fisher 112). Another adds: "We knocked on their doors many times and they wouldn't let us in" (qtd. in Fisher 113). The negotiations between the fathers and sons were hammered out on the women's backs in a move that Chambers has called "the back-grounding of the mediating instance" ("No Montagues" 10). The Madres have also been ignored by the Argentine media: "There is a conspiracy of silence. They never publish our communiques and they don't mention our participation in events or cover our demonstrations . . . The police filmed us, but the media, no." And because they know that publicity is essential to their group's survival, they realize that "if they don't write about us, we don't exist" (qtd. in Fisher 144).

The Madres' movement, the women seem to be saying, exists only in representation. I would agree but go further and say that, to a degree, the women were framed. It seems to me that the maternal role they chose to unite them was highly problematic. When the Madres decided to go beyond their individual search for their children and politicize motherhood, that decision was a conscious political choice—they could have (for example) performed as women, wives, sisters, or human rights activists. Motherhood seemed the logical choice for identity politics. The maternal image appears to be endlessly generous and expandable; it has a long and noble tradition in Argentina; many could identify with the mother figure and a whole group of women could share her suffering. Yet the assumption of sameness obscured real political, class, and social differences of Argentine women and limited the arena of confrontation. By the very fact that the maternal image subsumes boundaries, it also subsumes difference. What happens to other Argentine women who want to speak and act for themselves rather than for or through their children? What happens to the other issues (in addition to human rights violations) and other roles (in addition to motherhood) that need to be publicized and politicized? By taking on that one role to the exclusion of others (as one does in theatrical performance) the Madres were unable to maximize their political options in order to modify the environment that had proved so damaging not only to their children, but to women in general. It is not, I believe, that they did not want to include these other issues. Their individual statements attest to their concern with many social and political issues. However, the role did not allow for their politicization. Rather, the maternal role once again relegated the women to the subordinate position of mediators in an old drama between fathers and sons. Communication took place through and around them, yet they were dismissed and ignored as background noise. Once again, much as in the military discourse, the historical and material conditions of real women are eclipsed behind the image of Woman. As the women marched around the plaza, as they were harassed, arrested, tortured, and disappeared, the battle continued to be fought on the female body.

On one level, then, I have to conclude that the military and the Madres reenacted a collective fantasy, a *paso de dos*, that reaffirmed the negativity of the female partner and made it difficult for her to extricate herself. The performances staged by each reconstituted the stereotypical binaries: the military acted, the Madres reacted; the junta's narrative had a linear progression while the circular, repetitive nature of the Madres' demonstrations suggested—from a representational point of view—that they weren't going anywhere. The Madres challenged the military but played into the narrative. The junta might be performing the authoritarian father while the Madres took the role of the castrated mother, but both parties were reenacting the same old story. Their positions were, in a sense, already scripted. Their participation in the national tragedy depended little on their individual position as subjects. On the contrary: their very subjectivity was a product of their position in the drama.

Looking beyond the maternal role, however, and looking at the individual women who walked away from the plaza, I see a group of women who redefined the meaning of *mothers, family,* and *home* in a patriarchal society. Mothers, flesh-and-blood women, are now more free to act and take to the streets. They can be bold, independent, political, and outraged even as they take on the role of the submissive, domestic creature. Their new "home" is a negotiated space; their new "family" founded on political rather than biological ties. What has been accepted as the Madres' traditionalism in fact has more to do with the negotiated alliances of feminists. Their new family reminds me of what Cherríe Moraga, in *Giving Up the Ghost,* calls "making familia from scratch / each time all over again . . . with strangers / if I must. / If I must, I will" (58). The women may choose to adhere to their old ways, re-create a "familia," and cook for the younger members of the group, but that is now a choice they exercise. Their political activism, explicitly designed to empower the new Man, in fact made new people out of the Madres, people with options. As Hebe de Bonafini says, "For me cooking for twenty is the same as cooking for one, and we like to eat together because this is also a part of our struggle and our militancy. I want to continue being the person I've always been. Sometimes I'm criticized for wearing a housecoat and slippers in public but I'm not going to change. Of course my life is different" (qtd. in Fisher 158). The performance of motherhood has created a distance between "I" and the "person I've always been." It is as if the women's conscious performance of motherhood—restrictive and problematic though it was—freed them from the socially restrictive role of motherhood that had previously kept them in their place. The performance offered that disruptive space, that moment of transition between the "I" who is a mother and the "I" who chooses to perform motherhood.

The performative aspect, as I see it, was a politically vital and personally liberating aspect of the Madres' movement in several ways. For one, the demonstrations offered the women a way of coping with their grief and channeling it to life-affirming action. Rather than trivialize or eclipse their loss, the performative nature of their demonstrations gave the women a way of dealing with it. Much as in the case of mourning rites, aesthetic distancing is an enabling response to pain, not its negation. For another, the ritualistic and "restored" nature of their demonstrations succeeded in drawing much-needed public attention to their cause, both nationally and internationally. This put them in contact with human rights organizations worldwide and provided them with financial and moral support as well as the much needed legitimacy to offset the junta's claims that the women were only raving madwomen. Moreover, the "restored" nature of their public action in itself was a way of restoring the disappeared into the public sphere, of making visible their absence. And, by bringing motherhood out of the home, the Madres showed up the predicament facing women in Argentina and the world over. Traditionally, mothers have been idealized as existing somehow beyond or above the political arena. Confined to the home, they have been made responsible for their children. But what happens to the mothers who, by virtue of that same responsibility to their children, must go looking for them outside the home and confront the powers that be? Do they cease to be mothers? Or must onlookers renounce notions of mothers as apolitical? Their transgression of traditional roles made evident how restrictive and oppressive those roles had been. Thus their performance of mothers as activists challenged traditional maternal roles and called attention to the fact that motherhood was a social, not just biological, construct.

The Madres' performance, like all performances, challenged the onlooker. Would the national and international spectators applaud their actions or look away? join their movement or cross the street to avoid them? One letter to the editor of *La nación* asked the authorities to put an end "to the sad spectacle that we must endure week after week" (June 1, 1981, p. 6). But there were spectators who were able to respond as reliable audiences/witnesses, either because they saw the event from a safe distance or because they felt they had nothing more to lose. They helped introduce different perspectives and disrupt the show the military was staging about itself. Thus, though the Madres were caught within an ideological web of signification, their performance allowed them to destabilize it. The fact that the Madres could not do *everything*—that is, seriously challenge patriarchal authority—does not mean that they did *nothing* to challenge its defenders. Being trapped in or by the drama, extremely limiting though it was, need not imply that there is no "outside." One way of imagining an "outside" is perhaps implicit in the performance model itself. Performance, as a carrying through, needs the audience to complete its meaning, to tie the pieces together and give them coherence. The Madres relied for their efficacy and survival on capturing the attention of spectators—Argentines who might dare to reinterpret the junta's version of events as well as the foreign spectators who might feel compelled to bring pressure to bear on their governments. Moreover, the spectacle that the women made of their aged, maternal, yet nonetheless resistant bodies has prompted feminists from various backgrounds to rethink the seemingly unbridgeable schism between women's grassroots and feminist movements.[20]

The Madres had the courage to show the world what was happening in Argentina. They still continue their walk around the plaza at 3:30 on Thursday afternoons. They vow to do so until the government officially explains what happened to their missing children and brings their murderers to justice. There has been no closure. The drama is not over.

Trapped in Bad Scripts: Antígona furiosa *and the Madres de la Plaza de Mayo*

. . . all narrative may well be obituary in that it seeks a retrospective knowledge that comes after the end, which in human terms places it on the far side of death.—Elisabeth Bronfen, *Over Her Dead Body*

In the last part of this chapter I will explore how the Argentine feminist playwright Griselda Gambaro looks at the Madres in her play *Antígona furiosa* in an attempt to rearticulate and position the "feminine" in a masculinist structure and language predicated on its erasure. *Antígona furiosa* was written and premiered in Buenos Aires in 1986, the year after the sensational Trial of the Generals. The Dirty War was "over," at least, as Gambaro's play suggests, *for now*. Given the Oedipal overtones to the script, it is hardly surprising that an Antigone play should surface in relation to the Dirty War. The repeating narratives have explanatory and organizational power in interconnected social systems of representation, though traditionally we tend to think of them as divided into the seemingly separate categories of "art" and "life." The conflicts encapsulated in these stories, and the logic of their resolution, sometimes mirror each other self-consciously, but more often they seem to "appear" unselfconsciously in both. George Steiner, in listing the various versions of *Antigone,* notes that the motif comes up time and again not only in scripted form, but also spontaneously in the actions of real people:

> Even more pervasive, and altogether impossible to index, has been the role of the matter of Antigone in the actual lives of individuals and communities. It is a defining trait of western culture after Jerusalem and after Athens that in it men and women re-enact, more or less consciously, the major gestures, the exemplary symbolic motions, set before them by antique imaginings and formulations. Our realities, as it were, mime the canonic possibilities first expressed in classical art and feeling. In his diary for 17 September 1941, the German novelist and publicist Martin Raschke recounts an episode in Nazi-occupied Riga. Caught trying to sprinkle earth on the publicly exposed body of her executed brother, a young girl, entirely unpolitical in her sentiments, is asked why. She answers: "He was my brother. For me that is sufficient." (109)

The Dirty War, as I have argued throughout, was orchestrated by the military leaders in such a way as to exploit the foundational myths associated with nation-building. In their staging of power and order, the junta leaders re-enacted the "major gestures, the exemplary symbolic motions" referred to by Steiner. Given the narrative framework underwriting their rise to power, it seems inevitable that opposition to that heroic scenario should also be cast in terms of "antique imaginings and formulations." As I argued in terms of the Madres' movement, the junta's heroic self-representation simultaneously positioned the opposition. Unlike the Oedipal script, which focuses on generational father-son conflict and the male ruler's attempts to put an end to social crisis and *disease* through self-knowledge and the discovery of the Truth, the Antigone story illustrates the role allotted women in the dramatic dénouement.

Griselda Gambaro explicitly calls attention to the fact that she too will "mime the canonic possibilities first expressed in classical art and feeling" in order to stage women's defiance. She, like the Madres of the Plaza de Mayo, reappropriates the roles and language of heroic formulations and struggles to make them venues of resistance.

In *Antígona furiosa,* written and premiered three years after the fall of the military dictatorship, the characters speak to us from the far side of death. To paraphrase Bronfen's words, the play is both an obituary and a memento mori. It not only seeks "a retrospective knowledge that comes after the end" but is a warning that civil conflict and human sacrifice seem never-ending. Like Gambaro's other plays, beginning with the study of Argentina's quasi-fascist politics in *The Camp* (1965), *Antígona* places the current crisis in the context of a larger history of violence and criminal politics. In the first glimpse we have of Antígona, the protagonist removes the noose from her neck and returns to life, resuscitated from death, resuscitated from and through art. Once again her presence signals a national tragedy of civil violence, resistance, and enforced absenting, the death-in-life fate of both Antígona and the disappeared.

Clearly, there are many reasons why Gambaro would choose to draw on *Antigone* to represent the atrocities of the Dirty War. Latin American playwrights have long reworked classical material, sometimes to cast national conflicts in a "tragic" light, sometimes in order to circumvent censorship.[21] But the *Antigone* plot specifically raises questions about political leadership and misrule, about the conflict between the so-called private and public spaces, about public fear and complicity, about a population's duty to act as a responsible witness to injustice, and about social practices and duties predicated on sexual difference that were as urgent during the Dirty War as they were in 441 B.C. Sophocles' Creon sounds much like the junta leaders in his opening address when he announces the restoration of peace: "My countrymen, / The ship of state is safe" (ll. 179–80). He speaks of the "awesome task of setting the city's course" and adopting "the soundest policies" (l. 200). He seems entirely reasonable at the beginning, and is heralded by the Chorus as "the new man for the new day" (l. 174). But as in the case of the Argentine junta, it soon becomes clear that "the new man" is a tyrant and that ideological bonds outweigh the rights accorded to kinship and citizenship. Creon posits that "we can establish friendships, truer than blood itself" (l. 213), a position that relates closely to the junta's version of community and nationhood: "We cannot and should not consider the Marxist subversive terrorist our brother just because he was born in our Motherland. Ideologically, he has lost the honor of calling himself Argentine" (Frontalini and Caiati 22). When Sophocles' Antigone refuses to obey

Creon, she (like the *subversivos*) is reduced in status to a noncitizen, even a non-person, to "be stripped of her rights" (l. 976) and banished "alive to the caverns of the dead" (l. 1012). Like the *desaparecidos,* she "has no home on earth and none below / not with the living, nor with the breathless dead" (ll. 941–42).[22]

Gambaro's *Antígona furiosa* is both a quasi-faithful reworking of Sophocles' *Antigone* and a culturally specific reflection on the atrocities of the Dirty War. Gambaro uses the same plot: the fight to the death between Eteocles and Polynices, Antígona's decision to bury Polynices' exposed corpse, the argument between Creon and Haemon, Antígona's dirge, Tiresias's prophecy, and Antígona's death. She stages all this using only three characters, Coryphaeus, Antinous, and Antígona, who in turn represent the other figures, the Chorus, Creon, Tiresias, and Haemon.[23] The figure of Creon is represented by an empty shell that the different characters put on in order to give official orders—a gesture that undercuts the individuality that in Sophoclean tragedy accompanies tragic grandeur. The action of Sophocles' play (which runs 1470 lines—over sixty book pages) is telescoped into twenty pages. However, the explicit resuscitation of Antigone as the protagonist and the use of the three characters to enact all the others call attention to the fact that this is a highly self-conscious *re*writing. In certain parts of the play the characters recount the story, as if it had happened long ago (Coryphaeus: " 'Then she will die, but she will not die alone,' answered Haemon" [149]); or they anticipate a famous line from the Sophoclean script (Coryphaeus: "He'll make use of a masterly saying." Antinous: "Which one?" Coryphaeus: "One can rule a desert beautifully alone" [147]). Gambaro's version does not adhere to the linear development of the Greek original. Antígona, for example, continues to speak and narrate the actions taking place around her well after she has died in the earlier version.

The rewriting is both the theme and the strategy of Gambaro's enterprise. She constantly maintains a back-and-forth tension between Sophocles' work and her own, indicating that it is not only the universality of the subject matter that appeals to her but the specificity of her application of it to the Argentine situation. Thus, Sophocles' meditations on misrule, on woman's defiance, on death in Thebes provide a springboard for Gambaro's reflections on military misrule, on the Madres' movement, and on disappearance and death in Argentina. And, just as Sophocles' Chorus fails to understand the nature of the tragedy that it participates in and blames Antigone for her own fate (i.e., "Your own blind will, your passion has destroyed you" [l. 962], Coryphaeus and Antinous reflect the passivity and cynicism of much of the Argentine population that opted not to interfere with the atrocity taking place around them.[24] "I don't want to see it. I've already seen too much" (146).

The restaging serves several functions simultaneously. For one thing, by maintaining the tension between the two historical frames, Gambaro measures the distance/proximity between the "uncivilized" world and the contemporary horror of Argentine politics. If the struggle against barbarism has obsessed Argentine intellectuals and leaders since the time of Sarmiento, *Antígona furiosa* suggests that little progress has been made. In 1853, Matthew Arnold wrote that *Antigone* had lost its relevance because its subject matter—the desecration of the dead—was too barbaric and distant an act for contemporary audiences.[25] But the distance from barbarism, Arnold and Argentina's liberal founding fathers notwithstanding, cannot be measured in terms of chronological time or geographic space. Exposing the corpses of the military's victims was only part of the junta's horror show. Like Polynices' corpse, "an obscenity for the citizens to behold" (l. 231), the bodies of the junta's enemies were a message directed at the population as a whole. Much as in theatre, the bodies turned up as a revelation of obscene (etymologically related to off-scene, offstage) violence just beyond our field of vision. Moreover, the practice of disappearing bodies could, if anything, qualify as even more barbaric than exposing them—if ranking obscenities were the thing to do—for it precludes the very possibility of actions such as Antigone's mourning, burial rite, and defiance. The Madres have no bodies to honor and reclaim.[26]

The lines from *Hamlet,* the first uttered by Antígona onstage after the two *porteños* (natives of Buenos Aires) mistake her for Ophelia, further mark the distance between the past and the present.

> He is dead and gone, lady,
> He is dead and gone,
> At his head a grass-green turf,
> At his heels a stone.
> (137)

Instead of the "he is dead and gone" we have the reality of disappearance—"he" is gone and presumed dead, the terrifyingly ambiguous status of the junta's enemies. Death no longer has any markers: there are no visible tombs, no headstones, no grassy plots to attest to the event.

By rewriting these deaths, Gambaro not only shows that death isn't what it used to be; art isn't what it used to be either. Like many other Argentine writers and playwrights living during the Dirty War, Gambaro indicates that the function of art changes as history becomes a fiction. The erasure of death contributes to the erasure of history, the move on the part of the junta and on the part of Coryphaeus/Creon (the junta's counterpart in Gambaro's play) of burying factual specificity under universalities: "Always fights, battles, and blood" (140). The word "always" suggests that violence has become normative and that people no longer recognize it as such. The junta, as I have proposed, elevated their mission to heroic, transhistorical proportions, in part to obscure the atrocious particulars underwriting their project. Gambaro, on the contrary, situates the universalist qualities of Sophocles' play against the all-too-factual particulars in order to highlight the latter. History for the junta becomes "poetic," while tragic art, in the hands of Gambaro, becomes "historical." One of the reasons for restaging the Antigone story against the backdrop of a classical tragedy is to underline the specificity of the recomposition, the history of Argentina in the 1970s and 1980s. Death and sacrifice were not only *always* recurring, universal themes; there were very specific reasons why death and sacrifice occurred during the Dirty War. In order to further its economic agenda and secure absolute control over the population, the military targeted all those who got in its way. General Iberico Saint Jean, governor of Buenos Aires, summed up the military's position two months after the coup in May 1976: "First we will kill all the subversives; then we will kill their collaborators; then . . . their sympathizers, then . . . those who remain indifferent; and finally we will kill the timid."[27] But, as I suggested at the beginning, the historical imperative of communicating real facts to a population is also linked to its flip side: the specificity of the struggle can at times best be staged and made meaningful through the use of these universally recognized symbolic gestures.

By yoking together the writing-rewriting, Gambaro also emphasizes the role of the spectator or witness in atrocity. Antígona seems to exist on a separate, distant, "tragic" plane, a dislocation made immediately evident in the play by the fact she does not know what coffee is, and which was highlighted in Laura Yusem's 1986 production by the fact that Antígona was in a pyramidal cage throughout (see figures 50a and b). The other two characters occupy the roles of contemporary spectators watching Antígona's ordeal and enablers who contribute to the current tragic dénouement: they are Coryphaeus (literally, the leader of the Chorus) and his vaudevillesque sidekick Antinous ("the most insolent of Penelope's suitors and the first to be killed by Odysseus")[28] (see figure 50c). Sophocles is clearly concerned with the responsibility involved in seeing and knowing. The insistence on witnessing in Antigone is obvious from only a few examples: "Don't you see?" Antigone asks Ismene in the opening scene (l. 11); "how can I keep from knowing," Antigone responds when Creon asks her if she knows that she must die (l. 513); and the Sentry's admission that finding out about Polynices' clandestine burial puts "a terrific burden" (l. 288) on the guards. Gambaro builds on the theme of witnessing in her version, continuing her preoccupation with responsible witnessing, as opposed to what I call *dangerous seeing* or illicit or unwilling witnessing that spectators want to avoid because it puts them at risk. In Gambaro's *Information for Foreigners,* as I argued earlier, fearful spectators attempt to negate the reality of the violence they see with their own eyes by isolating it as theatre. Like an obedient audience, some members of the population can remain passive in the face of the most extreme brutality. Their leaders, after all, assure them that everything is under control. So too, the two *porteños* watch Antígona's tragedy and fail to see it as their own. They are both culturally incompetent and unreliable witnesses/ spectators: "Who is that? Ophelia? (They laugh. Antígona looks at them.) Waiter, another coffee!" (137). They are unwilling to recognize Antígona and understand her fate in relation to the criminal politics that afflicts their society. They prefer instead to hold onto the less threatening explanation of unrequited love associated with Ophelia's death. This displacement suggests that for the Argentine "man in the street/café," the atrocity of the Dirty War remained largely unrecognizable. Like recollections of the Holocaust analyzed by Shoshana Felman and Dori Laub, the Dirty War "functions as a cultural secret which, essentially, we are still keeping from ourselves" (*Testimony* xix). The witnesses were reluctant witnesses; they didn't know and they didn't want to know, for not knowing became the source of their sense of well-being.

Perhaps the most telling variation between Sophocles' play and Gambaro's, however, is the representation of the role of women in civil conflict. In order to explain why Antigone disappears well before the end of Sophocles' text, scholars such as H. D. F. Kitto have long suggested that she may not be the principal character of the play. Simon Goldhill, in *Reading Greek Tragedy,* sums up how scholars read *Antigone* in light of the paradoxical status of women in Greek drama and society, for while "explicit ideology . . . indicates a specific linking of the women with the inside, with the house, and with a denial of public life and language, nevertheless tragedy flaunts its heroines on stage in the public eye, boldly speaking out" (113). P. Slater posits that Greek tragedy demonstrates Athenian social pathology in its attitude toward women: "Women, repressed in life by men, find a voice through men in the institution of tragedy. The tension is, for Slater, a tension in Athenian life between the rejection or repression of women and the guilty projection of their power in the special worlds of myth and literature" (Goldhill 113). M. Shaw "has coined the phrase 'the female intruder' for the role of women on stage" (Goldhill 114).

I will return to a couple of these comments, but first it seems useful to outline briefly how Gambaro's version differs from Sophocles' in regard to the status, and representation, of women. In terms of representation, Gambaro's offers a

Figure 50a, b, and c. Laura Yusem's 1986 production
of *Antígona*. (Photos by Graciela Yentil)

more central and human role for Antígona, who is very much the principal character. She (unlike Antigone) is onstage throughout, and we actually see her burying Polynices (whose body is represented only by a shroud). Through the ventriloquism of the play, she speaks many of the majestic lines that Sophocles had allotted Haemon.[29] The play starts and ends with her, and her last lines indicate that she is furious at having to accept her fate of self-sacrifice: "I was born to share love, not hate. (long pause) But hate rules. (furious) The rest is silence! (She kills herself, with fury)" (159).

However, like her original, Antígona both fulfills the traditional roles assigned to women in ancient Greece by washing and preparing her relative's body for burial and lamenting his death, and transgresses them by claiming a body in which the state has demonstrated proprietary interests. But Gambaro's Antígona seems more loving and vulnerable than Sophocles' heroine, against whom Normand Berlin (in *The Secret Cause*) has leveled charges of "inhumanity" (21). Gambaro's Antígona "turns pale" when she hears that her sister Ismene might also be condemned to death and dissociates herself from her in order to save her (146). She also admits that she, like everyone else in the tyrannized population, feels fear (144), though she refuses to be silenced by it. But more importantly, because *Antígona* is the product of such a recent sociopolitical conflict, there is a way in which the historical and symbolic function of the character differs from anything we associate with Antigone. She does not simply "represent" the interior, household spaces normally assigned to women in ancient Greece or contemporary Argentina. She does not, in the Hegelian sense, embody divine (versus human) law. While the Latin Americanist Silvia Pellarolo suggests that Antígona stands for the "rebellion of the weak" (79) and that she is "representative of the people" (80), it seems clear to me that Gambaro's portrayal of the *porteños* as complicitous in the tragedy makes it impossible to sustain this argument in any straightforward way. Moreover, while Pellarolo makes a passing reference to Antígona's link to the Madres de la Plaza de Mayo, the gender issues so central to Gambaro's play fall out of her analysis.

Antígona furiosa, to my mind, prompts reflection on at least two of the most fundamental gender issues facing Argentine feminist writers: What are the repercussions on women of the junta's move to stage conflict—metaphorically and literally—on the female body? and Is it possible for women to appropriate roles and language developed by patriarchal discourse and turn them into vehicles for their own empowerment? I will explore this last question by looking both at Gambaro's allusions in this play to the Madres de la Plaza de Mayo and at the advantages and limitations she encounters in her attempts to appropriate the "masterly" words and roles of Sophocles' *Antigone*.

Gambaro, echoing the military discourse, represents the civil war as being fought on and in Antígona's flesh:

> The battle. An eruption of metallic clanging of swords, stamping of horses, screams and cries. ANTÍGONA moves away. Watches from the palace. She falls to the ground, hitting her legs, rolling from one side to the other, in a rhythm that builds to a paroxysmic crescendo, as though she endures the suffering of the battle in her own flesh. (139)

As in the case of the *Patria*, the vision of the feminine motherland belabored endlessly by the junta, Antígona's body is the site of conflict—configured in both discourses as a conflict between men, between brothers (even if the junta attempted to disqualify them as brothers and even though one third of the disappeared were women). The war was being fought in the interstices of the Mother *Patria*, in her bleeding entrails. Antígona, too, the play tells us, "endures the suffering of the battle in her own flesh." As with the image of the *Patria*, Antígona occupies a space of mediation between men. The junta could argue that Argentines were related and united as "authentic national beings" through their proximity to the *Patria*. This empty, feminine figure endows them with status, identity. Antígona, locked and constricted in the pyramidal cage, also mediates between and among men. Although the conflicting pulls created by the Creon/Zeus tension of the Greek version are gone, Antígona finds herself in a triangular formulation between Creon and Polynices on one hand, between Polynices and Eteocles on another, between Antinous and Coryphaeus on yet another, and between the modern reader and the Sophoclean original and between the Argentine spectator and the national tragedy on two more. She, like the "feminine" trope, is the conduit, the empty vessel; "she" is the one that has no power but who nonetheless becomes the figure of exchange, mediation, or interaction among those who do (Creon, Zeus, et al.). Antígona simultaneously fulfills her mediating role and warns us against it. What happens when the female body is used as the site of political conflict? Women are trapped in roles that prove as confining as the bars on Antígona's cage. Real-life women, like the *desaparecidas* that Antígona conjures up, die violent, untimely deaths. By staging the conflict literally on Antígona's body, Gambaro stresses the connection between the metaphorical practice of staging conflict on and in the *Patria* and the fate of historical women in recent Argentine history.

But Antígona not only conjures up the *desaparecidas*, her circular movements as she makes visible the city of the dead clearly recall the Madres' movement as well. The Madres, too, function as mediators in a triangular formulation between the pseudo-paternalistic junta and the threatening, disappeared "son." Like the Madres, who orchestrated the display of silhouettes of disappeared persons in Buenos Aires, Antígona makes the missing come to light. For both the Madres and Antígona, the dead are accessible only through representation. Walking around an empty square, the Madres display their photographs and silhouettes. Antígona, on her bare stage, exposes the corpses on which Creon's peace and order are founded:

> (Antígona walks among her dead, in a strange gait in which she falls and recovers, falls and recovers.)
> ANTÍGONA: Corpses! Corpses! I walk on the dead. The dead surround me. Caress me . . . embrace me . . . (140)

Antígona furiosa conjures up the image of the Madres de la Plaza de Mayo in ways that for an Argentine audience would have been immediately recognizable. Antígona's determination to give her brother's corpse a decent burial echoes the Madres' struggle to make the military government assume responsibility for their children's disappearances. Estela de Carlotto, a Madre, tells how she pleaded with General Bignone in 1977 to release her daughter: "He said that they didn't want to have prisons full of 'subversives,' as he called them . . . that they had to do what was necessary, by which it was clear he meant to kill them. I was now certain that Laura was dead so I asked please, would he at least return the body because I didn't want to search cemeteries amongst the anonymous graves for the body of my daughter" (qtd. in Fisher 20). Soon afterwards, however, the women started walking in a circle around the Plaza de Mayo, in front of the presidential palace or Casa Rosada, demanding "Aparición con vida [Back alive]." Both Antígona and the Madres consciously perform tragic, vaguely ahistorical roles in order to communicate the urgent nature of the civil confrontation with their fellow citizens. Antígona recognizes that she is forever trapped in the role of the self-sacrificing sister: "I will *always* want to bury Polynices. Though I a thousand times will live, and he a thousand times will die" (158; original emphasis). In *Hebe de Bonafini: Memoria y esperanza*, Alejandro Diago documents how the Madres consciously put on tragic roles and icons (the lamenting woman of Greek tragedy and the Virgin Mary among them) in order to carry on with their protest. In order to protect the rights and integrity of the "private," however, both Antígona and the Madres had to renounce the *familiar* roles (in both senses of the word) historically reserved for them in society. Antígona understands that "[f]or me there will be no wedding . . . Nor children. I will die . . . alone" (139). So too, the Madres' activism, which stemmed from their commitment to defending their families, threw many of them into direct conflict with their husbands and other family members who refused to validate their new roles. Both Antígona and the Madres took to the streets, although their physical environment (as reflected by the cage onstage) is alienating and restrictive. Antígona, like the Madres who were called the "madwomen of the Plaza de Mayo" is also "mad," *furiosa* like Orlando. The *porteños* taunt Antígona much as Reneé Epelbaum recalls some fellow Argentines jeering at them or, more often, crossing the street to avoid being seen close to them. Gambaro captures both of these images in the lines "Let no one come near—dare—to come near, like the mad girl / circling, circling the unburied unburied unburied corpse" (141). The Madres' public demonstration of loss belied the military's assurance that everything was under control, that their fight was a "clean" fight and that punishment came only to those who deserved it. The women's performance, much like Antígona's, created a chain between the living and the dead. So too, Antígona not only refers to memory as a "chain" (142) that links the living to the dead; her death reenacts that principle. Like her mother Jocasta before her, Antígona too dies by hanging herself. Antígona forges the chain that links the fate of women in social conflict; men seem destined for the more heroic fate of dying by the sword in direct confrontation while women, the generally silenced and unheroic victims, are forced to turn their violence in on themselves and take their own life. (Recall that Antigone's death was not the climactic moment of the Sophoclean version; the play culminates with the image of the shattered Creon walking onstage accompanying the corpse of his dead son.) Moreover, as Coryphaeus states, and as the Argentineans were beginning to realize by the time this play was written, "[m]any women have known a similar fate. When power is affronted and limits transgressed, my girl, payment is always in the currency of blood" (154). One of Antígona's final indictments is directed at the population that refused to face up to the catastrophe taking place around them: "Hiding in [your] houses, devoured by fear, the plague will follow [you]" (155).[30]

Antígona furiosa captures not only the strength and power of oppositional movements such as the Madres', it also points to some of its contradictions. As Ross Chambers writes in *Room for Maneuver,* oppositionality is not and never can be revolutionary because it works "*within* a system of power even as it works against it" (xvii; original emphasis). The Madres risked their lives by confronting one of the most brutal dictatorships of the twentieth century in order to protest the human rights abuses by the military government. They did not (at least initially) challenge the social system nor women's positions within it. They simply wanted their children back. If and when the Madres' position changed, it was because they were caught in the contradiction built into their patriarchal society: as mothers, they had to look after their children; as mothers, their place was the "private," apolitical sphere. No matter how much they may have wanted to comply, the Madres clearly could not adhere to both of these conditions simultaneously. Accepting one meant abdicating the other. Thus their decision to leave the private realm in search of their children was not, in itself, a revolutionary or radical move. Much like the tragic heroines that Goldhill refers to, the Madres defy "explicit ideology" in times of tragedy and command the "public eye, boldly speaking out." But because they did not want to or were unable to challenge some of the social mores governing women's lives, the Madres were framed by the social construction of acceptable, self-abnegating "feminine" roles (lamenting mother, Virgin Mary) even as they tried to manipulate them in defense of their children. Thus the Madres were trapped in a bad script, a narrative activated by the junta and which they themselves, no doubt unconsciously, reenacted. It is not without a certain irony that they too mimed the canonic possibilities of classical art when they accepted the Jocastian logo for their movement: "Our sons [hijos] gave birth to us; they left us pregnant forever" (qtd. in Diago 119).

The sexual ambiguity and feminine self-abnegation underlying this aspect of the Madres' discourse finds its way into Gambaro's *Antígona* as well; whether this is a conscious reflection of the Madres' language or not is open to debate. Antígona, while embodying the political spirit of sisterhood, is simultaneously mother, lover, and sister to her dead: "Antígona throws herself on [Polynices], with her own body covering him from head to toe . . . She pants as though she would revive him" (141).

Moreover, her readiness to give herself up—body and soul—for her brother reaffirms the erasure of "feminine" individuality and specificity in Western culture, in which individuality has been equated with masculinity. Thus her line "I will be your body, your coffin, your earth!" (142) maps out the process of feminine disintegration: first she loses her body, then she becomes the site and symbol of death (which even in this play is configured as feminine: "Death: bride, mother, sister" [156]), and finally she slips altogether into the vastness of "mother" earth. The feminine, once again absent of subjectivity, is no more than the vessel, the object (coffin or earth) housing male individuality. She too must sacrifice herself so that society might live. Thus Gambaro reactivates one of the oldest dramas in the world, "representations involving a social sacrifice of the feminine body where the death of a beautiful woman emerges as a requirement for a preservation of existing cultural norms or their regenerative modification" (Bronfen 181).

Nonetheless, to return to my original question, is it even possible to hope that women will empower themselves by appropriating the roles and discourse of a tradition that has historically disempowered them? Can the Madres performance of self-sacrificing women ever align human rights with women's rights? Can Gambaro, an avowed feminist, rewrite the canon or the position of women in it by taking *Antigone* and placing the woman center stage? It seems clear to me that Gambaro wants to write women's activism into her script. She turns the mask on Greek tragedy by having Antígona take on the role of the male heroes (Haemon, most notably), much as the male actors used to put on female roles in Attic tragedy. This ventriloquism, in Gambaro's hands, empowers women for they now have access to an entire canon of "masterly saying[s]" and make them their own—not as echo but as a subject with agency who uses the words for their own needs. It is no longer Haemon who is furious, heroic, and individuated, but Antígona who, at least, is meant to be. It is she who dominates the discourse and, within the limits that I am exploring, uses that discourse to make her own position heard. In my reading of the play, Gambaro is conscious of the limitations imposed on women, perhaps herself most specifically. Moreover, she like Antígona is "furious" at having to live within the canonic possibilities that, seen from this anti-Steiner perspective, are as much a cage as a means of making visible.

So why do it? Why speak a language that leads women inevitably—time and time again, as this play indicates—to a position of self-sacrifice and silence? Because, I would answer for Gambaro, there doesn't seem to be another. Those who speak "in the voice of a woman" (148) are still trapped in a discursive system that cannot hear them as anything other than irrational, transgressive, "perverse," and "indomitable" (147–48). If we lived in a different universe, one that was not predicated on the gender divide that casts males as actors, movers, and doers and women as other, death, and extremity, then this narrative would not be self-perpetuating.[31] But, as Gambaro writes in *Antígona*, "hate rules . . . The rest is silence!" (159). Hate was the language of currency in Dirty War Argentina; the rest really was silence. Gambaro's reclaiming Antigone to portray the Dirty War was, like that character's, also an act of defiance, a defiance of the silence and memory loss dictated for Argentine society. Like the Madres with their placards, or writings by the disappeared like Alicia Partnoy, Gambaro too tries to pull off a "reappearing" act. Only through art and representation, as artists and activists in Argentina committed to resistance knew, could the dead come "back alive." The three characters (like the Madres) quite literally stage absence; the other characters become visible only through them. The ventriloquism of the characters underlines that (as in Partnoy's testimonial writing) the voices of the missing can only be heard through the mouths of those who are willing to tell their stories. Recomposition, then, is the theme of *Antígona*, with all the limitations that the term implies. Recomposition through art functions as a kind of mourning—an obituary—that completes the life-death cycle and restores a sense of wholeness to the community. But recomposition is also a disavowal: the dead do not come back to life except as icons. The fractured community that tried to mend itself with the Trial of the Generals was ultimately made to surrender to the official denial.

Gambaro, like her Antígona, both assumes and expands on the role traditionally allotted women. In this play Gambaro mourns the deaths that took place in the Dirty War and functions as a hinge between the military atrocity and her audience in order to initiate a process of social recomposition. She goes further, though, moving into the role of authorized witness, a position that many male Latin American writers have claimed as their own. As Jean Franco writes, "the role of the one who commemorates the dead and does not permit them to be consigned to oblivion is taken by the writer who 'masculinizes' the Antigone position" (131)—that is, writers such as García Márquez, Augusto Roa Bastos, Ernesto Sábato, Carlos Fuentes, and others. Thus while Gambaro cannot change the role of Antigone, who is doomed to sacrifice herself time and again, this play expresses outrage at the discursive and representational limits placed on women.

Antígona is not so much about some sort of mythical feminine moral superiority and self-sacrifice (another form of extremism imposed on the "feminine") as about a woman who is furious at having to continue sacrificing herself and being silenced. Gambaro writes within the canonic limits produced by Western culture, but she writes with a vengeance. She appropriates the immediately recognizable role of Antigone because it offers the same paradoxical visibility and invisibility that the Madres found in the maternal role. Can feminist writers open new roads for themselves through ventriloquism? Can mother activists continue to exploit roles that have been socially sanctioned—even invented—by patriarchal structures? Gambaro's *Antígona*, like the Madres' movement, suggests that we won't have new answers until we have more choices.

most abhor. Thus I don't maintain
mimicry and even parody, pote
imacy of accepted order. Ra
for its capacity to provi
"feminine" space of si
gender anxiety by
women, wome
ambiguity a
inist an
rethi
th

8 Staging Battles of Gender and Nation-ness: Teatro Abierto 1981

We don't have any other weapons—they're all in the hands of
the people who burn things down—we only have the theatre.

—Osvaldo Dragún, video *Pais Cerrado*

Theatre as a Desiring-Machine

Throughout this study I have focused on the underside of social spectacle, on the way that those in power can manipulate the population and render it passive and blind through the theatrical control of the visual sphere. My observations on the numbing power of spectacle are not meant to contribute to the age-old strain of antitheatricalism. It's not that the theatricality of spectacle and theatre is deceptive or untrue because it's mimetic, and thus separated or opposed to the "real." In contrast to commentators in the antitheatrical vein, I, as a Latin Americanist, feminist, and performance scholar deeply invested in questioning and even challenging established power relations, relish what they

...hat theatre is nefarious because it involves
...tially undermining the stability or the legit-
...her, theatricality is to be celebrated, not blamed,
...e sensual pleasures. Theatre, considered at times a
...mulation and prostitution, has long provoked sexual and
...blurring the lines between the sexes. Boys pass for young
...n dress up in male attire and perform maleness. While sexual
...nd gender destabilization has frightened many commentators, fem-
...queer theory scholars find performativity a promising opening for
...nking and opening up gender categories. Still, the unease surrounding
...heatricality continues to be strong, sometimes even among feminist scholars.
Arguments dating from the time of Tertullian, ca. A.D. 200, to the present
pornography debates warn of the dangers of representation, afraid that spectators cannot differentiate between the representation of an act onstage and the
act itself, that appearance might lead to, indeed incite, "reality."

Theatre, its enemies and its proponents have always known, has power. It
deals in desire; it fascinates. It is a part of that desiring-machine that both
produces and is the product of group fantasy. Artaud understood theatre's
power of fascination and communication: "The mind believes what it sees and
does what it believes: that is the power of the fascination" (27). Thus he called
theatre a "disease" and a "delirium" that could externalize the terrors within
and lead to "extreme purification" (31). Grotowski speaks of the theatre as "a
place of provocation" in which "what is dark in us slowly becomes transparent"
(21). Barba, while referring to theatre as a "fiction" (24), claims that it gives us
the "possibility of changing ourselves and thereby of changing society" (26)
if only we are "disciplined" and "ruthless" enough to "ride the tiger," rather
than "be devoured by it" (25); God forbid that we, like amateurish actors, get
"bogged down in a biological chaos, in impotence" (25).

Clearly, theatre's power to fascinate can be anything from perverse to empowering—it's all a question of whom, why, and when it fascinates. Even the
most revered and visionary theatre theorists such as Artaud are blinded, I
believe, by the potentially fascist power of this potent desiring-machine. Artaud, for example, longed for a return to the mythical times of heroic men
capable of changing desire itself, "capable of imposing this superior notion of
the theatre, men who will restore to all of us the natural and magic equivalent of
the dogmas in which we no longer believe" (32). The fascist potential of theatre
is evident not only in the ideology of purification we encounter again and again
but, just as troubling, in its very operational mode, in its control of the gaze and
manipulation of desire. This controlling *practice* manifests itself in a whole

spectrum of works—from "leftist" productions ranging from the experiments in collective and "open" theatre of the 1960s (such as Judith Malina and Julian Beck's) to the Pip Simmons Group of the late 1970s to current productions focusing on the social control of the public and neo-Nazi chic (e.g., the brilliant Catalán company La Fura dels Baus). Interestingly, in Argentina as elsewhere, there are few examples of current fascistic theatre from the extreme Right, in part because the radical Right tends to dismiss theatre as a "leftist" place and concentrates more of its energy on public spectacles such as the parades and flag wavings of the Dirty War or the cross burnings and exhibition of the body-as-spectacle associated in the United States with the KKK and the skinheads. But there's a great deal of theatre that functions within the "rightist" ideology of conservatism (capitalist, masculinist, and Eurocentric) that passes itself off as apolitical, supposedly depicting the immutable world of "universal" value. This theatre certainly doesn't look radical or extreme. On the contrary, it projects its worldview as both natural and inevitable. All attempts to challenge that world-view seem somehow illogical. The so-called natural is the most difficult to decode. As Brecht put it: "When something seems 'the most obvious thing in the world' it means that any attempt to understand the world has been given up" (71). Theatre's power of fascination can lull the audience into hanging "its brains up in the cloakroom along with its coat" (27). Such theatre induces a trance and its spectators become little more than "sleepers" (187).

Those who decry the dark power of theatricality are just as mistaken (to my mind) as those who fail to take its power seriously—and for the same reason: they oppose "theatricality" to the "real." So, while commentators such as Deleuze and Guattari, for example, state that "the work of art is itself a desiring-machine" (32), they underestimate the particular power of spectacle as both a site and vehicle of such desiring. Arguing that psychoanalysis fails to deal adequately with desire, seeing it only as the product (or object) of fantasy, they write: "But even when the fantasy is interpreted in depth, not simply as an object, but as a specific machine that brings desire itself front and center, this machine is merely theatrical, and the complementarity of what it sets apart still remains" (26). I don't believe in the "merely" theatrical, or in the theatrical as a surplus or add-on to the "real." The "real," I have argued, is shaped through various kinds of enactments in the public sphere. Even the most basic and so-called natural things—from the way that we inhabit our bodies to our sense of nation-ness—are unthinkable without taking into account their performative character. The theatrical, rather, is a system of communication activated by desire as well as one that transmits and shapes desire. The exchange between consumers and producers of desire takes place in the sensual sphere, in which vision is, in late capitalism, particularly privileged, manipulated, and mass-produced.

What constitutes the power of theatre? Where or in what does that power reside? Theatre, like the more general spectacle, simplifies, makes visible/invisible, concentrates issues and communicates meaning while it organizes and situates spectators. Theatrical power is not limited to the play and its internal content or organization, though I spent the last chapter focusing on the power-to-limit of scripts and roles. Theatre's greatest power, I think, lies in its ability to command attention and focus the view—the made-you-look quality of performance. The audience's look casts it, making any response—from identification to witnessing to looking away—tacitly acknowledge the centrality and dominance of the show that is being presented to, and at times even thrust upon it. Looking can affirm identity and create community, but it can also trap the viewer in a contract of disempowerment. The show always insinuates that there is more to be seen, some repository of power concentrated just beyond view. Someone has access to it: those in control, not us, the powerless. Thus the "dangerous" power of theatrical spectacle is tied to its instability. It is open to manipulation. Those who control the spectacle, whether theatre or public display, control its meaning and impact to a significant degree.

Theatre, of course, is not synonymous with "theatricality" or "spectacle" or "performance," being on one level a specific and artistic (not "real") system of representations. A play is not true; actors don't really die. Nonetheless, it's impossible to separate out theatre from the "real" altogether. In the *paso de dos* between theatre and the real, theatre is the self-conscious partner, the one that either dances along, subverts, or mimics the other's moves. Theatre, as I will submit in this chapter, is deeply implicated in the construction of gender and nation-ness. Social hierarchies, gender roles, and national values become visible (and are challenged) not only in the content of the plays or in the racial and sexual makeup of the cast and audience, but also in the spatial layout of the theatrical event. Since the late eighteenth century, when the first professional theatre was inaugurated in Argentina, theatre was heavily policed in order to control not only the play's content and the actors' gestures and body language, but also to oversee audience behavior and ensure that the population was segregated by sex, class, and race. Since the wars of independence in the early nineteenth century, any desire for the beloved was performed as coalescing with the passionate love for the nation. Theatres (as public spaces) continue to be the very real site of political contestation, as acts ranging from the burning of theatres in Buenos Aires to the attack on funding for the arts in the United States today make clear. Plays, performances, and the theatrical spaces themselves are very much part of wider social struggles. "Theatre," in its traditional use as the sum total of the above, participates in the shaping, transmitting, and at times challenging of group fantasies and desires. Therein lies the danger and the hope.

Staging Battles of Gender and Nation-ness

Bad plays, everywhere and always, are the fault of literary mercenaries . . . These authors who have prostituted themselves to the tastes of the mindless masses have, in their artistic perversion, switched their spiritual sex. Instead of being the ones who, in the intellectual marketplace, inseminate the population with their ideas, they have let themselves be inseminated. The dramatic author who is authentically *masculus,* engenders his thoughts in the listener who receives the germ of the lesson and conceives actions and habits. Nothing is more imitable than the lessons from the theatre. But the author who is monstrously feminine receives the imposition of the public will and produces whatever it demands.—Mariano G. Bosch, *Teatro antiguo de Buenos Aires*

It should come as no surprise that theatre in Argentina, introduced by the missionaries after the Conquest and primarily controlled since by the state, has served as an instrument in the creation of the model subject/citizen. Theatrical presentations have given form, life, and passion to various political imaginings of what constitutes an ideal community and people's place within it. And given the centrality of gender in the spectacles of nation-building that I have examined thus far, it should by now seem predictable that the struggle to control theatre would be cast in terms of the "authentic" masculine will imposing itself on the feminized social body. Mariano Bosch, the eminent Argentine theatre historian writing at the beginning of the twentieth century, lays out the struggle in so many words: the truly *masculus* playwright should "inseminate the population with [his] ideas." If not, if he receives ideas from the public, he becomes a "prostitute," a sellout (mercenary), a traitor who "switche[s] spiritual sex" as others might switch political alliance. This "monstrously feminine" specimen, impregnated by the populous, produces a bastard culture. Bosch's diagnosis of the state of Argentine theatre echoes the nation-building scenarios that I mapped out in chapter 2: the authentic man imposes his will; he usurps birthing capabilities and "creates" civilization. Theatre's problems, like Argentina's problems (this scenario goes) result from the male's inability to stand firm. His feminization leads to bad coupling, producing bastard and contentious offspring.

Theatre's job, according to those in power, is to produce "good" children.

That potentially dangerous feminine space is considered beneficial when kept under the control of strong authority figures. Theatre—as opposed to the various kinds of performances that existed before the arrival of the Spaniards in the fifteenth and sixteenth centuries—was introduced by missionaries in order to hasten the transformation of the native populations into good Christians and submissive subjects. Since the sixteenth century, the clergy have used theatrical presentations in indigenous languages to teach the holy doctrine to native populations. As a new criollo population took root in the Rio de la Plata area in the early seventeenth century, the clergy retained control of theatrical activity. Aside from the public stagings in honor of religious celebrations, they tended to limit its practice to the male students in their schools and universities. Women had no access to theatre, in part because they had no access to education. But their exclusion was more deliberate than that: females could neither see nor be seen; they were not only prohibited from attending productions, but the clergy made special efforts to ensure that they could not catch a glimpse of the representations, even from the sidelines (Seibel 43). Female roles, of course, were played by boys. Long before the feminist movement, theatrical productions demonstrated that sex and gender were separate categories indeed—one did not have to "be" a woman in order to perform femininity. Theatre's citizen-building function was predicated on the absenting of real women, while the "feminine" was appropriated to consolidate patriarchal authority in a Christian, all-male, though strictly hierarchical, society.

Theatre, however, was soon recognized as an attractive instrument for civil education as well. Since the late eighteenth century, the theatre served as a rehearsal space for civic character. Although religious officers tried to control, then stifle, its growth and outreach, secular officials argued that theatre helped shape the model citizen because it "was one of the best schools for manners, language and urbanity, and thus useful in a city that lacks other healthy diversions."[1] The theatre space itself, they recognized, could also be used to dramatize the preeminence of civil authority. The first stable theatre, Teatro de la Ranchería (1783), boasted a special section or *palco* reserved for the viceroy. The luxurious balcony, with the official insignia surrounded by velvet and gold, reaffirmed the supremacy of state power. The play could not begin until the viceroy occupied his exalted place and was properly saluted by the actors (Klein 1:12).

Notwithstanding its obvious civic usefulness, Viceroy Vériz y Salcedo conceded that theatre—always potentially dangerous and immoral—had to be kept in line. His 1783 decree mandated that dramatic texts be censored, that actors' body language be controlled, that actors be prohibited from "executing any movement or action . . . that might cause the slightest scandal" (Klein 1:11), and that audiences be segregated by sex, race, and social class.[2] White men sat in the front rows, men of color (mulattos, mestizos, and blacks) stood at the back of the room, and women were confined to *la cazuela* (the pot), a balcony with standing room only reserved for women of all races (Casablanca 19).[3] Breast-feeding was prohibited. The restriction and physical arrangement of bodies highlighted the regulatory function that civil authority sought to confirm in and through theatre. In the theatre, then, part of the show was the audience. Men and women of color always had to view the stage from behind the white men, *seeing* them as privileged.

The performances, however, indirectly subverted the norms that held the white, upper-class male as the privileged spectator and physically pushed men of color and women to the sidelines. Even though the civil authorities occupying the *palcos* and the white men in the front rows were the principal spectators, minority men and women of all races had access to the performance and could interpret what they saw in ways they saw fit. Moreover, the professional theatre allowed women to gain visibility onstage. Not only could they act, interact with men, earn wages, and expose their bodies (all previously forbidden), but the newly arrived European plays—whose plots were rife with disguises, role switching, and gender confusion—permitted some gender-bending. Women of color and slaves were also allowed to act and coexist onstage and in theatre companies before society at large was ready to sanction any such interactions. Yet stipulations remained. Women were not allowed to dress as men from the waist down or show their ankles or feet (a wooden board blocked the audience's line of vision). Thus there was a complicated play of restrictions and transgressions going on as women and people of color strove for more options in their late-eighteenth-century society.

Though women gained some visibility, their roles were limited to two main categories: the superhuman or symbolic Woman (with roles ranging from Greek goddesses to the embodiment of virtues such as la Libertad and la Patria) or that of the subjugated, humiliated, or conniving woman (see Seibel 57). While women's roles were always subordinate, ironically women played a vital function. Female subordination was the centerpiece that held together the dominant worldview. In a moment of criollo expansion into indigenous territories, the white male's defense of the pure, white Woman served to legitimate the practice of genocide that accompanied nation-building. Not surprisingly, the first play by a local author to be staged in the Ranchería was Manuel de Lavardén's *Siripo* (1789), about none other than the famous *cautiva*, Lucía de Miranda. As I discussed in chapter 2, the myth of the loyal and loving wife captured by the ferocious and treacherous natives proved that the whites had been justified in waging war against them. Thus the subordinate role that women played in theatre should not mislead one into thinking that gender issues were not central to the drama of nation-building. As the women protagonists died, disappeared into convents, or effervesced into disembodied Woman, the boundaries of national/gender identity coalesced.[4]

Several battles were being fought simultaneously onstage in the early period of Argentine theatre. Rivalries between civil and religious authority were bitter, with clergy threatening to excommunicate actors and audiences alike. The Teatro de la Ranchería was mysteriously burned to the ground, ignited by a firecracker launched from the nearby church. Civil authorities, meanwhile, maintained that the theatre taught the population to distinguish between good and evil, to love the former and abjure the latter. A new building, the provisional Coliseo, was built, and theatre continued to perform its mandated mission: to shape and educate the ideal citizen. Guards were stationed in the theatre to assure that both the actors and the public behaved correctly (Casablanca 23–24).

During the first decade of the nineteenth century, a period marked by the British invasion (1806) and Argentina's independence from Spain, theatre's mission included forging feelings of national identity. Actors performed great battle plays full of patriotic heroism. In the midst of the 1806 invasion, the theatre and its actors provided a perfect foil for a plot to topple the enemy. As the Argentine theatre historian Teodoro Klein puts it, "there's nothing better than theatrical activity to cover up plans for rebellion" (*El actor* l. 59). The English general discovered the plot, and in a cruel dramatic reversal, he upstaged the rebel actors who saw him occupying the viceroy's *palco* when the curtain went up. Notwithstanding the setbacks, spectacles of nation/gender continued as Nymphs played the roles of Buenos Aires and Montevideo in the drama of Buenos Aires's revenge.[5] Argentina won independence, and the Coliseo joined in open support of the revolutionary fervor, presenting plays that affirmed the greatness and autonomy of the Argentine nation. Theatre musicians were the first to play the national anthem in 1813.

During the early years of independence, theatre became the cultural instrument in the battle for national autonomy. The theatre fanned desires for national unity and legitimacy. Many of the works promoted not only a passion for the new nation, but attempted (despite all the facts) to present an image of Argentine unity based on the assimilation of its racial, gender, and even national others. Plays presented romantic passion as inextricably linked to national liberation. Matilde, in *Libertad,* decries the loss of her lover (Adolfo) as equivalent to loss of freedom; she cannot live without one or the other. Another scene presents a glorious reunion—of Matilde, Adolfo, a Spaniard, and "various Indians"—in front of the temple to Liberty extolling the virtues of the *Patria*. As the Spaniard puts it, even he is obliged to the *Patria*, who has taken him to her breast and sheltered him (see Casablanca 59). In *Tupac Amaru*, Morante's 1821 play about the indigenous revolutionary hero, Amaru's wife, Micaela Bastide, loves him as intensely as she loves peace and freedom. She chooses to die rather than submit to Spanish rule. This play, too, illustrates the political realignment taking place in this postindependence period. The Spanish colonizer, not the native, is the archenemy. *Tupac Amaru* expresses the desire for an inclusive Argentina united against the tyrant. The fantasy works when the political situation requires broad-based cooperation and when, as in this play, the indigenous heroes and heroines are not only noble but dead. (Parenthetically, it is interesting to note how women, so central to the production of these all-inclusive fantasies, were still excluded from society. Trinidad Guevara, the most famous female actor of the period, was condemned as "a prostitute . . . a woman who has excited the hatred of society's matrons due to her criminal conduct." Nonetheless, theatre itself was recognized "as a most useful moral and political establishment" [qtd. in Seibel 131–33].)

The imagining of the new nation was unthinkable without gender—*la Patria* inspired blind devotion and passionate allegiance. And gender "difference" was created as part and parcel of the nation-building project. Women were first excluded altogether and then incorporated as the subordinate other who defined the male self as active hero and legitimated his striving for national/ gender autonomy and supremacy.

Under Rosas, as I noted in chapter 2, spectacle became the property of the state. When Rosas forced many theatre people into exile, there was a dismal drop in the quality of productions. The decline in theatre coincided with a rise in more class-inclusive or "popular" forms of entertainment such as the circus, magic shows, and cockfights. However, two new theatres were built during the period: the open-air Parque Argentina (1827) and the luxurious Teatro de la Victoria (1838), complete with the decoration of three roses (*rosas*) growing from a single stem—the dictator, his wife, and their daughter. Nonetheless, the stages were dominated by mediocre European plays. Local authors were used only to produce plays attacking Rosas's enemies, such as *The Duel between a Federal and a savage Unitarian, in which the former cuts the throat of the latter in full public view* (1841). The theatre continued in its function training the ideal citizen—an effort that still depended on segregation and policing. Men who sat in the balconies were accused of being "effeminate" (Castagnino *El Teatro*, 58);

they were charged with being uncivilized for smoking wherever they pleased in the theatre (there was a no smoking section in the Victoria); their unruly behavior provoked one commentator of the period to write that "this multitude of boys should be made to disappear" (qtd. in Castagnino, 59).

Until the end of the century, these theatre spaces continued primarily to house foreign plays and theatre companies, especially as more and more European immigrants landed in Argentina in the late eighteenth century. Majestic theatres—Teatro Colón (1857), Opera and Variedades (1872), Liceo (1876), Politeama (1879), Nacional (1882), San Martin (1887), Onrubia (1889), de la Comedia (1891), Apolo, Casino, Argentina, and Odeon (1892), Mayo (1893)—were built, demonstrating the power of the new Europeanized hegemonic culture.

Theatre in Argentina, as elsewhere in Latin America, has been in an unenviable double bind since its beginnings: those in power have tended to attack theatre as a hotbed of resistance, while popular theatre practitioners have looked at theatre as a machine of the state and an enemy of the people. The art form that had participated so actively in the independence struggle was, once again, at the service of the elites and a looming tribute to hegemonic power.

The 1850s, however, also saw the rise of *circo criollo*—a regionalist, popular theatre that staged works by local authors in *carpas,* circuslike tents. Commentators generally date the origins of Argentine national theatre to 1886, though clearly there had been considerable theatrical activity long before then, as this brief overview suggests. The popular circus personality José J. Podestá starred as the gaucho Juan Moreira in a pantomime dedicated to Argentine issues.[6] The show, first staged in 1884 by the foreign circus company of Carlo Brothers—starring Podestá—was reproduced by Podestá and his circus two years later, this time with dialogue. The production was staged on and off for the next years and gave rise to a whole new genre that became known as *drama gauchesco.* As Teodoro Klein points out, this genre marks a new period in Argentine theatre, not its origin (*El actor* 2:199). However, there was opposition to popular theatre, and in 1894 the *capra* of Gabino Ezeiza, one of the practitioners of *drama gauchesco,* was burned down. The opposition to popular theatre continued in the early twentieth century. Frank Brown, an English Shakespearian actor who moved to Argentina, entertained children by staging plays in a tent, until the children of the fascist Liga Patriótica burned his *capra* in 1910.

During the first part of the twentieth century, commercial theatres started springing up in Buenos Aires, prompted by the demand for popular entertainment created by the new wave of immigrants. Many mediocre productions dominated the stage. The first generation of Argentine playwrights, such as Florencio Sánchez, Roberto J. Payró, Martín Colorado, and Nicolás Granada y

Gregorio de Laferre`re, was over. In 1927–28 the *Anuario Teatral* stated: "It's impossible to fool ourselves. The National Theatre, with very few exceptions, is nowadays a commercial scandal of adulterated materials that seriously and profoundly poison the spiritual essence of Argentineness" (Ordaz, "La historia," in *Capítulo* 15, 193). The exceptions, of course, were important playwrights such as Francisco Defilippis Novoa, Armando Discépolo, Samuel Eichelbaum, and Roberto Arlt. But the banality of the commercial theatre was also challenged directly by a new theatre movement, known as independent theatre or *teatro independiente*. Again, these were popular, antihegemonic theatre groups that sprang up throughout Argentina, most of them staging amateur productions focusing on local or national issues. Notwithstanding the Great Depression and Argentina's first military coup in 1930, the new independent theatres made an impact throughout the decade. Teatro del Pueblo (The People's Theatre), one of the most important groups in the movement, was a communist theatre committed to working collectively to improve the "moral and physical" conditions of the general population (see Ghiano 17). It staged a wide range of national and international productions and acquired a large following among students and workers who could afford the reasonably priced tickets. In 1938, the theatre group was expelled from its location and moved to their own theatre, the Teatro Corrientes. In 1942, the fascists burned their new space. Nonetheless, the *teatro independiente* movement continued to thrive.

The attacks against noncommercial theatre that reflected local or national issues also continued. During the 1970s and 1980s other theatres were burned. Stink bombs were thrown in among the audience. Increasingly, theatre people were threatened and attacked. López Rega, the so-called *brujo* or warlock behind Perón and Isabelita, accused playwrights of exerting a nefarious influence on the population. During the mid- and late 1970s, theatre artists once more went into exile. Theatre schools closed; university programs in dramatic art disappeared. The potential for an oppositional theatre no longer seemed to exist.

Teatro Abierto 1981

At this brutal historical moment, during which the military dictatorship policed and targeted cultural production, a group of Argentine theatre people came together to challenge political repression. The Teatro Abierto event is generally considered by Latin American theatre practitioners to best exemplify theatre's liberating and contestatory power. Teatro Abierto (Open Theatre) was a cycle of twenty-one one-act plays conceived originally by Osvaldo Dragún in conjunction with other major Argentine playwrights to resist the dictatorship's attack on theatre and its practitioners.[7] Everyone donated their talents—21 playwrights, 21 directors, 150 actors, numerous composers, musicians, costume designers, stage and lighting designers. Even the owners of the 340-seat theatre, Teatro Picadero, where the cycle was first held, offered their space for free. The idea was that if a whole group of blacklisted people worked together, the dictatorship would not be able to clamp down on them all. The staging of the cycle was, in itself, an act of defiance. The artists would no longer be silenced and made invisible, though the media gave them no coverage. The media focused all its attention and resources on Frank Sinatra, who had come at the invitation of the junta and was offered presidential treatment. While Argentina's best theatre artists were working for nothing, Sinatra was paid $1.6 million, a sum that would have paid one thousand Argentine actors for a year.[8] Nonetheless, the excitement and collaborative effort that went into Teatro Abierto once again gave theatre people a sense of community and shared purpose.

The initial success of Teatro Abierto surprised everyone. Though the general population was terrified during the Dirty War, and though the show began at the unusually early hour of 6:30 P.M., tickets sold out for every performance. The population, attracted by the renewed cultural vitality and the affordable prices, overcame their fear. For the audience, too, Teatro Abierto implied an act of defiance: as audience members lined up for blocks to buy tickets, they formed part of the spectacle of resistance. In the middle of the night that Sinatra sang at Luna Park, one week after Teatro Abierto had opened on July 28, the Picadero was burned to the ground (see figure 51).

The military, of course, denied involvement in the destruction of the theatre. If the armed forces assumed that by destroying the theatre they would dampen the widespread interest in the theatrical phenomenon, they underestimated the resolve of all those participating in the Teatro Abierto project. After the burning of the Picadero a news commentator declared: "Too bad, an illusion was burned." But Dragún, speaking for Teatro Abierto, said, "Nothing has been burned." A few hours after the destruction of the Picadero, nineteen theatre owners offered their space to host the cycle. The designers agreed to re-create the sets and costumes, albeit on a more modest scale. After considerable discussion, which I will return to, the group voted to continue their work in the Teatro Tabarís, a cabaret-type locality with six hundred seats right on Corrientes, the theatre strip.

After the burning of the Picadero, the public showed massive support for the cycle, which became transformed instantly into a symbol of freedom; 25,000 spectators attended Teatro Abierto during its two-month run in 1981. In their introduction, "Teatro Abierto: Fenomeno socio-teatral argentino," the editors

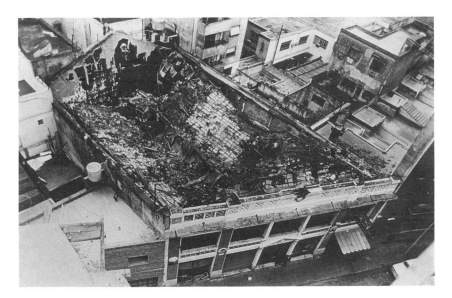

Figure 51. "Teatro Picadero." (Courtesy of Julie Weisz)

of *7 dramaturgos argentinos* call the event the "most important Argentine theatre movement of all times" (Giella and Roster 7). Surprisingly, the introduction fails to note that the event was staged during the Dirty War, that most of the participants were blacklisted, and that everyone but the military acknowledges that the destruction of the Picadero was politically motivated.

All the plays for Teatro Abierto were written specifically for the occasion, and they covered a wide range of topics. Several of them dealt with an aspect of Argentine history. Aida Bortnik, one of the three female playwrights and author of the script for the film *The Official Story,* wrote *Papá Querido* (Dear Father). In this play, four adult children of a recently deceased father (very much a Perón figure) meet for the first time at his funeral only to discover that they know very little about him, nothing about each other, and had all received different messages from this looming but absent figure. Much like the widely disparate groups of *peronists* found after the death of Perón, the only thing that united them was a great man who gave them very conflicting messages. Ricardo Monti's *La cortina de abalorios,* which I will discuss in some detail, is about Argentina's long history of colonialism. Ricardo Halac's *Lejana tierra prometida* (The distant promised land) expresses a painful loss of illusion, suggesting that Argentina itself was once that promised land. Some of the plays are more immediately about the experiences brought about by the Dirty War: exile

(Cossa), silencing (Goroztiza), acquiescence (Gambaro, Raznovich), survival through negation (Drago), militaristic thinking (Pavlovsky). Dragún's play *Mi obelisco y yo* (Me and my obelisk) asks the audience to view this monument of Argentineness from a new perspective, to examine how a symbol of liberation becomes part of a wider system of tyranny and oppression. Soto's *Trabajo pesado* (Heavy work) depicts a post*proceso* wasteland in which people have nothing, remember nothing, and end up participating in the violence. Esteve's *For Export* is about fear and "otherness"; O'Donnell's *Lobo . . . ¿estás?* (Wolf, are you there?) is about fear and political violence; Carlos Pais's *Juego de la oca* (something like "snakes and ladders") shows characters trapped in a snakes-and-ladders kind of game, going backward, forward, falling down stairs, paying fines. Then there were seemingly random plays such as Pronzato's *Ciau rubia* ("Bye, Blondie"), which depicts a generation of men coming of age in adoration of Marilyn Monroe; while tangential to the obvious political issues of the Dirty War, the play reproduces the paradigm I have noted throughout in which men define themselves specifically in relation to the idealized female other. The participants of Teatro Abierto—like the characters in the plays—seemed to be doing the impossible. As Goroztiza put it, "everything was impossible, we were a bunch of crazies who wanted to sing what couldn't be sung . . . a crazy possibility."[9]

Interestingly, given the iconic role of Teatro Abierto in Latin American theatre and the Dirty War, few people write about it. Participants such as Osvaldo Dragún and Patricio Esteve have commented on their intentions; commentators such as the Uruguayan Roger Mirza have asked why a similar phenomenon didn't occur in their country. Scholars such as Miguel Angel Giella, Edith Pross, and Olga Cosentino have edited the works and given general overviews of the movement or the period. These authors, however, tend to focus more on the *idea* of Teatro Abierto than on the plays themselves.[10] In part, the scarcity of critical commentary is understandable. Given the conditions of its emergence, Teatro Abierto was (and is) known more as a spectacle of resistance than for its quality as "theatre." While the works have artistic pretensions—and a couple of them are excellent—they were primarily conceived as responding to a political emergency. Thus two dynamics work simultaneously and interactively in Teatro Abierto. On the one hand, as art, these works look, and are, rather "traditional." The performance bases itself primarily on the text, thus reproducing the hierarchies that hold the literary text to be prior to and superior to performance, seen basically as a mise-en-scène. The plays set up a standard relationship between spectacle and audience. The actors work there, onstage, in person, in front of the audience; the audience has paid admission to the show. The critical response focuses on the artistic achievement rather than on the audience's response.

On the other hand, given its explosive context, Teatro Abierto was also political theatre. As such, it functioned more like performance art, which values the artist's performance over the text. Insofar as the text had to be available to censors, the political relevance of the piece depended on the artist's ability to transmit a critique through nonexplicit means—through improvisations, gestures, parodic inflection, and timing. The words, suddenly resemanticized, took on different meanings and opened up new levels of intelligibility. The participants, given the context, went to the theatre with a heightened consciousness; every word carried an innuendo, every gesture was a sign. While some of the words themselves might have been banal, the art of spectatorship had grown sharper during the Dirty War; people had become good "interpreters" or readers of signs. The drama was no longer in the text but in the urgency of creating meaning. The actor's body language contributed to the audience's understanding of oppositionality without being as vulnerable to government control. Censors would have had to police every performance of every show in order to clamp down on all antimilitary expression. Because of these challenges to censorship, by 1981 theatre was not as vigorously controlled as film or television, which had massive audiences (Esteve 64). Thus as political spectacle Teatro Abierto generated far more enthusiastic audience response than any critical reading of the works themselves might do. The need to reaffirm a different sense of community was so vital in Argentina in 1981. The audience that lined up to see Teatro Abierto was aware of the enormous political risks it was taking. Even after the Picadero Theatre was burnt down, the producers, playwrights, directors, actors, technicians, and audience continued to manifest their commitment to political change. The astonishing success of the Teatro Abierto cycle, most of those involved in the project would agree, had more to do with its political, rather than its strictly artistic, value. When, night after night, the audience rose to its feet and applauded euphorically, it applauded not just the individual plays but the entire enterprise. Teatro Abierto is admired as a courageous act of cultural affirmation, a bid for freedom of expression.

The critical silence surrounding Teatro Abierto might stem, in part, from the project's dual status as art and political spectacle. But Teatro Abierto also suffers from the troubling contradiction that I have observed throughout this study: acts of resistance tend to reproduce the language and logic of oppression in their attempts to challenge them. Again, my intention is not to attack the people who risked their lives by participating in this project. Rather, I think it's important to indicate the difficulties of oppositionality, so often trapped in the very ideological systems it aims to dismantle. Time and again in my research on Teatro Abierto I came across an oppositional discourse that echoed the military's. The composer Rodolfo Medero, for example, who worked with other composers and musicians to create the music for Teatro Abierto, replicated the military's fascistic harangue on purity and authentic Argentineness by speaking of Argentina as an infirm social body that had to be purged of contaminants: "We are saturated with things that are not national, not just in the theatre but in the culture at large. Artists, by and large, have become contaminated, and they're producing contaminated products, and the population is getting contaminated by receiving those products. We need a medical system to de-contaminate ourselves."[11] Teatro Abierto, though a strong affirmation of "open" cultural production and expression, was also the mirror that all too honestly reflected the image of Argentine national identity and its turbulent context (Pross 85).

In this section, I explore how Teatro Abierto in 1981 reenacted the struggle between men, staged on and through the "feminine," that I've looked at throughout this study. I will begin by exploring the masculinist organization and staging of Teatro Abierto before turning to an examination of two plays that highlight the violent positioning of the "feminine" in Argentina's struggle for national identity: Ricardo Monti's La cortina de abalorios (The glass-bead curtain) and Diana Raznovich's El desconcierto (Disconcerted).

Teatro Abierto, from its inception, was envisioned as an all-male show. Though theoretically Teatro Abierto was to be an "open" cultural act, as the name suggests, the spectacle reproduced the gendered reality of Argentina. Conceived originally by the eminent playwright Osvaldo Dragún, there seemed to be little or no consciousness on the part of the organizers that "open" was not synonymous with "all-male." Griselda Gambaro was the only woman included initially. After playwright Diana Raznovich complained that women were being excluded, she and Aida Bortnik were included among the twenty-one playwrights.[12] There were no women directors even though Raznovich insisted on having a female director for her play (her ex-husband Hugo Urquijo ended up directing her El desconcierto). There were very few women actors, and the roles available to them reproduced the whore/mother/young woman stereotypes. Both the music and the lighting were done by males. Women, again in keeping with the gendered division of labor, were in charge of costuming.

Furthermore, the decision to stage Teatro Abierto at Tabarís after the burning of the Picadero also served to underline the all-male nature of the event. As before, Teatro Abierto started early, at 6:30 P.M. At night, the Tabarís continued its regular programming—a cabaret featuring scantily dressed showgirls and livened up with misogynist jokes. When women in Teatro Abierto complained about housing their politically "progressive" and oppositional theatre event in that location, they were overruled. The argument was that Teatro Abierto would "subvert" the space and give it new meaning. But rather than subvert the space of ritualized misogyny, Teatro Abierto decided to exploit it to ensure its own survival and continuity. The military males, who frequented the cabaret during its regular hours, would be less likely to destroy a space they associated with their own pleasure.

This strategy of protecting political content behind or within the context of female sexual exploitation was not new to the period. The eminent filmmaker Adolfo Aristarain, who directed *Time for Revenge* in 1981, admitted to doing the same. He included long and unnecessary sexual scenes in the film, he explained in an interview with Annette Insdorf, " 'so the censors took five days and questioned things—*not* politics or ideology, but sex. All I had to do was cut a few frames at the end of some scenes, like one of a strip-tease. It doesn't hurt the scenes—especially if you made them longer than they should have been,' he said with a knowing smile" (17). After the film was shown, pro-military forces threatened to bomb the movie theatre. Someone wrote to the editor complaining: "What's going on with the Argentine censors? They're just watching breasts and they forget about ideology. Ban this picture!"[13] The consequence of this strategy, of course, was that gender inequality and female sexual exploitation could never be the topic of analysis since the transmission of the political message was seen as contingent on their continuing exploitation. Exploitation of women became the common denominator between pro- and anti-military factions.

In like manner, Teatro Abierto set up a situation in which theatregoers, prepared to find a critique of their repressive society, would have to walk past the posters of seminaked women to get into the theatre. The juxtaposition of the political event against the seminude female body reproduced the visual strategies I noted in regard to pro-military magazines such as *Gente* that superimposed headlines of the atrocious events of the Dirty War on the female bodies in bikinis that graced many of their covers. Again, the female was reduced to pure body and backgrounded as the site of violence and political conflict. The female subject could lay no claim to political participation or to nonexploitative representation; she served as the scenario on which the struggle between men—political agents—could take place.

Ricardo Monti's La cortina de abalorios

The female as scenario for the male contest for domination is, moreover, an explicit theme in several of the plays featured in Teatro Abierto, most notably perhaps Ricardo Monti's *La cortina de abalorios* (The glass-bead curtain). This play, set in an Argentine whorehouse at the end of the nineteenth century, begins with Mamá, the Frenchified and withered madam. Mamá, like Sarmiento's evocation of Buenos Aires as a lady mediating between the unruly interior provinces and the European cities across the ocean, is the space of economic and cultural exchange between men. Her body is a commercial zone. As a whore, she serves both her local master (Bebé) and his boss (the Englishman, in this case). She simultaneously taunts the "inferior" local (the servant) with the possibility of access and humiliates him. As the play opens, she sits open-legged on a table, instructing her quivering male servant:

> I'm going to show you who I am . . . (she opens her legs and points toward her sex).
>
> Do you know what this is? (Brief pause). A museum. Let's call it a museum of the imagination . . . Look closely, not just anybody can look in this mirror. Here you can leaf through the most brilliant pages from universal history . . . You are before an open book . . . This is where substance lies . . . El tout . . . The absolute . . . Am I being clear? Another comparison: a scenario. The folds of the curtain are separated, the protagonists jump onto the boards, a pirouette, they sink back deep in the shadows, curtain; the folds open again, and like that, forever. (210)

The play, we soon learn, is "about" the violence of imperialism, "about" the relationship between economic systems of domination and the practice of torture. It rises out of the spectacle of Mamá's genitalia—a "mirror" in which not only the servant but the audience at the theatre are supposed to see themselves reflected. And because the female body is the "museum" or "scenario" in which these social ills are to be exposed, the sexual exploitation of women can never be the subject of analysis. Mamá continues her monologue, referring to her sex as a diamond that "shines in the depths," promising eternal life and infinite pleasure (211)—to men, we must presume. Mamá is about to seduce the sweaty servant when the master, Pezuela, whom she calls Bebé (literally baby) enters, back from the wars. As he looks at himself in the mirror—the one on the wall this time—Mamá quickly tries to compose herself. He throws her a wrapped war booty which, when she unwraps it, we assume is the severed penis of the enemy, the "Indio." "Erect?" she asks. "Rigor mortis," he answers (212).

Bebé notices the servant's undone fly, suspects the worst, and shoots him dead. "Ah my dear friend," Mamá laments, "Good help is so hard to find" (214).

The "real" conflict of the play, it seems, is between Popham, a British magnate based perhaps on Sir Home Popham, who led the 1806 British invasion of Buenos Aires, and Pezuela, who probably represents General Joaquín de la Pezuela, a Spanish general who, during the independence wars, tried to strike a deal with the Uruguayan federalists against Buenos Aires. Whether these historical allusions refer precisely to these men, or to foreign colonizers in general, is not clear, though my guess is that the play, set specifically at the end rather than the beginning of the nineteenth century, is alluding to ongoing colonization in a general manner. In any case, Popham appears and demands payment for Bebé's loans. In order to distract him, Mamá flirts outrageously. As the object of exchange between men, she placates him with promises of sex. Bebé suggests that they have a drink and a game of cards. Popham, discovering that the deck is marked, shoots the new servant dead and brings out his own deck. He proceeds to take Bebé's last penny, as well as a fortune in public lands under Bebé's stewardship. Intent on recuperating his losses, Bebé offers his last remaining asset. He calls Mamá and asks her to cooperate by getting down on all fours. But it's not enough to have Mamá, the whore, used as an object of exchange: "I'm sorry Pezuela, but in England we also have a good supply of whores" (226). However, it's not just whores Pezuela is selling, but meat: Mamá is now the stand-in for a cow. Pezuela strokes Mamá's haunches, lifts her robe, invites Popham to touch the merchandise.

> PEZUELA: And not just fresh meat, Mister Popham . . . We have milk too, fresh, creamy, frothy . . . Milk her, go on, milk her. Taste.
> POPHAM: May I?
> PEZUELA: As if I weren't here.
> (He closes his eyes. Popham fondles Mamá's breasts.)

Mamá says only "you're tickling me! (laughing scandalously)." When the taste test is over and the men are negotiating, Mamá—still on all fours—asks: "Excuse me, are you finished with me yet?" (227). The woman, literally reduced to a piece of meat in this play, participates in her own dehumanization.

Popham agrees to allow Pezuela to put himself further in debt, but only on the condition that he be allowed the "privileges" of a free market. Sure, the men recognize, the deal will hurt local producers, but that's the price of "free" trade. Argentina, Mamá on all fours suggests, is pulled between two greedy masters. The language echoes not just the squabbles among foreign imperialists as to who would control the country's natural resources, it also resonates in the

Argentina of the Dirty War, in which local industry was being crippled by Martínez de Hoz's decision to open the market to free trade. Popham obliquely refers to the current situation when he claims that his "civilized" country is providing the durable goods—"cloth, jewels, railroads, artifacts, money! I sell money!" "And what do you have to offer?" Popham rhetorically asks Pezuela: "Dead meat . . . Instincts, brute force, destructible elementality. I sell civilization and you nature and barbarism" (228). Popham represents not only civilization but the scientific progress that he claims accompanies social improvement. But entry into the free market, then as during the Dirty War, necessitates the use of violence against the working class. Popham pulls out a long needle with a hook at the end of it which, he insists, will lead to the improvement of their subhuman race. Grabbing the last remaining servant, Popham asks: "What's this? An ape . . . In order to inoculate this subject with a sense of duty . . . sacrifice and productivity . . . meekness . . . discipline . . . resignation . . . respect for order and hierarchies . . . awareness of his nothingness . . . in short, all the attributes that adorn the honorable worker," Popham will apply the instruments of civilization. As in torture during the Dirty War, Popham too will produce a docile and submissive worker for the new economic age. But, as in the Dirty War, this play makes it difficult to understand that the "real" conflict in both scenarios is about Argentina's entry into the new international markets. The misogyny of both is so violent, the writing of and on the body so torturous, that it makes it hard to differentiate between the military's discourse and Monti's own.

Monti's representation of the female body (like Pavlovsky's) encourages the audience to see women as anything *but* human beings with their own political and economic struggles. This play is not "about" female exploitation. Mamá is depicted as a whore, but this play is not concerned with prostitution in Argentina at the turn of the century. Though historians like Donna Guy have studied "white slavery" and prostitution in Buenos Aires during this period, this play is not about social systems that force women into humiliating positions of servitude—sexual and otherwise.[14] Rather, Monti further exploits women by further degrading them and stripping them of any last shred of humanity: Mamá is a whore/animal/scenario—the site of deviance, the commodity for economic exchange. And what's more, no commentator has ever noted that Monti's "allegory" of Argentina's "national history" is written on female flesh.[15]

What's going on in Teatro Abierto? Again I ask, as I asked of Pavlovsky's *Paso de dos* at the beginning of this work, what kind of a play is this? a political commentary on imperialism? Isn't this just one more example of how the exploitation of the female body becomes backgrounded even in the effort to transmit the corrosive effects of imperialist exploitation?

Diana Raznovich's El desconcierto

Fewer questions, my manager says. Success smiles on us, the audience claps, the theatre is full and your personality eradicates an overflowing magnetism that doesn't need sound in order to shine. Maybe he's right. Maybe we're all right. Maybe you, by participating in this humiliating act, feel that you have truth on your side.—Diana Raznovich, *El desconcierto*

Diana Raznovich's one-act, one-woman play *El desconcierto* (*Disconcerted*), a feminist counterpart to Monti's play, calls attention to the violent positioning of the "feminine" in this misogynist system of representations. Raznovich, like Gambaro in *Information for Foreigners,* highlights the issues of audience self-blinding (or percepticide) as Argentine society under the military dictatorship became caught up in the active production of national fictions. The production of fictions, as both playwrights make clear, effectively equals public silencing.[16] Raznovich both portrays the silencing of the Argentine social body and exposes the gender violence at the center of the struggle for male power. In *El desconcierto,* the artist Irene della Porta and her audience are committed to creating silence. Her manager pays her handsomely to play Beethoven's *Patetica* on a piano that emits no sound. The audience buys tickets to watch Irene wrench sounds out of nothingness: "It is as if she and the audience, knowing that Beethoven could not be heard, were capable of constructing 'that other concert' which, though nonexistent, they had mysteriously pacted," reads the opening stage directions.[17] At the end of the play, the piano regains its sound as if by magic. But after so many silent concerts, Irene della Porta no longer knows how to make "real" music. Desensitized fingers produce harsh, discordant notes. Shocked and defeated by her ultimate failure as an artist, she rejoices when the piano once again becomes mute.

On the most obvious level, *El desconcierto* is a critique of Argentine artists and audiences alike who were willing to go along with the censorship imposed by the military dictatorship, convincing themselves that they were engaging in meaningful communication. What draws the members of the audience into the theatre night after night is, in part, a sharing of collective complicity that they can interpret as "resistance." Although they produce no sound, the reasoning seems to be that by their presence alone, audience members defy those who impose censorship and self-censorship. It is interesting to note that muteness and public silence were interpreted both as acts of complicity and acts of

Figure 52. To speak or not to speak? cartoon by Quino. (*Potentes, prepotentes e impotentes* Buenos Aires: Ediciones de la Flor, 1991)

resistance during the Dirty War (see figure 52). On the one hand, those who did not speak out against government brutality enabled the criminal practices of abduction, disappearance, and torture to continue. However, *not speaking* was also seen as a heroic defiance against a system that demanded conformity, just as it was seen as defiance against the torturer who demanded "information" during the act of torture.[18] The idea that mere public presence at a theatrical event functioned as an act of resistance in part underlay the entire Teatro Abierto project. The fact that thousands of people lined up to see plays *bajo vigilancia* (under surveillance)[19] was interpreted by the military leaders and by the population at large as an oppositional move.

El desconcierto, however, seems directed at those Argentines who were complicitous with the dictatorship and whose passivity in the face of governmental brutality made a new social order—the culture of terror—possible. Clearly the play refers to the Dirty War, which Irene della Porta refers to as a seductive aberration in Argentine history:

> This has got to stop . . . This has been a wonderful vacation on a desert island. This has been an amusing parenthesis. A white wind swept me away; a storm uprooted me from my piano stool. And now, where am I? I've reached the pinnacle of success. The concert hall is packed! We've made lots of money. What a wonderful desert! . . . Sometimes one even wants to stay here and never go back . . . stay here with you. (She weeps inconsolably.) (320)

The deterritorialization associated with the *proceso,* the storm that uprooted her from her artistic expression, becomes desirable. As former modes of existence lose viability, she comes to cling to her own silencing.

The "show," far from being oppositional, is produced by the power brokers themselves. By their very presence and willingness to be part of the performance, the spectators contribute to the construction of a new community, one that is grounded in fictions. Through performance, which involves everything from the staging of illusions to the suspension of disbelief, they constitute the new, silenced Argentina. The original meaning of *theatre* (from the Greek *theatron,* a place to see) has become perverted—the audience can no longer see, or recognize, the atrocity of which they are a part. Their sense of perception, whether visual or auditory, has been assaulted. Thus, the show functions as a metaphor of percepticide, the assassin of insight and perception that results in the spectators' diminished capacity for recognition and understanding, their inability to differentiate, their loss of memory. But the spectators do not recognize themselves in the scenario; they think that the drama (which seemingly eludes them as the sound eludes Irene) is taking place somewhere else. Yet this silencing and displacement were precisely what the *proceso* was all about.

The performative process of communal binding/blinding depicted by Raznovich points to two forms of gender violence. On one level, "femininity" is a performance that Irene enacts on a daily basis. Clad in her low-cut, tight red gown and dripping with jewels she becomes the other that the audience pays to see. She even speaks of herself in the third person, as Irene della Porta, as a commodity who has agreed to play along with her objectification and degradation because she gets some tangible benefits out of it: "Interminable years of comfort for accepting to be Irene della Porta playing in silence" (318). Raznovich presents gender as performative, much along the lines of Judith Butler's theory that "gender is an act which has been rehearsed, much as a script survives the particular actors who make use of it, but which requires individual actors in order to be actualized and reproduced as reality once again."[20] Few roles available to women in patriarchy offer visibility—the "star" is one of them. But, the star, as Irene explicitly notes, embodies the male spectators' desires. It is Woman as a projection of patriarchal fantasies who performs onstage. She is their mirror; like Monti's Mamá, her body reflects their struggles and desires. As in much Argentine art of the period, the recurring image of the mirror in *El desconcierto* indicates that individual and public identity is a deformed reflection of exterior forces—there is little in the way of an "inside."[21] The social "body" is in a process of dissolution and boundary loss: "One day, I will look in the opaque mirror and see my own face, blurred by time, and I will ask, 'why?' . . . It's so easy to explain things to a mirror" (320–21). All she sees is someone who has sold out, someone who has "made a pact with mediocrity" (318) and who can judge herself only through the eyes of others:

> Mirror mirror on the wall
> Who's the fairest of them all?
> The most talented?
> The most intelligent?
> The most attractive? (She laughs)
> Mirror mirror
> Who is the most successful of all women?
> (321)

On another level, *El desconcierto* signals that the project of community building undertaken by the junta is also gendered. The feminine image (*Patria*, Irene della Porta) serves a real function in community building by uniting all those who imagine themselves bound or loyal to her. However, the "feminine" is useful to the power brokers only as long as she remains an image without real agency. As such, "she" gives the spectators their identity. Just as the armed forces defined "true" Argentines by virtue of their loyalty to the *Patria* (and by extension, to the armed forces as her defenders), Irene della Porta's fans form a group (an "imagined community") because of their relationship to her: "Who am I? Who are you?" (319). The nature of this community building is circular—

the feminine image is the creation of the patriarchal order, but "she," in turn, is constructed as a "door" (*Porta*), giving access to the nation's image of itself. So, Irene della Porta candidly admits that she is the creation of her fans: "[They] have made me what I am. But who am I?" (317). And yet her tenuous, rehearsed "identity" unites the audience.

While the woman "disappears" in the image of *Patria*, Raznovich does not allow her audience to overlook the misogynist violence of this community-building discourse. Her character makes it clear that the audience is drawn to the "show" of public humiliation that she performs on a nightly basis. Raznovich illuminates what plays like Monti's and Pavlovsky's attempt to hide: that the audience desires and will pay to see the woman's degradation. Not for nothing are the themes of collective complicity, silencing, and disempowerment played out on the exposed and humiliated body of Woman. Irene della Porta forces the question: "What do you want of me? (She suddenly pulls open her dress and begins to strip.) Do you want to delve into some hidden truths? Do you want to see me without disguises? (She strips down to her underwear.) . . . Now that you see me like this, stripped of everything including my life's breath, do you know more about me than before? . . . Does my nakedness bring success? What is a naked woman? An exposed skeleton, with its fragile, vital membrane?" (319). This is not the desiring and/or desirable female body of *La cortina de abalorios* or *Paso de dos*. This female body is not backgrounded but, rather, the subject of debate. Rather than allow her to function unproblematically as a "door," a way through, Raznovich foregrounds her character. As a feminist, Diana Raznovich understood an aspect of the cultural production of community and silencing that other playwrights reproduced but failed to recognize—that the social pact between power brokers and complicitous audiences is being negotiated (both in the military discourse and in much of this "art") on the body of Woman. The audience searches for its identity in her bodily interstices and looks for "truth" on her naked flesh. Her body functions as a text on which the community's fate is inscribed. But by challenging the desirability of this construction, and by highlighting the *habits* of a desiring machine, Raznovich attempts to influence and modify desire itself.

Raznovich's highly conscious framing of the "feminine" in representation makes visible the masculinist trope of framing and erasing the "feminine" as the center, dead center, the portal of nation-building. Read in conjunction with Griselda Gambaro's *Antígona furiosa*, the play illustrates the ambivalent positioning of Woman in Argentine culture, a positioning augmented during the Dirty War. While civil conflict is represented on and through their bodies, Antígona and Irene della Porta occupy two opposite positions. Antígona defies civil authority and thus demarcates the very limits of society. She risks everything by taking on the role of moral agent and is consequently fated, like the *desaparecidos*, to "disappear from the world, alive" (152, Feitlowitz translation). Antígona signals moral extremity. She chooses to die rather than give in to unjust civil authority, but that extremity signals too the erasure of the feminine. She too must sacrifice herself so that society might live.

Irene della Porta, while exposed and sacrificed symbolically if not literally, occupies the position of decay and disintegration *within*, at the very heart of, the social body. Raznovich illustrates how the woman's body works as a trope of social dissolution and boundary loss. "She" is the mediator between power brokers (impresarios) and audience (population). Through her public demonstration of suffering and humiliation, she makes visible their own loss and pain. Her undoing is that she works actively in the system and is thus deformed by it. Yet even here, society acquires meaning and cohesion through her sacrifice: "I participate in my own suicide and that is also a crime," Irene says. "You are killing me. You've already killed me. I am a corpse that ambles across a dead stage, representing the same thing time and time again, my own death, mummification and failure. (She laughs)" (319). Her pain, humiliation, and erasure are made to look like a "show." Unlike Antígona, who is killed by her oppressors, Irene is killed by her fans, her own side, as it were, the "progressives" who continue to sacrifice the well-being and dignity of women in order to further their political agenda.

How does the act of participating in a woman's failure and degradation get read as an act of resistance? Instead of using Woman as a metaphor for everything from death and destruction to resistance and communal identity (the way that Pavlovsky's *Paso de dos* does), Raznovich forces the audience to look at real-life women as human beings, complete with their "exposed skeleton" and their "fragile, vital membrane" and to recognize misogynist violence for what it is. Raznovich drags out the body, exposing the literal effects of its symbolic positionings. Irene's performance, reenacted nightly before an explicitly male, adoring audience, underlines the violence of the scopic economy in which women are cast as the object of exchange between (male) producers and (male) spectators: "You, sir. You who used to come to all my concerts. You who still come to my concerts. You, with that profound and secret gaze. You who used to send me roses and who continue to send me roses—why do you come? Does my downfall amuse you?" (319). The strip-show quality of Irene's performance underlines the link between male power, self-definition, and pleasure and female degradation and powerlessness. He watches, controls; she reveals, exposes. But Raznovich makes us question the connection between the sexualized display and exposure of a woman and violent politics that progressive playwrights such as Pavlovsky and Monti both assume and elide. How does one get "read" as the other? As feminist scholars have indicated, the relationship between power and degradation has to do with the structure (rather than content) of representational practices. Who controls what we see? Who authorizes it? In 1981 Argentina, the answer to both has to do with the masculinist representational structure that grounded and conflated gender formation and state formation. The military man comes into being with the *Patria;* together, they form a nation of authentic beings. The problem is, of course, that the self-definition and authority of the military male is predicated on the construction of an illusory feminine foundation, the *Patria,* which is both the ground for sameness (national identity) and the institutionalized "other" which the masculinist "self" defends, negotiates, competes for, and erects. She is that which he maintains as the groundwork for his virulent/violent masculinity. The authentic national being (implicitly male) to whom they give birth is, as the junta stated, to follow in the footsteps of the glorious father. Thus women in this narrative are reduced to the masculinist projection of its own fantasies and prohibitions in a closed system whose only referent is male. Female subjects are forever linguistically absent and unrepresentable. When Irene della Porta opens her dress, it's not she, in all her vulnerable materiality, that the audience sees. It sees itself. It sees the projection of its own habitual desires. She becomes a mirror: her pain gets read as its pain, her silencing as an artist is heard as public silencing.

There is violence in this process of erasure that simultaneously exposes and eliminates the feminine. Irene represents her public exposure almost as an act of torture: "Why do you come to every show and wait for me to confess everything? Why do I have to confess . . . You already know everything" (318). Later, she refers to herself as being "tied up in front of you and you celebrate this with your attendance" (318). Nonetheless, the rage she feels has been incorporated into the show (or has the rage itself been reduced to a show?). Every night she walks to the piano, lifts the cover and takes out a pistol (see figures 53a and b):

> I speak of my mummification and my failure and then I take out the revolver and I aim it at you. (Aims at the spectators). You all know that the revolver is loaded and yet, you're not afraid. You've seen me take aim before without anything happening. (She laughs). You've also waited for me to turn the pistol to my own head (She does so) and you've seen that in spite of the suspense (She creates suspense), I always lower the weapon and put it away. Tonight will not be the night that you see me fall, nor will it be the night that you'll weep for me or throw flowers on the inert body that once was Irene della Porta. (320)

Figure 53a and b. "Irene della Porta" (in the German production the piano was replaced by a cello). (Photo by Jurgen Musolf, courtesy of Diana Raznovich)

The rage felt by women, as *Antígona* and *El desconcierto* illustrate, often propels the women to turn the violence on themselves. The sacrifice of Woman that underwrites the project of communal cohesion is usually presented as *self-sacrifice*, a *choice* taken by the victim, be it Antígona, who literally hangs herself, or Irene, who participates in her own death. Not only is the collective guilt localized on one female body (*she* killed herself), but collective aggression is also displaced onto the victim: *she* is the angry, dangerous, uncontrollable woman. Doesn't Antígona threaten to undermine state authority? Doesn't Irene della Porta point a pistol at the audience?

Irene della Porta is a fabricated image that sells itself as a cultural commodity or fetish on a nightly basis. She has been reduced (and has participated in her reduction) to a fiction that facilitates the production of other fictions. She magically orchestrates dreams of passion with unknowable others, dreams of destiny that she knows to be "fictions" based on "an idiotic pact" with a nonexistent God (319). She plays up her role as muse, oracle, or mysterious figure who has the answers. She "mystically opens her fingers" (319), as if conjuring up realities that the audience would not be able to see without her. The reality—on the contrary—is straightforward, banal, and anything but mystical, as she well knows: her degrading performance allows the audience to both

Figure 54. "Blues de la Calle Balcarce." (Photo by Julie Weisz)

"see" and displace its complicity. But the seeing constitutes an act of percepticide in that it allows for displacement rather than recognition, evasion rather
than responsible witnessing.

El desconcierto paradoxically signals both the failure and power of art in the
context of the Dirty War. The play's presentation of Irene della Porta's body as
violently exposed, rather than seductively naked, and the grotesque sounds
emanating from the piano defies the aestheticization of violence and the com-
modification of culture even as it portrays it. Raznovich decries fetishization
even as Irene della Porta succumbs to it. Her play is a work of "committed art"
even as it laments the nonexistence of such a thing. As Theodor Adorno noted
in the late 1960s, "A work of art that is committed strips the magic from a work
of art that is content to be a fetish, an idle pastime for those who would like to
sleep through the deluge that threatens them, in an apoliticism that is in fact
deeply political" (177). Diana Raznovich makes clear that noncommitted, eva-
sive art during periods of social catastrophe helps constitute and cement a
culture of terror in which people ultimately lose their capacity for real insight.
Even if restrictions were suddenly lifted, and the piano magically regained its
sound, those involved in the production of fiction would not be able to re-
establish real communication.

El desconcierto, not surprisingly, provoked anxiety both within the circle of

Figure 55. "Official 1°'" by Carlos Somigliene. (Photo by Julie Weisz)

Teatro Abierto and in the militarized state. According to Raznovich, some of her colleagues in Teatro Abierto criticized her play as "frivolous." Who could possibly be interested in a female pianist who can't play the piano in the context of the Dirty War? Though she was asked to withdraw the play and submit another, she refused.[22] The military reacted more violently, burning down the Picadero on the night that *El desconcierto* was presented (Arancibia and Mirkin 21).

Teatro Abierto 1981 reaffirmed the vitality of Argentine theatre, and inspired other similar events, such as *danza abierta, arte abierto,* and finally the Teatrazo, an international Latin American "open theatre" festival in 1985. While it challenged the military dictatorship, it did not radically challenge its ideological underpinnings. In several important ways, Teatro Abierto succeeded in doing exactly what the military had prohibited: it repeated and parodied the military gesture. The military had insisted they were the doers, the population the viewers. Playwrights delighted in usurping the military performance, in mimicking and subverting it (see figure 54). The 1982 and 1983 seasons continued to depict the human carnage that resulted from militarism (see figure 55). Nonetheless, the artists also reiterated the ideology that backgrounded women, objectifying them into the battleground for competing males. They seemed not to recognize how their bid for contestatory and "free" expression led them to brand and demonize the feminine. In a final blind gesture, the 1983 season of Teatro Abierto began with a public parade that included puppets and masks. "One of those dolls," a document notes, "was a formidable woman named Censorship. They marched her [through Buenos Aires] . . . and in a ritual act, they set fire to her, which symbolized the destruction of censorship" (Arancibia and Mirkin 24). Another Thatcheresque woman went up in flames to celebrate communal survival. Just as the military forever reenacted their same old claims to founding the "new" nation, resistance movements, too, are stuck in their slate-cleaning gestures. How many more women must be burnt in effigy so that "we," this specular community, might live? I, too, repeat Sarmiento's question: Don't people tire of these spectacles?

9 Crossing the Line: Watching Violence in the "Other" Country

> Young woman: . . .
> I will defeat 'it's not my concern' with my anguish
> blast their alien sleep with fireworks, horrible and
> indecent
> with countless shootings I will fall on the
> indifference
> of those who pass by
> until they begin to ask, to ask themselves
> Three men: (in an even tone)
> Why fear?
> Why torture?
> Why death?
> —Gambaro, *Information for Foreigners*

In bringing this study to an end I feel little of the elation, relief, and (admittedly false) sense of closure that I felt five years ago when I arrived in Buenos Aires in 1990. Then, I believed, the Dirty War was "over." Alas, I've come to conclude, there is no "over." But there is an irony to this realization. In one sense, there is a happy ending to this story—at least for now. For the fact is that. *now,* twelve years after the "end" of the Dirty War, people in Argentina are beginning to talk about the violence they endured. Since March 1995, when the first military officer confessed to committing human rights abuses, more and more military men from the navy and army have started admitting to their crimes. Some of the tormentors spoke out because they felt betrayed by the military leadership. While the upper echelons continued to enjoy raises and promotions in spite of their complicity, members of the rank and file were being denied advancement. Adolfo Francisco Scilingo, a naval officer, decried the unfairness of the situation, adding that he hadn't been able to sleep since his involvement in the Dirty War.[1] *El vuelo,* by Horacio Verbitsky, which broke Scilingo's account of the military's weekly death flights, became a national best-seller overnight. The red band wrapped around the book announced: "ESMA's pact of silence is broken." Other confessions followed. The "show" of atonement dominated the social sphere, replayed in newspapers and magazines and on radio and television programs.

As more information about the wrongdoings continues to come to light, the disappeared have, again magically, begun to reappear. The victimizers have started to name names and supply the specifics of the brutality that took place. In one particularly painful moment on the Argentine television program, *Hora clave,* a military man told a mother how he had thrown her nineteen-year-old son, drugged but alive, from an airplane. She thanked him for the information that would enable her to come to terms with the finality of her son's death, rather than live in the limbo of disappearance. While she vented no rage, she asked only that the military man be punished for his crime. But in another televised interview, a former torturer took evident pleasure in describing his firsthand experiences; prompted by the interviewer, he gloatingly confessed to more and more. Other torturers related how the military drew up lists of their members interested in "adopting" the newborn children of the disappeared, and how they disposed of the mothers' bodies after they gave birth.[2] What do viewers and readers learn from these accounts, except that human brutality knows no bounds and that these tormentors got away with murder? What does the public learn, or even want, from these "confessions"? Will anyone be held responsible? Will ordinary people begin to speak about their own role in the scenario? Or will the disappeared once again be exposed, this time to sell newspapers and boost ratings?

If anything positive has come from the show-and-tell it might be that some Argentineans who have clung to denial and deniability might finally accept that the atrocities reported by the Madres and other human rights organizations "really" happened. In April 1995, the army chief of staff announced that the military "employed illegitimate methods, including the suppression of life, to obtain information."[3] In his address, he stated that he wished to open a "painful dialogue about the past that had never been faced, a past that hovers over the collective consciousness like a ghost."[4] He stressed that the blame for what happened did not fall on a small group of individuals: "almost all of us are responsible for the fight among Argentines, either by act or omission, by absence or excess, by consent or advice . . . the deep-seated blame lies in the collective unconscious of the Nation." He closed his statement accepting responsibility for military actions and asking that "all men and women of our beloved country initiate a dialogue that will restore harmony to the Argentine familial wound." Jorge Balán, a sociologist at the Center for the Study of State and Society, believes that the official statement of culpability "will have a cathartic effect because it will free people to say what is in their minds and hearts." Even Menem has been embarrassed into admitting that his *indulto* or pardon might have to be rescinded.[5]

In spite of all the evidence, however, some people still don't believe that inadmissible things happened and others don't see them as inadmissible. Neo-Nazi activities continue unchecked in Argentina, such as the bombing of the Israeli Embassy in 1992 and the bombing of the Jewish community center in 1994. Anti-Semitic members of the military are now suspected of committing the crimes but, as one Argentine commentator put it, "it's obvious that the intelligence services don't investigate the neo-Nazi groups, because they will reach themselves. Just today I received photos of neo-Nazis meeting in Buenos Aires—they are all in black uniforms with insignia."[6] But there are even more blatant examples that some members of the population simply don't care about what happened. Antonio Bussi, one of the military leaders responsible for orchestrating over six hundred disappearances when he was governor of the state of Tucuman in 1976, was reelected governor in July 1995.

So, while I "see" the show of atonement, I don't buy it. I don't trust that the brutal repercussions of civil disputes will be "over" until the conceptual frameworks that "disappear" the feminine/feminized other in the name of male bonding and community building also "disappear." Civil conflict, clearly, is never "over" for good. But when civil conflict automatically gets played out as a battle to the death between the macho, "authentic" us and the effeminate them (consisting of penetrable, disposable bodies), then dirty wars are not far away.[7] There is a strange spectacularity to this moment. Time has been kept in abeyance by the haunting presence/absence of the disappeared and suspended between the not-yet-said and the not-yet-forgotten. Verbitsky's epigram to *El vuelo* sums it up: "History is a nightmare from which I am trying to awake" (James Joyce).

But there is a second, broader, basis for my unease. Ironically, while the quasi-fascist military forces that terrorized Argentina are being threatened with retribution, quasi-fascist sentiments and authoritarian politics have increased worldwide since I began this project. This week's news—to look no further—is filled with reports on hate crimes: the crimes against humanity committed by the Bosnian Serbs in their attempts at "ethnic cleansing"; the right-wing extremists' bombing of a federal building in the United States that killed over 160 innocent women, men, and children; the Russian efforts to mop up civilian blood in Chechnya; the massacre of an estimated four thousand Rwandans in a refugee camp; the rising tension in Japan in the aftermath of the gas attack by the Aum Supreme Truth cult; and U.S. officials and congressmen trying to figure out what to do about the "leaked" information that the C.I.A. not only trained but financed the Guatemalan military that has exterminated 300,000 civilians in the past decade. And that's just this week.[8]

While one war seems (momentarily) to be "over," a new "war" seems to be surfacing in the United States. The language U.S. terrorists use to describe their war sounds painfully familiar. Theirs, they affirm, is not an assault on innocent, unarmed civilians but a war (they too call it a holy war) on a godless enemy. It is a war of militaristic white men who think of themselves as true patriots, armed against all their others who do not fit into their image of America: Jews, minorities, women, and homosexuals. Where have we heard this before? Unlike Argentina during the Dirty War, in which most of the violence stemmed from state terrorism, the U.S. terrorists imagine themselves as profoundly antistate. They advocate "urban guerrilla" action executed with "the greatest coldbloodedness." Their acts of sabotage are intended "to cripple the economy of the country, agricultural or industrial production, transport and communication systems, the military and police systems."[9] Nonetheless, their antistate actions are closely linked to the currently dominant political rhetoric and policies designed to deny women, minorities, and homosexuals access to equal social participation through the dismantling of affirmative action, the welfare system, gun control laws, and anti-discrimination legislation.¹⁰ Although Rush Lim-baugh and other spokespeople for the rabid Right claim that we have to sepa-rate out the activities of the armed Right from their run-of-the-mill hate speech ("Blame the Bombers—Only"),¹¹ the Argentine example as well as other fas-cisms before it should have taught us the dangers of disconnecting violent inci-dents from the economic and ideological factors that gave rise to them. While I disagree with the Argentine chief of staff's claim that "almost all of us are responsible . . . either by act or omission," I do so only in degree. Without let-ting the culprits off the hook, it is vital to recognize that we participate in creat-ing the environment in which certain acts become thinkable, even admissible.

This study has advocated for the need to look at violence both globally (in an age of expanding "free" markets and policed borders) and locally (through the specific images and myths that populations hold about themselves). But how to "look" when the politics of viewing are so daunting? We are always looking across borders, whether national, ethnic, or cultural. The issue is not *if*, but *how*, we look. The encounters are staged in various ways—from the surveillance practiced by the U.S. border patrol or *migra* to the 'no se paga por ver' (you don't pay to look) of the street vendors. We participate in acts as disparate as witnessing, watching, peeping, as well as percepticide or self-blinding. Those acts entail different modes of identification, misidentification, seeing, or dis-believing what we see with our own eyes. Here, I will briefly sum up a couple of the problems I have argued attend the visual, beginning with the seeming non-encounter that results from denial and percepticide.

Martin Jay has recently argued that we have entered into an age of anti-ocularcentrism in which, after one trompe l'oeil too many, we question the relationship between the seen and the known. Our distrust of vision has been brought about by the very instruments—the telescope, the microscope, the camera—that theoretically were meant to enhance and expand our visual con-trol ("Photo-Unrealism" 344–360). Extending this observation from the realm of the epistemic to the political, we might say that part of our resistance to engaging politically (rather than emotionally) with the problems in the world around us is a product of studied disbelief. Viewers, often quite rightly, have come to suspect the way events have been structured as "problems," as "news." Not only does the media traffic in violence, milking catastrophes to excite viewers and hook them to the nightly news,¹² but there's the violence we don't see or, better put, that's not staged as *violence*. Poor children in the United States go without adequate food, education, and health care because white men in silk socks and Italian shoes want to save "us" money. The way that spectacles are framed and transmitted through the mass media threatens the truth value of what we see, turning any and all "real" occurrences into one more exotic commodity on our screen.

But denial stems not merely from the questionable linkage between the seen and known. We are so thoroughly submerged in the scopic field that at times we find it necessary to disengage from what we see or know to be "true." Devastating images from around the world lead to "compassion fatigue"—how many famished children and trainwrecks can we take in without feeling that we have to turn a blind eye for the sake of self-preservation? As waves of undifferentiated violence wash over us, differentiation seems impossible—after a while, it's all the same. We either resist identification—what happened in Argentina is not about me—or we over-identify. Identification, understood in psychoanalytic literature as the "internalization of the other" (Fuss, *Identification Papers*, 4), functions as an act of metaphoric substitution, supplanting the "you" with the "as-if-it-were-me." All of a sudden, the specificity of the problem vanishes. Watching the blows during *Paso de dos*, I might feel as if I were the torturer's next victim. Instead of reacting politically to end torture or violence against women, for example, we are paralyzed by extension. It's only one more step before we feel that these images tyrannize us and that *we* are their victims. The double mechanism of undifferentiation and over-identification results in percepticide, for the same gesture that denies specificity ("it's all the same after a while") commands our over-identification (it's about us—our money, our security, our national well-being). But this drama is not about me—as such—for I am neither the victim (who is helpless), nor the perpetrator (who is guilty). My role is neither to take on one's fear or the other's guilt, but to understand my role as *spectator* in enabling or disrupting the scenario.

Peeping and watching, which pertain to a different kind of cross-border looking, more explicitly call attention to the relationship between the see-er and the seen. Rather than the disavowal or cannibalism of percepticide—which supplants the relationship or questions the objective truth value of "the seen"— peeping and watching set up a unidirectional gaze. Both depend on perspectival vision that locates the seen within the scopic field while leaving the viewer safely out of the picture. We see as through the keyhole—the unseen see-er. Those who "just watch" what happened in Argentina risk engaging in Said's orientalism. Argentina is turned into a spectacle of excess (be it brutality or inflation) that feminizes it. It is "out of control." There's something fishy about the showy, macho, "Latin" virility. The military's performance of masculinity is overstated, if not parodic. The "othering" mechanism situates Argentina as the spectacle of transgression and the "body" of deviance. It serves as a cautionary message: that way disorder, dissolution, and danger lie. Moreover, it invisibly posits the watching "us" as the stable center. This unreciprocal seeing is part of the colonialist and militarist gesture of appropriation and internalization of the other to reenforce the defining self.

But the "looking" which I have called witnessing (in Boal's sense of the spect-actor rather than the passive spectator)[13] functions within a different scopic economy than peeping or watching. Gone is the comfort of perspectival vision—the safe vantage point from which the visual field is opened up and organized before the seeing "I," but which leaves the viewer out of the frame. On the contrary, witnessing belongs to the Lacanian field of the gaze, that register which locates us, and within whose confines we look at each other. The border has suddenly moved; it's no longer a question of the outer looking at the inner—we inhabit the expanded border zone of the inner. There is no stable footing here: the viewing subject is also the object of the gaze; the outsider is incorporated into the play of looks. We were all looking, looking at each other looking. The same scopic structure that situates the object to be looked at puts "us" in the picture. We are all caught off balance in the spectorial gaze, suddenly aware that the object of our gaze is also a subject who looks back, who challenges and objectifies us. Instead of the power and authority of the unseen seer looking down from some higher place, reciprocity upsets and destabilizes the authoritarian vantage point. What becomes immediately visible are the specificities of our position, and the ensuing limits to our perspective. We can't see everything; we can't occupy the visual vantage point of those located somewhat differently in the frame. What we see is clearly a function of where we happen to be standing—literally, politically, economically, and metaphorically. Though mutuality can be profoundly disconcerting and uncomfortable—perhaps the terms Yusem and I would have applied to our encounter—it stops us short, obliging us to rethink and look again. This pause, as Doris Sommer has so eloquently argued in her recent work, is not a bad thing if it encourages us to question easy notions of free access and rights of passage.[14]

Witnessing presupposes that looking across borders is always an intervention and that the space of interlocution is always performative. It works within an economy of looks and in a scenario where positions—subject/object, seer/seen—are constantly in flux, responding to each other. Each staging, as my example of the forum illustrates, makes visible and/or challenges certain relations of power, whether we like it or not. The physical setup of the encounter influences the dénouement of events. If Yusem and I had had the same conversation in private, my guess is that the outcome would have been different. As it was, our interface made evident the degree to which we were both trapped in our performative traditions—me, speaking with the authority of a first world feminist who is free to come, critique, and go, and Yusem, authoritarianly defending boundaries that had been negotiated away long ago. Recognizing the performative frame of the encounter allows us to recognize how both of us were caught in the spectacles we critiqued.

The scopic economy that has historically been established between the so-called First World and Third World reactivates and exacerbates these problems of viewing. There is no reciprocity of the look here. I will use these terms First and Third Worlds with great caution, for clearly this is one world, and the demarcations bespeak ideological as well as economic barriers and hierarchies. "First Worlders" refers to those from the so-called developed countries who economically benefit from the distribution of wealth and natural resources ensured by the corporate system and who contribute to its hegemony either through consent, identification, or lack of resistance. But there are many Third Worlders in the United States, for example, many native peoples and disenfranchised minorities who neither consent to, buy into, nor benefit from the dominant corporate, capitalist state. And the Third World certainly has its share of billionaires whose affiliations lie with Western banks rather than with their fellow citizens. There is no monolithic First World and Third World. Even allowing for a certain destabilization of the terms First and Third Worlds, which fuels my utopian fantasies that someday the ideological boundaries may be expanded and renegotiated, the terms refer to systems of power, wealth, distribution, and consumption that are differentiated enough to validate their (cautious) usage.

Viewing between the First and Third Worlds replays the same discrepancies in power I have outlined throughout. First Worlders have long been the powerful object of the look—looked at even when envied or despised. Images of the First World dominate the world. The media globally broadcasts and advertises the exuberance and youthfulness of its populations. Third Worlders represented in the media generally tend to be the topic of ethnographic study. The music and photography used to represent Them usually alert us that we are scopically entering some other space and time. We are enticed into something like the Twilight Zone, though we travel backwards, to peep at strange people and animals.

The fact of the matter is that most Third World peoples know far more about the First Worlders than the other way around. They need to in order to survive. International systems of power have made Third Worlders economically and politically dependent on "developed" countries. First Worlders, on the other hand, usually know very little about their many others, whose lives are nonetheless affected by the policies and images that reach them from "above." Argentineans might have an intense love-hate relationship with Britain; they drink tea and dress in the tweeds and plaids they buy at Harrods in Buenos Aires. But judging from British bookstores, this neocolonial benefactor of Argentine raw materials doesn't seem to know that Argentina exists. So while First Worlders may be looked upon, they seldom acknowledge or return the look.

The viewing other of the Third World tends to be denied subjectivity and legitimating power by conservatives and progressives alike. Right-wingers often promote the closing and policing of U.S. borders even as they themselves infiltrate other countries in the interests of so-called national security. Progressive leftists often overlook the effects of U.S. policy in the Third World. It seems interesting and ironic to me that even while many progressive First World intellectuals in the U.S. academy today endlessly evoke *positionality* and the *politics of location* in their work, they usually refer to geographic space only as metaphor. Scholars use terms such as *inclusivity* and *exclusivity, centrality* and *marginality* to describe relations of privilege and domination situated firmly within national lines. This elision, too, is a sign of power. Just as the terms of engagement, such as *straight, white, male,* and *class privilege,* fall out of discussions of power relations, issues related to positionality in terms of nation-ness (*First* and *Third* Worlds) underwrite all modern cultural projects and yet seem to be invisible, unspoken. Even when scholars in the United States refer to "nation," the concept is often applied nationally—to the U.S. nation and its multiple internal nations, the many Native American nations, the Chicano nation, the queer nation, the Aryan nation, and the nation of Islam being just some of them.

The resistance to letting down one's national guard is, not surprisingly, expressed from many in the Third World. A sense of national identity is particularly urgent given Latin America's history of colonialism. The struggle for national identity, fought through the various wars of independence in the nineteenth century, enabled most of these countries to free themselves from some sorts of foreign political and economic domination. But the continuing pressures of economic, political, and cultural imperialism intensify nationalist feelings. The sense of cultural superiority, combined with ignorance, manifested by the leaders of the First World, reminds the most open-minded Third Worlders that international "dialogue" is really power's misinformed monologue. (Remember when Dan Quayle, as vice president, visited Latin America and stated that he was pleased to have the opportunity of brushing up on his Latin?) Critiques of cultural colonialism, ethnocentricity, of lack of sensitivity and understanding about intercultural issues have long been waged against

First Worlders. Latin American theories of transculturation, *mestizaje*, and hybridity were developed to highlight cultural specificity and national "difference." Not only right- and left-wing nationalists, but progressive artists and intellectuals have felt it vital to essentialize difference from others (rather than differences within and among members of populations) and make difference visible. Even when First and Third Worlders struggle for similar issues, the alliances and interactions are fraught with dangers and tensions. For the last decades, feminist scholars from Third World countries have warned "white" feminists about engaging in discursive colonization, which "almost invariably implies a relation of structural domination, and a suppression—often violent— of the heterogeneity of the subject(s) in question."[15] Who can blame countries that have suffered centuries of colonization and neocolonialism for bolstering "national" identity and barricading their borders in an effort to keep community in and violence out?

Rather than argue that as a Canadian-Mexican feminist these warnings don't apply to me, I feel the sting from both sides. The tensions run right through me. I share the anger at the ignorance and cultural arrogance of some First Worlders who look "down" at Latin America as the site of fascinating excess. Yet I know people on both sides of the many "borders" dedicated to the principles of equal exchange and dialogue. I see informed debate about, among, and between these communities and negotiated alliances as absolutely essential in the struggle to alter or dismantle the conceptual paradigms that put us all at risk.

So what is to be done? How can we, as spectators in a global, scopic economy, look across national borders? What is the spectator's role in violence, especially in what can be constructed as the "other" country? We need, I believe, to recognize that "looking" is always an intervention, whether we like it, or accept it, or not. Not intervening, turning away, is its own form of intervention. Social scientists (most notably anthropologists) in the last few decades have noted that their very presence affects the nature of their analysis. They are no more "out" of the picture than any of us are "outside" the structural framework of the gaze. It's only within/from our system of positionalities, values, hierarchies that we recognize ourselves/each other. I can only play "self" to your "other." We're all actors and this, in the most global sense, is our *paso de dos*. Our choice is how, not whether, to participate.

Spectacles work internationally. People cross borders, capital moves invisibly from one location to another. Fantasies, too, are exported and imported; staging techniques travel; speech acts echo each other. The neo-Nazis in the United States today who advocate white supremacy belong to the same world as the neo-Nazis in Argentina with their black shirts, and both groups mimic Hitler's performance. The totalitarian spectacle of the Dirty War was one more "damnable iteration." It was a repetition with no single original. Through what act of negation, of self-blinding, can we maintain that what happens in another country has nothing to do with us?

Witnessing entails the acceptance of the "heavy weight of sorrow," and it entails responsibility. And it's not without its own risks. *Se paga por ver* (one pays for looking). Like others who write against violence, I too have wished for more options, better scripts, braver interventions. But witnessing, however singular and limited, is vital. It might help broaden the scope of the possible, expand the audience, and allow for a wider range of responses. Thus I join my perspective to others'—internal and external witnesses, historians, researchers, artists—who have struggled with the problem of documenting and representing violence.[17] My role in this drama is not to keep quiet, but to be a better spect-actor. For it is against the diminishment of our complex and interconnected visions that we must struggle.

Notes

1 Caught in the Spectacle

1 The production of *Paso de dos* was based on Pavlovsky's 1989 script, *Voces* (Voices), although it had undergone considerable change due to the year and a half of rehearsal with director Laura Yusem and the addition of another actor, Stella Galazzi, who played She's voice. The quotes that I cite (and translate) from *Voces*, however, were the words used in the play.

Throughout this book, I will give the Spanish title of all works first, then the translation in parentheses. If the work has been translated and published in English, I will also underline the English title. I will quote from the English translation whenever possible. When translations are not available, I will translate the sections myself.

2 I use "pornography" in the most general sense to refer not so much to content (the female's exposed body) as to the structural relationship of domination in which (generally) the woman-object is nothing but a victim to be violently exposed/raped by the aggressive subject for his enjoyment and the pleasure of a paying audience. What Susanne Kappeler writes in *The Pornography of Representation* sounds strikingly like what I describe in *Paso de dos:* "The so-called female point of view is a male construction of the passive victim of his own scenario, the necessary counterpart to his active aggressor: whether 'she' resists her own violation, whether she enjoys it in involuntary bodily response and against her will, or whether she is voluntarily

and infinitely available to his impositions—all available alternatives serve to enhance the pornographic pleasure, the active subjectivity of the male, his feeling of life. The options are strictly defined within the one imperative that it *will* happen to her; 'she' can choose an attitude" (91).

3   Horacio Verbitsky, *Página 12*, April 29, 1990.

4   Roberto M. Herrscher, "The Never Never Land," *Buenos Aires Herald*, May 28, 1990.

5   In "Torturadores y heroes," interview with Pavlovsky by Adriana Bruno, *Página 12*, April 29, 1990.

6   See the description of the film in Linda Williams's study of pornography, *Hard Core*, 61.

7   I am thinking specifically of stories such as Valenzuela's "Cambio de armas" (Other weapons) and novels such as Lynch's *Informe bajo llave* (Confession under lock and key). The motif of torture as a love story, of course, is not limited to Argentina. Liliana Cavani's film *The Night Porter* is another example of a work that stages violence against a woman as an act of "love."

8   In her essay "Frame-Up: Feminism, Psychoanalysis, Theatre," in *Performing Feminisms*, ed. Sue-Ellen Case, 59.

9   I realize that some might argue that I, not the play, am obliterating She's pleasure, her delight in this mad tango, this *pas de deux*. After all, Susana Evans insisted in an interview, she liked the physicality of the production. Even though it literally rendered her speechless, it "relaxed" her. "For me," she says, "there's a great deal of pleasure in it" (Feitlowitz, "Dance of Death," in *The Drama Review* 69). Without foreclosing the possibility of pleasure in the object position, or of s/m, I think it is crucial to differentiate between relations between consenting adults and the objectification and extermination of a political opponent. In the context of *Paso de dos*, set specifically in the Dirty War, defending She's right to pleasure in pain only reiterates what the Argentine military, wife abusers, and, ironically, Pavlovsky, are already saying: She likes it! It's all right to kill her because she enjoys the intensity.

10   The term *percepticide* was coined by the Argentine psychoanalyst Juan Carlos Kusnetzoff to describe the military's attack on the perceptual organs of the population (see Súarez-Orozco, "The Heritage of Enduring a 'Dirty War' " 492).

11   Almirante Emilio Massera, May 1976, documented in Avellaneda 150.

12   Nothing, the junta decreed, should "diminish the image of the guardians of order" or illustrate "any deterioration in the image of parents, or justify the rebellion of their children" (Avellaneda, 155).

13   "In all cases," the decree continued, "the resolution of the issues must lead to a positive ending" (Avellaneda 155).

14   Interview with author, Buenos Aires, September 1994.

15   Works such as Jacobo Timerman's *Preso sin nombre, celda sin número* (*Prisoner Without a Name, Cell Without a Number*, 1980) were followed by works such as *Todos somos subversivos* (We're all subversives) by Carlos Gabetta (1983) and Andrew Graham-Yooll's *A State of Fear* (1986).

16   Oscar Troncoso's collection of documents pertaining to the Dirty War, *El proceso de reorganización nacional* (The process of national reorganization), was published in 1984, and Andrés Avellaneda's *Censura, autoritarismo y cultura: Argentina 1960–1983* (Censorship, authoritarianism and culture) came out in 1986. Emilio F. Mignone's indictment of the supportive role of the Catholic Church in the *proceso*, *Iglesia y dictadura* (Church and dictatorship), was also published in 1986.

17   The draconian cuts sharply increased unemployment and also had a devastating effect on the

economic status of retired people, some of whom committed suicide in the Plaza de Mayo to call attention to their plight. (For unemployment figures, see "Boom Bypasses Argentina's Jobless," *New York Times*, February 5, 1995.

18   Gary Marx, "Argentina's President Pardons Leaders of 'Dirty War' on Leftists," *Chicago Tribune*, December 30, 1990.

19   *Brecha*, July 24, 1992. Qtd. in Petras and Vieux, "The Transition to Authoritarian Electoral Regimes in Latin America" 5.

20   "Crece la polémica por la guerra sucia," *Clarín* (edición internacional), November 1–7, 1994.

21   "Argentine Tells of Dumping 'Dirty War' Captives into Sea," *New York Times*, March 13, 1995.

22   Renan, "What Is a Nation?" in *Nation and Narration*, ed. Homi K. Bhabha 11.

23   Roach, "Culture and Performance" in *Performativity and Performance*, ed. Parker and Sedgwick.

24   Richard Schechner, *Between Theater and Anthropology*, p. 36. Jacques Derrida, "Signature Event Context," in *Margins of Philosophy*, p. 315.

25   See Lacan's *Four Fundamental Concepts of Psycho-Analysis*, especially "The Eye and the Gaze" and "What Is a Picture?"

26   See Doris Sommer's analysis of how the populist rhetoric blurs "left" and "right" in the suppression of the "feminine" within the patriarchal family in *One Master for Another*.

27   I have, in fact, begun looking at the attack on poor women in the United States in articles ("Welfare Mothers: The War on Poor Women and Their Children," coauthored with Annelise Orleck and Alexis Jetter) and through a series of conferences and workshops.

2   Gendering the National "Self"

1   "CELAM declara guerra a conferencia de mujeres," *Plou*, Buenos Aires, June 5, 1995.

2   Luis de Miranda, "Romance Elegíaco," in *Cautivas y misioneros* ed. Iglesias and Schvartzman, 20.

3   Ibid., 14–15.

4   Legends such as the one of the *cautiva* Lucía de Miranda written in 1612 by Ruy Díaz de Guzmán (in *La argentina*) and rewritten in numerous versions in following centuries, and Esteban Echeverría's nineteenth-century *La cautiva*, show the enduring and compelling interest in this myth. While there is a historical basis for these legends—there were white *cautivas* abducted by indigenous men—Susana Rotker, in an unpublished work, has illustrated by tracing the actual fate of these women that no one was interested in the women themselves. Once they had been freed and restored to "civilization," many of them went unclaimed by their families. As in Echeverría's version, once the woman is suspected of having been violated by the indigenous male, she is no longer reassimilable into the marriage or family.

5   Also quoted in Masiello, *Between Civilization and Barbarism* 27. See too Elizabeth Garrels's study on Sarmiento's *Facundo, A Myth Like a Hero* (forthcoming).

6   Since the time of the independence struggles at the beginning of the nineteenth century, two factions coalesced in opposition to each other. The Federalists wanted to empower the provinces as quasi-autonomous entities and preserve parochial traditions and popular culture. Their opponent, the Unitarians, were centrists, privileging Buenos Aires as the country's economic and governmental center. As Nicolas Shumway observes in *The Invention of Argentina*, "Argentine society from the first days of independence appeared to be built on a seismic fault" (44).

7   I use *fetish* much the way Michael Taussig does in his essay "Maleficium: State Fetishism," in Apter and Pietz's collection of essays, *Fetishism as Cultural Discourse.* Taussig draws his concept of the fetish from the Frankfurt School's theory of commodity fetishism, from French radicalism, and from Durkheimian sociology.

8   Susana Rotker is currently exploring the topic of the *cautivas:* see "Captives in the Border" (Rutgers University, 1994); "Dichos y des-dichos" (MLA, 1994); "Los otros desaparecidos: Las cautivas argentinas del siglo XIX (Anacitec-United Nations, 1995).

9   In part, Sarmiento's accusation of Inquisitional politics belong to the long line of liberal demonization of their opponents by associating them with the *leyenda negra.* However, the Nationalists in general, and the junta of 1976 specifically, claim the Inquisition as a model.

10   Esteban Echeverría's short novella, *El matadero* (The stockyard, 1830), is an apt nineteenth-century rendition of this violent opposition. While the Federalists' *mazorca* tried to reduce liberals to feminized bodies by threatening to rape the protagonist with a corncob, the liberal author discredits the enemy as a brutish thug, equating the Federalists with the bare-chested butcher covered with blood, surrounded by a horde of black and mulatto women groveling for the entrails (100).

11   Francine Masiello, in *Between Civilization and Barbarism,* writes of the effects of Rosas's assault on the collective imagination: "Argentine cultural texts of the period appear rich in the details of gender switching, designed to elude the tyrant . . . [I]n the age of Rosas, when masculine triumph is reserved for the dictator, all other men will be reduced in stature and deprived of the power identified with their sex" (28). Clearly, the diminishment of male opponents to "feminine" status ushered in new images of the feminine but these, paradoxically, undermined the status of "real" historical women by establishing a new paradigm for male bonding. Masiello continues: "Yielding the site of masculinity to the federalists, the unitarian men . . . assume a feminized pose. Yet despite this apparent gesture towards feminization, a snare lies in the author's final proposal, whereby men find new sources of bonding with one another and eliminate the need for women entirely" (28).

12   José María Ramos Mejía, *Rosas y su tiempo,* qtd. in J. M. Taylor, *Eva Perón: The Myths of a Woman* 118.

13   In Alberto Baldrich, "Las instituciones armadas," qtd. in Potash 102. See, too, Lugones' *La patria fuerte* and *La grande Argentina.*

14   Qtd. in Potash 103.

15   See, for example, how the military gains status through coverage in popular magazines dating back to the turn of the century, such as *Caras y caretas.*

16   See Molloy, "Too Wilde for Comfort."

17   Qtd. in Jorge Salessi, "Militant Histories of the Turn of the Century" (unpublished manuscript).

18   In Taylor and Villegas, *Negotiating Performance* 261.

19   Juan Bialet-Massé, *El estado de las clases obreras argentinas a comienzos de siglo* (1904), qtd. by Jorge Salessi in a work in progress, *Medics, Crooks, and Tango Queens: The Argentine Construction of the Homosexual Subject* 5 (Salessi's translation).

20   Newman, "The Modernization of Femininity: Argentina, 1916–1926," in *Women, Culture and Politics in Latin America,* ed. Bergmann et al. (Berkeley: University of California Press, 1990) 78.

21   The Uruguayan feminist Paulina Luisi, head of the National Women's Council in 1918, described the struggle of Argentine and Uruguayan women over the past several years: "Two years ago, we would scarcely dare pronounce the word *feminism;* it was synonymous with

machismo, with revolution, with the family's dissolution. It evoked rebellion and rupture, a threat to the family and to the center of our social structure . . . By now, we have convinced all attentive ears that what we want is not a destructive revolution at all, but rather a healthy and constructive evolution that will rebuild the crumbling structure of the family with the stone foundation of women's emotional and spiritual equality with men . . . We want to reclaim women's rights as social entities" ("Feminism," in *Women's Writing in Latin America*, ed. Castro-Klarén, Molloy, and Sarlo 251).

22 Nancy Leys Stepan writes in *"The Hour of Eugenics": Race, Gender and Nation in Latin America:* "Negative eugenics made women's fertility seem a crucial resource to the nation, thus locking women into reproductive roles. It supported racist ideas by proposing that maintaining distance between various ethnic and racial groups was necessary for the prosperity of the nation" (122).

23 Masiello, "Women, State, and Family in Latin American Literature of the 1920s" in *Women, Culture and Politics in Latin America* 32.

24 See Ximena Bunster-Burotto, "Surviving beyond Fear: Women and Torture in Latin America," in Nash and Safa, *Women and Change in Latin America*.

25 Often referred to as a fascist, Perón freely admitted that he had modeled his policy on fascist doctrine. He developed his concept of *justicialismo*, what he called "the third position" between the capitalist and communist world powers, from Mussolini. His plans to restructure Argentina were inspired by Nazi Germany, which, he thought, "was undergoing a similar process, . . . an organized state for a perfectly organized community . . . That is how I discovered the whole doctrine . . . People will say that it was a simple reflection of what was happening in Europe, and I will answer that is so, because that is the way our country has always been. What happens in Europe reaches us ten years later" (qtd. in Rock, *Authoritarian Argentina* 146). But *peronismo*, which began as a hybrid nationalist-fascist doctrine, became increasingly eclectic. Perón spoke of democracy as a desired goal, in large part to appease the United States. He drew freely from Marxism, with allusions to the proletariat and the bourgeoisie. He started marginalizing the church, a move that profoundly alienated the Nationalists. While he reaffirmed his commitment to the Nationalist doctrine based on principles of political sovereignty and nonalignment, the Nationalists who helped him to power felt betrayed as *nacionalismo* gradually gave way to *peronismo*.

26 In spite of the Hollywood image of unity promoted by Perón and Evita, his sexuality was a cause of speculation and concern among the population. It was rumored that the couple did not have sexual intercourse—in part explained by the fact that Eva developed cancer early in their life together. Notwithstanding the intensely exhibitionistic nature of his power-play, he is said to have been a voyeur attracted to young girls. After Evita's death, he spent more and more time in the girls' branch of the Union of Secondary School Students (UES), supposedly watching the young women undress through a one-way mirror in the locker room. Robert Crassweller, in *Perón and the Enigmas of Argentina*, maintains that Perón's interest was more that of a father than a pederast, but acknowledges that Perón took a fourteen-year-old student from the UES, Nelly Rivas, to live with him (275).

27 Qtd. in Rowe and Schelling 171.

28 Though a member of the military, Perón alienated his colleagues in the armed forces who, considering him dangerously ambitious and self-serving, arrested him on October 9, 1945. He gained the upper hand (and the presidency) by encouraging his mistress (later wife) Eva Duarte and his followers to organize a mass labor movement on October 17 to demand his release.

29 See Eva Perón's *La razón de mi vida*, ch. 6. Some acquaintances of Eva's, of course, did not believe this self-representation. In *Todas mis guerras*, the Mexican actress María Felix writes that Eva Perón's marriage was merely one of convenience. Felix writes: "When we were alone, Eva would confide in me. For example, that her husband was worthless both as a president and as a public figure; but she had to build him up to an extraordinary degree so that people thought that he ran the State" (21).

30 See García Canclini's illuminating discussion of the popular and popularity in his *Culturas híbridas*.

31 Tomás Eloy Martínez, *Santa Evita* (Buenos Aires: Planeta, 1995).

32 Qtd. in Navarro, *Evita* 289; my translation.

33 Qtd. in Navarro, *Evita* 306; my translation.

34 See J. M. Taylor, *Eva Perón: The Myths of a Woman*, ch. 4, and Mary Main, *Woman with a Whip: Eva Perón*.

35 After the fall of Isabelita in 1976, the weekly magazine *Gente* published a retrospective issue with a photograph of Evita's body returned to Argentina in 1973: "For the past twenty years, her body has been the protagonist of an incredible novel. It had been used for political ends. It was said to be at the bottom of a river, in an Italian convent, in a Spanish monastery. A thousand whereabouts and histories were assigned to it. When it arrived here, an impressive entourage marched around the car that transported it to the Presidential residence. Men armed to the teeth with modern machine guns and clutching walkie-talkies watched over the coffin. They looked like metal dummies, automatons. Their faces epitomized the times they were living in" ("Fotos hechos, testimonios de 1035 dramáticos días: 25 de mayo de 1973–24 de marzo de 1976," *Gente*, 191).

36 Qtd. in Troncoso, *Presidencias y golpes militares del siglo xx* 3:12.

37 Roberto Cossa's play, *El avión negro* (1970), stages the return of the repressed Perón and the power of the unsaid, as I explore in the chapter on the fight for public space.

38 Following the dissolution of political parties after the Onganía coup in 1966, politicized and often militarized groups, ranging from extremely violent neofascists (of the Nazi or falange model) to leftist anti-imperialists, appeared on the Argentine scene. Many of these conflicting groups, ironically, looked to *peronismo* as their source and worked to bring about its resurgence. After the *Cordobazo* of 1969, a popular outbreak in Córdoba that brought down the Onganía dictatorship, guerrilla warfare became, to paraphrase Carl von Clausewitz, the continuation of politics by other means. The *montoneros,* the Peronist Armed Forces (FAP), and the Revolutionary Armed Forces (FAR) came into being as three separate branches of armed *peronist* forces. Left-wing parties, such as the People's Revolutionary Army (or ERP, a small Trotskyite armed force) and the Revolutionary Workers' Party (PRT), also sprang up. General Alejandro Lanusse, who supplanted Onganía as president of Argentina, remarked in hindsight that his and Onganía's greatest political blind spot "was our inability to see that politics existed and that nothing could be more dangerous than the arrogance of considering it non-existent" (Troncoso, *Proceso* 68). Lanusse sought to minimize the increasingly violent effects of repressed *peronismo* by making secret overtures to the exiled ex-president Perón himself. However, Perón had a history of using the very people who were using him, and true to his record he succeeded in turning the secret negotiations against Lanusse. He eventually unseated the president and reinstated himself as a political leader. In 1973, Perón's stand-in, Héctor Campora, was voted into office, and in October of that same year Perón himself regained the presidency with Isabelita as his vice president on a Perón-Perón ticket.

Although *peronismo* reappeared as a legitimate political force, its legal status did not cement the diverse groups that had used the term to consolidate themselves. *Peronist* groups ranged from the violent, ultra-right-wing AAA to the *montoneros* and the Peronist Youth. While all his disciples awaited his return to Argentina, a violent outbreak occurred at the airport on the day of his arrival. Perón sided with the ultra-right, and used the AAA, made up of new paramilitary forces and death squads, to target the *montoneros* and the Peronist Youth for elimination. However, one of the most puzzling and ironic aspects of the conflict was the difficulty of differentiating among the various groups on ideological grounds, although they were brutally fighting each other. But these two groups could not be called "leftists" in the conventional meaning of that term because they were fighting the extreme right wing. The umbrella terms covered a broad ideological range that included positions normally associated with both the Left and the Right—divergencies that were not always apparent to the groups' members, many of whom were young and politically unsophisticated. As Rock writes, "the Montoneros became yet another example of 'that strange fusion or marriage between the Left and [Right]' that characterized so many of the political movements of the late 1960s and early 1970s" (*Authoritarian Argentina* 219). They not only organized themselves in a strict hierarchical and authoritarian fashion, but they even drew from the same xenophobic, misogynist, and palingenetic discourse that throughout this study I have associated with the Nationalists. Eugenio Méndez, in *Confesiones de un montonero*, documents that women in the *montonero* movement were treated as sexual objects by the male leaders. The bosses got to choose the prettier women, while the others were distributed among the more lowly men. He quotes from the *montonero* doctrine that sounds much like the Nationalists: "there should be a wall between revolutionaries and traitors, a wall grounded in national conscience, in the determination to execute solutions, in the love for the Patria, loyalty to our martyrs and hate unto death of everything that represents the enemy" (98). Rock cites Guillermo O'Donnell's idea that the *montoneros* bore "a striking resemblance to a seldom recognized precursor: the radical wing of the European fascist movement [in their] hostility to foreigners per se; an extraordinarily chauvinistic affirmation of the nation; exaltation of the leader in the person of Perón; the worship of violence [and] military hostility to both Marxism and Liberalism. [The Montoneros upheld] profoundly militarist, authoritarian and elitist conceptions . . . of politics and their own organizations" (*Authoritarian Argentina* 220). So while the violence among the factions was undoubtedly real, it is not clear that their ideologies were always radically divergent.

39 Aside from the fact there is no neat left-wing/right-wing distinction, there is even evidence that oppositional forces had been infiltrated by government agents. Mario Firmenich, leader of the *montoneros*, is said to have been a double agent (see Martin Edwin Anderson, "Dirty Secrets of the 'Dirty War'" 340), thus opening to question how much of the oppositional violence was orchestrated by the military in order to justify their imposed rule on Argentina. To complicate matters further, members of the *montoneros* and other opposition groups also welcomed the social disruption and looked forward to the military coup, not simply because they had little use for "Martínez," as they now called their president, but because they thought that a coup would motivate oppositional groups and the Argentine population to form a united resistance. No doubt most of the *montoneros* did not recognize the degree of their miscalculation, nor did they understand that they had in fact played into the military's hands, until most of their members had been eliminated.

40 Document reproduced in Vázquez 36.

41   Qtd. in the special issue of the weekly magazine *Gente, Lo mejor de Gente y la actualidad*, 1977, "Palabras de Isabel" 228–29. Interestingly, there is a book on Evita, Perón's popular wife, entitled *Evita: Woman with a Whip.*

42   See, for example, "La historia secreta de la caída de Isabel Perón," in the special issue of the weekly magazine *Gente, Lo mejor de Gente y la actualidad*, 1977, p. 186. It is of interest to note that this article, like many in *Gente*, calls attention to its testimonial nature: "What follows is an exact and faithful testimony of the final act of the *proceso*," it announces, though the observer is never identified. Moreover, the unidentified author notes, the tape recorder that was to capture Isabelita's words after her abduction and overthrow was not turned on: "Maybe because of the tension or maybe because of a technical error, the play button was not activated. The exact words of the dawn of the 24th are not recoverable. They are locked in the memory of the protagonists. Only they can repeat them" (185). Nonetheless, the author goes on to "quote" the conversation and mention Isabelita's remark about her wardrobe.

43   See Eva Gilberti and Ana María Fernández's anthology of feminist essays, *La mujer y la violencia invisible*, for a discussion of the status of women in Argentina during the 1970s and 1980s.

44   See the documentary *Las Madres de la Plaza de Mayo* by Susana Muñoz and Lourdes Portillo for an interview with the U.S. military commander in charge of this training. See, too, Noam Chomsky and Edward S. Herman, *The Washington Connection and Third World Fascism*, ch. 2.

45   The authoritarianism that has dominated twentieth-century politics in Argentina is not, strictly speaking, fascist. *Nacionalismo*, the Argentine ideology often confused with fascism, is an ultraconservative, antirevolutionary, Catholic, and "macho" form of authoritarianism that has, at times, existed alongside fascism but has just as often worked against it. *Nacionalismo* tends to differ from fascism by not being a charismatic or populist form of power. With the exception of Juan Perón, who at times was arguably closer to fascism than to *nacionalismo*, the Nationalists have seldom sought enthusiastic and active popular support. Rather, they posit the military as a chosen elite, destined to guide the country toward its grand destiny. The Nationalists highlight the role of the Catholic Church (as evident in their visible coalition with the clergy) and appeal to their Catholic traditions to justify their actions as a crusade for "Truth" and "purity." I refer the reader who is interested in these issues to historical works such as David Rock's *Authoritarian Argentina* (1993), Marysa Navarro's *Los nacionalistas* (1968), Robert Potash's *The Army and Politics in Argentina* (1969), Tulio Halperín Donghi's *El revisionismo histórico argentino* (1971), and intellectual histories such as Francine Masiello's *Between Civilization and Barbarism: Women, Nation, & Literary Culture in Modern Argentina* (1992) and Nicolas Shumway's *The Invention of Argentina* (1991) for a more complete account of the historical, intellectual, and social forces leading to the Dirty War.

3   *Military Males, "Bad" Women, and a Dirty, Dirty War*

1   The exception to the general ban was the soccer game scheduled for that day. See note 3.

2   Larsen, "Sport as Civil Society: The Argentinean Junta Plays Championship Soccer."

3   Larsen's example of soccer as a spectacle related to civil society is an interesting one, though the 1978 World Cup restaged, in a supposedly nonpolitical space, the same contentious world-view and masculinist values endorsed by the military. The all-male world divided into the "us" versus the enemy "them," the rigorously trained and disciplined male body as the embodi-

ment of national identity and aspirations, the role of the spectators on the sidelines who could only manifest their feelings of national identity by feminizing and symbolically violating the enemy other can be seen as an extension of the military spectacle.

4 See Turner, *The Anthropology of Performance.*

5 Juan Carlos Onganía, who led the 1966 coup, stated: "Today we initiate once and for always the march towards the conquest of a glorious destiny for the Patria." Jorge Rafael Videla, president of the junta of the 1976 coup, stated: "The immediate past has been left behind and we embark on a future that will lead to the greatness of the Patria. The events that just happened [the coup] represent a definite closure to one historical cycle and the beginning of a new one." For a study of "new beginning" speeches by Argentine leaders see Graciela Scheines, *Las metáforas del fracaso* (Buenos Aires: Editorial Sudamericana, 1995).

6 The cover of the weekly magazine *Tal Cual* during the Malvinas war depicted Thatcher, dressed in a Wonder Woman costume, under the headline: "Thatcher Is Crazy: She Thinks She's Wonder Woman."

7 It apparently also circulated within the armed forces as a poster. If this is so, its meaning in that context would vary somewhat from what I argue if the general public is the intended audience, though here too, the lone soldier tries to convince his peers that this is a good, "clean" fight and casts a suspicious look behind in case any in the military don't support him.

8 See de Lauretis, *Alice Doesn't.*

9 The speech was printed in its entirety in *La nación* on the day of the coup. It is also reprinted in Oscar Troncoso's collection of documents, *El proceso de reorganización nacional.* (All translations from Spanish are mine unless otherwise noted.)

10 All references to this document are from Troncoso's collection of documents, though the pronouncement also ran on the front page of *La nación* on the day of the coup.

11 "Ilegó el momento en que asumimos nuestra mayoría de edad y aplicamos nuestra propia doctrina" (*La Prensa* April 1, 1981), qtd. in Frontalini and Caiati, *El mito de la "Guerra Sucia,"* 32.

12 Michael Taussig, "Maleficium: State Festishism," in Apter and Pietz, *Fetishism as Cultural Critique.*

13 See Francine Masiello and Beatriz Sarlo's essays in *Ficción y política,* ed. Balderston et al. for discussions of the representation of the military as a unified subject. In fact, however, the three branches of the armed forces were bitter rivals; the *desaparecidos* were sometimes tortured and killed as retribution to another branch.

14 Qtd. in Feitlowitz, *Lexicon of Terror,* 30.

15 See "Interview" in *La maga,* June 21, 1995, p. 4.

16 Fisher, *Mothers of the Disappeared* 65.

17 Emilio Massera's public speeches, collected in a volume entitled *El camino a la democracia,* are interesting, in part because he is the junta leader most directly involved in the tortures, personally directing paramilitary death squads or *grupo de tareas* to carry out the abductions and killings (see Raúl David Vilarino's account, *Yo secuestré, maté y vi torturar en la Escuela de Mecánica de la Armada*). Moreover, his collection of essays maps out the ups and downs of the nationalist discursive terrain—the progression from prelapsarian myths of origin to a dangerous present threatened by insidious enemies to glorious visions of collective triumph. Massera's speeches provide the most coherent picture of the military ideology as represented by one of its own.

18 Eugenio Méndez, in *Confesiones de un montonero,* reports how women were treated as sexual

objects for the leadership and repeatedly equates the "feminine" with weakness, sissiness, and betrayal.

19   I want to thank Elizabeth Garrels and an anonymous reader for helping me clarify this connection.

20   The military's move to claim "national" subjectivity for itself while relegating nontranscendence to the feminine is an example of Judith Butler's observation in *Gender Trouble* 11–12: the male subject "is abstract to the extent that it disavows its socially marked embodiment and, further, projects it on to the feminine sphere, effectively renaming the body as female. This association of the body with the female works along magical relations of reciprocity whereby the female sex becomes restricted to its body, and the male body, fully disavowed, becomes, paradoxically, the incorporeal instrument of an ostensibly radical freedom."

21   McGee, "The Visible and the Invisible Liga Patriótica Argentina, 1919–28."

22   *Gente*, May 6, 1976, pp. 12–13. Editorial Atlántida, publishers of *Gente* and *Somos*, elaborated on these themes in their women's magazine, *Para tí* (For you).

23   In *Lo mejor de Gente y la actualidad: las grandes notas, las grandes fotos, los grandes viajes, los grandes reportajes*, Buenos Aires, 1977.

24   Ximena Bunster-Burotto, "Surviving beyond Fear: Women and Torture in Latin America," in Nash and Safa 299.

25   Pedro Pablo Carballo, in "La elección de las embarazadas," *Página 12*, July 1, 1995, p. 2.

26   See Verbitsky, *Rodolfo Walsh y la prensa clandestina, 1976–1978* 87–88. See also "La elección de las embarazadas," *Página 12*, July 1, 1995, p. 2.

27   A confession by concentration guard Pedro Pablo Carballo in "La elección de las embarazadas," *Página 12*, July 1, 1995, p. 2.

28   Adriana Calvo de Laborde's testimony in *El libro del juicio: Testimonies* 38–39.

29   General Ramón J. Camps explained the rationale for disappearing babies: "It wasn't people that disappeared, but subversives. Personally I never killed a child; what I did was to hand over some of them to charitable organizations so that they could be given new parents. Subversive parents educate their children for subversion. This has to be stopped" (qtd. in Fisher, *Mothers of the Disappeared* 102). Vertibsky cites several instances in which children were killed by the military. In one case, witnesses heard one of the members of the armed forces who was taking away a ten-year-old boy, "We'd better kill you now, so you don't grow up." The boy was never seen again (*Rodolfo Walsh* 62).

30   Redefining Motherhood conference, Dartmouth College, May 1993.

31   The letter is published in Verbitsky's *Rodolfo Walsh* 119–20.

32   Agustín Feced, head of the Gendarmerie (qtd. in Frontalini and Caiati's *El mito de la "Guerra Sucia"* 22).

4   The Theatre of Operations: Performing Nation-ness in the Public Sphere

1   Eduardo P. Archetti, "Masculinity and Football: The Formation of National Identity in Argentina," in Giulianotti and Williams, *Games without Frontiers* 236.

2   The term *nation-ness* was coined by Benedict Anderson in *Imagined Communities* to encompass concepts as disparate as nation, nationality, and nationalism. Though clearly the three are not synonymous, there is a certain slippage even in Anderson's use of the terms: "My point of departure is that *nationality*, or, as one might prefer to put it in view of the word's multiple significations, *nation-ness*, as well as *nationalism*, are cultural artifacts of a particular kind" (13;

italics added). "Nation-ness," Anderson states, "is the most universally legitimate value in the political life of our time" (12). Although he doesn't define the term, I take it to mean the *idea* of nation, which includes everything from the bureaucratic fact of citizenship to the nationalist's mythical construct of nation as an eternal entity.

3   Beatriz González Stephan, "Las escrituras de la Patria: Constituciones, gramáticas y manuales," *Estudios: Revista de Investigaciones Literarias* 3.5 (January–June 1995): 19–46.

4   Judith Butler, "Performative Acts," in Case, *Performing Feminisms* 270.

5   I am indebted to my colleague, Rodolfo Franconi, who has shared his work on modern Brazilian cultural studies with me.

6   Qtd. in Rowe and Schelling, *Memory and Modernity* 170.

7   Qtd. in Rowe and Schelling, *Memory and Modernity* 170.

8   The film *Man Facing SouthEast* beautifully captures the isolation and compartmentalization of space under the junta. Rantes, a patient who claims to be an alien from a more humanitarian planet, leaves the psychiatric ward and initiates a spectacle of joy and inclusivity at a concert. His transgression ultimately leads to his death.

9   David Rock notes that the brutality of the Dirty War went hand in hand with the economic restructuring undertaken by Martínez de Hoz: "the butt of both was the urban sectors: the unions, industry, and much of the middle class. The Army's task, with the war against subversion in part as pretext, was to shatter their collective bargaining power and their means of resistance; Martínez de Hoz's role was to weaken and ultimately destroy the economy on which they subsisted" (*Argentina* 369).

10 Foucault, *Discipline and Punish* 201.

11 Admiral César A. Guzzetti put this clearly: "My concept of subversion refers to terrorist organizations on the left. There is no right wing subversion or terrorism. The social body of this society is contaminated by a disease that erodes its entrails and forms antibodies. Those antibodies cannot be considered in the same way that one considers a microbe. As the government controls and destroys the guerrilla, the action of the antibodies will disappear. I am convinced that in the next few months there will be no more action from the right, something that is already underway. It is only a natural reaction to a social body" (*La Opinión*, March 10, 1976, qtd. in Frontalini and Caiati, *El mito* 21).

12 One example of the military exercises in population control, documented in the daily *La razón* on December 19, 1976, illustrates how the theatre of operations worked: "An operation of population control, similar to earlier ones, was carried out this morning by the joint forces of Villa Comunicaciones and Retiro. This included the identification of persons, the registration of documents, and an intense sanitary control of the population. The operation, which began at five this morning, was completed by 1,500 men from the joint forces, and 500 collaborators from the Departments of Migration, Social Welfare, Public Health and the Municipality of Buenos Aires" (qtd. in Frontalini and Caiati, *El mito* 37).

13 Renee Epelbaum's three children were disappeared in 1976–77. Her cook, Ester, not only stayed with her during that period and up to the present but she and her young daughter were submitted to a terrifying raid by paramilitary forces after the children's abductions. The "task force" took everything—all the photographs of the children, the soap, the toilet paper. Ester remembers lying that the children were away on holiday so that the soldiers would not take out their anger on her and her child (interview with author, Buenos Aires, July 1994).

14 Private instruction was offered by some of Argentina's bravest and most eminent academics. Entire disciplinary groups, such as women's studies, moved to relatively hidden spaces, such as

the *ático* Gloria Bonder describes, with its labyrinthine approach (interview with author, Buenos Aires, July 1994).

15   AIDA, *Argentina: Como matar la cultura* 19–20.

16   The controls did not let up even when the government started moving toward privatization as part of their effort to dismantle the unwieldy state bureaucracy and enter into a neoliberal economy. When the radio stations were privatized in 1980, for example, a new law was passed, containing eighty-seven articles controlling the content of broadcasted materials.

17   *Gente*, April 15, 1976, p. 17.

18   AIDA, *Argentina: Como matar la cultura* 249.

19   *La nación*, June 1, 1976.

20   Ad in *La nación* for *Gente*, July 8, 1976, p. 16.

21   Ministry of Middle and Higher Education, Ministry of Culture and Education, Circular 137, qtd. in AIDA, *Argentina: Como matar la cultura* 245.

22   See Kordon, *Psychological Effects of Political Repression*.

23   "Algo que espanta," *Gente*, August 26, 1976, pp. 4–7.

24   The feminist scholar Gloria Bonder recounts how she and the group of women who organized an interdisciplinary seminar on women's studies were forced out of the university. In 1979 they founded the Centro de Estudios de la Mujer (CEM), which they located in an attic with a labyrinthine approach to it. The women felt relatively safe there. This was one of the "alternate" spaces that, when they did not entirely disappear, the junta pushed out of sight. When the women left their attic to speak in public or to organize work groups in the poor districts, they would dress up, put on furs and earrings like good *burgesas* to avoid being seen as active women by the military or as lesbian feminists (terms perceived as synonymous) by the nonpoliticized women they worked to help.

25   *La nacion*, January 2, 1977, p. 15.

26   *La nación*, May 11, 1976, p. 14.

27   *La nación*, April 21, 1976, p. 16.

28   The ad is included in the video, *Pais cerrado, Teatro abierto*.

29   *La nación*, April 18, 1976.

30   *La nación*, May 27, 1976.

31   *La nación*, April 14, 1976.

32   It seems clear that the images circulating in the public sphere were also absorbed and transmitted less consciously as well. For example, a picture of a woman screaming on the cover of an Ellery Queen mystery magazine was accompanied by the caption "No se descuide al salir a la calle [Be careful when you go out on the street]" (*La nacion*, May 3, 1976, p. 8). The cover was not meant to comply with the military's strict "guidelines"; nonetheless, it manifests the feelings, fueled by the military and experienced by the population, that public space had become a terrifying hunting ground. Women and, more generally, the "feminine," were under attack. The headline in an ad for a children's encyclopedia read: "How do we measure the speed of falling solid objects?" Ordinarily, this headline might not signal an alarm, but in the context of a regime that eliminated their opposition by flinging the drugged bodies of their opponents out of airborne airplanes, the image of solid bodies falling produced terror. In the marketplace, a battle was waged against a toy rifle called the Guerrillero: "The country is also killed with toy rifles" (*Gente*, April 22, 1976, pp. 68–69). The toy, the article explains, is inoffensive. But the name: "a word that everyone identified with violence and death was being used as bait to sell toys to children" (68). The company withdrew the toy and published its

apologies, and *Gente* concluded the article by saying: "The toy rifle, 'Guerrillero,' is no longer on the market. It's no longer being made. It's no longer a threat. The error was corrected" (69). It's not rifles that disappear from the public sphere—just *guerrilleros.*

33 *La nación,* May 3, 1976, p. 7.

34 Taussig, *The Nervous System* 2.

35 See Rowe and Schelling, *Memory and Modernity* 138.

36 Pierre Bourdieu, "How Can One Be a Sports Fan?" in *The Cultural Studies Reader,* ed. During 340.

37 Eduardo P. Archetti, "Masculinity and Football: The Formation of National Identity in Argentina," in *Games without Frontiers,* ed. Giulianotti and Williams, p. 225.

38 Simpson and Bennett, *The Disappeared* 287.

39 "Campiones de Verdad" *Siete días,* June 29–July 5, 1978, p. 6.

40 "Campiones de Verdad" *Siete días,* June 29–July 5, 1978, pp. 3–13.

41 "In the smaller, less-known stadiums, I would argue soccer is an all-male affair, with all-male fans. Females are sporadically seen, in the more modern and bigger stadiums, always accompanied by males, and only in the expensive plateas, or covered seats under a roof, section of the stadium. This more expensive, rather small section, reserved for officials and the upper classes, that occasionally find amusement in the spectacle, is separated from the larger terraces by wire fences. Note that for all practical purposes females are the 'real' fans, and go to the stadiums by and large to find exotic amusement" (Suárez-Orozco, 25n "A Study of Argentine Soccer" 10).

42 Suárez-Orozco, "A Study of Argentine Soccer" 9.

43 Social scientists Suárez-Orozco, A. H. Chapman, Ralph Bolton, Stanley Brandes, Alan Dundes, and others have noted the macho's fear of homosexuality. As Dundes puts it, the macho must expend great energy protecting his "mas(male)culus(anus)" or masculinity (qtd. in Suárez-Orozco, "A Study of Argentine Soccer" 18).

5   *Percepticide*

1 The caption, not legible in this particular photograph, reads: "Now to the Death: To All Argentines: We have demonstrated our pacifist vocation. Now we will demonstrate our spirit of struggle. Two virtues, equally real for Argentineans. Both with many historical antecedents. We knew how to give up our lives for our Malvinas. Now, we will kill whoever tries to take them away."

2 See Iain Chambers, "Narratives of Nationalism: Being 'British,'" in Carter, Donald, and Squires, *Space and Place.*

3 Here I elaborate on an earlier version of an essay, published in 1991, which explored the theatrical representation of a terrorist space.

4 Terrorism, Herbert Blau notes in *Take Up the Bodies: Theater at the Vanishing Point,* "has always been designed theatrically. There is a plot, choreography, coup du théâtre, and all the attendant apparatus of the staged performance" (272). Elaine Scarry, in *The Body in Pain,* repeatedly refers to torture, metaphorically, as theater: as the "mime of uncreating" (20), as an "acting out" (27), as an "obscene and pathetic drama" (56). The torturer, to Scarry, "dramatizes the disintegration of the world" (38).

5 All translations are by Marguerite Feitlowitz in her edition, *Information for Foreigners: Three Plays by Griselda Gambaro.* While several of Gambaro's novels were published in Argentina

during the 1970s (Gambaro is also an award-winning novelist), her plays were not published in Argentina during this period. The collection of Gambaro's plays published by Ediciones de la Flor came out in 1984. *Information*, included in this collection, circulated in manuscript form before its publication and has never been performed in its entirety. This circumstance does not invalidate the work's attempts to reach different audiences, including the reading (foreign) audience of the title. The questions we could pose about its performance, such as what would happen if a member of the real audience offered the Tortured Girl some dry clothes, or if someone walked out, are still valid. What would happen if someone responded? The question is not hypothetical. The answer is that it has not happened, and that acts of repression (the censorship of this play included), keep happening in Argentina and elsewhere. The play's intent is to scrutinize the public's ability to deny the facts that it knows to be true.

6   These incidents are detailed in press reports from April to December 1970; see *La prensa, La nación*, and *Clarín*, for example, and Rock, *Argentina: 1516–1987* 441.

7   General Jacques Massu's memoirs of the Algerian war, *La Vraie Bataille d'Algers*, became a classic defense of torture, giving rise to expressions such as Massuism and Massuist. Michael Levin follows the Massuist line of argument in "The Case for Torture," in *The Norton Reader: An Anthology of Expository Prose*, ed. Caesar R. Blake et al. (New York: Norton, 1988) 619. For a general study on torture see Edward Peters, *Torture*.

8   Lifton, *The Nazi Doctors* 420. See also Alice Yaeger Kaplan, *Reproductions of Banality: Fascism, Literature, and French Intellectual Life* (Minneapolis: University of Minnesota Press, 1986); and Saul Friedlander, *Reflections on Nazism*, trans. Thomas Weyr (NY: Harper and Row, 1984).

9   See Scarry, *The Body in Pain* 28; Peters, *Torture*; and Timerman, *Prisoner Without a Name*. The situation described in *Nunca Más* succinctly states a conclusion about the gratuitous nature of the interrogation that coincides with the findings reported in the different studies: "They were tortured, almost without exception, methodically, sadistically, sexually, with electric shocks and near drownings and constant beatings, in the most humiliating possible way, not to discover information—very few had information to give—but just to break them spiritually as well as physically, and to give pleasure to their torturers. Most of those who survived the torture were killed"; see *Nunca Más: The Report of the Argentine National Commission on the Disappeared.*

10   In *Argentina: 1516–1987*, Rock notes that Martinez de Hoz's economic measures to stabilize Argentina "through the aggressive pursuit of foreign investment" were inseparable from the military's repression of the population, specifically labor leaders and union workers. "The Army's war on subversion and Martinez de Hoz's program elicited opposite responses from outside observers, who detested the extreme brutalities of the former but generally praised the latter. In many respects, however, the two policies were complimentary and inseparable" (369). On public complicity, see Peters, *Torture* 179–84.

11   Argentine president Menem's decision to pardon the criminals of the Dirty War is only the most current example of the inversion attested throughout the literature on torture. Jacobo Timerman's testimony of the torture inflicted on him in Argentina in *Prisoner Without a Name* was discredited by many reviewers who defended the regime and accused Timerman of bringing "his own troubles, including his own torture, on himself" (Peters, *Torture* 160–61). *Torture in Brazil: A Report by the Archdiocese of Sao Paulo*, documents that torture victims and/or their families asking that the torturers be punished were called vengeful; they were encouraged to forget, to "let bygones be bygones" (xii). Peters reports that in 1973, UNESCO refused to allow Amnesty International to convene in its Paris center because Amnesty's report

on torture reflected unfavorably on sixty of UNESCO's member-countries currently practicing torture (160).

12   Anthony Kubiak, "Disappearance as History: The Stages of Terror," *Theatre Journal* 39 (1987): 84.

13   Gambaro, in a 1982 interview, insists (with an anti-Aristotelian inversion) that theatre must enable the audience to see again, for the public has lost its capacity to see reality: "the dead are numbers, statistics . . . we can read about the war in Lebanon and it means nothing to us . . . The aesthetic act has to wake us up, we have to come round, out of the anesthetizing misinformation, the emotional deformation, and the ideas that are the very basis of our society"; see Griselda Gambaro, *Teatro* (Ottawa: Girol Books, 1983), 31.

14   For a discussion of the disappearance of self in the field of other, see Lacan, *Four Fundamental Concepts of Psycho-Analysis.* The audience's situation in *Information* recalls Jean-Paul Sartre's example of the individual peering through the keyhole: "My consciousness sticks to my acts, it is my acts; and my acts are commanded only by the ends to be attained (the spectacle to be seen), a pure mode of losing myself in the world . . . But all of a sudden I hear footsteps in the hall. Someone is looking at me! . . . the person is presented to consciousness in so far as the person is an object for the Other. This means that all of a sudden I am conscious of myself as escaping myself. Not in that I am the foundation of my own nothingness but in that I have my foundation outside of myself. I am for myself only as I am a pure reference to the Other" (*Being and Nothingness* [ ]).

15   Foucault, *Discipline and Punish* 195.

16   Metz, *The Imaginary Signifier* 63.

17   Berger, *Ways of Seeing* 58 (emphasis is Berger's).

18   See Chomsky and Herman, *The Washington Connection and Third World Fascism: The Political Economy of Human Rights.*

19   Simpson and Bennett, *The Disappeared: Voices from a Secret War.*

6   Disappearing Bodies: Writing Torture and Torture as Writing

1   See Horacio Verbitsky, *El vuelo;* and "Argentine Tells of Dumping 'Dirty War' Captives into Sea," *New York Times,* March 13, 1995.

2   Qtd. in Fisher, *Mothers of the Disappeared* 102.

3   In Blonsky, *On Signs* 40.

4   See Simpson and Bennett, *The Disappeared* 225.

5   Torture was not used primarily to ensure national security (not that it would be justified in any case). Six months before the coup, Videla estimated that the opposition amounted to little more than three thousand people. A year later he claimed "the virtual elimination of the subversive organizations with the loss of approximately 90% of [the] cadre" (qtd. in English in Tina Rosenberg, *Children of Cain* 123).

6   Qtd. in English in Tina Rosenberg, *Children of Cain* 117.

7   Salessi quotes Ramos Mejias, who goes to great lengths to equate the Jews to the *invertidos* by noting "a bizarre fusion of the economic type of man and the sexual invert . . . The acquisition and conservative energies of the usurer, in his tranquil intensity and in his hidden pleasure, are only comparable to the lust of the sexual invert, essentially shameful" (*Médicos maleantes* 32).

8   David Halperin, "Sex before Sexuality," in *Hidden from History: Reclaiming the Gay and Lesbian Past,* qtd. in Salessi, *Médicos maleantes* 49.

9   Chambers, "No Montagues Without Capulets" 2. In this, I disagree to some extent with Susanne Kappeler's argument that "gratuitousness" motivates torturous crimes against the defenseless, supposedly inferior other—the murder and photographing of eighteen-year-old black farmer Thomas Kasire by the white farmer van Rooyen: photographing the torture and the corpse "is for sheer surplus pleasure, as is the torture itself, which has nothing to do with fighting so-called terrorists or any other utility in the world. It serves the leisure and the pleasure of the white man . . . it is a form of his free expression of himself, an assertion of his subjectivity" (10). While no doubt the ability to inflict pain and death on another is a form of expression, privilege, and invulnerability for the powerful, it still serves some "useful" purpose. But maybe it was the "pleasure" of it that made it so widespread a practice during the Dirty War.

10   Alicia Partnoy, interview with author, Dartmouth College, May 14, 1993.

11   My quotations of Alicia Partnoy come from her written material, *The Little School* (1986) and *Revenge of the Apple* (1992), and from a personal interview (Dartmouth, May 14, 1993) and a conference presentation by Partnoy at the Redefining Motherhood conference at Dartmouth on May 16, 1993.

12   "Now, it's getting harder for me to talk about what happened. At first, it wasn't so difficult because I had an urgent need to tell people what was going on. But after the military were granted amnesty, I noticed that I was getting tired, and sick even, whenever I spoke. It must have been the frustration of talking and knowing that nothing was getting done" (interview).

13   While the military kept accurate records of the disappeared and clearly used them as hostages and pawns in a national and international drama, the fate of the individual *desaparecidos* was somewhat random. Neither young age, political inactivity, nor collaboration with the military ensured their survival.

14   Diana Taylor, "Alicia Partnoy: A Portrait," in *The Politics of Motherhood: Activist Voices from Left to Right,* ed. Orleck, Jetter, and Taylor (Hanover: University Press of New England, 1996).

15   See *Nunca Más* (208), and Taylor, "Alicia Partnoy: A Portrait" for this information.

16   Elaine Scarry, in *The Body in Pain,* writes: "Even when the torturers do not permanently eliminate the voice through mutilation or murder, they mime the work of pain by temporarily breaking off the voice, making it their own, making it speak their words, making it cry out when they want it to cry, be silent when they want its silence, turning it on and off, using its sound to abuse the one whose voice it is as well as other prisoners" (54).

17   Carmen González, "Violence en las instituciones juridicas," in *La mujer y la violencia invisible,* ed. Giberti and Fernández 181.

18   Alicia Partnoy discusses how torture was tailored differently for women and men. She refuses to discuss the differences in terms of "more" or "less," insisting that it is not ethical to do so, but she specifies that female *desaparecidas* and political prisoners were tormented by threats to their children and, when they were in jail, the women were not allowed to hold or touch their children, while these restrictions did not apply to male prisoners.

19   Doris Sommer, " 'Not Just a Personal Story': Women's *Testimonios* and the Plural Self," in *Life/Lines,* ed. Brodzki and Schenk 109.

20   For a detailed report on the short- and long-term effects of torture, see Eric Stover and Elena O. Nightingale, *The Breaking of Bodies and Minds: Torture, Psychiatric Abuse, and the Health Professions.*

21   These particular problems do not vex victims/witnesses like Rigoberta Menchú. After all, she did not "write" her story. When critics raise valid objections to mediated forms of testimonial

writing such as hers, the objections have to do with the transparent yet all too powerful role of the writer: Does the cultural and experiential divide between the writer and the speaking, testimonial subject invalidate the account? Whose story are we really reading? Who shapes it? Whose fears and fantasies are these? See Elzbieta Sklodowska, "Testimonio Mediatizado: ¿Ventriloquia o Heteroglosia?" and Doris Sommer, " 'Not Just a Personal Story': Women's Testimonies and the Plural Self," in *Life/Line*, ed. Brodzki and Schenck.

22   See *Historia de la tortura y el orden represivo en la Argentina: Textos documentales*.

23   Juri Lotman, "The Origin of Plot in the Light of Topology," *Poetics Today* 1 (1979): 161–84. Summarized in Bronfen, *Over Her Dead Body* 65.

24   Dauster, introduction to *El Señor Galíndez* in *3 dramaturgos rioplatenses*.

25   Bixler and Foster, for example, suggest that the torturers are the victims. Bixler writes: "The total paralysis displayed by the men suggests that they are as much victims of Galíndez as they are victimizers of their own political prey. They are imprisoned, not only by the four walls and the darkness that surrounds them, but also by the telephone upon which their livelihood, and perhaps even their life, depends . . . Beto and Pepe try not to think of their 'laburo' as anything more than a source of steady income. The two veterans are merely cogs in a wheel whose mechanism they cannot begin to comprehend" ("Toward a Reconciliation" 71–72). Foster writes that though they seem in control of the situation, the three men "are in reality also the victims of forces and influences beyond their control and knowledge" (108; my translation).

7   Trapped in Bad Scripts: The Mothers of the Plaza de Mayo

1   Mothers' movements inspired by the Madres of the Plaza sprang up in Chile, Brazil, Nicaragua, El Salvador, Guatemala, and other Latin American countries. Women's groups such as the Women in Black from the Gaza Strip, the Kenyan Mothers, and the Yugoslavian Mothers are recent examples of the political mobilization organized around motherhood.

2   See Judith Butler's formulation of this problem in the first chapter of *Gender Trouble*.

3   I disagree with Ann Snitow's assessment in "A Gender Diary" (in *Rocking the Ship of State*, ed. Harris and King) that the Madres split "along the feminist divide" (49). Both groups, as I see it, have an ambivalent relationship to feminism. According to the Madres de la Plaza faction, tensions started in the group after Alfonsín came to office at the end of 1983. The Linea Fundadora, they maintain, wanted to negotiate with Alfonsín and take a more pacifist line. There was also an election in the movement in January 1986, which intensified the suspicion and resentment among the women and provoked the final rupture (see Diago 193–95).

4   Only five of the leaders were convicted. Videla, president of the first junta, received the most severe punishment: life imprisonment. His sentence was lifted in December 1990 by President Menem after repeated uprisings from the right wing in the military. Everyone else has been acquitted.

5   Laura Rossi states that, without being feminists, the Madres have actually come to the same realization that underlines feminism, that the personal is political (152). I think that the Madres have become increasingly feminist, except that feminism is largely misunderstood in Argentina (and Latin America as a whole) to mean radical separatists, men-haters. The word feminism, moreover, is too loaded with imperialist, "First World" connotations to be considered useful to the Madres. Hebe de Bonafini, the leader of the Madres, states the following: "I don't think the Mothers are feminists, but we point a way forward for the liberation of women. We support the struggle of women against this *machista* world and sometimes this

means that we have to fight against men. But we also have to work together with men to change this society. We aren't feminists because I think feminism, when it's taken too far, is the same as *machismo*. So yes, we want to say that we agree women should have the same place as men, not above or below, but equal, and we have pointed a very clear way forward to this. I think we have also raised some new possibilities for women, the most important of which is the possibility of the socialization of motherhood. This is something very new" (qtd. in Fisher 158).

6   "The Challenge of Constructing Civilian Peace: Women and Democracy in Argentina," in *The Women's Movement in Latin America*, ed. Jaquette 77.

7   "Women in Transition to Democracy," in *Women and Social Change in Latin America*, ed. Jelin 91.

8   J. Colotto, in homage to former chief of the federal police Alberto Villar, qtd. in María del Carmen Feijoó and Mónica Gogna, "Women in Transition to Democracy" 111 n. 18.

9   There was a pro-military league of mothers, who called themselves La Liga de Madres de Familia, that organized to ask the junta for a more forceful implementation of "family values": "Of our leaders we ask for legislation to protect and defend the family, the pillar of society: an ordinance in favor of education that secures traditional and Christian values, and the necessary means so that the media can be a true instrument of culture, broadcasting good example and healthy diversion" (Avellaneda 148).

10   *Casa Matriz*, in *Salirse de madre*, ed. Hilda Rais 179.

11   Women in Argentina today are legal minors; they are bound by law to show "reverential fear" for their husbands (see Graciela Maglie's "Violencia de genero y television el recurso del silencio" and Gloria Bonder's "Las mujeres y la educacion en Argentina," in *La mujer y la violencia invisible*, ed. Giberti and Fernández). Universities are considered a "factory for spinsters" (Fisher 37). There is little or no justice or recourse for battered women. These conditions indicate that socioeconomic and historical conditions, rather than "natural" or "biological" ones, keep women fixed in their subservient roles onstage and off. Both in social and theatrical representations, women are defined primarily in relation to male needs and desires.

12   Franco writes: "to describe someone as a 'public woman' in Latin America is simply not the same as describing someone as a public man . . . The public woman is a prostitute, the public man a prominent citizen. When a woman goes public, she leaves the protected spaces of home and convent and exposes her body" ("Self-Destructing Heroines" 105).

13   Qtd. in Chaney, *Supermadre* 21.

14   Graciela de Jeger, a Madre, states that they believe in the "liberation of men and women. Clearly, women are doubly oppressed, especially in Catholic-Hispanic countries. We are oppressed as workers in a dependent capitalist country, because women work in the lowest paid, least qualified work and we also have housework to do. This makes it more difficult for women to take part in the struggle" (qtd. in Fisher 155).

15   In Jaquette, *The Women's Movement in Latin America* 77.

16   Qtd. in Laura Rossi, "¿Cómo pensar a las Madres de Plaza de Mayo?" in *Nuevo Texto Crítico*, ed. Pratt and Morello Frosch 149.

17   Ross Chambers, "No Montagues Without Capulets: Some Thoughts on Cultural Identity." My discussion later on "identity politics" and "cultural politics" is based in part on his observations.

18   Jane Jaquette, in her introduction to *The Women's Movement in Latin America*, writes: "The

search for human rights was tied to women's rights, and the critique of military authoritarianism became a critique of authoritarianism in the family. The treatment of women political prisoners (which often involved rape and other forms of sexual abuse), the cynical manipulation of family ties to enhance the effectiveness of torture, the breaking up of families and the parcelling out of the children of the 'disappeared'—all revealed the hypocrisy behind the glorification of motherhood and made it impossible to evade the issue of women's sexuality. Awareness of violence against women in the prisons made it acceptable to talk about violence against women in the home and on the street. These experiences gave Latin American feminist theory a unique vantage point from which to analyze the boundaries between private and public, to debate how women's groups 'make politics' to bring about social change" (6). Carmen González, in "Violencia en las instituciones jurídicas" (in *La mujer y la violencia invisible,* ed. Gibert and Fernández), notes that 95 percent of the victims of domestic violence are women (181). See too Graciela B. Ferreira's study, *La mujer maltratada.*

19 "Revolutionizing Motherhood," unpublished manuscript, p. 10.

20 Jaquette's example is only one of several; scholars such as Temma Kaplan, Ann Snitnow, Sara Ruddick, Marysa Navarro, and the Argentine feminist scholars I cited in this chapter have found themselves forced to renegotiate these divides.

21 The meaning of the reworkings often departs from the original to directly address Latin American concerns and values. In most Latin American readings of the Antigone story, Polynices is the hero. Discussing versions of or allusions to Antigone other than Gambaro's, Jean Franco notes "the interpretation of Antigone undergoes a sea change in Latin America, where Polinices is identified with the marginalized" (*Plotting Women* 131). In Gambaro's play, Antígona is loyal to both her brothers, though she calls Polynices "my most beloved brother" (141). Even Coryphaeus blames Eteocles for the civil conflict: "Eteocles didn't want to share [power]" (139).

22 All references to *Antigone* are from Sophocles, *The Three Theban Plays,* translated by Robert Fagles, with introduction and notes by Barnard Knox. Quotation numbers refer to line numbers. All English quotations from *Antígona furiosa* are translated by Marguerite Feitlowitz, unless otherwise noted, and reference numbers refer to page numbers in her edition of *Information for Foreigners: Three Plays by Griselda Gambaro.* All other translations from Spanish are my own, unless otherwise noted.

23 Silvia Pellarolo, in "Revisando el canon," sees the three-character cast as the influence of Augusto Boal's "Joker" system, in which an actor takes on several roles in order to discourage empathetic identification on the part of the audience (see Boal, *Theatre of the Oppressed*). It might also, at the same time, reflect the tradition in Attic tragedy of using three masked characters to play all the parts. Throughout this play, Gambaro draws on both classical and modern Latin American theatrical traditions.

24 Marcelo M. Suárez-Orozco, in "The Heritage of Enduring a 'Dirty War': Psychological Aspects of Terror in Argentina, 1976–1988," writes that "the great majority of Argentines . . . developed conscious and unconscious strategies of knowing what not to know about events in their immediate environment" (469).

25 See Bernard Knox's introduction to Sophocles, *The Three Theban Plays* 35.

26 The fight over the bodies of the disappeared in fact split the Mothers' movement. One faction, La Linea Fundadora, led by Reneé Epelbaum, proposed that the Madres accept the dead bodies finally offered them by forensic specialists once the mass graves started to be unearthed after the fall of the dictatorship. The other group, led by Hebe de Bonafini, refused to

acknowledge the bodies or accept them until the government investigated how the disappeared had died and justice had been meted out to the executioners.

27 Qtd. in Simpson and Bennett, *The Disappeared: Voices from a Secret War* 66.

28 Tripp, *The Meridian Handbook of Classical Mythology* 55. Silvia Pellarolo, in "Revisando el canon" (82), explains the specific Argentine flavor of the two characters by relating them to a figure originating in the tango: *el vivo* (the wiseguy) who develops from *el guapo* (the goodlooker, the inflexible macho who toughs out his insecurity and cowardliness).

29 Pellarolo notes that Antígona speaks some of Haemon's lines (83), but she fails to consider that Antígona is actually "playing" Haemon when she does so, a fact that sets up a complex and interesting ventriloquism that she fails to notice.

30 Marguerite Feitlowitz translated this as "Hiding in *our* houses, devoured by fear, the plague will follow *us*" (emphasis added) but "your" and "you" are the faithful translation of "Escondidos en sus casas, devorados por el miedo, los seguirá la peste" (214). The "you" also makes more sense in terms of the scene, for Antígona has already offered up her flesh to the carrion-feeders and accepted the responsibility of living in a society contaminated by violence and fear.

31 Bronfen notes how Western culture associates women with extremity: "Woman comes to represent the margins or extremes of the norm—the extremely good, pure and helpless, or the extremely dangerous, chaotic and seductive" (181).

8 Staging Battles of Gender and Nation-ness: Teatro Abierto 1981

1 Argentine theatre historian Adolfo Casablanca in *El teatro en la historia argentina* (18), summing up the position of the viceroy, Don Juan José de Vériz y Salcedo.

2 Viceroy Juan José de Vértiz y Salcedo, "Ynstrucción que deverá observarse para ls representación de comedias en esta ciudad" (1783), in Luis Ordaz, "La historia de la literatura argentina" Capítulo 15 (1979): 315. See the following for further information: Teodoro Klein, *El actor en el Rio de la Plata*, vols. 1 and 2; Beatriz Seibel, *De ninfas a capitanas* and *Historia del circo*; Raúl Castagnino, *Teatro argentino premoreirista* and *El teatro en Buenos Aires durante la época de Rosas* (1830–1852); Ernesto Morales, *Historia del teatro argentino*; Mariano Bosch, *Teatro antiguo de Buenos Aires*, *Historia del teatro en Buenos Aires*, and *Historia de los orígenes del teatro nacional argentino*; Vicente Rossi, *Teatro nacional rioplatense*; Adolfo Casablanca, *El teatro en la historia argentina*, Luis Ordaz, "Nacimiento del teatro"; in *Capitulo 15* and Arturo Balassa's video *Pais cerrado, Teatro Abierto* (1985). Interestingly, most accounts of the history of theatre in Argentina fail to mention the consistent attacks on theatre practitioners and buildings by those in power.

3 Castagnino suggests that women of all classes and races shared the balcony (*El teatro en Buenos Aires* 1: 57).

4 Offstage, women in the theatre also found themselves in an ambiguous position. On one hand, they were breaking ground for women. The criollas started earning wages, though their husbands or fathers had to sign the contracts for them, as only widowed women enjoyed some measure of legal and financial independence. Yet the women were socially stigmatized for participating in a profession regarded as morally depraved and that placed them in direct contact with men. In an important legal battle in 1788, a twice-widowed actor, mother of three children, went to court to complain that her father prohibited her from acting. The woman, María Mercedes González y Benavídez, argued that she supported herself and her three

children with the money she earned. The theatre manager argued that all professions were equal and that the theatre needed her. The father maintained that his daughter not only brought disgrace onto herself but onto her family through her profession, which, among other things, allowed "the vilest and most despicable persons, such as that mulata slave who acts," into the company (qtd. in Klein, *El actor* 1:23). Deliberations lasted six months. María Mercedes González y Benavídez won the case and was given a 100 percent raise plus a large sum of money to buy a new outfit. See Klein, *El actor* 1:22; and Seibel 95.

5   *La lealtad más acendrada y Buenos Aires vengada*, by Juan Francisco Fernández, 1808.

6   The pantomine of Juan Moreira was based on the novel of the same name by Eduardo Gutiérrez that enjoyed great popularity in the 1880s.

7   Only twenty of the plays were staged in 1981. Oscar Viale's play, *Antes de entrar dejen salir*, though written specifically for Teatro Abierto, was not staged "due to technical reasons," according to Miguel Angel Giella's edition of the plays, *Teatro Abierto 1981*, vol. 2. (All page numbers refer to this edition. All translations are mine.) The empty time slot reserved for the missing play became known as *espacio abierto* (open space) and was filled with readings, concerts, and performances by different artists.

8   Video, *País cerrado*.

9   Video, *País cerrado*.

10   Although Miguel Angel Giella does have a book-length study in which he analyzes the plays (a companion volume to the plays themselves—*Teatro Abierto 1981*, vols. 1 and 2), his discontextualized approach seems to miss the sociopolitical point of the plays.

11   "Estamos muy saturados de cosas que no son nacionales, no solo en el teatro sino en la cultura general. Los artistas en general se han contaminado y producen productos contaminados, y la gente se ha contaminado de recibir esos elementos contaminados. Haría falta un sistema médico como para descontaminar, ¿no?" (*Pais cerrado, Teatro Abierto*).

12   Diana Raznovich, interview with author, Buenos Aires, 1994.

13   In Vincent Canby's view of *Time for Revenge, New York Times*, January 14, 1983.

14   See Donna Guy, *Sex and Danger in Buenos Aires: Prostitution, Family and Nation in Argentina;* "Prostitution and Female Criminality in Buenos Aires, 1875–1937," in *The Problem of Order in Changing Societies*, ed. Johnson; and " 'White Slavery,' Citizenship and Nationality in Argentina," in *Nationalisms and Sexualities*, ed. Parker et al.

15   Introductory remarks to Monti's play in *7 dramaturgos argentinos*.

16   Michael Taussig, I believe, is quite right when he states (in *The Nervous System*) that "Above all the Dirty War is a war of silencing . . . This is more than the production of silence. It is silencing, which is quite different. For now the not said acquires significance and a specific confusion befogs the spaces of the public sphere, which is where the action is" (26).

17   All translations from Spanish are mine except for those from *Antígona furiosa*, translated by Marguerite Feitlowitz, or unless otherwise noted. I was not familiar with Victoria Martínez's translation of *Disconcerted* until I had finished this section.

18   The film *Tiempo de revancha* (released in Buenos Aires in 1981) ends with the hero cutting his tongue out as an act of defiance against a brutal corporation that is determined to prove that he can speak. In his essay, "Torture: A Discourse on Practice" (in *Tattoo, Torture, Mutilation and Adornment*, ed. Mascia-Lees and Sharpe), Ñacuñán Sáez writes that in "Argentina, in the 1970s, power was the power not to speak" (137). The cartoonist Quino has a cartoon showing the public confrontation of two resistance groups—those who carry placards of mouths open in a scream and those who carry placards of silenced lips (*Potentes, prepotentes e impotentes* 23).

19   This is the term used by Miguel Angel Giella to describe Teatro Abierto in his study/anthology: *Teatro Abierto, 1981: Teatro Argentino Bajo Vigilancia.*

20   Judith Butler, "Performative Acts and Gender Construction" in *Performing Feminisms: Feminist Critical Theory and Theatre*, ed. Sue-Ellen Case 277. See also *Gender Trouble* and *Bodies That Matter.*

21   The image of the accusing, distorting or broken mirror occurs repeatedly in art of the period, in Griselda Gambaro's *Decir sí* (also Teatro Abierto, 1981), and films such as Aristarain's *Tiempo de revancha* (1983) and Olivera's *No habrá más penas ni olvido* (1983).

22   Interview, Dartmouth College, September 1994.

9   Crossing the Line: Watching Violence in the "Other" Country

1   *El vuelo*, by Horacio Verbitsky, first reported Scilingo's confession. The account was picked up by news agencies around the world. In "Argentine Tells of Dumping 'Dirty War' Captives into Sea," *New York Times*, March 13, 1995, Scilingo says he confessed to what happened because "I feel like the navy has abandoned us, left us to the wolves, the very ones who were loyal and followed orders."

2   *Página 12*, July 1, 1995, pp. 1–13.

3   Army Commander's 'Dirty War' Admission Ungags Argentines," *New York Times*, April 27, 1995.

4   The text of Lt. General Martín Braza's speech was reprinted in *La nación*, April 27, 1995, section *Política* (my translation).

5   "Army Commander's 'Dirty War' Admission Ungags Argentines," *New York Times*, April 27, 1995.

6   James Brooke, quoting Jorge Lanata, founder of *Página 12*, in "Argentines Protest Bombing as Death Toll Reaches 44," *New York Times*, July 21, 1994.

7   While the situation has changed considerably, I feel that, once again, women's rights are being sacrificed in the interests of so-called national interests. Menem aligned himself with the church in his bid for reelection. The trade-off was a simple one: Menem could count on support if he upheld a stiff anti-abortion platform. Menem's political well-being depends on the negation of women's rights.

8   April 13–20, 1995.

9   "Manual for Terrorists Extols 'Greatest Coldbloodedness,'" *New York Times*, April 29, 1995.

10 See "Programs Based in Sex and Race Are Under Attack," *New York Times*, March 16, 1995, which discusses attempts to cut Affirmative Action even while studies indicate that women and minorities are discriminated against in the workplace: "Women and Minorities Still Face 'Glass Ceiling': White Men's Fears Are Barriers, Report Says" (*New York Times*, March 16, 1995). See also "Deciding Who Gets What in America" (*New York Times*, November 27, 1994), "House G.O.P. Would Replace Scores of Programs for the Poor" (*New York Times*, December 9, 1994), "Gap in Wealth in U.S. Called the Widest in West" (*New York Times*, April 17, 1995). "The Battle Against Gays" (*Boston Globe*, April 24, 1995) documents that the Montana state legislature "recently passed a proposal requiring homosexuals to register with police" by a margin of 41 to 8. Public outrage forced the measure to be rescinded.

11 Limbaugh, "Blame the Bombers—Only," *Newsweek*, May 8, 1995, p. 39.

12 Max Frankel, "The Murder Broadcasting System," *New York Times Magazine*, December 17, 1995, pp. 46–48.

13 Augusto Boal interview in video "Como querem beber agua: Augusto Boal and the Theatre of the Oppressed in Rio de Janeiro," a documentary by Ronaldo Morelos.

14 Doris Sommer, *Proceed with Caution: The Rhetoric of Particularism,* in process.

15 "Under Western Eyes," in *Third World Women and the Politics of Feminism,* ed. Mohanty, Russo, and Torres 52.

16 Historical studies by scholars such as David Rock, Marysa Navarro, Robert Potash, Tulio Halperin Donghi, and others look at the period of the Dirty War or events leading up to it. Frank Graziano's *Divine Violence: Spectacle, Psychosexuality, and Radical Christianity in the Argentine "Dirty War"* also looks at spectacle during the Dirty War but leaves gender issues out of the equation. Other noted scholars such as Jean Franco, Doris Sommer, Francine Masiello, Elizabeth Garrels, and Donna Guy explore gender issues in the construction of Argentine nationhood, but not during the period that I am working on and not in relation to the creation of gendered images in the public sphere. Jean Franco comes closest to my approach in a recent essay entitled "Gender, Death and Resistance: Facing the Ethical Vacuum," but again, the scope of her article is more limited than my book-length project and she does not turn her attention to public spectacle. Thus fine scholarship has already been done in these related fields. They have greatly influenced my work, and I hope that my perspective, too, will contribute to future scholarship on Argentina's Dirty War.

Bibliography

 Adorno, Theodor, et al., eds. *Aesthetic and Politic*. London: Verso, 1986.

Agosin, Marjorie. *Circles of Madness: Mothers of the Plaza de Mayo*. Fredonia: White Pine Press, 1992.

——, ed. *Surviving beyond Fear: Women, Children and Human Rights in Latin America*. Fredonia: White Pine Press, 1993.

AIDA (Asociación Internacional para la Defensa de los Artistas víctimas de la represión en el mundo), ed. *Argentina: Cómo matar la cultura*. Madrid: Editorial Revolución, 1981.

Althusser, Louis. *Lenin and Philosophy*. New York: Monthly Review Press, 1971.

Amar Sánchez, Ana María. *El relato de los hechos*. Buenos Aires: Beatriz Viterbo Editora, 1992.

Amnesty International. "Argentina: The Military Juntas and Human Rights: Report of the Trial of the Former Junta Members, 1985." London: Amnesty International Publications, 1987.

Anderson, Benedict. *Imagined Communities: Reflections on the Origin and Spread of Nationalism*. London: Verso, 1983.

Anderson, Martin Edwin. "Dirty Secrets of the 'Dirty War.'" *Nation* (March 13, 1989): 339–41.

Apter, Emily, and William Pietz, eds. *Fetishism as Cultural Discourse*. Ithaca: Cornell University Press, 1993.

Arancibia, Juana A., and Zulema Mirkin, eds. *Teatro argentino durante el proceso (1976–1983).* Buenos Aires: Editorial Vinciguerra, 1992.

Arditti, Rita, and M. Brinton Lykes. " 'Recovering Identity': The Work of the Grandmothers of Plaza de Mayo." *Women's Studies International Forum* 15.4 (1992): 461–71.

Aristotle. *The Politics.* Trans. T. A. Sinclair. Harmondsworth: Penguin, 1977.

Artaud, Antonin. *The Theater and Its Double.* Trans. Mary Caroline Richards. New York: Grove Press, 1958.

Austin, J. L. *How to Do Things with Words.* Cambridge: Harvard University Press, 1962.

Avellaneda, Andrés. *Censura, autoritarismo y cultura: Argentina 1960–1983.* Vol. 2. Buenos Aires: Biblioteca Politica Argentina, 1986.

Balderston, Daniel, et al. *Ficción y política: La narrativa argentina durante el proceso militar.* Ed. Hernán Vidal. Madrid/Minnesota: Alianza Editorial/Institute for the Study of Ideologies and Literature, 1987.

Barba, Eugenio. *Beyond the Floating Islands.* Trans. Judy Barba, Richard Fowler, Jerrold C. Rodesch, and Saul Shapiro. New York: PAJ Publications, 1986.

Barish, Jonas. *The Anti-Theatrical Prejudice.* Berkeley: University of California Press, 1981.

Barthes, Roland. *Mythologies.* Trans. Annette Lavers. New York: The Noonday Press, 1972.

——. *Camera Lucida: Reflections on Photography.* Trans. Richard Howard. New York: Hill and Wang, 1981.

Bataille, Georges. *Erotism: Death and Sensuality.* San Francisco: City Lights, 1986.

Berger, John. *Ways of Seeing.* Harmondsworth: Penguin, 1972.

Berlin, Normand. *The Secret Cause.* Amherst: University of Massachusetts Press, 1981.

Bergmann, Emilie, et al. *Women, Culture, and Politics in Latin America.* Berkeley: University of California Press, 1990.

Bersani, Leo, and Ulysse Dutoit. *The Forms of Violence.* New York: Schocken, 1985.

Bhabha, Homi K., ed. *Nation and Narration.* London: Routledge, 1990.

Bignone, Reynaldo B. A. *El último de facto: La liquidación del proceso. Memoria y testimonio.* Buenos Aires: Planeta Espejo de la Argentina, 1992.

Bixler, Jacqueline Eyring. "Toward a Reconciliation of Text and Performance: How to Read *El Señor Galíndez*." *Gestos* 13 (April 1992): 65–77.

——. "Signs of Absence in Pavlovsky's 'teatro de la memoria.' " *Latin American Theatre Review* 28.1 (1994): 17–30.

Blau, Herbert. *Take Up the Bodies: Theater at the Vanishing Point.* Urbana: University of Illinois, 1982.

Blonsky, Marshall, ed. *On Signs.* Baltimore: Johns Hopkins University Press, 1985.

Boal, Augusto. *Theatre of the Oppressed.* Trans. Charles A. McBride and Maria-Odilia Leal McBride. New York: Theatre Communications Group, 1985.

Bornstein, Kate. *Gender Outlaw: On Men, Women and the Rest of Us.* New York: Routledge, 1994.

Bosch, Mariano G. *Teatro antiguo de Buenos Aires.* Buenos Aires: Imprenta El Comercio, 1904.

Bouvard, Marguerite. *With the Mothers of the Plaza de Mayo.* Bedford, N.H.: Igneus Press, 1993.

——. *Revolutionizing Motherhood: The Mothers of the Plaza de Mayo.* Wilmington, Del.: Scholarly Resource Books, 1994.

Brecht, Bertolt. *The Caucasian Chalk Circle.* Trans. Eric Bentley. New York: Grove Press, 1947.

——. *Brecht on Brecht.* Ed. and trans. John Willett. New York: Hill and Wang, 1957.

Brodzki, Bella, and Celeste Schenck, eds. *Life/Lines: Theoretical Essays on Women's Autobiography.* Ithaca: Cornell University Press, 1989.

Bronfen, Elisabeth. *Over Her Dead Body: Death, Femininity and the Aesthetic.* New York: Routledge, 1992.

Brown, Cynthia, ed. *With Friends Like These.* New York: Pantheon Books, 1985.

Burgin, Victor, James Donald, and Cora Kaplan, eds. *Formations of Fantasy.* London: Methuen, 1989.

Butler, Judith. *Gender Trouble: Feminism and the Subversion of Identity.* New York: Routledge, 1990.

———. *Bodies That Matter: On The Discursive Limits of "Sex."* New York: Routledge, 1993.

Canby, Vincent. "Film: Argentine *Time for Revenge.*" *New York Times* January 14, 1983, p. C-8.

Cárdenas, Gonzalo, et al. *El peronismo.* Buenos Aires: Carlos Perez Editor, 1969.

Caro, D. Carlos Augusto, and et al. "Observaciones y comentarios críticos del gobierno Argentino al informe de la CIDH sobre la situación de los derechos humanos en Argentina." Círculo Militar, 1980.

Carter, Erica, James Donald, and Judith Squires, eds. *Space and Place: Theories of Identity and Location.* London: Lawrence & Wishart, 1993.

Casablanca, Adolfo. *El teatro en la historia argentina.* Buenos Aires: Edición del Honorable Consejo Deliberante de la ciudad de Buenos Aires, 1994.

Case, Sue-Ellen, ed. *Performing Feminisms: Feminist Critical Theory and Theatre.* Baltimore: Johns Hopkins University Press, 1990.

Castagnino, Raúl H. *Teatro argentino premoreirista.* Buenos Aires: Plus Ultra, 1969.

———. *El teatro en Buenos Aires durante la época de Rosas (1830–1852).* Vols. 1 and 2. Buenos Aires: Academia Argentina de Letras, 1989.

Castillo, Marcial Castro. *Fuerzas armadas, ética y represión.* Buenos Aires: Editorial Nuevo Orden, 1979.

Castro-Klarén, Sara, Sylvia Molloy, and Beatriz Sarlos, eds. *Women's Writing in Latin America.* Boulder: Westview Press, 1991.

Celiberti, Lilian, and Lucy Garrido. *Mi habitación, mi celda.* Montevideo: ARCA, 1990.

Chambers, Iain. *Migrancy, Culture, Identity.* London: Routledge, 1994.

Chambers, Ross. *Room for Maneuver: Reading (the) Oppositional (in) Narrative.* Chicago: University of Chicago Press, 1991.

———. "No Montagues Without Capulets: Some Thoughts on 'Cultural Identity.'" Lecture, School of Criticism and Theory, Dartmouth College, 1992.

Chaney, Elsa M. *Supermadre: Women in Politics in Latin America.* Austin: University of Texas Press, 1979.

Chomsky, Noam, and Edward S. Herman. *The Washington Connection and Third World Fascism: The Political Economy of Human Rights.* Montreal: Black Rose, 1979.

Chumbita, Hugo. *Los carapintada: Historia de un malentendido argentino.* Buenos Aires: Planeta, 1990.

Colomina, Beatriz, ed. *Sexuality and Space.* New York: Princeton Architectural Press, 1992.

Corradi, Juan E., Patricia Weiss Fagen, and Manuel Antonio Garretón, eds. *Fear at the Edge.* Berkeley: University of California Press, 1992.

Cosentino, Olga. "El teatro en los '70: Una dramaturgia sitiada." *Latin American Theatre Review* 24.2 (Spring 1991): 31–40.

Crassweller, Robert. *Perón and the Enigmas of Argentina.* New York: W. W. Norton and Company, 1987.

Dauster, Frank. "Eduardo Pavlovsky" in *3 dramaturgos rioplatenses.* Ed. Frank Dauster, Leon Lyday and George Woodyard. Ottawa: Girol Books, 1983.

de Certeau, Michel. *The Practice of Everyday Life*. Trans. Steven Rendall. Berkeley: University of California Press, 1984.

de Lauretis, Teresa. *Alice Doesn't: Feminism, Semiotics, Cinema*. Bloomington: Indiana University Press, 1984.

———. *Technologies of Gender: Essays on Theory, Film and Fiction*. Bloomington: Indiana University Press, 1987.

———, ed. *Feminist Studies/Critical Studies*. Bloomington: Indiana University Press, 1986.

Deleuze, Gilles, and Félix Guattari. *Anti-Oedipus: Capitalism and Schizophrenia*. Trans. Robert Hurley, Mark Seem, and Helen R. Lane. Minneapolis: University of Minnesota Press, 1983.

Derrida, Jacques. *Margins of Philosophy*. Trans. Alan Bass. Chicago: University of Chicago Press, 1982.

———. *Specters of MARX*. Trans. Peggy Kamuf. New York: Routledge, 1994.

Diago, Alejandro. *Hebe Bonafini: Memoria y esperanza*. Buenos Aires: Ediciones Dialectica, 1988.

Diamond, Elin. "Brechtian Theory/Feminist Theory: Toward a Gestic Feminist Criticism." *The Drama Review* 32.1 (Spring 1988): 82–94.

Dolan, Jill. *The Feminist Spectator as Critic*. Ed. Oscar G. Brockett. Vol. 52. Ann Arbor: UMI Research Press, 1988.

Dragún, Osvaldo. "Dramatugia nacional y realidad política." *Conjunto* 60 (April–June 1984): 57–60.

Dubatti, Jorge A. "Teatro Abierto Despues de 1981." *Latin American Theatre Review* 24.2 (Spring 1991): 79–86.

Duhalde, Eduardo Luis. *El estado terrorista argentino*. Buenos Aires: Ediciones El Caballito, 1983.

Durberman, Martin, Martha Vicinus, and George Chauncey Jr., eds. *Hidden from History: Reclaiming the Gay and Lesbian Past*. New York: New American Library, 1989.

During, Simon, ed. *The Cultural Studies Reader*. London: Routledge, 1993.

Echeverría, Esteban. *El matadero/La cautiva*. Ed. Leonor Fleming. Madrid: Cátedra, 1986.

Eckstein, Susan, ed. *Power and Popular Protest: Latin American Social Movements*. Berkeley: University of California Press, 1989.

Eloy Martinez, Tomás. *Santa Evita*. Buenos Aires: Planeta, 1995.

Esteve, Patricio. "1980–1981—La pre-historia de Teatro Abierto." *Latin American Theatre Review* 24.2 (Spring 1991): 59–68.

Feitlowitz, Marguerite. "A Dance of Death: Pavlovsky's *Paso de dos*." *Drama Review* 35.2 (1991): 60–73.

———. *TDR*.

———, ed. *Information for Foreigners: Three Plays by Griselda Gambaro*. Evanston: Northwestern University Press, 1992.

———. *Lexicon of Terror*. (Unpublished manuscript.)

Felix, María. *Todas mis guerras*. Mexico City: Editorial Clio, 1993.

Felman, Shoshana. *The Literary Speech Act*. Trans. Catherine Porter. Ithaca: Cornell University Press, 1983.

Felman, Shoshana, and Dori Laub. *Testimony: Crisis of Witnessing in Literature, Psychoanalysis, and History*. New York: Routledge, 1992.

Fernández, Ana María. "Violencia y conyugalidad." *La mujer y la violencia invisible*. Eds. Eva Giberti and Ana María Fernández. Buenos Aires: Editorial Sudamericana, 1989.

———, ed. *Las mujeres en la imaginación colective: Una historia de discriminación y resistencias*. Buenos Aires: Paidos, 1992.

Ferreira, Graciela B. *La mujer maltratada: Un estudio sobre las mujeres víctimas de la violencia doméstica*. Buenos Aires: Editorial Sudamericana, 1989.

Fisher, Jo. *Mothers of the Disappeared*. Boston: South End Press, 1989.

Foster, David William. *Contemporary Argentine Cinema*. Columbia: University of Missouri Press, 1992.

———. "Ambigüedad verbal y dramática en *El Señor Galíndez* de Eduardo Pavlovsky." *Latin American Theatre Review* 13. 2 (Summer 1980): 103–110.

Foucault, Michel. *The History of Sexuality*. Vol. 1. Trans. Robert Hurley. New York: Vintage, 1980.

———. *Discipline and Punish*. Trans. Alan Sheridan. New York: Vintage, 1979.

Franco, Jean. *Plotting Women: Gender and Representation in Mexico*. New York: Columbia University Press, 1989.

———. "Gender, Death, and Resistance: Facing the Ethical Vacuum." In *Fear at the Edge*. Ed. E. Corradi et al. Berkeley: University of California Press, 1992.

Fraser, Howard M. *Magazines and Masks: Caras y Caretas as a Reflection of Buenos Aires, 1898–1908*. Tempe: Center for Latin American Studies, 1987.

Fresán, Rodrigo. *Historia Argentina*. Barcelona: Editorial Anagrama, 1991.

Freud, Sigmund. *The Standard Edition of the Complete Psychological Works of Sigmund Freud*. Vol. 14. Ed. James Strachey. London: Hogarth, 1957.

———. *Civilization and Its Discontents*. Ed. James Strachey. New York: Norton, 1961.

———. *Three Essays on the Theory of Sexuality*. Ed. James Strachey. New York: Avon, 1962.

———. *New Introductory Lectures on Psycho-Analysis*. Ed. James Strachey. New York: Norton, 1989.

Frontalini, Daniel, and María Cristina Caiati. *El mito de la "Guerra Sucia."* Buenos Aires: Editorial CELS, 1984.

Fuss, Diana. *Essentially Speaking*. New York: Routledge, 1989.

———. *Identification Papers*. New York: Routledge, 1995.

Gabetta, Carlos. *Todos somos subversivos*. Buenos Aires: Editorial Bruguera, 1983.

Gambaro, Griselda. *Teatro 3*. Buenos Aires: Ediciones de la Flor, 1989.

———. *Information for Foreigners: Three Plays by Griselda Gambaro*. Ed. and trans. Marguerite Feitlowitz. Evanston: Northwestern University Press, 1991.

Garber, Marjorie. *Vested Interests: Cross Dressing and Cultural Anxiety*. New York: Harper Perennial, 1993.

García Canclini, Nestor. *Culturas híbridas*. Buenos Aires: Editorial Sudamericana, 1992.

Garrels, Elizabeth. *A Myth Like Its Hero: Sarmiento's Facundo Retold by a Woman*. In progress.

Geis, Deborah R. "Wordscapes of the Body: Performative Language as Gestus in Maria Irene Fornes' Plays." *Theatre Journal* 42.3 (October 1990): 291–307.

Ghiano, Juan Carlos. *Teatro argentina contemporaneo: 1949–1969*. Madrid: Aguilar, 1973.

Giberti, Eva, and Ana María Fernández, eds. *La mujer y la violencia invisible*. Buenos Aires: Editorial Sudamericana, 1989.

Giella, Miguel Angel. "Teatro Abierto 1981: De la desilusión a la alienación." *Latin American Theatre Review* 24.2 (Spring 1991): 69–78.

———, ed. *Teatro Abierto 1981*. 2 vols. Buenos Aires: Corregidor, 1991.

Giella, Miguel Angel, and Peter Roster, eds. *7 dramaturgos argentinos*. Ottawa: Girol Books, 1983.

Giulianotti, Richard, and John Williams, eds. *Games without Frontiers: Football, Identity and Modernity*. Hampshire, England: Arena, 1994.

Giussani, Pablo. *La sombra armada*. Buenos Aires: Tiempo de Ideas, 1984.

Gledhill, John. *Power and Its Disguises: Anthropological Perspectives on Politics.* London: Pluto Press, 1994.

Goldhill, Simon. *Reading Greek Tragedy.* Cambridge: Cambridge University Press, 1986.

Gómez-Peña, Guillermo. *Warrior of Gringostroika.* Saint Paul: Graywolf Press, 1993.

Gramsci, Antonio. "The Modern Prince." *Prison Notebooks.* New York: Columbia University Press, 1975.

Graziano, Frank. *Divine Violence: Spectacle, Psychosexuality, and Radical Christianity in the Argentine "Dirty War."* Boulder: Westview Press, 1992.

Grecco, Jorge, and Gustavo González. *Argentina: El ejército que tenemos.* Buenos Aires: Editorial Sudamericana, 1990.

Griffin, Roger, ed. *Fascism.* Oxford: Oxford University Press, 1995.

Grosz, Elizabeth. "Bodies-Cities." *Sexuality and Space.* Ed. Beatriz Colomina. Princeton: Princeton Architectural Press, 1992.

Grotowski, Jerzy. *Towards a Poor Theatre.* New York: Touchstone, 1968.

Guerra Cunningham, Lucía, ed. *Splintering Darkness: Latin American Women Writers in Search of Themselves.* Pittsburgh: Latin American Literary Review Press, 1990.

Guy, Donna J. *Sex and Danger in Buenos Aires: Prostitution, Family and Nation.* Lincoln: University of Nebraska Press, 1991.

Halperín Donghi, Tulio. *El revisionismo histórico argentino.* Mexico: Siglo Veintiuno Editores, 1971.

——. "Argentina's Unmastered Past." *Latin American Research Review* 23.2 (1988): 3–24.

——. *The Contemporary History of Latin America.* Durham: Duke University Press, 1993.

Handelman, Don. *Models and Mirrors: Towards an Anthropology of Public Events.* Cambridge: Cambridge University Press, 1990.

Harris, Adrienne, and Ynestra King, eds. *Rocking the Ship of State: Toward a Feminist Peace Politics.* Boulder: Westview Press, 1989.

Hegel, G. W. F. *The Phenomenology of Mind.* Trans. J. B. Lichtheim. New York: Harper Torchbooks, 1967.

Hirsch, Marianne. *Family Frames: Photography and Narrative in the Postmodern.* Cambridge, Mass.: Harvard University Press, forthcoming.

"La historia secreta de la caída de Isabel Perón." *Gente* (1977): 180–87.

Horno-Delgado, Asunción, et al., eds. *Breaking Boundaries: Latina Writing and Critical Readings.* Amherst: University of Massachusetts Press, 1989.

Horvath, Ricardo. *La trama secreta en la radiodifusión argentina: Los medios en la neocolonización.* Buenos Aires: Editorial Rescate, 1988.

Iglesias, Cristina, and Julio Schvartzman. *Cautivas y misioneros: Mitos blancos de la conquista.* Buenos Aires: Catalogos Editora, 1987.

Insdorf, Annette. "Time for Revenge: A Discussion with Adolfo Aristarain." *Cineaste* (1983): 16–17.

Jaquette, Jane S., ed. *The Women's Movement in Latin America: Feminism and the Transition to Democracy.* Boston: Unwin Hyman, 1989.

Jara, René, and Hernán Vidal, eds. *Testimonio y literatura.* Minneapolis: Institute for the Study of Ideologies and Literature, 1986.

Jassen, Raul. *Seineldin: El ejercito traicionado, la patria vencida.* Buenos Aires: Editorial Verum et Militia, 1989.

Jay, Martin. "Photo-Unrealism: The Contribution of the Camera to the Crisis of Ocular Centrism." In *Vision and Textuality.* Ed. Stephen Melville and Bill Readings. Durham: Duke University Press, 1995.

Jeffords, Susan. *Hard Bodies: Hollywood Masculinity in the Reagan Era*. New Brunswick: Rutgers University Press, 1994.

Jelin, Elizabeth, ed. *Women and Social Change in Latin America*. London: Zed Books, 1990.

Johnson, Lyman L., ed. *The Problem of Order in Changing Societies: Essays on Crime and Policing in Argentina and Uruguay, 1750–1940*. Albuquerque: University of New Mexico Press, 1990.

Kappeler, Susanne. *The Pornography of Representation*. Minneapolis: University of Minnesota Press, 1986.

Kertzer, David I. *Ritual, Politics, and Power*. New Haven: Yale University Press, 1988.

King, John, and Nissa Torrents, eds. *The Garden of Forking Paths: Argentine Cinema*. London: National Film Theatre, 1988.

Kitto, H. D. F. *Greek Tragedy*. New York: Doubleday, 1954.

Klein, Teodoro. *El actor en el Rio de la Plata*. Vol. 1: *De la colonia a la independencia nacional*. Buenos Aires: Ediciones Asociación Argentina de Actores, 1984.

———. *El actor en el Rio de la Plata*. Vol. 2: *De Casacuberta a los Podesta*. Buenos Aires: Ediciones Asociación Argentina de Actores, 1994.

Kohut, Karl, and Andrea Pagni, eds. *Literatura argentina hoy: De la dictadura a la democracia*. Frankfurt am Main: Vervuert Verlag, 1989.

Kolodny, Annette. *The Lay of the Land: Metaphor as Experience and History in American Life and Letters*. Chapel Hill: University of North Carolina Press, 1975.

Kordon, Diana R., ed. *Psychological Effects of Political Repression*. Buenos Aires: Editorial Sudamericana, 1988.

Kristeva, Julia. *Tales of Love*. Trans. Leon S. Roudiez. New York: Columbia University Press, 1987.

Kusnetzoff, Juan Carlos. "Renegación, desmentida, desaparición y percepticidio como técnicas psicopáticas de la salvación de la patria." *Argentina Psicoanálisis Represión Política*. Ed. Oscar Abudara et al. Buenos Aires: Ediciones Kargieman, 1986: 95–114.

Lacan, Jacques. *Ecrits: A Selection*. Trans. Alan Sheridan. New York: Norton, 1977.

———. *Four Fundamental Concepts of Psycho-Analysis*. Trans. Alan Sheridan. New York: Norton, 1981.

LaCapra, Dominick. "History and Psychoanalysis." *Critical Inquiry* 13.2 (1987): 222–46.

———. *Representing the Holocaust: History, Theory, Trauma*. Ithaca: Cornell University Press, 1994.

Lacoste, Pablo, ed. *Militares y política 1983–1991*. Buenos Aires: Centro Editor de America Latina, 1993.

Laitin, David D. *Hegemony and Culture*. Chicago: University of Chicago Press, 1986.

Landes, Joan B. *Women and the Public Sphere in the Age of the French Revolution*. Ithaca: Cornell University Press, 1988.

Laplanche, Jean, and Jean-Bertrand Pontalis. "Fantasy and the Origins of Sexuality." *Formations of Fantasy*. Ed. James Donald, Cora Kaplan, and Victor Burgin. London: Methuen, 1986.

Larsen, Neil. "Sport as Civil Society: The Argentinean Junta Plays Championship Soccer." In *The Discourse of Power: Culture, Hegemony and the Authoritarian State*. Ed. Neil Larsen. Minneapolis: Institute for the Study of Ideologies and Literature, 1983.

El libro del juicio: *Testimonios*. Buenos Aires: Editorial Testigo, 1985.

Lifton, Robert Jay. *The Nazi Doctors: Medical Killing and the Psychology of Genocide*. New York: Basic Books, 1986.

López-Saavedra, Emiliana. *Testigos del "proceso" militar (1976–1983)*. Vols. 1 and 2. Buenos Aires: Centro Editor de America Latina, 1984.

Loveman, Brian, and Thomas M. Davies, eds. *The Politics of Antipolitics: The Military in Latin America*. Lincoln: University of Nebraska Press, 1978.

Ludmer, Josefina. *El género gauchesco: Un tratado sobre la patria*. Buenos Aires: Editorial Sudamericana, 1988.

——. "Tricks of the Weak." *Feminist Perspectives on Sor Juana Inés de la Cruz*. Ed. Stephanie Merrim. Detroit: Wayne State University Press, 1991.

Lugones, Leopoldo. *La grande Argentina*. Buenos Aires: Babel, 1930.

——. *La patria fuerte*. Buenos Aires: Circulo Militar, 1930.

——. *Antología poética*. Buenos Aires: Espasa-Calpe, S.A., 1946.

Main, Mary. *Woman with a Whip: Eva Perón*. Garden City: Doubleday, 1952.

Malloy, James M., and Mitchell A. Seligson, eds. *Authoritarians and Democrats: Regime Transition in Latin America*. Pittsburgh: University of Pittsburgh Press, 1987.

Martínez Estrada, Ezequiel. *X-Ray of the Pampa*. Trans. Alain Swietlicki. Austin: University of Texas Press, 1971.

Mascia-Lees, Frances E., and Patricia Sharpe, eds. *Tattoo, Torture, Mutilation, and Adornment*. Albany: State University of New York Press, 1992.

Masiello, Francine. *Between Civilization and Barbarism: Women, Nation, and Literary Culture in Modern Argentina*. Lincoln: University of Nebraska Press, 1992.

——. "Women, State, and Family in Latin American Literature of the 1920s." *Women Culture, and Politics in Latin America*. Ed. Emilie Bergmann, et al. Berkeley: University of California Press, 1990.

Massera, Emilio E. *El camino a la democracia*. Caracas: El Cid Editor, 1979.

——. *El pais que queremos*. Buenos Aires: Editorial F.E.P.A., 1981.

Mazziotti, Nora, ed. *Teatro Abierto 1982*. Buenos Aires: Puntosur Editores, 1989.

McGee, Sandra F. "The Visible and the Invisible Liga Patriótica Argentina, 1919–28: Gender Roles and the Right Wing." *Hispanic Historical Review* 64.2 (1984): 233–58.

Menchú, Rigoberta, and Elisabeth Burgos-Debray. *I . . . Rigoberta Menchú*. Trans. Ann Wright. London: Verso, 1984.

Méndez, Eugenio. *Confesiones de un montonero*. Buenos Aires: Planeta, 1985.

Metz, Christian. *The Imaginary Signifier: Psychoanalysis and the Cinema*. Trans. Celia Britton, Annwyl Williams, Ben Brewster, and Alfred Guzzetti. Bloomington: Indiana University Press, 1982.

Mignone, Emilio. *Iglesia y dictadura*. Buenos Aires. Ediciones Pensamiento Nacional, 1986.

Miller, Francesca. *Latin American Women and the Search for Social Justice*. Hanover, N.H.: University Press of New England, 1991.

Millett, Kate. *The Politics of Cruelty: An Essay on the Literature of Political Imprisonment*. New York: Norton, 1994.

Mohanty, Chandra Talpade, Ann Russo, and Lourdes Torres, eds. *Third World Women and the Politics of Feminism*. Bloomington: Indiana University Press, 1991.

Molloy, Sylvia. "Too Wilde for Comfort." *Social Text* 31–32 (1992): 187–201.

——, ed. *Hispanisms and Homosexualities*. Forthcoming.

Monti, Ricardo. "La cortina de abalorios." *Teatro Abierto, 1981* Vol. 2. Ed. Miguel Angel Giella. Buenos Aires: Corregidor, 1992.

Moraga, Cherríe. *Giving Up the Ghost*. Los Angeles: West End Press, 1986.

Morales, Ernesto. *Historia del teatro argentino*. Buenos Aires: Lautaro, 1944.

Morgon, Michael, and James Shanahan. "Television and the Cultivation of Political Attitudes in Argentina." *Journal of Communication* 41.1 (1991): 88–103.

Moyano, María José. *Argentina's Lost Patrol: Armed Struggle 1969–1979*. New Haven: Yale University Press, 1995.

Mulvey, Laura. "Visual Pleasure and Narrative Cinema." *Screen* 16.3 (1975): 6–18.

Murray, Gilbert, ed. *Euripides: The Trojan Women*. London: Allen & Unwin, 1967.

Nash, June, and Helen Safa, eds. *Women and Change in Latin America*. Boston: Bergin & Garvey, 1986.

Navarro, Marysa. *Los nacionalistas*. Buenos Aires: Editorial Jorge Alvarez, 1968.

——. *Evita*. Buenos Aires: Ediciones Corregidor, 1981.

——. "The Personal Is Political: Madres de Plaza de Mayo." *Power and Popular Protest*. Ed. Susan Eckstein. Berkeley: University of California Press, 1989.

Nelson, Cary, and Lawrence Grossberg, eds. *Marxism and the Interpretation of Culture*. Urbana: University of Illinois Press, 1988.

Newman, Karen. "Directing Traffic: Subjects, Objects, and the Politics of Exchange." *Differences* 2.2 (Summer 1990): 41–54.

Newman, Kathleen. *La violencia del discurso: El estado autoritario y la novela política argentina*. Buenos Aires: Catálogos Editora, 1991.

Nixon, Richard. *The Real War*. New York: Simon & Schuster, 1980.

Nunca Más: The Report of the Argentine National Commission on the Disappeared. New York: Farrar Straus Giroux, 1986.

Ordaz, Luis. "La historia de la literatura argentina: El nacimiento del teatro." *Capítulo* 15 (1979): 313–36.

——. "El teatro: Desde Caseros hasta el zarzuelismo criollo." *Capítulo* 30 (1980): 169–92.

——. "El teatro: Cierre de un ciclo, 1970." *Capítulo* 111 (1981): 577–600.

Ortúzar, Ximena. *Represión y tortura en el cono sur*. Mexico City: Editorial Extemporaneos, 1977.

Oszlak, Oscar, ed. *"Proceso," crisis y transcición democrática*. Vols. 1 and 2. Buenos Aires: Centro Editor América Latina, 1984.

Parker, Andrew, et al., eds. *Nationalisms and Sexualities*. New York: Routledge, 1992.

Partnoy, Alicia. *The Little School: Tales of Disappearance and Survival in Argentina*. Trans. Alicia Partnoy, Lois Athey, and Sandra Braunstein. Pittsburgh: Cleis Press, 1986.

——. *Revenge of the Apple/Venganza de la manzana*. Trans. Richard Schaaf, Regina Kreger, and Alicia Partnoy. Pittsburgh: Cleis, 1992.

Pavis, Patrice. *Languages of the Stage: Essays in the Semiology of the Theatre*. New York: Performing Arts Journal Publications, 1982.

Pavlovsky, Eduardo. *El Señor Galíndez y Pablo*. Buenos Aires: Ediciones Busqueda, 1986.

——. *Voces*. Buenos Aires: Ediciones Busqueda, 1989.

——. *La ética del cuerpo: Conversaciones con Jorge Dubatti*. Buenos Aires: Libros Babilonia, 1994.

Paz, Octavio. *The Labyrinth of Solitude: Life and Thought in Mexico*. Trans. Lysander Kemp. New York: Grove, 1961.

Pellarolo, Silvia. "Revisando el canon/La historia oficial: Griselda Gambaro y el heroismo de Antígona." *Latin American Theatre Review* 7.13 (April 1992): 79–86.

Penguin, Carlos. "Las guerrilleras: La cruenta historia de la mujer en el terrorismo." *Somos* December 2, 1976, pp. 10–17.

Perón, Eva. *La razón de mi vida*. 13th ed. Buenos Aires: Ediciones Peuser, 1952.

——. *My Mission in Life*. Trans. Ethel Cherry. New York: Vintage, 1953.

Peters, Edward. *Torture*. New York: Basil Blackwell, 1985.

Petras, James, and Steve Vieux. "The Transition to Authoritarian Electoral Regimes in Latin America." *Latin American Perspectives* 21/4.83 (1994): 5–20.

Phelan, Peggy. *Unmarked: The Politics of Performance*. New York: Routledge, 1993.

Pinkus, Karen. *Bodily Regimes: Italian Advertising under Fascism.* Minneapolis: University of Minnesota Press, 1995.

Pla, Alberto J., et al., eds. *La década trágica: Ocho ensayos sobre la crisis argentina, 1973–1983.* Buenos Aires: Editorial Tierra del fuego, 1984.

Potash, Robert A. *The Army and Politics in Argentina, 1928–1945.* Stanford: Stanford University Press, 1969.

Pratt, Mary Louise, and Marta Morello Frosch, eds. *Nuevo Texto Crítico 4 (Año 2): Segundo semestre.* Stanford: Stanford University Press, 1989.

Propp, V. *Morphology of the Folktale.* Trans. Laurence Scott. 10th ed. Austin: University of Texas Press, 1988.

Pross, Edith E. "Open Theatre Revisited: An Argentine Experiment." *Latin American Theatre Review* 18.1 (1984): 83–94.

"¿Qué es Teatro Abierto?" *Conjunto* 60 (April–June 1984): 51–56.

Quino. *Potentes, prepotentes e impotentes.* Buenos Aires: Ediciones de la Flor, 1989.

Rais, Hilda, ed. *Salirse de madre.* Buenos Aires: Croquiñol Ediciones, 1989.

Raznovich, Diana. "El desconcierto." *Teatro Abierto 1981.* Vol. 2. Ed. Miguel Angel Giella. Buenos Aires: Corregidor, 1981.

——. *Cables pelados 1.* Buenos Aires: Ediciones Lúdicas, 1987.

——. "Disconcerted." Trans. Victoria Mártinez. *The Literary Review* 32.4 (Summer 1989): 568–72.

Reati, Fernando. "Argentine Political Violence and Artistic Representation in Films in the 1980s." *Latin American Literary Journal* 17.34 (1989): 24–39.

Reinelt, Janelle G., and Joseph R. Roach, eds. *Critical Theory and Performance.* Ann Arbor: University of Michigan Press, 1992.

"Report on the Situation of Human Rights in Argentina." Organization of American States, 1980.

Retamar, Roberto Fernández. *Caliban and Other Essays.* Trans. Edward Baker. Minneapolis: University of Minnesota Press, 1989.

Roach, Joseph R. "Theatre History and the Ideology of the Aesthetic." *Theatre Journal* 1.2 (1989): 155–68.

——. "Culture and Performance." *Performativity and Performance.* Eds. Andrew Parker and Eve Kosofsky Sedgwick. New York: Routledge, 1995.

Rock, David. *Argentina 1516–1987.* Berkeley: University of California Press, 1987.

——. *Authoritarian Argentina: The Nationalist Movement, Its History and Its Impact.* Berkeley: University of California Press, 1993.

Rodríguez-Molas, Ricardo, ed. *Historia de la tortura y el orden represivo en la Argentina: Textos documentales.* Buenos Aires: Editorial Universitaria de Buenos Aires, 1985.

Rogoff, Edmond. "His Master's Voice: Television in Argentina. A Case of Cultural Penetration." *Journal of Popular Culture* 18.1 (1984): 92–100.

Rose, Jacqueline. *States of Fantasy.* New York: Oxford University Press, 1996.

Rosenberg, Alfred. *Der Mythus des 20 Fahrhunderts.* München: Hoheneichen=Berlag, 1934.

——. *Selected Writings.* Ed Robert Pois. London: Jonathan Cape, 1970.

Rosenberg, Tina. *Children of Cain: Violence and the Violent in Latin America.* New York: Penguin, 1991.

Rosencof, Mauricio. *Los caballos; El combate en el establo; El saco de Antonio.* Montevideo: Libros, 1985.

Rossi, Laura. "¿Cómo pensar a las madres de Plaza de Mayo?" *Nuevo Texto Crítico.* Ed. Mary Louise Pratt and Marta Morello Frosch. Stanford: Stanford University Press, 1989. 4:145–53.

Rossi, Vicente. *Teatro nacional rioplateuse*. Buenos Aires: Solar/Hachette, 1969.

Rouquié, Alain. *The Military and the State in Latin America*. Berkeley: University of California Press, 1989.

Rowe, William, and Vivian Schelling. *Memory and Modernity: Popular Culture in Latin America*. London: Verso, 1991.

Rubin, Gayle. "The Traffic in Women: Notes on the 'Political Economy' of Sex." *Toward an Anthropology of Women*. Ed. Rayna R. Reiter. New York: Monthly Review Press, 1975.

Ruddick, Sara. *Maternal Thinking: Toward a Politics of Peace*. New York: Ballantine Books, 1989.

Sabato, Ernesto, ed. *Nunca Más: The Report of the Argentine National Commission on the Disappeared*. New York: Farrar, Straus & Giroux, 1986.

Salessi, Jorge. *Médicos maleantes y maricas*. Buenos Aires: Beatriz Viterbo Editora, 1995.

Sarlo, Beatriz. *La imaginación técnica: Sueños modernos de la cultura argentina*. Buenos Aires: Ediciones Nueva Visión, 1992.

Sarmiento, Domingo F. *Facundo*. México: Editorial Porrúa, 1985.

——. "De la educación popular de las mujeres." *Educación Popular*. Buenos Aires: Juan Roldan, 1915.

Savigliano, Marta. *Tango and the Political Economy of Passion*. Boulder: Westview Press, 1995.

Scarry, Elaine. *The Body in Pain: The Making and Unmaking of the World*. Oxford: Oxford University Press, 1985.

Schechner, Richard. *Between Theater and Anthropology*. Philadelphia: University of Pennsylvania Press, 1985.

Scheines, Graciela. *Las metáforas del fracaso*. Buenos Aires: Editorial Sudamericana, 1995.

Schirmer, Jennifer G. " 'Those Who Die for Life Cannot Be Called Dead': Women and Human Rights Protest in Latin America." *Feminist Review* 32 (Summer 1989): 3–29.

Sedgwick, Eve Kosofsky. *Between Men: English Literature and Male Homosocial Desire*. New York: Columbia University Press, 1985.

Seibel, Beatriz. *De ninfas a capitanas*. Buenos Aires: Editorial Legasa, 1990.

Senkman, Leonardo, ed. *El antisemitismo en la argentina*. Buenos Aires: Centro Editor de America Latina, 1989.

Shumway, Nicolas. *The Invention of Argentina*. Berkeley: University of California Press, 1991.

Silverman, Kaja. *The Acoustic Mirror: The Female Voice in Psychoanalysis and Cinema*. Bloomington: Indiana University Press, 1988.

Simpson, John, and Jana Bennett. *The Disappeared: Voices from a Secret War*. London: Robson Books, 1985.

Sklodowska, Elzbieta. "Testimonio mediatizado: ¿Ventriloquia o heteroglosia? (Barnet/Montejo; Burgos/Menchú)." *Revista de Crítica Literaria Latinoamericana* 19.38/2 (1993): 81–90.

Skloot, Robert. *The Theatre of the Holocaust: Four Plays*. Madison: University of Wisconsin Press, 1982.

Sommer, Doris. *One Master for Another: Populism as Patriarchal Rhetoric in Dominican Novels*. New York: University Press of America, 1983.

——. *Foundational Fictions: The National Romances of Latin America*. Berkeley: University of California Press, 1991.

Sontag, Susan. *Under the Sign of Saturn*. New York: The Noonday Press, 1980.

Sophocles. *The Three Theban Plays: Antigone, Oedipus the King, Oedipus at Colonus*. Trans. Robert Fagles. Middlesex, England: Penguin, 1987.

Sosnowski, Saúl, ed. *Represión y reconstrucción de una cultura: El caso argentino*. Buenos Aires: Editorial Universitaria de Buenos Aires, 1988.

Steiner, George. *Antigones*. Oxford: Oxford University Press, 1984.

Stepan, Nancy Leys. *"The Hour of Eugenics": Race, Gender, and Nation in Latin America*. Ithaca: Cornell University Press, 1991.

Sternbach, Nancy Saporta, et al. "Feminisms in Latin America: From Bogotá to San Bernardo." *Signs* 17.2 (1992): 393–434.

Stoller, Robert J. *Perversion: The Erotic Form of Hatred*. New York: Pantheon, 1975.

Stover, Eric, and Elena O. Nightingale, eds. *The Breaking of Bodies and Minds: Torture, Psychiatric Abuse, and the Health Professions*. New York: W. H. Freeman, 1985.

Suárez-Orozco, Marcelo M. "The Heritage of Enduring a 'Dirty War': Psychosocial Aspects of Terror in Argentina, 1976–1988." *Journal of Psychohistory* 18.4 (1991): 469–505.

——. "A Study of Argentine Soccer: The Dynamics of Its Fans and Their Folklore." *Journal of Psychoanalytic Anthropology* 5.1 (1982): 7–28.

Suleiman, Susan Rubin, ed. *The Female Body in Western Culture*. Cambridge, Mass.: Harvard University Press, 1985.

Taussig, Michael. *The Nervous System*. New York: Routledge, 1992.

Taylor, Diana. "Alicia Partnoy: A Portrait." In *The Politics of Motherhood: Activist Voices from Left to Right*. Hanover: University Press of New England, 1996.

——. *Theatre of Crisis: Drama and Politics in Latin America*. Lexington: University Press of Kentucky, 1991.

——. "Transculturating Transculturation." *Performing Arts Journal* 38 (1991): 90–104.

Taylor, Diana, and Juan Villegas, eds. *Negotiating Performance: Gender, Sexuality and Theatricality in Latin/o America*. Durham: Duke University Press, 1994.

Taylor, J. M. *Eva Perón: The Myths of a Woman*. Chicago: University of Chicago Press, 1979.

Tedlock, Dennis. *Breath on the Mirror: Mythic Voices and Visions of the Living Maya*. New York: Harper Collins, 1993.

Theweleit, Klaus. *Male Fantasies*. Vol. 1. Minneapólis: University of Minnesota Press, 1987.

——. *Male Fantasies*. Vol. 2. Minneapolis: University of Minnesota Press, 1989.

Thompson, Currie K. "Against All Odds: Argentine Cinema, 1976–1991." *Post Script* 11.3 (1992): 32–45.

Timerman, Jacobo. *Prisoner Without a Name, Cell Without a Number*. Trans. Toby Talbot. New York: Vintage, 1982.

Torture in Brazil: A Report by the Archdiocese of Sao Paulo. Trans. Jaime Wright. New York: Vintage, 1986.

Traba, Marta. *Conversación al sur*. Mexico City: Siglo Veintiuno Editores, 1981.

Tripp, Edward. *The Meridian Handbook of Classical Mythology*. New York: New American Library, 1970.

Troncoso, Oscar. *El proceso de reorganización nacional: Cronología y documentación*. Vol. 1. Buenos Aires: Centro Editor de America Latina, 1984.

——, ed. *Presidencias y golpes militares del siglo xx*. 3 vols. Buenos Aires: Biblioteca Política Argentina, 1986.

Turner, Victor. *The Anthropology of Performance*. New York: PAJ Publications, 1986.

Ulla, Noemí, and Hugo Echave. *Después de la noche: Diálogo con Graciela Fernández Meijide*. Buenos Aires: Editorial Contrapunto, 1986.

Uriarte, Claudio. *Almirante cero: Biografía no autorizada de Emilio Eduardo Massera*. Buenos Aires: Planeta, 1991.

Vazquez, Enrique. *PRN la ultima: Origen, apogeo y caída de la dictadura militar.* Buenos Aires: Editorial Universitaria de Buenos Aires, 1985.

Verbitsky, Horacio. *Rodolfo Walsh y la prensa clandestina, 1976–1978.* Buenos Aires: Ediciones de la Urraca, 1985.

———. *Civiles y militares: Memoria secreta de la transición.* Buenos Aires: Editorial Contrapunto, 1987.

———. *El vuelo.* Buenos Aires: Planeta, 1995.

Victor, J. *Confesiones de un torturador.* Barcelona: Editorial Laia, 1981.

Vidal, Hernán, ed. *Fascismo y experiencia literaria: Reflexiones para una recanonización.* Minneapolis: Institute for the Study of Ideologies and Literature, 1985.

Vilarino, Raúl David. *Yo secuestré, maté y vi torturar en la Escuela de Mecánica de la Armada.* Buenos Aires: Editorial Perfil, 1984.

Walsh, María Elena. *Desventuras en el País-Jardín-de-Infantes.* Buenos Aires: Editorial Sudamericana, 1993.

Walsh, Rodolfo. *Los oficios terrestres.* Buenos Aires: Ediciones de la Flor, 1986.

White, Hayden. *Tropics of Discourse: Essays in Cultural Criticism.* Baltimore: Johns Hopkins University Press, 1978.

Williams, Linda. *Hard Core: Power, Pleasure, and the "Frenzy of the Visible."* Berkeley: University of California Press, 1989.

Yudice, George, Jean Franco, and Juan Flores, eds. *On Edge: The Crisis of Contemporary Latin American Culture.* Minneapolis: University of Minnesota Press, 1992.

Zantop, Susanne. *Colonial Fantasies in Pre-Colonial Germany.* Durham: Duke University Press, forthcoming.

Zimbardo, P. G., et al. "A Pirandellian Prison." *New York Times Magazine* (April 8, 1973): 36–60.

Index

About the Author

Diana Taylor is Chair of the Comparative Literature Program and Professor of Spanish and Comparative Literature at Dartmouth College. She is the author of *Theatre in Crisis: Drama and Politics in Latin America* and co-editor (with Juan Villegas) of *Negotiating Performance: Gender, Sexuality, and Theatricality in Latin/o America* (Duke, 1994).

Library of Congress Cataloging-in-Publication Data
Taylor, Diana.
Disappearing acts : spectacles of gender and nationalism in Argentina's "dirty war" / Diana Taylor.
Includes bibliographical references and index.
ISBN 0-8223-1877-6 (cloth : alk. paper). — ISBN 0-8223-1868-7 (pbk. : alk. paper)
1. Theater—Political aspects—Argentina. 2. Argentine drama—20th century—History and criticism. 3. Argentina—Politics and government—1955–1983. 4. Violence—Argentina—History—20th century. 5. Disappeared persons—Argentina. I. Title.
PN2451.T28 1997
792'.0982'09045—dc20   96-22185CIP